SHAMELESS SHORTCUTS

1,027 TIPS AND TECHNIQUES

That Help You Save Time, Save Money, and Save Work Every Day!

**Edited by Fern Marshall Bradley
and the Editors of** YANKEE MAGAZINE

Notice

The information in this book has been carefully researched, and all efforts have been made to ensure accuracy. Rodale Inc. and Yankee Publishing Inc. assume no responsibility for any injuries suffered or damages or losses incurred during or as a result of following this information. All information should be carefully studied and clearly understood before taking any action based on the information or advice in this book.

Mention of specific companies, organizations, or authorities in this book does not imply endorsement by the publisher, nor does mention of specific companies, organizations, or authorities imply that they endorse this book.

Internet addresses and telephone numbers given in this book were accurate at the time it went to press.

Library of Congress Cataloging-in-Publication Data

 Shameless shortcuts : 1,027 tips and techniques that help you save time, save
money, and save work every day! / edited by Fern Marshall Bradley and the editors of
Yankee Magazine.
   p. cm.
 Includes index.
 ISBN-13 978-0–89909–390–6 hardcover
 ISBN-10 0–89909–390–6 hardcover
 ISBN-13 978-0–89909–391–8 paperback
 ISBN-10 0–89909–391–4 paperback
 1. Home economics. I. Bradley, Fern Marshall.
TX145 .S527 2004
640—dc22   2003023556

Distributed to the trade by Holtzbrinck Publishers

    8 10 9   hardcover
2 4 6 8 10 9 7 5 3   paperback

Shameless Shortcuts

YANKEE PUBLISHING STAFF

PRESIDENT: Jamie Trowbridge
BOOK EDITOR: Fern Marshall Bradley
CONTRIBUTING WRITERS: Alexandra Benwell,
Jeff Bredenberg, Tom Cavalieri, Sally Cunningham,
Melanie DeVault, Barbara W. Ellis, Rose Kennedy,
Dougald MacDonald, Margaret McVeigh, Arden Moore,
Donna Shryer, Delilah Smittle
BOOK DESIGNER: Jill Shaffer
ILLUSTRATOR: Jill Weber
COPY EDITOR: Barbara Jatkola
INDEXER: Nanette Bendyna
PROOFREADERS: Nancy Rutman, Emily Williams

RODALE INC. EDITORIAL STAFF

EXECUTIVE EDITOR: Ellen Phillips
EDITORIAL PRODUCTION MANAGER: Marilyn Hauptly
COVER DESIGNER: Anthony Serge

Contents

Shortcut Solutions for Everyday Life

When you think of a shortcut, you probably remember a favorite childhood path through neighborhood yards. But shortcuts are for grown-ups, too! Today's fast-paced world leaves us too little time, energy, and money to get everything done. We could all use a few good shortcuts to help us get through the day. That's why the editors at *Yankee* Magazine put their heads together to create *Shameless Shortcuts*.

In this book, you'll find more than 1,000 tips and ideas for saving time, money, and effort on cooking, cleaning, shopping, exercise, pet care, kid care, paperwork, decorating, home repairs, yard work, crafts, holiday planning, gardening, and more. There are shortcuts for every hour of every day of your daily routine, as well as for the leisure activities and special events that we all look forward to.

Shameless Shortcuts begins with Part 1: Reduce the Weekday Rush. Those ingenious *Yankee* editors have come up with shortcuts to help you save precious minutes and avoid aggravation in the daily whirl of life. You'll find shortcuts ranging from a three-step approach to assembling an outfit to five quick tricks for bad hair days, a generous helping of fast, nutritious breakfast ideas, and simple techniques for ensuring that you leave for work on time. Because we know that house-

cleaning is not your favorite chore (we hate it, too), we've filled a whole chapter with great ideas for staying caught up on cleaning during the week with minimal time and effort. You'll find five fabulous household cleaners you can make with ingredients you already have on hand, as well as an ingenious game that will inspire your family to help with cleaning chores (without whining). Part 1 also includes a hefty helping of shortcuts for daily exercise, pets, commuting, shopping, weeknight dinners, and planning ahead.

If you enjoy being at home and doing home projects, you'll love all the shortcuts in Part 2: Chop a Chunk out of Chores. Going room by room, the *Yankee* editors have assembled a terrific collection of in-depth tips for cooking, cleaning, organizing, decorating, and making the best use of every room in your house, plus your garage and yard. Here's just a sample of the hundreds of tips: a simple strategy for ending the accumulation of moldy leftovers in your refrigerator, an ingenious do-it-yourself project that doubles your bedroom closet space, a labor saving way to clean your patio furniture and outdoor grill, and foolproof ideas for organizing your workbench.

In Part 3, there are tips for the pleasures of life: making crafts and gifts, gardening, taking leisure trips, and enjoying the holidays. Here the emphasis is on maximizing the time spent on enjoyable tasks, minimizing the time spent on routine tasks (such as weeding the garden), and getting the most for your money. You'll love the simple, money-saving ideas for making gifts and crafts, such as how to assemble a gift basket of flowers for a fraction of the store price and how to launch kids on homemade gift projects that they really can complete themselves (leaving you time to enjoy your own hobby). RV enthusiasts will want to check out the great tips for outfitting an RV on the cheap and making meals in advance for a weekend RV trip. And everyone will appreciate the suggestions for making a holiday centerpiece in less than 5 minutes and a child's Halloween costume in under an hour.

Throughout *Shameless Shortcuts,* you'll find tried-and-true tips provided by real-life "everyday experts." The *Yankee* editors consulted more than 200 people from all around the coun-

try who are experts by virtue of their professions (garden tips from organic market gardeners), their hobbies (packing tips from a retired Scoutmaster), or their everyday life experiences (quick dinner ideas from a working mother of three). Many of the tips in *Shameless Shortcuts* reflect the ingenious responses of these folks to their real-life needs to save time and money in the day-to-day business of raising a family, taking care of a household, and paying the bills.

While editing this book, I couldn't resist trying many of the shortcuts myself. I've discovered a new way to tie my shoes so that they never come untied, a simple trick that cuts laundry-folding time by a third, and a shamelessly quick way to clean my microwave oven. I've enjoyed several of the easy breakfast and dinner ideas (especially Rose Kennedy's Mediterranean pasta dish on page 138). And my handyman husband, Tom, is tickled pink with the new built-in light on his portable drill (see page 237).

I'm sure you'll find your own personal favorite tips in *Shameless Shortcuts* just as I have. Aim to add one new short-cut to your routine each day or week. Doing so will add a spirit of adventure and achievement to everyday tasks—and you'll be amazed how the time and money savings add up.

Fern Marshall Bradley
Editor, *Shameless Shortcuts*

PART 1

Reduce the Weekday Rush

Managing the Morning Madness

Navigating the weekday morning rush—filled with toilette timetables, wardrobe requirements, nourishment needs, and schedule accommodations—is a major accomplishment. Knowing the right short-cuts can turn mayhem into a well-managed routine. Read on to find energy- and timesaving tips for bathing, dressing, making breakfast, packing lunches, dealing with kids, and getting out the door on time. Sometimes the best way to avoid morning madness is to start the night before, so check out "Planning Ahead to Save Time Tomorrow" on page 114, too.

STARTING OUT ON THE RIGHT FOOT
Dual-Duty Conditioning

When dry, brittle hair cries out for a deep-conditioning treatment, knock off a few chores in the shower while waiting the requisite 5 minutes for your conditioner to do its thing. Hand-wash some panty hose or those delicate unmentionables that you don't dare machine-wash. Attaching an antifogging magnifying mirror to the shower wall allows men the option of shaving while conditioning (the steam from the shower softens a beard); women can pluck stray eyebrow hairs (again, the steam softens the hairs). An added bonus to all this shower activity is that the steam helps the conditioner penetrate the hair shafts.

Superfast Outfit Assembly

For those mornings when you have no time to think about what you're going to wear, rely on this no-nonsense approach to getting dressed.

1. Choose a skirt or a pair of trousers in black or a neutral dark color (pants are faster because you can wear knee-high hose rather than struggling with panty hose).
2. Add a white or pastel blouse, preferably one designed to be worn over the waist, so there's no need to put on a belt.
3. Tie a colorful oblong silk scarf loosely around your neck.

Total dressing time: 3 minutes flat.

Accessible Accessories

Accessories make the outfit, but who has time to search for just the right accessories on a busy morning? To simplify the process, hang your accessories right with the outfit they're meant for. Got the perfect choker to go with that little black dress? Stick the choker in a clear plastic bag and poke the hook of the hanger through the bag.

Step-Saving Shelves

Who can afford the time to run back and forth between the dresser and the

3 MINUTES A DAY

The Smarter, Shorter Shower

A long, lazy shower is a luxury just about everyone enjoys. But your morning shower presents an opportunity to trim a few minutes off your daily routine by multitasking. Here's how.

- Buy a pair of shower gloves so you can scrub dry skin from your elbows and knees as you wash your body. The gloves, found in the beauty aisle at any supermarket or home store, are a modern-day version of a pumice stone.
- Use a liquid body cleanser that also contains a moisturizer, so you'll be softening your skin while you shower.
- Use a combination shampoo and conditioner to halve the time spent washing your hair.
- After you step out of the shower, apply a moisturizing body spray or lotion—one with a fragrance you particularly like—and you can skip using cologne or perfume.

A Messy Wardrobe

Problem:

So many of the items in your closet are in disrepair that you waste precious minutes every morning trying to assemble a presentable outfit.

Do This Now:

This week, set aside 1 hour for making vital repairs, says Susan Fignar, an image consultant from Itasca, Illinois. Sew loose buttons and ripped seams on everyday essentials, such as your navy blue blazer. Polish the shoes you wear most often and clean out your everyday purse. If a repair is beyond your skills, place the item in a tote bag beside the front door so you can whisk it off to the appropriate repair shop tomorrow. This 1-hour fix will result in a basic wardrobe that's in good shape.

Do This for Good:

Devote 1 afternoon each season—spring, summer, fall, and winter—to closet and dresser inventory. Tidy your closet and dresser and switch seasonal apparel. Repair all clothing in the mending basket. Polish all shoes and check the heels. Treat leather goods—such as wallets, belts, handbags, and briefcases—with a leather cleaner. If straps or seams look shabby, have them repaired. (Most shoe repair shops repair all sorts of leather goods.) This investment of 4 afternoons per year will make getting dressed all 365 mornings a breeze.

closet in search of coordinating items? To save steps and avoid frustration, follow this advice from JoAnn Marra, an apparel design consultant from West Bay Shore, New York. JoAnn recommends moving key wardrobe items such as sweaters and T-shirts from crowded dresser drawers onto closet shelves, where they'll be handy and visible for fast pairing with pants and skirts.

Finally, a Tie That Binds

For umpteen years, you and the children in your life have been tying shoes with a bowknot. Trouble is, a single bowknot slips undone maddeningly often. Double-knotting solves that problem, but double-knotted laces are difficult to untie. That's why it pays to learn an easy variation on a bowknot that almost never comes undone on its own.

First, picture the steps for tying your shoes conventionally.

1. Cross the two shoelaces and wrap one lace around the other. Pull the laces snug.
2. Form a loop with one lace and hold it in place with your thumb and forefinger.
3. Wrap the second lace around the loop one time. Poke a section of that second lace through the "hole" you just made at the base of the loop, thus creating a second loop.
4. Pull both loops snug to secure the knot.

Now for the never-comes-untied variation, which involves step 3. Instead of wrapping the second lace around the loop once, wrap it around twice. Complete the knot in the usual fashion. Untying this type of knot is as easy as ever—just pull on the free end of one of the laces.

Caddy-Gorize

A makeup drawer can be a hodgepodge of tubes, jars, bottles, wands, and compacts that take forever to sort through. To solve this problem, buy three caddies or other containers. Spread an old sheet, tablecloth, or shower curtain on a flat surface such as your bed. Pile every item of makeup you own on the sheet. Place daily essentials in one caddy, special occasion makeup in another, and products you cannot bear (yet) to give up in the third. Now you have an easy-to-use makeup inventory. If you wish, keep your daily essentials in the drawer, but leave the other collections in their caddies.

As you sort, throw out any makeup that you never use or that has expired. If you have not used something in the last 6 months, it counts as never used.

Baby Your Makeup Brushes

Washing your makeup brushes will help keep your makeup cleaner, so it will last longer and be less likely to carry harmful bacteria. Wash natural bristle brushes once a month and synthetic brushes weekly. You can buy special brush cleaners, but baby shampoo or a mild soap works just as well. If you buy a generic brand of shampoo, you'll save about half the cost of a snazzy brush cleaner.

Good Things Come in Small Packages

Assembling a mini–makeup kit for your purse or briefcase more than pays for itself in time saved transferring makeup into and out of your purse every day. Choose a small zippered case and makeup products packaged in slim compacts or thin tubes that fit inside the case. Watch for gift-with-purchase promotions, which often include downsized versions of mascara, eye shadow, or perfume, for example. As for lipstick, keep a neutral shade in the kit, so if you're too hurried to pack that luscious fuchsia you applied at 7 A.M., you'll have a perfectly acceptable backup at noon.

Other handy items for a mini–makeup kit include cotton swabs, a small comb, a travel-size bottle of anti-bacterial hand sanitizer (no water necessary), and hair spray. This compact assortment should fit in a bag no larger than a 3-by-5-inch index card.

File This under Fast

When your nails are a mess but you've got to run, try this fast fix. File your nails and buff them to create a bit of a shine. Then apply one thin coat of clear polish—no base or top coat needed. When the polish is dry (about 10 minutes), rub cuticle oil around the edges of your nails and moisturize your hands. Total time: less than 15 minutes. And if someone else is available

Date Your Makeup

Makeup can be a breeding ground for bacteria, and those bacteria can cause annoying skin and eye infections, including pinkeye (caused by using old mascara). It's easy to avoid such problems by culling your makeup regularly and tossing out older products. The trick is to remember what's old and what's new. Keep a small roll of mailing labels or masking tape in your makeup box. Every time you buy a new product, label the item with the purchase date. Then follow these guidelines for how long to keep various products.

Product	How Long to Keep
Liquid foundation	6 months
Concealer	8 months
Pressed or loose powder	1 year
Mascara and eye shadow	3 months
Lipstick	1 year
Cosmetic pencil*	1 year
Cleanser	6 months
Moisturizer	6 months
Toner	1 year

*Sharpening the pencil will prevent bacteria buildup.

All-natural and organic cosmetics often have shorter shelf lives than those listed here. If any cosmetic changes in texture, smell, or consistency, toss it immediately.

3 Professional Polish Tricks

A flaw in your manicure is no cause to start again from scratch. Instead, repair the damage in a jiffy with one of these ingenious tricks.

Smooth a smudge. If you smudge the polish before it's dry, dab a tiny bit of nail polish remover on the tip of a finger on the unsmudged hand. Very gently tap the smudge with the remover. This will dissolve the polish, which will smoothly resettle on its own.

Fix a chip. To repair a small chip in your manicure, moisten a cotton swab with nail polish remover and gently swipe the chipped area until all the edges are feathered smooth. Then apply one or two coats of nail polish.

Patch up a break. For a broken nail, apply a little nail glue (superglue will work in a pinch) along the break line. Let the glue set for about a minute as you hold the break in place. Apply another drop of glue and cover the break line with a tiny piece of a tea bag or facial tissue. Let the glue and covering dry for about 5 minutes, then file smooth. A few coats of nail polish will make the patch invisible.

* * *

to drive, you can accomplish the drying and moisturizing while you're in the car.

Better Blow-Drying

Even on a busy morning, you'll have time to wash and style your hair if you follow this quick blow-drying technique offered by beauty expert Mary Beth Janssen of Palatine, Illinois.

1. Spray your hair with a light-hold styling spray, then power-dry it by setting the dryer on high, holding the nozzle about 3 inches from your scalp, and moving the nozzle constantly around your head. (The continuous movement means you won't overheat your scalp or your hair.)

2. When your hair is about 80 percent dry, turn the dryer off and finger-comb your hair into place.

3. You have two options for this step, depending on whether you want a natural look or a finished style. For a natural look, scrunch your hair: Gently grab a small section of hair, close your hand over the section, hold for a second or two, and then release. Continue until dry.

For a finished look, use a round or vent brush and the blow dryer set on low. Work the brush through the hair ends to add control and polish. If you want extra hold, apply a light mist of non-aerosol hair spray.

Color Me Happy

Donna Shryer wears so many hats that she often forgets whether she's coming or going. But here's one hat this busy Chicagoan loves to wear. "When I have less than two minutes to get out the door, I put on a bright red baseball cap, a pair of matching red sunglasses, and red lipstick," Donna says. "Add a black or navy jogging suit, and it's all systems go, go, gone!"

 Quick Tricks for Bad Hair Days

You look in the mirror and want to scream when you see your hair. Not to worry! Here are five rescue strategies for times when your hair just won't cooperate.

Capture it. Pull long hair back into a low ponytail at the nape of your neck. Fasten the ponytail with a pretty barrette, or use an elastic ponytail holder and cover it with a scrunchie or ribbon. Rub a little styling gel between your hands and smooth the sides and top of your head to secure stray hairs.

Go trendy. For shorter hair, rub a little gel or styling mud (which looks like natural shoe polish but is a wonderfully handy hair care product) between your fingertips, place your fingers just above your ears at the hairline, and sweep your fingers back, slicking the sides sleek and flat. Leave the hair on the top and back of your head loose and tousled. For a more festive look, place a small flower (real if you can, silk as a standby) behind one ear. A gardenia or orchid works well.

Take a powder. If your hair looks greasy but there's no time to shampoo, sprinkle a little talcum powder or baby powder on your fingertips and massage it into the roots. Then comb the powder through your hair.

Use H$_2$O and go. Spritz your hair with plain water, being careful to not soak it, then scrunch it to release the natural waves.

Try a bang-up solution. Put on a shower cap and use the handle of a rat-tail comb to pull out just your bangs. Wash, dry, and style your bangs. You'll be amazed what a difference this can make.

GETTING YOUR KIDS GOING

Ease the Kids out of Bed

Here's a smart way to end the battle of getting children out of bed. Set the alarm clock—or schedule rise-and-shine kisses—5 minutes earlier than necessary. During this extra time, invite your child to enjoy a glass of juice or a small sweet treat. The catch is, he must sit up to munch or sip. And once a child is sitting up, you've won 90 percent of the battle.

Timed for Morning Success

Turn the morning routine into a game, and kids will beg to speed things up. Carol Kriebel of Deerfield, Illinois, mom to three and frantic-morning veteran, suggests playing right into kids' hands. On Sunday evening, she assigns her children a goal for the upcoming week, such as getting completely dressed or being seated at the breakfast table. After waking the kids up each morning, she sets her kitchen timer. Whoever completes the goal and beats the bell wins. Prizes, Carol says, are optional.

Check the Fine Print

If your kids can't seem to remember the morning routine no matter how many times you've nagged them about it, try giving them a checklist they can use each morning. Buy a small dry-erase board and marker for each child. Write each one's morning routine on the board (for example, "Wake up," "Get dressed," or "Eat breakfast"). Hang the board on the door of the child's room. As she completes each task, she checks it off. When all the tasks are done, she wipes off all the check marks for a fresh start the next day. For preschoolers who can't read, draw visual checklists. You could include a picture of the sun for waking up, a shirt and pants for getting dressed, a bowl and spoon for eating breakfast, and so on.

Brush First, Play Later

Nine-year-old Anna Cieslik of Chicago recently discovered Sparkle City on the Internet (www.sparkle-city.com). This Web site includes a series of entertaining and somewhat educational games. Anna's mom spun this fact to her advantage: Anna can log on and play only if she has brushed her teeth before school without a fuss. The results? Persuading Anna to brush now takes zero minutes.

Peanut Butter Banishes Chewing Gum

How chewing gum gets stuck in children's hair is a mystery. All we know for sure is, it does. To remove chewing gum, the experts (aka grade school teachers) recommend massaging plain peanut butter into the gum. The gum will begin to dissolve, and you can simply pick the bits out of the hair.

Conditioner Saves Combing Time

Combing kids' hair consumes precious morning minutes. You can speed up the task by helping your kids establish a nighttime habit of rinsing their hair with a detangling conditioner after shampooing. The next morning, their hair will be considerably less tangled. If they forget the rinse, immediately after they jump out of the shower, put a pea-size dot of conditioner and a quarter-size dot of styling gel in your palm. Rub the two together, smooth through freshly shampooed hair, and comb as usual.

Tangles with a Twist

When a child wakes up with fierce tangles, use a distraction to prevent time-consuming whining and fidgeting during the detangling process. Choose a small amusement that fits in a child's lap, such as an Etch-A-Sketch or Silly Putty.

BREAKFAST SHORTCUTS

Oatmeal at the Ready

Oatmeal with raisins and brown sugar is a favorite old-fashioned breakfast. Try this new-fashioned way to prepare oatmeal in next to no time. Allrecipes.com (www.allrecipes.com) offers this recipe submitted to the Web site by "Joanne." Mix together 5 cups unsweetened instant oatmeal, $1/4$ cup brown sugar, 1 cup raisins, and 3 tablespoons dry milk. Store the mixture in an airtight container. It takes only 3 minutes to whip up

5 Healthy, Fast Breakfasts

Even when you need to eat breakfast quickly, you can eat wisely. Nutrition counselor Monique Ryan, owner of Personal Nutrition Designs in Evanston, Illinois, offers a week's worth of healthy breakfasts.

Cereal plus. Sprinkle wheat germ over a bowl of whole grain cereal. Add fresh fruit and ½ cup skim milk.

Lunch for breakfast. Place 2 slices of low-fat cheese, a few slices of tomato, and 2 slices of lean turkey inside a whole wheat pita pocket and microwave long enough to melt the cheese. (There's absolutely no reason you cannot enjoy traditional lunch-meats for breakfast, Monique says.)

Easy egg. Sprinkle salt and pepper on a hard-boiled egg, or slather it with mustard. (Monique notes that, barring doctor's orders, even those on low-cholesterol diets can eat three eggs a week.)

Peanut butter and banana. Spread natural peanut butter on a slice of whole grain bread, a bagel, or crackers, then mash half a banana on top.

Yogurt on the side. Smear 100 percent fruit jam on a whole grain muffin and eat it with a side of yogurt.

a bowl of oatmeal using the mix. In the morning, place 1 cup of the dry mixture in a bowl and stir in ½ to ¾ cup boiling water, depending on how thick you like your oatmeal.

This recipe makes enough for about 5 servings. If you'd like, you can multiply the ingredients to make enough to last several months. This special oatmeal mix makes a nice gift, too.

Creamsicle Smoothie

Here's a quick breakfast you and your kids are sure to love. In a blender, combine ½ cup skim milk, 1 cup vanilla yogurt, and a dollop of frozen orange juice concentrate. Serve fruit chunks on the side, to eat plain or dip in the smoothie.

A New Slant on Toast

When time is tight, toast is a tried-and-true breakfast. To boost the nutritional value, skip the butter and top your toast with peanut butter and thin slices of apple instead, suggests Monique Ryan.

Be Nutty with Cereal

Cold cereal is certainly one of the fastest breakfasts you can serve your kids or yourself. To renew your enthusiasm for breakfast cereal, perk it up by sprinkling peanuts or almonds on top, suggests Monique Ryan. Add some sliced fruit for extra vitamins and fiber.

The 2-Minute Breakfast

For a quick eye-opener with more staying power than a slice of toast, try microwaved eggs. Use a fork to beat 2 eggs and a dash of pepper in a microwave-safe cereal bowl. If you like spicy eggs, add a few drops of Tabasco sauce. Microwave, uncovered, on high for 2 minutes. Eat the eggs right out of the bowl or, for a heartier meal, slide them between 2 slices of toast or a split English muffin. Top with a slice of cheese and lunchmeat, if desired.

Two more bonuses of microwaved versus stove-cooked eggs: You'll save time on cleanup (no messy pan), and you'll be doing your heart a favor (no butter or cooking oil is needed).

Freezer Breakfasts from Scratch

As a busy person, you must know about prepackaged freezer breakfasts. But have you ever considered freezing your own? Simply prepare a double batch of pancakes and place the extras on a cookie sheet lined with waxed paper. Stack one pancake on top of another, with a 1/4-inch-thick pat of butter in between. Place the cookie sheet in the freezer. When the pan-

My Favorite
Shortcut

Burrito Boogie

At home, many kids eat healthy food, or they face Mom's wrath. At Nana's house, however, they can get away with almost anything. But when Charlene Shryer of Glenview, Illinois, invites any of her six grandchildren for a sleepover, she outfoxes them by rolling a few vitamin-packed ingredients into the kids' breakfast of choice—pancakes. First she prepares a few microwaveable pancakes. While they cook, she cuts strawberries into small bits. When the pancakes are done, she removes them from the microwave and plops a spoonful of fruit on one half of each pancake. Then, starting on the side with the fruit, she rolls up each pancake like a burrito and wraps it in waxed paper. Her grandkids gobble them up, never catching on to the fact that they've just eaten a nutritious breakfast.

cakes are frozen, place each stack in a resealable plastic bag. To serve, remove a stack from its bag, place on a plate, and microwave on high for 1 to 2 minutes, depending on the type and size of the pancakes.

Prefer French toast? Follow the same procedure.

Breakfast on Four Wheels

Worst-case scenario: You have to eat breakfast in the car today. Rather than trying to down a crumbly muffin or messy breakfast sandwich while you drive, take along a resealable plastic bag of trail mix. You can prepare the trail mix in advance so it's always available when time runs short in the morning. Simply mix together 2 cups of any low-sugar, whole grain cereal (such as Cheerios); about 1 cup of dried fruits (such as apricots, cherries, bananas, or raisins); and a handful of nuts, pumpkin seeds, and/or sunflower seeds. To eat the trail mix without making a mess, pour some mix from the bag into a paper cup, and crease the rim of the cup to form a spout. To eat, just pour a mouthful of trail mix directly from the cup into your mouth. Between munches, store the cup in your car's cup holder. No sticky fingers either!

They Had *NO Shame*

Dishing Up Some Fun

Deerfield, Illinois, mom Carol Kriebel enlists the help of her two older kids by designating one night a week as Dishwasher's Delight. Whoever is responsible for doing the breakfast dishes each week wins the right to choose one night's dessert (usually a Friday). When Carol is feeling reckless, she allows the dishwasher to select the entire dinner menu, bracing herself for a main course of sundaes, a side dish of brownies, and apple pie for dessert.

Sipper Breakfast for the Drive

Another no-mess breakfast for the car is a breakfast smoothie. This takes a little time to prepare, but it's such a treat, you'll find the time.

To make a smoothie, put $1/4$ cup frozen strawberries, 1 cup pineapple juice, $1/4$ cup orange juice, and $1/2$ cup low-fat vanilla yogurt in a blender. Blend on high until smooth. Pour the smoothie into a large plastic cup with a lid and a straw, and you're ready to go. There are hundreds of variations on the recipe, so experiment.

PACKING LUNCHES

Peanut Butter Plus

There's no denying that fixing a peanut butter sandwich is fast and easy. To counter the boredom of eating the same thing day after day, take an extra minute to blend a custom peanut butter spread. To $1/2$ cup peanut butter, add a few tablespoons each of finely shredded carrot, sunflower nuts or pine nuts, raisins or currants, and honey. Spread as usual on bread. You should have enough for several sandwiches.

Don't Pay for Prepackaged

Prepackaged lunch kits from the refrigerator case at the supermarket are convenient but awfully expensive. It's not hard to make your own copycat version, and you'll save at least half the cost. The secret is to use a cookie cutter to cut cheese and cold cuts to fit round whole wheat crackers. Kids love these lunch treats, and so will you.

Give Your Kids Lunch Trumpets

For kids who resist eating traditional sandwiches, trim the crust from two slices of bread and flatten the bread with a rolling pin. Spread a thin layer of filling, such as chicken, tuna, or ham salad, not quite to the edges of the bread. Roll each bread slice into a cone shape, keeping one end open. Fasten with toothpicks.

A cone-shaped sandwich is a lunch box innovation that will win over fussy eaters.

Little Dippers

Sandwiches day after day in your brown-bag lunch can become mighty boring. For a fast alternative, fill a small drip-proof container with salsa, hummus, bean dip, or fruit dip. Add a bag of sturdy chips, veggie sticks, or fruit.

What to Do When There's No Dessert

Not a cookie or piece of candy in the house, but your child (or spouse) will be so disappointed if there's no treat in his lunch bag. Sure, he could live without it for a day, but here's an easy, innovative substitute. Just create a "Get Out of Doing the Dinner Dishes" or "Excused from Cleaning your Room" card and slip it in with his lunch. Up the fun factor by writing with crayons or markers on a 3-by-5-inch index card, or whip up something colorful on your home computer and print it out.

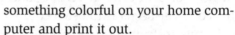

Give Kids the Big Chill

"I used to worry about lunch boxes sitting in a warm locker for three hours," says Wendy Andrews, a Chicago mom. "I could just imagine the tuna fish sandwiches and fruit cups wilting. I tried using freezable gel packs, but they're expensive and kept coming home with holes punched in them. So I started popping small disposable water bottles in the freezer." Wendy places one frozen bottle of water in each of her three children's lunch boxes. The cold bottle keeps food from spoiling, the water is thawed but still quite cold by lunch, and the bottles are reusable. If the bottles come home in one piece, Wendy refills and refreezes them. If they disappear, it's no great loss.

When the Bread's Gone, Waffle It

The bread bag is empty, but you have lunches to pack. Raid the freezer and pull out frozen waffles as a bread substitute. Just toast two waffles, spread them with peanut butter and jelly, and assemble them as a sandwich. This is guaranteed to give kids (and sometimes grown-ups) the giggles.

Easy-Wash Ideas for Lunch Boxes

Over time, a reusable lunch box or bag can become a breeding ground for bacteria, but cleaning lunch boxes isn't high on most folks' "to do" lists. Try one of these easy ways to clean a lunch box. If it's a soft plastic lunch bag, turn it inside out and toss it in the washing machine with your bleachable whites.

Crush-Proof Lunch Containers

Brown-bagging presents a challenge: how to avoid squashed soft foods, crushed chips, and liquid leaks. Here are four clever ways to solve the problem without spending much on fancy packaging.

Recycle margarine tubs and yogurt cups. Not only are you helping the environment, but you also won't be upset if the containers accidentally get lost or are thrown away.

Improvise juice boxes. Commercial juice boxes are pricey. Instead, buy a six-pack of 8-ounce plastic bottles of water. After you drink the water, fill the bottles with juice bought by the half gallon. You can wash and reuse the bottles ad infinitum.

Invest in mustard. Buy a few of the smallest, stubbiest mustard squeeze bottles you can find. This isn't as cost-effective as a jumbo bottle of mustard, of course, but you need to do it only once. After you've used the mustard, wash the bottles, and you'll have a set of long-lasting condiment containers. Simply spoon in mustard, mayonnaise, or salad dressing and pack the appropriate container with a lunch. That way, you can apply condiments when it's time to eat instead of in the morning, thus avoiding soggy sandwiches and salads.

Save spice containers. Spice containers with screw-on lids are great for small portions of creamy dips or yogurt to spoon on top of fruit.

Most soft plastic lunch bags are colorfast and will not run, bleed, or fade. Another option is to clean your lunch box, soft or hard, outside using a hose. Hook the power nozzle onto your garden hose and blast away every last speck of dirt. For older children and adults, tuck an antibacterial wipe inside the box each day. Instruct them to toss the garbage and wipe the box clean after they finish eating.

GETTING OUT THE DOOR ON TIME

Coffee to Go—From Home

Using a leak-proof travel mug for your coffee is a great shortcut, but not when you leave the mug in the car, at the office, or sitting on the counter unwashed overnight. For those mornings when your mug isn't at hand—or is a grimy mess—stock a supply of paper cups and plastic lids exactly like the ones your neighborhood coffee shop uses. For a stash of these commercial cups, check the paper goods aisle at your local grocery store or ask the manager at your favorite coffee shop for a few.

Drop Boxes for All

Your family's natural tendency is to drop belongings willy-nilly on entering the house, meaning that no one can find anything the following morning. It's probably futile to try to change their style, but don't despair. You can go with the flow and still be organized. Just provide a drop box for each family member near the front door. Use inexpensive plastic tubs, fruit crates, or laundry baskets. Then decree that any items not in the baskets (or put in the wrong basket) may be thrown out.

Hang Up Some Storage Space

If you have a small entry with a small coat closet, you may not have enough space to accommodate all the coats, boots, backpacks, briefcases, and bags that accumulate there. To create instant storage space for these important items that you need on a daily basis, install a heavy wire grid—the type meant for hanging pots and pans in the kitchen—on the wall. Be sure to secure the grid to wall studs (not just the drywall or plaster), and it will be sturdy enough to hold book-filled backpacks and heavy winter coats.

Conquer Your Coat Closet

When you open the coat closet door, mittens, hats, boots, parkas, and scarves come tumbling out about your feet. You'll be late for work if you stop to sort out the mess. To prevent coat closet mayhem from derailing your morning schedule, revamp the closet. Hang all long coats on the far end of the rod. Buy a few stackable plastic bins at a home center and arrange them in the middle of the closet, below short coats. Use the bins for less used items such as zip-out linings, snow pants, and bulky gloves. Then hang an over-the-door shoe holder inside the closet door. The pockets are perfect for mittens, knit hats, scarves, and even collapsible umbrellas. Important reminder: one item to a pocket.

Hardworking Message Centers

A central point for messages is essential in today's busy households. Try one of these ideas for a message center to keep you on track.

Clip it. To make this message center, you need a 1-by-2-inch piece of wood about 12 inches long, some screws, and several bulldog clips. Screw each clip into the wood strip. Place a label with the name of one family member above each clip. Use the clips to attach messages and other information to the board.

Post it. Materials for this message center are a corkboard; a shallow wall shelf, such as the type for displaying collectibles or framed photos; and pads of stick-on notes—a different color pad for each family member. Install the corkboard beside the most commonly used phone in your home. Install the shelf below the board. Place the stick-on notepads and several pencils on the shelf, then attach the notes to the board as needed.

Shutter it. This message center has country charm. To make it, find an old wooden shutter at a yard sale (or perhaps there's one in your garage). Place the shutter back side up on a flat surface. Cut a piece of heavy cardboard to fit snugly in the center inset section of the shutter back. Run a thin bead of all purpose glue around the outside edges of the inset and along the edge of each slat. Place the cardboard in the inset and apply pressure so that it will stick to the glue. When the glue is dry, hang the shutter beside your telephone, making sure that a message pad and a pen are nearby. Slip messages between the slats; the cardboard backing will prevent them from falling through.

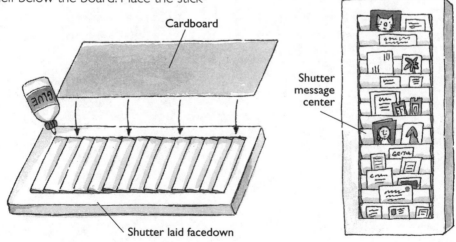

Cardboard

Shutter laid facedown

Shutter message center

Decorate a Coat Tree

Another way to simplify the morning search for outerwear is to buy a coat tree and position it near the front door. Enforce a rule that each person may hang only his most used coat on the tree. All other clothing items and backpacks belong elsewhere.

A Towering Shortcut

A bookshelf tower is a great shortcut solution for organizing your entry if you're short on both space and handyperson skills. Place a basket or plastic dishpan on each shelf of a tall, narrow bookcase. Designate one basket or pan for each family member, or one basket for keys, one for mail, and so on. If you don't like to fiddle with tools, have the furniture store deliver and assemble the bookcase for you.

Tie a School Ribbon

Tired of making extra trips to your child's school to drop off the book report, library book, or other item she forgot to take with her? Prompt her to remember those items by tying a brightly colored ribbon to her school backpack as a reminder. Keep the ribbons easily at hand by attaching them to the refrigerator with a clip magnet.

Weekday Cleaning Catch-Up

2

Weekday cleaning is a necessary evil. Although it's tough to find time (and motivation) to deal with dirt, messes, and clutter during the week, it's even worse if you postpone all the cleaning until the weekend. Look to the shortcuts in this chapter to learn how to whip up homemade cleaning products in a flash, conquer clutter on a daily basis, keep ahead of dust and dirt, and even enlist your family's help with cleaning chores.

HOMEMADE CLEANING SOLUTIONS

Give Furniture a Noncommercial Glow

When your container of furniture polish runs dry, whip up your own polish in seconds using common household ingredients. Dr. Sarah Kirby, associate professor of family and consumer sciences at North Carolina State University in Raleigh, suggests combining 3 cups olive oil and 1 cup white vinegar. Mix until thoroughly blended, dampen a soft cloth with the solution, and use it to polish your furniture.

Half-and-Half Works Wonders

Here's the world's easiest-to-make all-purpose kitchen and bathroom cleaner. Combine equal parts white vinegar and water in a spray bottle. Spray the solution on fixtures, sinks, and counters and wipe. Use the solution to clean the toilet as well. To deodorize the toilet, pour 3 cups vinegar into the bowl, let sit for 30 minutes, and then flush odors away. The vinegar cleans and kills germs at the same time.

Weekday Window-Washing Wisdom

Washing windows doesn't seem like a weekday cleaning job. Having to wipe down the panes two or three times to try to eliminate those inevitable streaks is such a time-consuming task. To cut window-washing time in half, mix this simple formula in a bucket: 1 quart water and 3 to 4 teaspoons plain ammonia (not the sudsy or lemon varieties). With this solution, windows will be crystal clear with just one wipe. You can clean several windows in 15 minutes, and there's nothing to brighten your spirits like a window unsullied by smears, streaks, grime, and fingerprints.

*Glorious
Gizmos*

Super-Simple Spray

Why should you spend your precious dollars for a commercial all-purpose cleaner when you can whip up your own for mere pennies? Fill a 32-ounce spray bottle with water and add 3 teaspoons dishwashing liquid. Screw the cap back on and shake. Ta-da! This simple mixture is a great light-duty cleaner for anywhere in the house. If you want it a tad stronger, add more dishwashing liquid—but not so much that the foam interferes with the spraying action. Use it anywhere you would use one of those high-ticket household cleaners. It smells great, too.

Put the Squeeze on Lime Deposits

Lime and mineral deposits on faucets and other fixtures have a tough reputation. You can scrub and scour for days and get nowhere. But those deposits will wilt and crumble in the face of this simple technique, says Dr. Sarah Kirby, associate professor of family and consumer sciences at North Carolina State University in Raleigh. Soak a few paper towels in white vinegar and wrap them around the lime deposit. Then go off and do something else for an hour, smug in the knowledge that you're "hard at work" cleaning. When you return, those stubborn deposits will be soft and easy to remove.

Fountain of Youth—For Aluminum

After years of service, your beloved aluminum cookware looks stained and beleaguered inside. But you can return those pots to their former glory while you're busy with some other week-day task, says Dr. Sarah Kirby. Combine 2 tablespoons cream of tartar and 1 quart water in one of your stained pots. Bring the solution to a boil, then reduce the heat and let simmer for 10 minutes. Wash and dry the pot as you normally would.

HOUSEWIDE HINTS

Small Moves Save Time

Here's the key to cleaning tabletops, counters, and shelves when you're short on time. Never move the objects on these surfaces far away from their correct positions, says Barbara Webster, president of Nice N Clean Maid Service in Miami. When you're cleaning a countertop, for instance, move any

My Favorite
Shortcut

The Ultimate in Caddy Convenience

For convenience and speed, there's nothing like premoistened towelettes, says Ruben Masas, manager of Maid of Honor cleaning service in Fort Lauderdale. Stock a cleaning caddy with these items, and you'll be covered for all your everyday cleaning needs.

■ Towelettes for windows and mirrors, such as Windex Glass and Surface Wipes.

■ Towelettes for furniture, such as Old English Furniture Wipes.

■ Kitchen and bathroom towelettes, such as Clorox Disinfecting Wipes.

■ A mop system with replaceable pads that are premoistened with a cleaning solution, such as Swiffer WetJet.

Using premoistened towelettes may cost a little more than using cleaning cloths, but the payoff in ease and time saved is worth it, Ruben says. With these products, there's no need to wash your cleaning rags, and you get just the right concentration of cleaning solution, which prevents waste. Also, all of these products are extremely lightweight, saving you effort as you carry them around the house.

objects forward on the counter, clean the newly opened space, and immediately return the objects to their proper positions. That way, you'll avoid losing objects or forgetting where everything goes.

A Damp Cloth Will Do It

Simplicity is often the key to a quick weekday cleanup. You'd be surprised what you can accomplish with only a damp cleaning cloth, says Barbara Webster, president of Nice N Clean Maid Service in Miami. Use it to wipe down counters, fixtures, and other hard surfaces. Every so often, run fresh water over the cloth and give it a good squeeze. (You don't want the cloth dripping wet, just damp.) Keep in mind that this is just to hold things over until you can clean with a capital *C*. If you come across any truly offensive messes, do a fast spot cleaning with an all-purpose cleaner.

5 Fab Multipurpose Cleaners

If you could select just a handful of commercial products for the full range of cleaning chores around the house, which would you choose? We put the question to professional cleaner Patty Metheny, who owns Sparklin Clean in Knoxville, Tennessee. Her choices are available in supermarkets, hardware stores, and discount stores.

Greased Lightning. A great all-purpose cleaner, particularly for bathrooms. Spray and wipe, or let the cleaner sit for a while on heavy stains.

Windex. This tried-and-true window cleaner is also handy for cleaning kitchen and bathroom countertops.

Mr. Muscle. This oven cleaner also makes porcelain bathtubs sparkle.

Clorox Clean-Up. Great for bathroom and kitchen cleaning, disinfecting, and killing mold.

OdoBan. An odor neutralizer handy for pet smells, bathrooms, kitchens, refrigerators, and carpets.

The ultimate efficiency for weekday cleaning would be to use only one cleaning product, Patty notes. And if she had to choose just one product from this list, it would be Greased Lightning. You can even use Greased Lightning on carpets, although it's a good idea to apply some to an out-of-the-way spot to test whether it will discolor the carpet. Don't use Greased Lightning on leather or on painted, varnished, or laminated surfaces.

Let the Windows Wait

On days when cleaning time is at a premium, save the windows for last. A dirty sink or tub is much more noticeable, so it gets priority, says Ruben Masas, manager of Maid of Honor cleaning service in Fort Lauderdale.

No Elbow Grease Required

Many cleaners need to soak in for several minutes to do their job thoroughly, so don't start scrubbing immediately after you spray a cleaner onto a surface, says Barbara Webster. Instead, spray on the cleaner and then find something else to clean— wipe down the smudgy front of your microwave, for instance, or do a top-to-bottom sweep of your fridge for leftovers that have lingered too long. When you return to the sprayed surface, you'll have an easy wipe-up job.

Beware the Dangerous Drip

The quick-cleaning approach for glass and other hard surfaces seems clear: Just spritz on some glass cleaner and wipe. But not so fast! If the cleaning solution runs down the surface and seeps inside, it can ruin the object that you're trying to be so kind to—the matting of framed pictures, for instance, or the inner workings of televisions, computer monitors, and other electronic equipment. Instead, lightly spray the glass cleaner onto your cloth and wipe as usual.

Freshen Carpets While You Sleep

You can deodorize a musty carpet or rug overnight with reliable, odor-busting baking soda. Sprinkle on the baking soda before you go to bed, then vacuum it up in the morning.

Clean Blinds on a Time Budget

Cleaning window blinds is an intimidating task. To speed up the process, close the blinds and run your dust cloth over the surface of the slats all at once, says Greg Longe, president and CEO of Molly Maid in Ann Arbor, Michigan. Then grab the bottom rail of each blind, pull it away from the window, and wipe the back of the slats. Next, close the blinds in the other direction and give both sides another quick wipe. You can use a multipurpose cleaner on metal or plastic blinds. Wipe fabric blinds with a dry cloth or use the brush attachment on your vacuum cleaner.

RALLYING THE TROOPS
Turn Rug Rats into Neatniks

Young children can handle a few weekday cleaning chores, and they'll even find the tasks fun if given the right kind of help, says Betsy Donoghue, a family educator and mental health coordinator at Parent-Child Development Corporation in Richmond, Virginia. For kids too young to read, cut out magazine pictures that depict the clothing that belongs in their dresser drawers and the toys that belong in certain bins. (Computer clip art works well, too.) Install low coat hooks and towel racks as needed so that kids can hang up their own jackets and towels. Start them out right, and they will be agreeable helpers for years to come.

Dialing for Dust Bunnies

Eliminate time-wasting arguments over whose turn it is to vacuum or dust by using a simple game. To start, choose one hour of the week as the time when every family member—including Mom and Dad—performs a cleaning chore, suggests Betsy Donoghue. Craft a spinner dial out of paperboard and a paper fastener or paper clip. Write one recurring household chore ("Vacuum the living room," "Mop the kitchen floor," or "Dust the dining room," for instance) in each of the dial's pie-

Use a homemade paperboard spinner to divvy up chores during family cleaning hour. Work together without a fuss, then treat yourselves afterward.

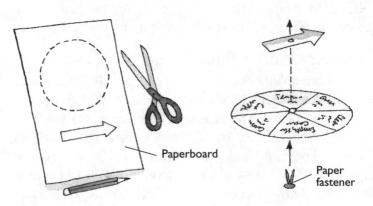

Paperboard

Paper fastener

A Better Way to Deal with Dishes

The typical family's breakfast routine goes something like this: Mom or Dad serves breakfast. The kids wolf down their food, dump their dishes in the sink, and vanish. Mom and Dad finish breakfast; then, finding the dishwasher full of clean dishes, they dump their dishes in the sink, too. Now there's a good chance that those dishes will occupy the sink until evening, when someone (probably you, saint that you are) finally empties the dishwasher and transfers the dirty dishes to the washer.

So much unnecessary effort and clutter! With a small change in your routine, you can ensure that dirty dishes are handled only once—by the person who used them—and that they spend not a moment in the sink, says Kathy Paauw, who runs an organizing and productivity firm called Paauwerfully Organized in Seattle. Just follow these two rules to reduce dish-related work by up to 15 minutes a day.

1. Empty the dishwasher while, or even before, the kids eat breakfast.
2. Enforce a rule that all members of the household must put their dirty dishes straight into the dishwasher, with no exceptions. If you leave one dirty dish in the sink, others will do the same.

shaped segments. Each person gives the dial a spin and tackles the assigned chore. When you're all working together, the team spirit will speed the work along. Plan for a treat or fun activity when the hour is up so that everyone will look forward to finishing.

Abuse It, You Lose It

Even the sloppiest kid will become an inspired neatnik under the dreaded "Out of Place, Out It Goes" rule. First, teach your children where all toys, books, games, and clothes are supposed to be stored. Then make sure they understand this rule: Whenever those items are found in an inappropriate place— say, the middle of the living room floor—they will be tossed out. (Okay, maybe you'll just hide them in the closet for a month, but you don't have to tell the kids that.) The rule sounds extreme, but invoke it once, and you may never need to enforce it again.

STALKING THE WILD DUST BUNNY

Try the Hoover Maneuver

You thought your vacuum cleaner was a simple device. Yes, it sucks up dust and dirt and takes it out of circulation. But there's more to the story. All of that machine-generated wind has to go somewhere once it's been filtered, and that somewhere is back into the room—which means that your vacuum cleaner can also blow other dust all over the place. What's a poor homemaker to do? Put vacuuming at the top of the chore list in the room you want to clean, says Ruben Masas, manager of Maid of Honor cleaning service in Fort Lauderdale. Then wipe up the dust that has collected on other surfaces in the room. Yes, this violates the old "Clean from the Top Down" rule, but it works.

Mist Those Dust Bunnies

Tired of chasing those wily dust bunnies under the bed or down the stairs? Ruben Masas gives them a light spritz of water with a spray bottle. Dust bunnies are attracted to the water—and weighted down by it—making them much easier to round up with a broom.

Let Your Furnace Do the Dusting

If your home has a forced-air heating system, you can cut your dusting chores in half by checking the furnace filters frequently, says Barbara Webster, president of Nice N Clean Maid Service in Miami. If the filters are matted with dust, they aren't able to do their job, and dust will build up much more quickly in your house. So check the filters every 2 weeks during heating season and replace them whenever they become clogged. (Replacement filters cost only a couple of dollars each.)

Dust—And Then Say Gesundheit?

Pretreated throwaway dust cloths are a boon for quick jobs during the week, but there's a cheaper alternative. Lotion-treated facial tissues work just as well for dusting touch-ups, particularly on books, televisions, and windowsills. The price is right—a box of 175 or more tissues costs only a couple of bucks. Plus, there's no storage involved, because unlike most cleaning supplies, you can put them in plain view on the coffee table. And if you use lotion-treated tissues for daily dusting, you're more likely to have them on hand if someone develops a miserably sore runny nose. What a relief!

Sock It to Dust

You've probably seen those mitt-shaped dust rags at the grocery store. You slip one on your hand, and you can dust everything from shelves and knickknacks to chair railings. Well, guess what? You already have perfectly good dusting mitts at home: orphaned socks. They're just taking up space in a drawer, so why not put them to work? Slip one over your hand, and you're ready to dust. (If you're going to use a cleaning solution or polish and you have sensitive skin, slip on a pair of latex kitchen or surgical gloves before donning the sock.) Use the flat of your palm to wipe surfaces and extend a single sock-covered finger to tease dust out of tight corners.

Tidy When Time Is Tight

No time to vacuum? Do what apparel design consultant JoAnn Marra of West Bay Shore, New York, does to keep pace with her shedding pets: Keep a pet hair or lint roller handy. You can roll it over upholstery or rugs to pick up dust bunnies or lint in a jiffy. Even if you don't have pets, use it to give your room a just-picked-up look until you have time to vacuum.

Safety First for Ceiling Fan Cleaning

Dust bunnies are big fans of ceiling fans. (Or should we call them dust birdies up there?) Patty Metheny, owner of Sparklin Clean in Knoxville,

Glorious Gizmos

Cobweb Collector

Dust and cobwebs like to collect in ceiling corners and hold conventions around light fixtures—out of reach, of course. If you attack the situation with a feather duster, you'll just spread the dust around the room, moving the dirt from one location to another, notes Patty Metheny, owner of Sparklin Clean in Knoxville, Tennessee. Here's a quick way to do high-altitude dusting. Wrap a cleaning cloth around the business end of a broom and secure it with a rubber band. Spray the cloth with a dust-attracting product (Patty uses OdoBan, but Endust will do the job, too), then make a clean sweep of the ceiling.

Tennessee, has a safe, no-nonsense approach to dispatching the offending critters: Stand on a step stool and use a dry cleaning cloth to knock the dust bunnies to the ground, then vacuum them up. Sure, it's a two-step process, but it actually saves time and is safer. Using a spray cleaner or a moist cloth could smear the dust onto the surface of the fan blades, and who wants to deal with wiping down fan blades while doing a high-wire act?

CONQUERING CLUTTER

Set Up a Mail Station

It's an age-old story played out in millions of households: The mail comes into the house, and most of it winds up in an ever-growing pile that will eventually take 2 hours to sort. Meanwhile, wedding invitations are ignored, and bills and medical

Glorious Gizmos

Bill Holder of Champions

When bills pile up in a stack, it's easy to lose track of their due dates. Be kind to your credit record and craft a simple bill holder to place in your kitchen or next to the spot where you sit when paying the bills. To make the bill holder, cut a cereal box in half lengthwise and place one half inside the other, says Raleigh, North Carolina, housewife Benedicte Whitworth.

Tape the two halves together and cover the holder with wrapping paper (if the Wheaties motif is not your cup of tea). For stability, rest the bill holder against a wall or other firm support. When bills come in, immediately write the due date on the end of the envelope and stand the envelope on end in the holder, with the due date showing. Your days of late payments will be over.

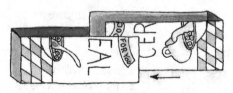

Push two halves together.

Cereal-box bill holder

records languish. If this sounds like your home, set up a simple mail-opening station, suggests professional organizer Patty Bareford, owner of Wide Open Space in Concord, Massachusetts. Pick up a rack for holding files upright (just a few dollars at an office supply store) and set it up in a place where there's a trash can within easy reach. Label a file folder for each member of the family, plus a file marked Urgent in bold red letters and positioned up front so it can't be ignored. As you open the mail each day, let nothing end up in a pile. Instead, put mail pertaining to a family member in the appropriate folder. Mail that requires immediate action goes into the Urgent folder, and all that junk mail goes in the circular file. You'll never have to dig through that mountain o' mail again!

Keep Junk out of the House

Here's a simple way to keep junk mail out of your home: As you walk back from the mailbox, quickly sort through your mail and stop by the recycling bin or trash can before you head inside. About half of the mail you receive is easy to identify as junk, and you can toss it without bothering to open it. The less mail you pile on the kitchen table, the less you'll have to cart back outside to the trash later.

Lean on Library Loaners

Cultivating the library habit will not only keep your book warehousing to a minimum, but it also will save you tons of money, says Patty Bareford. When you're ready to read a book, check it out of the library rather than buying it. (If your local library doesn't have the book, ask the librarian to obtain it through interlibrary loan. Or your library may be willing to buy it outright for its collection.) This approach saves you the cost of buying books, ensures that the only books lying around your den are the ones you're actively reading, and seriously reduces your dusting time.

Get the Hang of High Storage

If your home is tight for space, finding innovative ways to store bulky items will reduce your daily stress. To do this, think creatively about using your walls for storage. Hang a

My Big, FAT Filing Process

Kathy Paauw, who runs an organizing and productivity firm called Paauwerfully Organized in Seattle, has a three-step approach to whittling paper piles down to size. Memorize her approach by remembering FAT, which stands for file, act, and toss. Following her system will save you at least 20 minutes a week compared to random paper stacking and sorting.

Here's how it works. Grab a stack of papers and get ready to sort them into three piles. Put papers that you'll need for future reference in the "file" stack and put the stack in a file folder when you're done. Any papers that require you to "act" should be dealt with right away or placed in a dated tickler file so that they will be available at the right time. The rest go in the "toss" pile. You'll find that up to 80 percent of your papers will end up in this pile, Kathy says.

When you're trying to decide whether to keep a paper, answer these questions.

- What's the worst that could happen if you threw it away?
- Could you get another copy later if you needed it?
- Will it become obsolete by the time you retrieve it from a file?
- Will the paper play a significant role in your personal or professional life?
- Are there legal or tax reasons to keep the paper?

spare chair on the wall (and tell your guests it's pop art or Shaker style). Suspend your bicycle from the garage wall or ceiling using rubber-coated hooks. Wall-mounted lamps will conserve precious floor and tabletop space.

A Tidy Bedroom in 60 Seconds

One minute is all you need to tidy up even the messiest bedroom, says Barbara Webster, president of Nice N Clean Maid Service in Miami. Here's her five-step whirlwind formula. Got your running shoes on?

1. Make the bed: Pull up the cover and straighten the pillow.
2. Collect all the clothes that are flung about the room. Dirty stuff goes in the hamper. Clean clothes go in a "to be put away" basket or pile (an assignment for the owner of the bedroom).

3. Toss toys into toy bins or baskets.
4. Put books in a neat pile or on a shelf.
5. For a nice cosmetic touch, position the curtains so that each side is equally open. Either pull blinds up or leave them down but open.

Deep-Six the Duplicates

Take inventory of the items in your kitchen, and you're likely to find an array of duplicates: two corkscrews, three ice cream scoops, four sets of measuring spoons. Golly, you think, they cost money—better keep them! You're wrong, says Kathy Paauw. There's no value to these items if all they do is clutter up your life. In fact, those extra items cost you precious time as you sort them through to find the utensils you really need. Whenever you run across unneeded duplicates, pull them out of the drawer or cabinet and set them on course to a large cardboard box in your garage or basement marked Yard Sale.

Oh, My Darlin' Clementine

When your family has finished off those sweet little oranges called clementines, you're left with a little wooden crate. Benedicte Whitworth, a housewife in Raleigh, North Carolina, says that these crates are miracle organizers for the pantry. Use one to hold all the soup packets, hot chocolate envelopes, sauce mixes, and cake mixes. Another can serve as a storage basket for onions. What's more, they make cleaning the pantry a snap: Just lift the crate out, wipe the shelf, and put it back.

A Counter on Wheels

Have you ever had a kitchen with too much counter space? We didn't think so. Of course, there's no time during the week to redesign your kitchen, or even to rethink the overall arrangement of items on your kitchen counters. However, there is a way to create more counter real estate in your kitchen. Pick up a wheeled cart at a local kitchen store or home center. Some have butcher-block tops, cabinets, or open-shelf arrangements. In itself, the cart creates some new storage space. Plus, if you move your microwave oven onto the cart, you'll open up a huge chunk of counter space.

KITCHEN AND BATH TOUCH-UPS

Steam-Clean Your Microwave

The inside of your microwave oven probably looks like an abstract painting: spaghetti sauce from last Thursday, chicken soup from the weekend. And, of course, it's all baked on so hard that you'll need an archaeologist's chisel to chip it off (which you don't want to do, by the way, because you would damage the walls). There's a simple secret that will transform this cleaning nightmare into a simple weekday chore, says Greg Longe, president and CEO of Molly Maid in Ann Arbor, Michigan. Fill a microwave-safe dish halfway with water. Place the dish in the microwave and heat it for a few minutes, until the water boils. Open the door, and you'll see that the crusted-on grunge is now a steam-softened smudge that you can sponge away with ease.

Rub-a-Dub-Dub

Using an abrasive cleanser on dishware is a balancing act. Use a cleanser that's too wimpy, and you'll never remove that oven-hardened cheese. Use a cleanser that's too abrasive, and you'll permanently scratch the dish or pan. What to do? Scrub with a paste made from baking soda and water. If that combo doesn't rub your cares away, sprinkle on some Bon Ami, recommended by manufacturers as a dish-friendly abrasive cleanser. You'll get the job done in the shortest amount of time possible, and the finish on your dish or pan will remain sparklingly scratch-free.

Go for the Glitz

Nothing improves the look of a kitchen or bathroom like sparkling fixtures, and it's easy to get that shine. Just spray glass cleaner on the fixtures, wipe them down, and take a bow. If there's no glass cleaner handy, use rubbing alcohol. Or wipe the fixtures

The Second Time Around

Keep a Lid on That Pepper Mill

Those potato chips sold in cardboard tubes have little plastic lids that come in handy. North Carolina housewife Benedicte Whitworth sets her pepper mill on top of such a lid to keep the peppercorn fragments from littering up her spice shelf. (Weren't you looking for an excuse to put Pringles on your shopping list?)

Contaminated Sponges

Problem:
Kitchen sponges and washcloths can harbor nasty bacteria that could cause illness.

Do This Now:
Throw out those sponges and washcloths and whip out new ones. Even if the old cleaning implements appear pristine, assume that bad bugs are lurking there.

Do This for Good:
Once a week, douse your sponges and washcloths in a bleach and water solution. Combine one part chlorine bleach and four parts water in the sink. Toss in the sponges and washcloths and take off for a 2-hour lunch. When you return, rinse the sponges and washcloths thoroughly. They're ready for service, and your sink is sanitized to boot.

---

with toothpaste (a very mild abrasive) and rinse, says Barbara Webster, president of Nice N Clean Maid Service in Miami.

KEEPING UP WITH THE LAUNDRY

Lots of Laundry? Cool It!

As president of Miracle Maids in Brooklyn, Cindy Lebow knows a thing or two about laundry. She also has six children, which means that she has to run three loads of wash every day just to keep up. To fit that task into her busy weekday routine, Cindy skips the arduous process of sorting laundry. She throws whites and colors together and just washes everything in cold water. (Bonus: Her clothes never shrink, and she saves a bundle by not heating all that water.) For more cleaning power, she pretreats stains and adds a detergent booster such as OxiClean to the wash.

Bag the Socks and Undies

Figuring out whose socks are whose is never a problem if you don't mix your family's clothes together in the first place. To speed up your laundry routine, take this tip from professional organizer Pat Moore of McKenney, Virginia. Buy a mesh laundry bag for each family member and clip it onto a laundry

A Genie Sorts My Laundry

Not quite ready to abandon the practice of sorting your laundry before washing? If that's the case, try this tip that will cut the time you spend sorting laundry to nil, saving at least 15 minutes each week. The trick is to provide two laundry hampers in each room where dirty laundry collects, suggests Barbara Webster, president of Nice N Clean Maid Service in Miami. One hamper is for whites, and the other is for colors. For instant recognition, use one white and one brightly colored hamper. Or just label them, and make sure family members use them correctly. Dirty clothes will arrive in the laundry room presorted and ready to go straight into the washer.

hamper. Tell your family to put all socks and underwear into their individual bags. On washday, toss the bags into the washer and then the dryer, and return each bag to its owner intact. You'll never have to sort socks and undies again.

Strip and Spray

Why wait until your clothes get into the laundry room to treat them for stains? Organizing consultant Judy Brown of Yale, British Columbia, suggests keeping a container of stain remover in each laundry hamper. The moment a stained item of clothing goes into the hamper, it gets a squirt. Yes, the spray may dry out before washday, but this treatment will help break down the stain.

Treat Your Clothes to a Shake

The spin cycle usually leaves clothes twisted and mashed flat. If you toss your clothes into the dryer in this condition, you're making the whole laundry chore take longer than it needs to—and giving yourself some extra ironing to boot. Clothes take longer to dry when they're all balled up. So when you remove them from the washer, shake those duds out a bit. This little preventive measure also will reduce the wrinkles in your clothes.

Lighten the Load

Don't overload the dryer. To dry properly, your clothes need plenty of space to tumble around.

3

Don't Forget to Exercise

Fitting exercise into a busy day is a challenge, but the secret is to look for exercise opportunities all day long. We've discovered ingenious shortcuts to help you fit in simple exercises while you work, commute, clean the house, or even watch TV or lie in bed. As you test the exercise shortcuts in this chapter, always keep in mind that pain should *never* be part of any exercise or stretch, no matter where or how you do it. Stay within your comfort zone. If you do a lunge and it hurts your knee, for example, don't step so far forward.

EXERCISE GEAR AND GARB

The Smarter Dumbbell

There's an old saying, "A pint's a pound the world around," and that doesn't refer to the price of beer. It means that 1 pint of water weighs 1 pound. Thus you can fill a 2-liter (4-pint) soda bottle with water and know that you're lifting 4 pounds. A gallon jug weighs 8 pounds. By contrast, a gallon of paint in an aluminum can weighs 9 to 10 pounds, as does a gallon jug of olive oil or laundry detergent. (Paint and oil are both heavier than water, not to mention the weight of the containers.)

Build Strength with Beans and Rice

Peek into your kitchen cupboard, and you'll find objects that can serve as weights for arm and hand exercises. Rice, beans, split peas, and other legumes usually come in 1-pound plastic bags. Depending on your strength, a 1-pound weight might be heavy enough for you. If it's not, put two or more bags of beans in a plastic grocery bag and tie it tightly closed.

Work Out with Your Clothesline

Jumping rope is just about the best cardiovascular exercise there is, and a short session offers plenty of benefits. But you don't need to buy an expensive jump rope from the sporting goods store. An old-fashioned heavy cotton (not lightweight nylon) length of clothesline will do the trick. The thing to remember about jumping rope is to start slowly and gradually, so you don't overexert yourself.

Putty in Your Hands

Strengthening your hands can relieve that annoying ache that plagues you after a long session of knitting, crocheting, or typing. You can exercise your hands while you're riding in the car, watching TV, or waiting in the doctor's office, and the only gear you need is Silly Putty, Play-Doh, or modeling clay. Squeeze and release the putty in your clenched fists or between your fingers. Another way to strengthen your digits is to wrap a loop of clay around a bent finger. Slowly extend the finger to a pointing position, against the resistance of the clay. Keep a lump of the stuff in the glove compartment of your car. Squeeze it during your morning commute when you're stuck at a light or in traffic. It's exercise and stress relief at the same time.

Glorious Gizmos

Sock It to Yourself

If you have some old (uncooked) rice that you're ready to throw out, fill some orphaned socks with it. Tie the sock tops tightly and squeeze the socks to strengthen your hands.

4 Terrific Towel Exercises

Who says you need special time and equipment to exercise? Whenever you take a bath or shower, you have an exercise opportunity. A bath towel is so versatile, it may well be the duct tape of improvised exercise equipment. Here are four exercises to do right after you get out of the shower.

Arch scrunch. This exercise warms up and strengthens your arch muscles, which makes you less prone to foot injuries. Start by putting a towel on the floor. Place your heel on the floor so that just your forefoot is on the edge of the towel. Use your toes to pull the towel toward you without lifting your heel off the floor.

Triceps stretch. This one stretches and tones your triceps—the muscles at the back of your arms. Hold the towel in one hand. Raise it straight over your head and then bend your elbow and let the towel hang down your back. With your other hand, grab the other end of the towel behind your back and pull until you feel a gentle stretch in the triceps of the top arm. Next, hold the towel firmly with the bottom hand and pull with the top hand to tone the triceps.

Side stretch. Hold the towel between your hands and extend your arms over your head. Lean to one side and then the other until you feel a gentle stretch on each side. Don't bend forward as you do this stretch; keep your back straight.

Neck strengthener. You probably don't pay much attention to neck strength—until you go for a long bike ride or sit hunched over your desk and the muscles in your neck start to hurt. Here's the solution. Hold the towel taut with both hands in front of your forehead. Push against the towel until you feel resistance in your neck muscles. Hold for 5 seconds and repeat. Repeat, holding the towel against the back of your head and pushing your head backward.

Try the Tube Stretch

A 4-foot length of stretchy rubber surgical tubing is a low-cost, low-tech tool for stretching and strength workouts. This type of tubing is available from most hardware or medical supply stores. To turn the tubing into an exercise tool, tie the ends of the tubing together with a square knot to form a large loop. Hitch the loop to a doorknob or bedpost at waist height, grab the other end with your hand, and pull on the tubing to simulate many of the exercises you would do with a weight machine at the gym. For a leg workout, hitch the tubing to the leg of a bed or chair and slide your foot into the other end of the loop. Pull the tubing forward, as if you were kicking something with your foot, or sweep your foot sideways, alternating your stance so that you work the foot in both directions. Keep your upper body still during these exercises so that all the effort comes from your legs and hips.

Sleep in Your Sweats

If you're really pressed for time in the morning but you want to work out, be ready to go the minute you roll out of bed. Either go to bed in your workout clothes (sans sneakers, of course) or exercise in your pajamas. Pajamas are great workout clothes as long as they're loose and don't restrict your movement or breathing.

Call the Cops

Baseball coach Ryan Crawford of Oneonta, New York, knows that when an impromptu exercise opportunity crops up, there's no need to worry about donning special exercise shoes. He relies on black police shoes to take him seamlessly from work to play. "I got this idea from my mother, who was a cop when I was a kid," Ryan says. "She used to wear her black uniform shoes most of the time, even when she was off duty, because they were the most comfortable shoes she owned. She said they worked just as well if she was walking a beat, chasing a felon, playing catch with me in the yard, or doing anything adult like PTA meetings or court appearances. Cop shoes are pretty inexpensive compared to real dress shoes or even a good pair of sneakers. You can buy them in any army-navy or uniform supply store."

EVERYDAY EXERCISE SHORTCUTS

A Counter-Productive Exercise

Whether you're waiting for the microwave to ding, the copier to collate, or the laundry to dry, you are probably standing next to a counter. That counter is exercise equipment in disguise, just waiting for you to take the opportunity to exercise your chest and shoulder muscles.

Stand about 2 feet away from the counter with your feet together. Extend your arms and hold the edge of the counter with your hands. Without bending your knees or arching your back, bend your elbows and lower yourself toward the counter. Slowly raise yourself again.

You can do this exercise against a wall, too. Stand facing the wall. Extend both arms and place your palms on the wall at about shoulder height. Lean forward, bending at the elbows,

5 Exercises to Do before the Day Begins

Think you don't have time for a morning stretch routine? Here are some stretches to do before you leave your bed. They won't take much time, and you'll start the day warm and loose.

Stretch out. Extend your arms over your head, straighten your legs, and point your toes. Stretch your whole body—imagine that you're making yourself an inch taller. Hold for a moment, relax, and repeat.

Sign your name with your foot. Raise one foot in the air and with fluid, florid "strokes," slowly write your name. You can do this while seated on the edge of your bed, or for a harder workout, lie on your back or stomach. Work one foot and then the other. For a change of pace, occasionally do both feet at once. This stretch loosens and warms up your ankles.

Scrunch up the covers. Use your hands to gather up the blanket, top sheet, or comforter on your bed with a grabbing, scrunching motion. Stop every so often to vary the exercise by twisting the blanket as if you were wringing it out. This one warms up the wrists and forearms.

Build an arch. Lie on your back with your arms by your sides. Bend both knees, placing your feet flat on the bed. Raise your buttocks off the bed and hold for about 10 seconds. This works your thighs, buttocks, and back.

Make like a cat. Roll over and get on your hands and knees. Start with a flat back (don't let it sag) and look down at the bed (to avoid straining your neck). Arch your back up like a cat that has just awakened from a nap. Hold the position for a moment and then return to the flat-back position. Repeat a couple of times to warm up and stretch your upper and lower back.

until your nose almost touches the wall. Push away from the wall with your arms until you are standing up straight again.

Chair Squats

Here's an exercise to repeat each time you sit down in or stand up from a chair. Stand with a chair or sofa behind you. Sit down and then repeat the process of standing and sitting 8 to 10 times. Make sure to maintain proper form: Keep your back straight, not arched. Keep your head up; feet should be about shoulder width apart and flat on the floor. A good way to make sure your technique is correct is to look up at the ceiling while you sit.

Fast Lifting Lets You Down

In weight training, as your strength increases, you have to keep adding weight to achieve the same results. So it stands to reason that lifting faster must be better, too, right? Wrong. According to professional trainer Eric Hörst, author of *Training for Climbing*, most people would benefit more from their weight training if they slowed down. Slow, precise lifts and lowers maximize the work your muscles perform in a given movement, whereas faster lifts use momentum instead of muscles to complete the movement. To prevent yourself from rushing your lifts, Eric suggests mentally reciting a lifting cadence of "one-one-thousand [up], one-one-thousand, two-one-thousand [down]."

Carry Those Groceries

If you're just picking up a few items at the grocery store, carry a basket instead of pushing a cart. Each aisle you walk with a basket full of groceries is like another rep with weights.

Walk This Way for Mall Savings

Many malls are open several hours early for walkers, which accommodates even those who must exercise before the workday starts. Do a few rounds of all the mall corridors for a low-impact workout in any weather. As a bonus, you'll get to see the latest clothing styles and check storefront promotions to see what's on sale. And if all that exercise causes you to drop a clothing size, you'll know precisely where to shop for your new wardrobe.

Map a Museum Route

If walking at the mall doesn't excite you, try a local history or art museum.

If you cover every exhibit, taking the stairs instead of the elevator, you can rack up a couple of miles. And the mental stimulation from the museum is a good stress reliever, too.

Abs First

If you have time for only one strength exercise, work on your abs, says ace rock climber Arnould t'Kint. The abdominal muscles, he says, "are central to your overall body strength, and they don't require much time, or any special apparatus, to work on." Arnould avoids weight machines and gimmicky workout devices and focuses instead on basic crunches. To do crunches, lie on the floor, bend your knees, and put your hands by your ears (but not behind your head) and your elbows out. Lift your shoulders up off the floor, keeping your chin out, not tucked into your chest. Concentrate on lifting with your stomach, not your back. Release, let your shoulders go back, and repeat. To vary this exercise, try to touch your left knee with your right elbow, then your right knee with your left elbow, alternating with each lift. It's pretty tough to touch your knee, but the attempt puts a twist in your crunch that works your oblique muscles as well as your abdominals. Even a 5-minute ab workout each day will pay huge dividends in increasing strength and reducing back pain, Arnould says.

Exercise during Drive Time

Of course, you won't be doing jumping jacks while you're cruising down the highway, but you can do this simple sequence of isometric exercises while you're driving or stopped at a light. Hold each position for 10 to 15 seconds.
1. Pull in your abs, hold them, and then release.
2. Squeeze the wheel tightly, first with your left hand, then with your right hand.
3. Press your lower back into the seat back and then release.

Subway Strength Training

"When I used to ride the T to work in Boston, I'd try to make the best of it and get some exercise," says writer Dougald MacDonald. "I'd stand on the balls of my feet or alternately raise

9 At-Your-Desk Stretches

Sitting all day can make your whole body ache. Of course, the best solution is to get up and go for a walk. But when you don't have time to leave your desk, do one or more of the following stretches.

Toe touch. Slide your chair away from your desk and sit with your feet flat on the floor. Bend forward slowly as far as you can, reaching for your feet. Hold for 5 seconds. Use your leg muscles to push yourself back up.

Knee kisser. Sit up straight and pull one knee toward your chest. Clasp the knee with both hands for 5 seconds. Release the knee and then repeat with the other one.

Back arch. Sit with your feet about hip width apart and flat on the floor. Clasp your hands behind your head and slowly arch your back, bending your head backward as well. Hold this stretch for up to 5 seconds, relax, and repeat.

Shoulder circles. Let your arms relax at your sides, then raise your shoulders and rotate them up and back in a circular motion. Repeat up to five times, then change directions.

Neck stretch. Sit up straight. Slowly turn your head to the left and hold for 5 seconds. Then turn to the right and hold.

Over and out. Sit up straight in your chair. Interlace your fingers and lift both arms over your head. Keeping your arms straight, slowly lean to your right. Hold for about 5 seconds, then repeat to the left.

Hand waves. Hold your hands out in front of you with your fingers splayed. Rotate your hands in circles, gently working your wrists. Repeat several times.

Finger work. With your hands out in front of you, clench both fists and hold for 5 seconds. Then spread your fingers as far as you can and hold for 5 seconds. Repeat five times.

Palm push. Raise your arms over your head and interlace your fingers so that your palms are facing out. Push your palms out to stretch your arms and shoulders.

and lower my heels. With enough repetitions, it's a powerful workout for calf muscles." You can do these low-tech calf raises anywhere—in front of a sink or copying machine, for example—but the extra effort required to stay in balance on a rocking subway train offers an exercise bonus.

Double Dips

Sitting around waiting for a phone call? Use that time to give your arms a workout. Sit on the edge of a bed or chair with your feet flat on the floor in front of you. Place your hands on the edge of the seat on either side of your butt. Keeping your elbows close to your body, lift yourself off the seat so that you are supporting yourself on your hands. Slowly lower your body below the level of the seat by bending your elbows. Go only as low as you feel comfortable, and never let your elbows bend more than 90 degrees. Raise yourself back to the starting position. How many "dips" you should do depends on how fast your arms become fatigued. Work your way up to sets of five or more.

Exercise Your Eyes

Staring at a computer screen all day can cause eyestrain, fatigue, and headaches, but these woes are easy to prevent with just a few minutes of eye exercise each day. During the day, once every hour, take your eyes off the screen for about a minute and look at an object in the distance. Then roll your eyes and look side to side for another half minute.

Get on the Ball

Would you like to exercise all day long and never leave your desk? All you need is a fitness ball, also known as a Swiss ball. "These sturdy, large, inflatable rubber balls cost only about twenty-five dollars, and they're well worth the price," says Lori Baird, editor of *Powersculpt*. Use the ball as a desk chair. While you're sitting on the ball, you can do exercises to strengthen your lower back and abdominal muscles. Try this sequence.

1. Lift one foot a few inches off the ground and balance. Switch feet.
2. Roll the ball about a foot away from your desk. Plant both feet on the floor wider than shoulder width apart. Lean forward and stretch your back muscles. Hold for several seconds.

3. Squeeze the ball with your legs for a few seconds, then release to work your adductors (inner thigh muscles).
4. Place your feet shoulder width apart and put your hands on your thighs. Make small circles with your hips. Do several in each direction. This exercise loosens and stretches your lower back.
5. In the same position, gently rock your pelvis forward and backward to loosen your lower back. Moving your pelvis as little as 1 inch is beneficial.

EXERCISE WHILE YOU CLEAN

Dance the Dirt Away

To turn everyday housecleaning into a workout, you need to get in the mood to move with vigor. So turn up the stereo and dance the dirt—and weight—away!

Do the Vacuum Cleaner Lunge

You may think that only your arms and eardrums get a workout when you vacuum. But if you use an upright machine, you can involve your legs as well. Grab your upright vacuum cleaner by the handle. As you push it forward, step forward with one leg, bending the knee slightly. Keep your back straight and don't let your front knee go past the toes of the front foot. Push off the front foot and return to a standing position. Repeat the lunge with the other leg, then continue alternating sides for a complete lower-body workout—while you clean your house.

Reach for the Stars (and the Dust)

Dusting high shelves offers a wonderful opportunity to stretch and work your upper back and shoulder muscles. First, reach for the shelves without lifting yourself onto your toes; concentrate on making yourself longer. Then stretch again while going up onto your tiptoes.

Spin Your Laundry

Turn the dull chore of doing the laundry into a productive exercise for your core muscles—those in your lower back and abdomen. This exercise works best with top-loading washers and dryers, but it will work with front-loading machines, too.

Stand so that the laundry basket is on your right and the washer is on your left. Position the basket so that you can comfortably reach both it and the washer. Your feet should be about hip width apart. Keeping your hips facing forward as much as possible, turn from the waist and bend your knees to pick up some of the laundry in the basket. Turning at the waist again, place it in the washer. When you do this, you should feel a stretch in your abs and your obliques (sides). After 6 to 10 reps, turn so that the basket is on your left and the washer is on your right to work the other side of your body.

When the clean laundry is ready to go into the dryer, repeat the drill. You'll be getting an even better workout, because wet laundry is heavier than dry.

Lift That Laundry Detergent

Once the laundry is in the washer, you'll have to add some detergent, and that's yet another opportunity to squeeze in a little exercise. Imagine that you're going to pull the starter cord on a lawn mower—only the starter cord is actually your bottle or box of detergent. Slowly raise the bottle or box to your hip and bring it down again, repeating several times.

TV TIME EXERCISE TIPS

Plan an Exercise Program

To plan your exercise time for the coming week, pull out your copy of *TV Guide* and highlight your favorite programs. Then make a list of exercises you can do in 3-minute intervals and keep that by the TV, too. A 1-hour TV

Calorie Counts for Household Chores

Lose weight while you clean! Sounds like an infomercial, but it's true. You burn calories while you do housework just as you do at the gym. Here's a rundown of how many calories you consume during just 30 minutes of household activities. (Note: While you're cleaning, don't forget to switch hands frequently to work both sides of your body.)

Activity	Calories Burned per 30 Minutes
Cooking	105
Food shopping at a supermarket	135
Gardening	168
Making the bed	117
Mopping the floor	126
Polishing furniture	72
Scrubbing while standing	87
Sweeping the floor	51

program usually has four 3-to-4-minute commercial breaks. During just one of those breaks, you can do three different weight-lifting exercises or 4 minutes of aerobics. With your list by your side, the next time a commercial comes on, you'll be ready to go.

Try the Chair Slide

If you're older or are recovering from an illness, you may be worried that exercise isn't for you. Well, you haven't tried the chair slide. Not only can you perform this gentle doctor-approved exercise while you sit and watch TV, but it's an excellent introduction to an exercise program. All you need is a chair and two paper plates. Put one paper plate under each foot. As you pump your arms back and forth, slide your feet back and forth. Perform 10 times and repeat. As a variation, press your arms straight up over your head while you slide your feet.

Do Your Kegels

It's not uncommon for older women to experience loss of bladder control, or incontinence, as they age. If this has become a problem for you (or even if it hasn't), fight back by

3 Exercises for TV Time

Most evenings, you know where you're going to end up: parked in front of the TV, watching your favorite program. Why not turn that time into exercise time? Of course, you could ride an exercise bike or walk on a treadmill while you watch TV, but here are three simple exercises to do without buying any expensive equipment.

Leg lifts. Sit on the edge of the sofa and extend one leg, pointing your toe. Bend the leg again. Repeat 12 times to strengthen the tops of your legs (quadriceps) and your knees.

Ball rolls. Place a tennis ball on the floor and roll it back and forth under your foot to soothe your aching feet after a hard day's work.

Marble pickup. Place some marbles (or wads of paper) on the floor around your feet. Lifting first one foot and then the other, pick up the marbles or paper with your toes to stretch and strengthen your feet.

doing your Kegels while you watch TV or sit at your desk. Kegels are a simple exercise you can do to strengthen the pelvic floor muscles (which are related to bladder control). To find the pelvic floor muscles, pretend that you are trying to stop the flow of urine. Tighten and relax the muscles 10 to 20 times, holding each contraction for 3 to 4 seconds. Repeat several times a day.

Do the Refrigerator Chest Stretch

When a commercial comes on, you head straight for the refrigerator, right? Don't grab a snack, but instead do this stretch. Stand facing the front of the refrigerator. With your left arm extended in front of you at shoulder height, place your left palm on the left side of the fridge. Without moving your hand, turn your body to the right until you feel a gentle stretch in your chest and shoulder. Hold for 10 seconds, then repeat on the other side.

Take a minute to stretch instead of reaching into the refrigerator for a snack.

Roll It!

Tight calf muscles are the bane of a walker's existence. Not only can they make walking uncomfortable, but they also can lead to injuries such as shinsplints. The good news is that you can keep those muscles loose and warm while you watch TV. Next time you come home from your evening stroll with tight, achy calves, grab a rolling pin. While you watch your favorite show, roll the pin gently back and forth over your calves. The rolling will increase the blood flow to your muscles, which will help prevent injury.

EXERCISING OUTDOORS

Walk through Water

Even if you don't like to swim for fitness, you can get plenty of exercise at the beach or pool. Whether you're playing with the kids in the shallow end of the pool or walking alongside the surf, try striding purposefully through shin- to thigh-deep water. Do laps across the pool or count 20 strides in the ocean, with a rest between each set. You'll be amazed how much this works your legs and back.

Just Take One Step

Here's a trick from Pennsylvania-based professional trainer Eric Hörst for those days when you don't feel like exercising. "Just tell yourself you're going to do a scaled-back workout, not the full deal," Eric says. For instance, if you normally walk or run 2 miles, simply resolve to go outside for a brief walk around the block—much less of a mental hurdle to overcome on a "down" day. Interestingly, Eric says, "once you get out the door and start walking, you'll begin to feel better and usually decide to keep going—often for the full length of your workout."

Get a Grip!

If your bike handlebar grips are coming off, spritz a little hair spray inside the grips. While the hair spray is wet, the grips slide on with no problem. Once they're on, let them dry for a few minutes, and the grips will be on good and tight.

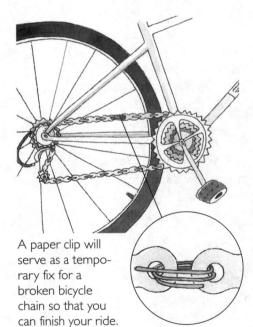

A paper clip will serve as a temporary fix for a broken bicycle chain so that you can finish your ride.

Clip Your Bike Chain

Pop a chain on your bicycle on your way to work? Don't despair—as long as you have a paper clip of any size (even a small one) with you. Just clip the broken links together, replace the chain, and you'll be off again in a flash.

Your Dog Will Make You Do It

People who want to stay healthy need to exercise for at least an hour a day—double the previous workout recommendation—according to a new study released by the Institute of Medicine. "Most people don't have time to exercise for one hour continuously, and it's just as beneficial to break it up

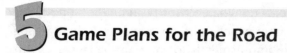

5 Game Plans for the Road

"I have to drive around a lot, especially when I'm on recruiting trips," says Ryan Crawford, a baseball coach at a small college in upstate New York. "After a while, you've got to stop to stretch your legs. Sure, walking around the parking lot at a rest stop is okay, but why not use that time to get some exercise that's a little more fun and challenging?" Here are some items Ryan suggests keeping in your trunk so that you can enjoy your driving breaks.

Frisbee. A game of Frisbee works your whole body—legs, torso, and arms. If you have a dog along on your trip, you can use the flying disc to help him burn off some excess energy, too.

Medium-size playground ball. A ball is good for spur-of-the-moment soccer or kickball games. It also can substitute for a volleyball or basketball in a pinch. Choose one that's all rubber and about the size of a soccer ball.

Golf driver and Wiffle golf balls. Don't just stand there—practice your driving!

Tennis balls. Play catch or handball, or juggle. Add a twig or frozen ice pop stick, and you've got a game of hit the stick.

Kite (and string, of course). Choose a style you can roll up or otherwise collapse so it won't take up much space.

● ●

throughout the day," says Andrew Flach, author of *Combat Fat!* Fitting exercise into your daily life is as simple as taking the stairs instead of the escalator; adopting an active hobby such as tennis, golf, or gardening; or riding your bike on local errands instead of driving. If you're not self-motivated, disciplining yourself to adopt these habits can seem overwhelming. If that's the case, take Andrew's pet approach: Visit the local animal shelter and adopt a dog. With a loving, playful pet to accompany you on your daily walk or jog, you'll have consistent, enjoyable motivation to exercise.

Volunteer for Exercise

Another way to motivate yourself to exercise consistently is to combine good exercise with good deeds, suggests active volunteer Judy MacDonald of Yarmouth, Maine. "Many people I know are involved in the Maine Handicapped Skiing program, helping those folks do whatever they can on the slopes," Judy says. "Also, I know people who raise and train therapy dogs, which they take into hospitals to cheer up patients. It's great exercise walking those dogs! Some people also work with horses that physically or mentally challenged kids can ride. Or people can go on fund-raiser walks—good cause, good fun."

Intensify with Intervals

Professional trainer Eric Hörst of Lancaster, Pennsylvania, says, "For time-efficient aerobic workouts, I love interval training." To do intervals, you alternate walking with jogging, or slow walking with faster-paced walking. If you're walking along a road, for example, you might choose to speed up for the distance between two telephone poles, starting every fifth or sixth pole. This strategy burns more calories for a given distance than constant-pace walking or jogging. As your fitness increases, increase the length of the fast intervals.

Ski Tramp

Backcountry skiing guidebook author Lou Dawson of Carbondale, Colorado, offers this simple preseason workout for skiers. "A trick I use is to jump on one of those minitrampolines in my ski boots," Lou says. "I tilt one side of the tramp by setting its legs on a plank, so the angle built into the boots doesn't feel too awkward. Then I do three jumps: one simply up and down to warm up, one from side to side to simulate ski turns, and then a one-legged jump. The single-leg jump is what gives you the strength training; the others help with balance. Put some music on and do three ten-minute sessions a week. It's really effective. You can hold ski poles in your hands for balance, but don't use them to assist the jumps."

Bottles for Bases

A vigorous game of keep away, tag, softball, or soccer is a great way to exercise while enjoying some fun with friends or family. To be ready for an impromptu game, fashion four homemade markers to serve as bases or show the out-of-bounds areas. All you need is four take-out food tubs or plastic soda bottles. Paint them orange and fill them with water or sand so they'll stay put. Stow your markers in the garage or a closet when not in use.

Making Time for Pets

4

W hen the whirlwind pace of life overwhelms us, pets are a comfort to come home to. Their tapping tails, bodies wiggling with delight, and cheerful woofs, meows, and whistles are our rewards as pet owners. Pets demand our time, too, though, and that's why we've included this chapter of pet care shortcuts. From the food bowl to the grooming brush to playtime, this chapter contains plenty of "pawsitively" pleasing ways to save time, money, and frustration while enjoying a happy, healthy relationship with your pet.

FEEDING YOUR FURRY (AND FEATHERY) FAMILY

Set Out the Welcome Mat

Cats detest messes, but some are slobs when they eat. Bits of cat food end up scattered and stuck on the floor, becoming a smelly problem unless you wash your floor daily. To end this grimy mess, set food bowls on vinyl place mats that you can pick up and wipe clean with a sponge.

Serve a Tuna Toothbrush

Ever try brushing your cat's teeth with a pet toothbrush? Who needs the fuss or the fight? Sidestep these tense moments by keeping her teeth white and her gums healthy with a tuna "toothbrush." The next time you're at the supermarket, buy a piece of fresh tuna about the size of a deck of cards. Cut it into thumbnail-size pieces and store them in a container in the freezer. Once a day, pull out one or two pieces. Let them thaw for a minute, then offer them as treats to your cat. The action of chewing the tuna will help rid her teeth of surface tartar and massage her gums, says Jill Richardson, DVM, a veterinarian in Secaucus, New Jersey.

Buy in Bulk

Karen Cichocki, a registered nurse from Dyer, Indiana, has reduced the number of trips to the pet supply store by buying 40-pound bags of dry kibble for her dogs, Max, Misty, and Oliver. Ounce for ounce, the bigger bag costs less than a 5-pound bag, so she saves money as well as time. At first there was a problem with her dogs chewing through the bags for unauthorized snacks. To prevent this, Karen now pours the kibble into an 18-gallon plastic bin that keeps the food fresh, dry, bug-free, and safe from doggy raids. A trash can with a tight-fitting lid also works well as a kibble container.

3 MINUTES A DAY

Feed a Menagerie Faster

Feeding their three dogs and two cats took too much time each day for Karen and Rick Cichocki. Karen and Rick discovered that they could shave minutes off mealtime by pouring dry kibble into self-feeding bowls that provide a full day or two's supply. To foil dogs intent on eating the cat food, they set the cats' chow on a shelf out of the dogs' reach.

Soothe Sensitive Stomachs

For dogs that can't digest fatty or low-quality commercial foods, do what Leslie Sinclair, a veterinarian from Montgomery Village, Maryland, does for her greyhound, Moses. While she's preparing a meal for her toddler son, Zachary, she fixes a treat for Moses, too. For example, Leslie warms up an extra veggie burger (patty only) or occasionally offers Moses the crusts cut from Zachary's peanut butter sand-

Leaping for Liver

The monthly food bill for three dogs can be expensive, but Karen and Rick Cichocki have discovered a real money-saver. Instead of buying high-priced treats, they make homemade liver treats. "Our dogs love these treats as much as Rick loves my chocolate chip cookies," says Karen. "I make enough in a batch to freeze some and hand them out as treats." Here's her technique, which requires only a 1-pound package of sliced beef liver, 1/4 cup water, and a 6-ounce package of corn muffin mix.

1. Preheat the oven to 350°F.
2. In a food processor, process the liver slices on high, adding one slice at a time, until liquefied. With each slice, add a little of the water to the food processor until all the water is used.
3. Pour the corn muffin mix into a large bowl. Add the liquefied liver and mix thoroughly.
4. Spray an 8 1/2-by-11-inch baking pan with nonstick cooking spray.
5. Pour the mixture from the bowl into the pan.
6. Bake for 20 to 25 minutes, or until the middle springs back at your touch.
7. Allow the pan of treats to cool and cut into bite-size cubes. Store the cubes in resealable plastic bags in the freezer.

wiches. Both treats are nutritious and don't take any extra time to prepare.

Hot Dog, Dog Treats!

If you love to reward your dog with a crunchy treat but hate to pay the high prices for store-bought treat sticks, try making your own. They cost a fraction of the price of a commercial brand, and you can whip them up in a jiffy. Cut a hot dog lengthwise into thin strips (1/4 to 1/2 inch wide). Spread the strips on a plate and cover them with a paper towel. Microwave until they're crispy and dry, with a texture something like Styrofoam. (When you first try this, cook the strips in short bursts of about a minute each, until you have figured out the right total cooking time for your microwave.) Use any brand of hot dogs, but choose reduced-fat ones for dogs that are watching their weight. Break the treats into bits to use as bait for training, or give your dog a whole strip at once just to say you love him. Two 25-cent hot dogs will yield 18 sticks, which would cost you $2 to $3 at the pet store.

Weight the Water Bowl

Ferrets love to spill and splash water from bowls. Counter these tendencies by using spill-proof or heavy bowls that are difficult to tip. Marylou Zarbock, editor of *Ferrets* magazine in Mission Viejo, California, says weighted glazed ceramic or stainless steel bowls work well as water dishes and are dishwasher-safe.

Veggies for the Birds

Like vegetables? So do your birds. Bird owner Laura Doering of Long Beach, California, saves time by steaming packages of frozen lima beans, carrots, peas, and corn once a week as she prepares her dinner. She spoons the steamed mixture into individual plastic bags, putting about 1½ cups of veggies in each bag. Laura stores the bags in the freezer. In the morning, she thaws one bag and serves ¼ cup of veggies to each of her two birds, Ollie and Sunshine. She returns the rest of the veggies to the refrigerator, and in the evening, she heats that portion for her own dinner. Laura does the same each week with steamed pasta, making sure that the portions for her birds do not contain any salt or butter.

Flock to This Morning Routine

In under 5 minutes each morning, Melissa Kauffman ensures that Carlisle and Natty, her pair of cockatiels, are enjoying their breakfast before she leaves for work as group editor of *Bird Talk* and *Birds USA* magazines in Mission Viejo, California. Melissa sticks with a steady routine of feeding her birds pellets, a handful of seeds, and some greens, which she hangs from food clips in their cages. For time efficiency, she stores all these foods in one location just a couple of feet from the cage. Carlisle and Natty are busy munching their meals as Melissa scoots out the door.

BATHING AND GROOMING

Fun Makes Bath Time Faster

Bathing a dog that doesn't like to be washed is misery for you and the dog. Ensure that your puppy's first bath is a positive experience, and you'll avert untold frustration in the future. Here's a bathing routine that will help your puppy feel comfortable at bath time, says Jill James, a lifelong dog owner and middle school teacher from Allen, Texas.

1. Put your puppy in the sink or tub and add only enough water to wet the puppy's feet.
2. Slowly add water to wet the puppy's legs and body; wet his head last.
3. Shampoo and rinse. The key to removing shampoo residue is to shampoo up the body and rinse down the body with warm water.
4. As you dry off your puppy with an absorbent towel, let him play tug with one end of the towel. That way, your dog will associate bath time with playtime.

Soak Your Dog Shampoo

It's important not to shock an older dog's body with cold liquids during bathing, or bath time can become a battle of wills—and you'll end up losing valuable time if your dog jumps out of the tub and you have to coax him back in. Robyn O'Donnell, a certified master dog groomer and owner of the Pink Poodle Parlor in Westerly, Rhode Island, suggests this shortcut. Soak the shampoo container in a bucket of hot water or dilute the shampoo with warm water before applying it to the dog's coat.

Warm Water, Please

Using warm water at bath time is important, too. That's no problem when you bathe your dog in the tub, but if you plan to bathe your dog outdoors, what can you do? Buy an inexpensive attachment that connects your garden hose to your kitchen faucet, says Gigi Gonzales, a United Parcel Service (UPS) driver who shares her Claremont, California, home with

Timesaving Bath Time Tactics

At-home baths for your dog don't have to be a time-consuming chore. The secret is to prepare the bathtub or sink before you call your dog, says Patty Allard, who operates the Furry Friends Pet Salon in Pascoag, Rhode Island.

■ Make sure the bathtub or sink is clean. (A kitchen sink is the ideal bathtub for dogs under 15 pounds.)

■ Lay a rubber mat on the floor in front of the sink or tub to give you traction and reduce stress on your joints.

■ Remove any items on the counter or sink that you won't need while bathing and grooming your dog.

■ Place a nonslip mat in the tub to provide stable footing for your dog.

■ Shake out your towels and hang them on a nearby hook, doorknob, or cabinet handle.

■ Pop open the lid of your shampoo container. Put the container, along with any sprays and combs that you'll need, in a small bucket on the counter or beside the tub.

three dogs. The attachments are available at hardware stores and home centers.

Serve Peanut Butter in the Bath

If your dog is not a big fan of baths, distract her attention as you bathe her by smearing a tablespoon of peanut butter on the tile wall near her face. She can lick off the peanut butter while you rinse out the soap.

Throw in Three Towels

Avoid a spatter of bathwater by wrapping your dog in two bath towels before he can get out of the tub to do a full-body shake. After you've rubbed him dry in the tub, grab a third towel and wrap him in it as you begin brushing him. These towel tactics prevent the mess made by the dog trying to shake himself dry.

Bath Time without Water

Does your dog smell like a dirty sock, but you don't have time to give her a bath? Or perhaps your dog is recovering from surgery and shouldn't have her stitches soaked with soapy water. When a bath is not an option, lightly spritz your dog with an antistatic or detangler product specifically made for dogs. (You'll find these products at major pet supply stores.) Select a product that does not contain silicone, which can damage her coat. Follow up by brushing the product through her coat to lift out loose hair and debris. The unpleasant odor will disappear.

Making Time for Pets

The Ultimate Grooming Setup

If you have a lot of grooming tools to keep track of, you'll save time in the long run by installing a magnetic strip on the wall in the area where you groom your dog. As you work, you can stick your clipper blade, scissors, nail clippers, and other steel tools right to the wall, so they'll never be out of reach. Pet grooming professional Patty Allard also suggests that you put up a small rack with hooks to hold your brushes and grooming tools so that each item has its own place and won't be misplaced.

Snip Spare Hair

When a dog's coat has become a matted mess, grooming is anything but pleasant for him or you. Prevent mats from forming with this grooming shortcut recommended by Jill James of Allen, Texas. Spend a few minutes once a month snipping feathery hairs on your dog's legs (the areas most likely to attract grass, mud, and other messes). Jill finds that this quick technique keeps the fine coat on her Labrador–Irish setter, Dixie, mat-free.

Stop the Static Greeting

If you live in an area with cold winters, there is a risk of the dry heat indoors creating static electricity in the coats of

My Favorite Shortcut

Giving Dogs the Brush-Off

Each Tuesday and Thursday evening, Carol Oddi of New Fairfield, Connecticut, sets up for multitasking while watching her favorite TV shows. She seats herself between a wastebasket and a plastic storage box that contains a slicker brush (the type with metal bristles), a wide-tooth comb, and a small plastic bag. Then Carol calls Max and Belle, her pair of Kerry blue terriers, for their grooming sessions. She spends 10 to 30 minutes grooming each dog, taking the time to check their coats for fleas and cuts and to give them lots of one-on-one attention. "I keep the grooming tools right there so I don't have to hunt for them," says Carol, a regulatory specialist for a pet company, who also trains dogs in obedience. "I think of this grooming time as a time for me to relax with my dogs. It also strengthens our friendship bond."

your cats and dogs. To prevent this, do what Karen and Rick Cichocki of Dyer, Indiana, do for their three dogs, Oliver, Misty, and Max. They keep the dogs' coats shiny and static-free by wiping their fur with an antistatic dryer sheet before grooming. It's an inexpensive way to stop any unintentional zaps from the buildup of static electricity, and it's safe even if your dog tends to lick his coat.

Tame Those Tangles

Removing tangles in your dog's or cat's coat can be time-consuming for you and painful for her. Treat those tangles by sprinkling a little cornstarch into any trouble spots. Work your fingers through the snarls to separate the hairs, then follow up by combing with a wide-tooth comb.

Painless Brush Cleaning with Panty Hose

The bristles of your dog's brush can hurt your fingertips as you attempt to remove the hair stuck in it. Protect your fingers and reduce the time spent cleaning your brush by cutting up panty hose into squares big enough to cover all of the brush's bristles. Before brushing your dog, place the panty hose square over the bristles and pull it down so that the bristles poke through. As you brush your dog, the excess hair will stick to the panty hose. When it's covered with hair, just lift off the panty hose and replace it with another square.

Stick a square of panty hose over the bristles of a dog brush. To clean the brush, just pull off the panty hose to remove the hair without a fuss.

Add a Little Aloe

After thoroughly brushing your dog or cat, dab a little aloe into his coat to restore the moisture. This quick step will prevent your pet's coat from drying out and will stave off any minor skin problems due to dryness.

Cornstarch to the Rescue

Keep a small box of cornstarch or styptic powder within reach when you're trimming your dog's or cat's nails. In case you accidentally cut too deeply and cause bleeding on the nail, you can sprinkle on either substance to stop the bleeding, says Jill Richardson, DVM, a veterinarian in Secaucus, New Jersey.

Touch, Tickle, and Massage

Do you dread trimming your cat's nails? Prevent prolonged battles and painful scratches by following these four easy steps each week.

1. Bring your cat into a small room such as a bathroom (to prevent distractions or escapes), close the door, and wrap the cat in a thick towel (this gives you better control).
2. Speak in a calm, reassuring tone as you cut one nail at a time.
3. Always finish the trimming with praise and treats—your cat may even learn to look forward to the sight of the nail clippers.
4. Open the door and let your cat exit. Wait 10 seconds and then calmly leave the bathroom. This delay will help your cat realize that you are not going to chase her and that her "peticure" is no big deal.

A Sprinkle a Day . . .

Fortunately, most cats keep their coats in tip-top shape with daily self-grooming sessions. For those times when

They Had NO Shame

Share Your Shower with Your Birds

Conserving water is important in Long Beach, California, where Laura Doering lives, so she's come up with this twist on the old saying "Save water; shower with a friend." Each morning, Laura brings her tropical birds, Ollie and Sunshine, into the shower, placing Ollie on a special bird perch that hangs off the showerhead and Sunshine on a perch on the shower curtain rod. The birds enjoy the hot, steamy moisture on their feathers as Laura showers. This morning routine allows the birds' feathers to dry during the day so that they don't go to bed at night with wet feathers.

your cat smells like a dog, you can restore his freshness without a drop of water. Simply sprinkle about a tablespoon of baking soda on the cat's back and work the powder into his coat with your fingers. Baking soda absorbs unwanted odors and is safe for your cat.

Pining for a Brush

When Barbara Lee of Lake San Marcos, California, misplaces her cats' brushes, she doesn't fret. She simply goes outside and picks up a pinecone. Then she carefully runs the pinecone over her cats' coats to remove loose hair. Her advice: "Be sure to choose a pinecone that's dry and sap-free. This works great when you're in a pinch."

AVOIDING PET-RELATED MESSES

Vacuum Your Dog instead of Your House

Using your vacuum cleaner to remove loose hair directly from your dog is much more efficient than vacuuming your entire house. To vacuum your dog, adjust your vacuum cleaner to reduce the suction. (Some vacuum models feature a sliding cover that enables you to decrease the suction. If you're not sure how to do this, check the operating manual.) Use the upholstery brush and carefully maneuver it over your dog's coat. Don't insist on vacuuming your dog if she doesn't like it, and always finish a vacuuming session by giving your dog a well-deserved treat.

Trap Pet Hair with Packing Tape

Beware of beagles, rat terriers, and other breeds with short-cropped hair. True, they may not shed like a golden retriever, but their coarse, stiff hair can easily weave itself into the fabric on your couch and other furniture. Follow the advice of Marylou Zarbock, the proud owner of Taffy, a 7-year-old Dalmatian, and Toby, a 7-year-old rat terrier. "The best way to remove their embedded hair from my furniture is to use packing tape on the fabric," says Marylou, editor of *Ferrets* magazine. "I press a strip of this tape down, and it lifts up the dog hair. This tape has a better grip than the types you find on rollers sold at pet supply stores, and it's cheaper."

Stash a Lint Brush in Your Dash

When you have pets, no matter how hard you try, you occasionally end up with an embarrassing coating of pet hair on your clothes. Those stray hairs are no worry if you keep a lint brush in your car for speedy hair removal before you enter a nice restaurant, a friend's house, or your workplace.

Crate the Dog for a Clean Car

Audrey Pavia of Santa Ana, California, loves to travel with Nigel, her Pembroke Welsh corgi. But when Audrey bought a new SUV, she didn't want the interior to feature wall-to-wall dog hair. To save herself the chore of vacuuming the car's upholstery, she decided to keep Nigel inside a pet crate in the backseat on trips. The crate also protects Nigel from harm should Audrey need to brake abruptly.

Layer Those Cage Liners

Save time and aggravation by precutting about a week's supply of newspaper pages to fit the bottom of your bird's cage. Cut six to eight layers of newspaper to the right size and lay them in the cage. Each day, roll up the top layer and discard it, leaving the next clean layer ready. You'll reduce daily cage cleanup time to mere seconds.

Try This Cagey Idea

The area under a birdcage can deteriorate into an awful mess. To prevent this, place the bird's cage on a tile or linoleum floor. These surfaces are easier to clean than carpet. Also, position a throw rug under the cage. Once a week, shake the rug outdoors and then toss it into the washing machine. It beats scrubbing the floor!

TRAINING AND EXERCISE

A Toy Chest for Your Dog

Tired of tripping over your dog's toys? Seek out a child's toy chest at a yard sale or thrift shop (or perhaps you still have one stashed in the attic). The chest will work perfectly for storing all your dog's playthings. Bring out one or two toys at a time to keep your dog occupied but not overwhelmed by too many choices. This strategy also accents your prestigious role as Keeper of the Toys in the eyes of your loyal dog.

Dog-Proof Door Latch

Training a dog to stay out of a particular room can be a lost cause (especially if that room is home to a cat litter box). Instead of spending time hauling your dog out of the room over and over, bar his way with a simple latch. To make the latch, you'll need a thin, 1-inch-wide strip of metal plate. The length of the strip will depend on how far you want the door to open. A 2-to-3-inch-long piece is sufficient to hold a door open a crack; a 5-to-6-inch piece will allow cats, but not larger dogs, to squeeze through.

Use a portable drill to drill a hole in one end of the metal strip and to open a notch in the other end. Use a small screw to attach the metal strip to the inside of the doorjamb. Make sure that it's tight yet has enough slack so that the strip can swing back and forth. The door should close without hitting the screw head. Put another screw into the edge of the door itself. To keep the door open a crack, fit the notch in the latch over the screw in the door. When you want to open the door fully, just push up on the latch with your thumb.

Slip the slot over the screw head.

Screw head

Install a simple metal latch in the door frame to keep dogs out of a room but allow cats to come and go as they please.

FIX IT FAST • FIX IT FOREVER

Shoe-Chewing Puppy

Problem:
Your young dog views your favorite pair of leather shoes as chew toys.

Do This Now:
Provide your dog with plenty of appropriate items to chew, says professional dog trainer Terry Long of Long Beach, California. Give your dog ice cubes or offer a hollow hard rubber dog toy, such as a Kong toy, that you can stuff with peanut butter or other tasty treats to preoccupy your dog and divert him from shoes and other no-chew items.

Do This for Good:
Learn to be a tidier housekeeper by puppy-proofing your home. Put shoes away in your closets, pillows up high, potted plants behind furniture, and other potential chew items out of your dog's reach.

Keep the Lid Down

Save yourself some potential veterinary bills by adopting the habit of putting the toilet lid down. To your dog, the toilet is a handy auxiliary drinking bowl, but the water in the toilet can harbor disease-causing bacteria, warns veterinarian Jill Richardson of Secaucus, New Jersey.

Master the Hands-Free Sit

Train your dog to sit on cue—without having to push down his rump. Terry Long shares her sit secret. Get your dog's attention by holding a tasty treat just above his head. Say "Sit" as you glide the treat over his head and toward his hind end. Your food-motivated dog will naturally move his head to follow the path of the treat, and that's where gravity kicks in. He will need to sit down to maintain his balance. Once his back end hits the ground, hand over the treat and say "Good sit."

Chill Your Puppy's Chewing Habit

Puppies and young dogs need to chew. Protect your shoes and other prized belongings by offering your puppy suitable chew objects. Do what Audrey Pavia, of Santa Ana, California, did for her puppy, Nigel. Audrey filled an ice cube tray with a

65

mixture of equal amounts of water and chicken broth. After the mixture froze, she rolled a few cubes onto the kitchen floor for Nigel. The teething puppy enjoyed chewing the tasty cubes and soothed his sore gums at the same time.

Put Your Dog on Remote Patrol

Here's the ultimate shortcut for couch potatoes. Since dogs like to have jobs, teach your dog to play the "get the remote control" game. You can sit back on the couch and relax as

5 Fun Feline Games

A playful cat is a happy cat and one that is less apt to get into mischief. Pet expert Arden Moore, the author of *The Kitten Owner's Manual*, offers these five interactive games you can play with your cat—and they're a lot cheaper than buying fancy pet toys at a pet supply store.

Hide-and-seek. With your cat at your side, toss a small treat across the room. As she darts after the treat, quietly slip around the corner out of sight and call her name. When she comes, praise her and give her another treat. Repeat as your cat desires.

Beam me up, Fluffy. Dim the lights and cast a flashlight beam on the walls and floors. Watch your cat take off in hot "purr-suit."

Shake, rattle, and roll. Fill an empty film canister with a teaspoon of uncooked rice and seal the cap with tape. Your cat will enjoy batting around this noisy toy.

Let's go fishing. Keep your cat's hunting skills honed by attaching a toy mouse to the end of a sturdy shoelace and flexible pole. Toss the mouse within sight of your cat. When he prepares to pounce, tug the pole so the mouse retreats. Move the mouse up and down and side to side to give your cat a good workout.

Kitty in the bag. Remove the handles and cut a 2-inch-diameter hole in the bottom of a paper shopping bag. Attach a toy mouse to the end of a long shoelace and thread the other end of the shoelace through the hole, with the mouse inside. Place the bag on the floor with the bottom facing you; pull on the shoelace to draw the mouse about midway inside the bag. Call your cat so that she faces the open end of the bag, then gently wiggle the mouse. Watch your cat dive in to capture the mouse as you reel it out through the hole.

Counter-Climbing Cat

Problem:
Your cat likes to walk on your kitchen countertops.

Do This Now:
Fill a cookie sheet with water and place it on the counter as a booby trap for your cat. Also, apply double-sided sticky tape to the counter. These solutions worked for family therapist Barbara

Lee of Lake San Marcos, California, who had grown tired of shooing her cats off the kitchen counters.

Do This for Good:
Cats instinctively seek high places to perch. Provide a few cat-friendly shelves or a cat tower with perches as preferred alternatives for your counter-top-cruising cat.

your dog reinforces his "Fetch" command skills. When he brings you the remote, reward him with a treat and plenty of praise. Then sit back and enjoy a good canine caper together—perhaps a *Frasier* rerun.

Nothing to Sneeze At

Keep your home-alone cat occupied by making this toy out of an empty tissue box. Remove the clear plastic over the opening in the box and pop one or two table tennis balls inside. If necessary, use scissors to widen the opening of the box, just enough so that it's barely big enough for the balls to come out. Your curious cat will spend hours trying to fish out the balls through the narrow opening.

Late Supper Stops Midnight Friskiness

Noisy bouts of feline play can ruin a good night's sleep. Curb that sleep-disturbing play by outfoxing your feline. Change his feeding time from early morning to right before bed, suggests Kevin Moore, a construction worker with the U.S. Navy, who shares his Laurel, Maryland, home with Lager, a tiger-striped cat. With a full belly, a cat is inclined to snooze longer. Kevin also spends 10 to 20 minutes before bedtime playing with Lager so that the cat will be tired and ready to sleep.

Stir In Some Bird Fun

When Laura Doering of Long Beach, California stops at her favorite coffee shop, she also remembers to bring home a few wooden coffee stirrers for Sunshine, her 9-year-old double yellow-headed Amazon. The bird loves to chew, and these freebies are safe selections. Laura checks to be sure that the stirrers have not been bleached and do not sport a shiny finish. She also offers Sunshine empty toilet paper and paper towel rolls to shred, which keeps him entertained.

Have a Ball with the "Come" Command

Got a smart dog who knows the "Come" command but doesn't always choose to obey? Stuff a tennis ball in your jacket pocket before you head out for a walk. If your dog playfully runs ahead of you, stop, show her the ball, and then turn and walk slowly away from her. Say her name, followed by "Come." Praise your dog when she comes to you, but never yell at her for running away. Once your dog returns and sits, toss the ball for her to fetch. This sequence makes obeying the "Come" command fun for your dog. In no time, she will realize that good things, such as ball games, happen when she obeys, says Carol Oddi, a dog owner from New Fairfield, Connecticut.

Haste Makes Waste

Start Your Day Off on the Right Leash

It may seem like a time-saver to rush your dog through his morning bathroom duties, but that could lead to problems. An underexercised dog may have an accident or trash your house out of boredom while you're at work during the day. You can avoid these headaches by devoting 15 minutes to your dog every morning with a brisk walk. Use this time to play one of his favorite games. Practice some tricks to give him the chance to unleash some pent-up energy, suggests Terry Long, a professional dog trainer and behavior consultant in Long Beach, California.

Double-Duty Dog-Walking Routines

Pet expert Arden Moore of Oceanside, California, incorporates basic obedience commands to her Pembroke Welsh corgi, Jazz, in a fun way each time they stride through the local park. As they walk, Arden will suddenly say "Sit," and as soon as Jazz does, she hands him a treat from a bag attached to her belt loop. During the 30-minute walk, Jazz also earns treats for other commands, including "Stay," "Come," and "Down." The obedience training breaks up the monotony of a walk and makes learning fun.

Put Your Dog's Best Paw Forward

Brrrr! When the ice and snow of winter strike, prevent the possibility of frostbite on your dog's paws (which could require a trip to the veterinary clinic). Before you head outdoors for a walk, apply a thin layer of aloe or petroleum jelly to your dog's footpads. Or try spraying the pads with nonstick cooking spray. These options provide a protective coating and keep snow and ice from accumulating between the toes, says Jill Richardson, DVM, a veterinarian from Secaucus, New Jersey.

Angling for Agility Hand-Me-Downs

Nigel, a Pembroke Welsh corgi, loves the sport of canine agility—much to the delight of his owners, freelance writer Audrey Pavia and her husband, Randy, of Santa Ana, California. Rather than immediately buy brand-new equipment, the couple decided to enroll in a few agility classes first. There, Audrey and Randy met other agility enthusiasts, and from these folks they bought used agility equipment in good condition—at major price savings—to install in their backyard for practice runs. "Who cares if the equipment isn't brand-new, as long as it's functional?" says Audrey.

Agility Training for Pennies

Carol Oddi and her dogs, Max and Belle, compete in agility, a canine version of an obstacle course, including hurdles to jump and poles to weave through. When Carol set up a mini obstacle course in her New Fairfield, Connecticut, backyard, she built her own wooden dog walk and A-frame rather than buying official equipment, thus saving about $450. Instead of buying a set of 12 weave poles, Carol bought 3-foot-long polyvinyl chloride (PVC) pipes fitted with plastic caps on each end. Carol removed one cap from each pipe and hammered a 3-inch-long nail through the cap so that the pointed end protruded through the outside. After replacing the caps on the pipes, she hammered the pipes into the ground; the nails acted as stakes to anchor the pipes. Total price for the pipes: $10, versus $40 or more for commercial weave poles. "My dad is a cabinetmaker, so he taught me at an early age how to use electric saws," says Carol. "It's paying off now with big savings on equipment for my agility dogs."

"By letting others know we were looking for used equipment, we saved a lot of money."

Broom Handle Hurdle

Daily practice is important for agility training, but the equipment you need can be expensive. Instead of buying a commercially designed hurdle, make your own for nothing. Position a broom handle on two chairs or boxes so it will easily roll off if your dog hits it while jumping over. Begin with a hurdle 8 inches high and gradually increase the height based on your dog's jumping ability.

Create a Poop Zone

In their sprawling, fenced backyard, Karen and Rick Cichocki of Dyer, Indiana, have designated a tucked-away area behind the garage as the bathroom area for their three dogs. Using treats and praise, the Cichockis guided Misty, now a 12-year-old Sheltie, to this area. After a few outings, she learned to identify this as her bathroom zone. Misty then trained her younger dog mates, Max and Oliver, to do the same. This saves cleanup time for the Cichockis and keeps the main part of their lawn poop-free.

The Second Time Around

Recycle Your Newspaper Bag

Pet stores try to entice you to buy special poop bags for your pooch, but why spend the money when a perfect poop bag is right in your driveway? When you take your dog out for his morning walk, stop and pick up your newspaper. Remove the plastic bag, stuff it in your pocket, and use it to pick up your dog's poop. Reach into the plastic bag and grab the poop, then turn the bag inside out and tie it shut. Toss the bag into an outside trash container with a lid. No fuss, no muss—and no expense!

Stuff Those Poop Bags

As the proud owner of two big dogs, Bubba and Hooch, veterinarian Jill Richardson, of Secaucus, New Jersey, knows the importance of practicing regular poop patrols in her yard. She saves time by stashing empty plastic bags from supermarket visits in one bag tied onto the back porch door handle. She just grabs a bag from her stash to collect the doggie doo. When she finishes the chore, Dr. Richardson drops the plastic bag into a specially designated garbage can that she takes out to the street for pickup once a week.

Going Places without Going Crazy

5

We have become a country of commuters. Our vehicles have become our second homes on wheels. We take pride in the creature comforts: no-spill cup holders, seat warmers, and even mini-TVs to keep our energetic children entertained while we weave through traffic. This chapter contains plenty of on-the-road shortcuts designed to help you steer clear of rush hour stress, carpooling snafus, and shopping trip headaches.

THE CLEVER COMMUTER

Fast Fix for Frosty Windshields

Welcome to Minneapolis—the cold capital of America. Dale Anderson, M.D., a doctor at a local urgent care clinic, is proud of being a lifelong resident of Minnesota, despite the winter storms that leave his car's windshield looking like an ice rink. Rather than try to muscle off the ice with a plastic scraper, Dr. Anderson reaches behind the driver's seat for the sturdy plastic tumbler that he keeps in his car specifically for ice-clearing duty. He uses the rim of the tumbler to scrape away the ice. "I've found that the plastic tumbler is easier to grip than an ice scraper, and it won't scratch the windshield," notes Dr. Anderson. "It removes the sheet of ice on the windshield quickly." So on your next trip to a discount store or home center, visit the housewares section to select your own "ice tumbler" in your favorite color.

Bag Your Windshield

Hate to spend time brushing snow off your windshield after a storm? With a little preparation, you'll never have to do it again. When the weather report says snow, cover the windshield with a heavy-duty plastic garbage bag. Cut the bag open along the sides so it'll fit all the way across. Close the front doors on the edges of the bag to hold it in place. When you want to drive, just open the doors and remove the bag—and all the snow with it. This trick works for the rear window, too.

Guarantee a Swift Start

Back into the garage when you come home from errands or work so that you can easily exit the next morning. This habit will also save you time and aggravation if you run into mechanical problems, such as a dead battery. With the engine facing front, the battery is within easy reach to apply jumper cables. Also, be sure to turn off the lights, radio, heater, or air conditioner before you turn on the ignition. With less drain on your car's battery, you'll save a few seconds per start-up.

Keep Your Key Warm

On a cold winter morning, there's nothing worse than being late for work *and* being stuck outside your car because the door lock has frozen. You can try heating the tip of the key with a disposable lighter, but you're just as likely to burn your fingertips as heat up the key. Here's a trick that'll warm up the key enough to defrost the lock—and keep your hands warm while you drive, too.

Before winter arrives, pop down to the local sporting goods or camping-supply store and pick up a few chemical warmers.

These little pouches are available in two sizes—hand and shoe. They're inactive until you open the package and give them a shake to start the chemical reaction. On a freezing morning, open a package (either size will do) before you leave the house and place it in the pocket or purse where you carry your keys. In just a few minutes, the key will be warm enough to open the lock. During your commute, slip the warmer inside one glove to keep your hand toasty. Switch off hands when you're stopped at red lights.

Lavender Cools Traffic Tension

Newspaper sportswriter Marcia C. Smith of Santa Monica, California, spends a lot of time in traffic around Los Angeles. But she never loses her cool while driving. What's her sanity-saving secret? She spritzes the interior of her car with lavender at the start of each ride. Some car supply stores and catalogs offer this "anti–road rage in a bottle," but you can save money by making it yourself. Just put a few drops of lavender essential oil (available at health food stores or drugstores) in a small plastic spray bottle. Fill the bottle with distilled water and shake to mix the oil and water, then spritz away.

Take Advantage of a Traffic Jam

Life on the road comes with some frustrations, such as traffic-clogging fender benders and rush hour traffic that moves like molasses. Use these jam-up times to your advantage by recognizing them as terrific times to think. Mentally draft a letter to your sister or decide on the menu for tomorrow's dinner. Brainstorm ideas for sprucing

Haste Makes Waste

Play a Little Game in Traffic

Everyone feels the urge to switch lanes in a traffic jam to try to get ahead. The problem is, there's no predicting a traffic jam. Lane switching in heavy traffic is dangerous, and it usually doesn't pay. You can prove this to yourself the next time you approach a congested stretch of cars on the highway. Watch for a motorist who's dodging from lane to lane and make note of the car's appearance or license plate. Stay in the lane you're in—don't switch (unless traffic signs say you must)—and note your progress versus that of the lane switcher. Very often, the same car that rushed to pass you will be halted in another lane as you catch up. You can smile to yourself as you note your car edging ahead.

up your flower or vegetable garden. Decide which outfit you will wear tomorrow or identify the perfect birthday present for your best friend.

If your memory is less than perfect, ensure that your thinking session doesn't go to waste by keeping a small tape recorder in your car. When traffic slows to a crawl, switch on the recorder and do your thinking out loud. That way, you can be mentally productive while still keeping your hands on the steering wheel. Either way, keeping your brain in gear will help you feel far less stress than focusing on the traffic delay.

Breathe Deep during Traffic Tie-Ups

Relieving tension during a traffic tie-up is as easy and natural as breathing. When you're tense, you tend to hold your breath or breathe shallowly. Restore your serenity by following the lead of Joely Johnson, a part-time yoga instructor who has lived and driven in high-traffic San Francisco, Philadelphia, and New York City. Joely keeps her cool during traffic foul-ups by practicing deep, relaxing breathing, a technique she learned from yoga. Concentrate on taking a deep breath through your nostrils so that your chest rises. Then exhale through your mouth slowly to the count of 3 seconds. Repeat.

Dial Around for Traffic News

Preset your car radio for a news station that reports traffic and weather every 8 to 10 minutes. These frequent updates can help you steer clear of major traffic congestion by offering better alternative routes.

Cruise through Those Tollgates

Save time and money when traveling on toll roads by paying the tolls in advance. In states such as California, Massachusetts, and Pennsylvania, savvy commuters no longer have to fumble for loose change to feed those toll baskets. Instead, they use their banking debit cards to pay for the tolls electronically. Each month, they receive an update on their toll charges. Plus, these toll payment plans offer discounts for commuters, as well as technology that allows them to slow down—but not stop—when passing through the tollgates.

Marcia C. Smith, a newspaper sportswriter who lives in Santa Monica, California, drives daily on toll roads. She estimates that by using the toll plan, she saves about $5 a month in tolls plus uncounted minutes of frustration and boredom waiting in line to pay them.

Pay Yourself a Commuter Tax

Remember the joy you got from plunking coins in a piggy bank as a child? Here's an adult version that can be a real shortcut to savings. Each time you get in your car, put a quarter in a special container that you stash under the driver's seat. At the end of each month, transfer those quarters to an interest-bearing account at your bank. You'll be surprised how quickly they add up. By the end of the year, you could have $200 or more—plenty to treat yourself to a nice gift, a superb dinner, or a quick weekend getaway at a bed-and-breakfast. The quarters also provide an in-car emergency fund if you find yourself short of cash at the restaurant drive-thru window, video store, or parking garage.

Barter Books on Tape

Listening to a tape-recorded book can certainly help a long commute seem to pass more quickly, but audiobooks can be pricey. To make the habit affordable, check with coworkers who also commute long distances; you'll probably find some who like to listen in the car as well. Swap books with one another, and you'll cut your costs considerably. Check your local library, too. Not only do libraries offer popular books such as murder mysteries, but they also have educational tape sets. For example, you could learn to speak a foreign language during your commute.

My Favorite Shortcut

Sweat but Never Fret

Magazine editor Laura Doering lives in Long Beach, California, 30 miles north of her office in Mission Viejo. Her commute can take as little as 30 minutes, but when traffic is heavy, the trip stretches to more than an hour. Laura has developed a shortcut strategy that's good for her health and frees her from wasting time in traffic. "I bring my workout clothes with me to the office," she says. "If I get off work at six P.M., the peak of rush hour traffic, I just change into my workout clothes and run at a nearby park for forty-five minutes or so. I look at it this way: I'd rather do something healthy and active like running than sit in traffic for an extra forty-five minutes. At the end of the run, the traffic has cleared, and I'm home by seven-thirty, feeling fit."

Soften Your Hands While You Drive

Moisturize your hands without removing them from the wheel. If you suffer from perpetually dry hands, especially during the winter months, try this technique. When you're ready to leave for your morning commute, slather on hand cream and then slip on a pair of white cotton gloves (available at a pharmacy). If it's a really cold day, put on your outdoor gloves over the cotton ones. While you drive, the moisturizer will be absorbed deeply into your skin.

Give Your AC a Head Start

Believe it or not, you can cool your car faster on a hot day by turning on the air conditioner and *opening* one of the windows. Start off with the air conditioner on high, then crack one of the windows about an inch—this gives the hot air trapped in the car a place to escape, so the interior air will cool down faster. As the temperature inside the car drops, close the window and adjust the air conditioner settings accordingly.

RUNNING ERRANDS

Remember the Lunch Hour Rush

Many supermarkets are open early and late. The busiest times tend to be during lunch hour, weekdays between 5 and 7 P.M., and Saturday mornings. Save yourself time and long lines by choosing to shop during off-peak hours, such as before 8 A.M. or after 8 P.M. You will breeze through the aisles and check-out line.

The Wheel Deal for Groceries

Lori Crouch loves living in the heart of Washington, D.C., but knows that maneuvering her car in the city is taxing and time-consuming. The nearest food market is only a couple of blocks from her apartment, but driving there eats up minutes, and there is no guarantee of an available parking spot. If you're a city dweller like Lori, follow her lead and keep your car in its parking stall on grocery day. Lori walks to the store with a collapsible two-wheel, lightweight cart in tow. This type of cart is available at luggage stores and through mail-order catalogs that cater to airline travelers. Lori keeps a couple of bungee cords in the cart to secure her bags in place. She picks out a week's worth of groceries, loads the bags on the cart, and wheels the food home. She gets a little exercise without the undue strain of carrying grocery bags, and there's no hassle looking for a parking space.

Never Get Keyed Up Again

For decades, Roberta Mulliner, a retired office manager from Cutchogue, New York, wasted time standing by her locked car, fingering through her big purse for her car keys. It seemed that the keys disappeared when she needed them most— when her arms were full of groceries or the rain was pouring down. If you have the same problem, do what Roberta did and have a combination lock added to the car door. Now Roberta just punches in her code and opens the door. Once in the driver's seat, she can take her time finding her elusive keys.

Do the Grocery Store Grab

You must pick up milk and eggs at the grocery store on the way home from work or a meeting, but you're starving. Head straight for the deli section and pick up a loaf of French bread, prepackaged slices of ham or turkey, cheese slices, and dill pickles. Then finish your shopping, content in the knowledge that you have the ingredients for an instant dinner when you arrive home.

Monday Is Washday

Take advantage of your age by taking your car to the car wash on days when

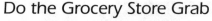

My Favorite Shortcut

Avoid Endless Excursions

Hate to shop? Always feeling like you need to dash off to the store? Take the advice of Roberta Mulliner, who has reduced her shopping trips to one morning or afternoon a week. Before Roberta grabs her keys, she maps out her route and writes down a list of must-get items. On a recent trip, Roberta needed to buy groceries, return library books, deposit a check at the bank, and mail packages. She plotted her route as a loop, ending with the grocery store so that the perishables would stay fresh. Spending a few minutes planning can save you hours shopping, says Roberta.

Note: If all your errands take you to stores located along one busy street, take care of the errands on the right-hand side of the street first, then tackle the errands on the other side of the street on the way back.

senior citizen discounts are offered. Typically, those are Mondays and Tuesdays, but check with your local car wash to be sure.

Prepare for Parking Fees

Adopt the Boy Scout motto and be prepared for parking fees and tolls. Keep a letter-size envelope with some paper money in your car in a secure hideaway such as the glove compartment, tucked inside the owner's manual, or underneath the driver's seat. Keep about $20 in singles, and you won't be delayed the next time you encounter an unexpected toll or have to pay to park when attending a sports or theater event.

Curb Those Parking Meter Blues

Fill an empty plastic film canister with quarters, dimes, and nickels. Seal the lid and stash the canister in the driver's side door panel. The next time you pull into a metered parking spot, you'll enjoy peace of mind knowing that you're guaranteed to find just the right change to feed the meter. Replenish the supply of coins with the change you receive at fast-food drive-thru windows.

Park Prudently at the Mall

The closest spot isn't necessarily the safest spot in a mall parking lot, and when it comes to safety, you don't want to take shortcuts. Play it safe by parking in lanes that allow you to exit either forward or backward so that you can't be blocked in. Park under lights when shopping at night, and request an escort by a shopping mall security officer when leaving the mall and carrying packages to your vehicle.

TIPS FOR FAMILY CHAUFFEURS

Never Waste Waiting Time

Don't waste those minutes that elapse while you are waiting in your parked car for your child to get out of school or finish soccer practice. The secret is to plan for this time before you leave the house. Bring a notebook and compile your grocery list, or use your cell phone to order a pizza that you can pick up on the way home. While you have the cell phone out, call one of your favorite friends or relatives for a nice chat. Sew a button on a shirt, file your nails, or write some checks for a couple of bills that are due (and drop them in the mailbox on the way home).

Fuss-Free Vehicular Video

A vehicle equipped with a small TV and VCR can be a blessing if you have to transport children frequently, but it can also lead to aggravating arguments among the kids about what to watch. Save yourself from refereeing fights by following this procedure. Rent several children's videos from the library (they are low or no cost compared to commercial rentals). Then flip a coin to decide which child will have the privilege of choosing the video.

Pass the Car Pool Clipboard

Carpooling is a must if your children are involved in lots of activities. Here's how to start a carpooling network and do a favor for other busy parents at the same time. At the first soccer (or football or baseball) practice of the season or the first Cub Scout meeting or dance class, bring along a clipboard, paper, and a pen. Put a sheet of paper in the clipboard with the following headings: Child's Name, Parents' Names, Address, Phone Number, E-Mail Address. Pass the clipboard around and ask everyone to fill it out. Type up the list and hand out copies to all the parents at the next practice or meeting. This approach is much more effective than trying to introduce yourself to other parents individually, and the time you invest in preparing the list will be rewarded with an immediate carpooling network. The list also will come in handy for those times when you need to arrange for a last-minute ride for your children.

GET ME THERE ON TIME

Be an Early Bird

Sometimes allowing extra time to reach a destination offers a payback that's truly worthwhile. For example, Frank and Flo Frum of Oceanside, California, never arrive late to church (a record they've maintained throughout 58 years of marriage). In fact, they are usually the first to arrive for the Sunday morning service. What's their motivation? "By getting there early, we get the choice of the parking spots and the best pew inside the church," says Frank, a retired postal worker. "We're spared the stress felt by some of our fellow churchgoers who are always rushing at the last minute to get to church."

Post Those Directions

To avoid making a wrong turn when you're en route to a new restaurant or other unfamiliar destination near home, write out the directions in bold letters (use a thick pen) on a sticky note. Stick the note on your steering wheel so you can easily read the directions and still drive attentively.

Stop Spinning Your Wheels

Lost? No problem. Find an intersection or business where you can pull over or park safely and use your cell phone to call for directions. Major cell phone providers can help with point-to-point directions: Just dial 411. A small service charge usually

Navigate Like a Pro

Los Angeles. Chicago. Philadelphia. Fort Lauderdale. In her decade as a newspaper sportswriter, Marcia C. Smith has had to hop into her car and head for sporting events in these major metropolitan areas and others. She also has had to map out the quickest route to hundreds of interviews. So Marcia has had plenty of experience with finding and following directions in a metropolis. She offers this three-step approach to navigating in unfamiliar territory.

1. Consult your computer before you turn on the ignition. Tap into direction-giving Web sites such as www.mapquest.com, www.rand mcnally.com, or www.travelocity.com, then type in your starting address and destination to plot out the fastest route.

2. To avoid having to squint to read the directions when your eyes should be on the road, enlarge and boldface the type before you print them out.

3. Fold directions in half and carefully tuck them between your front seat and the center console. Rather than fumbling with unwieldy maps, you'll be able to scan the directions quickly and reach your destination on time.

applies, but think of it this way: If you don't call, you'll end up spending the money on wasted gas as you drive around aimlessly looking for your destination. Keep a pen and notepad in the pocket of the driver's door so you can write down the correct directions. If dialing 411 doesn't work, try calling a road-savvy friend who gives good directions.

The Family Schedule Chain

Keeping track of who's where when during the week can be a real challenge, whether your household has 2 members or 10. Here's a creative tracking system that will end confusion and missed appointments. At a home store or toy store, buy hanging chains with attached clips (designed to be hung from the ceiling and hold stuffed animals)—one chain for each family member. Hang the chains wherever they will be most convenient to refer to. Divide each chain into several sections, using pieces of ribbon tied to links at the dividing lines. These sections represent the days of the week. Keep a stack of 3-by-5-inch index cards nearby. Instruct family members to jot down their activities for the week on the cards and clip each card at the appropriate spot on their personal chains. At a glance, you'll be able to review everyone's schedule for the day by reading horizontally across the chains. To peer into someone's future, read vertically down a chain. These schedule chains can also be the designated site for phone messages and family reminders—no more scraps of paper floating around the house.

MEALS TO GO

Fast Alternatives to Fast Food

Satisfy your hunger on the road by packing bite-size snacks such as apple slices, carrot sticks, pretzels, and small cookies. Stick with snacks that don't drip, crumble, or get sticky, and you'll steer clear of clothing and car messes.

Dining While You Drive

When Karen and Rick Cichocki of Dyer, Indiana, prepare to take a road trip with their two young grandchildren, Chrissy and Andy, they pack plenty of mess-free snacks. They wash and chop up red and green bell peppers, carrot sticks, celery sticks, cucumbers, apples, orange slices, and broccoli florets. They stash each fruit and vegetable in its own resealable plastic bag and keep things fresh inside a cooler with ice.

"The plastic bags keep water from reaching into the food," says Karen, a registered nurse. "We also stick a couple of soapy washcloths in resealable plastic bags so that we can quickly clean the faces of our grandchildren. We use the empty bags to store any food trash and throw them away at our next stop."

Nutty about Carfare

Dale Anderson, M.D., of Minneapolis knows the dangers of low blood sugar caused by going too many hours without eating. In case he misses a meal during his busy day as an urgent care physician, he keeps resealable plastic bags of his favorite nuts (pecans, almonds, and cashews) in the glove compartment of his car. These nuts provide a nutritional boost during his daytime drives. "The nuts keep my blood sugar level on an even keel and give me steady energy," says Dr. Anderson. "Sometimes I toss in some pieces of dried fruit—fast, healthy foods to counter my twelve-hour workdays."

TRAVELING BY BUS

Take a Seat, Please

Location, location, location. The mantra for real estate brokers is also good advice for bus riders. When you're pressed for time, select an aisle seat near the exit. Aisle seats also offer you more legroom to stretch your limbs.

A Budget Bus Plan for Outings

If you take a day off midweek for a family outing to the zoo or a museum, consider riding the bus instead of driving the car. Some municipal bus systems offer money-saving plans during the week. Montgomery County, Maryland, for example, offers a Kids Ride Free program for all metro buses running in the county between 2 P.M. and 7 P.M. Check to see what's available in your area. Taking the bus saves wear and tear on your car,

Pack a Bus Bag

When Roberta Mulliner of Cutchogue, New York, rides the bus to Philadelphia to visit friends and relatives, she doesn't just sit and stare out the window. By taking a little time to plan ahead, she is prepared to spend her time productively and enjoyably. The day before the trip, Roberta always prepares a tote bag of essential activities and goodies.

■ Crochet hooks, knitting needles, and yarn (to make a hat or afghan)

■ A can't-put-it-down book (to indulge herself without guilt)

■ Note cards (to write those long-overdue thank-you notes)

■ A bottle of water with a secure lid (in case she gets thirsty)

■ Hard candies (to ease minor hunger pangs)

■ Premoistened towelettes (for quick cleanups)

■ Earplugs (to block out noisy cell phone users)

and you can indulge in a heart-to-heart talk with your kids during the ride.

Swap Your Car for a Bus

If you love to shop at open-air flea markets or farmers' markets on weekends, you know that trying to find a parking spot for your vehicle can be a challenge. If you find a place, it is often blocks away and you're charged a parking fee. If you live in a city with dependable bus service, leave your car at home on market day. Grab a cloth shopping bag and board the bus to the market. You'll save wear and tear on your car, your feet, and your wallet.

TAKING CARE OF YOUR CAR

Book Two-in-One Appointments

You've no doubt become a multitasker at work, but you can use those timesaving skills in caring for your car as well. Ask the garage to perform necessary repairs and standard maintenance tasks in the same visit to save you extra service charges and time. For example, when you schedule an oil change, have the shop flush the coolant, too.

Dipstick Squint Saver

If you can't see the "full" and "add" lines on your oil dipstick without wearing your reading glasses, this trick will save you the trouble of pulling out your glasses when you need to check your oil. Just drill tiny holes in the dipstick at the "add" and "full" marks. You'll be able to see the holes even without your cheaters. Be sure to clean off any metal shavings before you replace the dipstick in its slot.

Keep a Car Diary

Spend a few seconds a day maintaining a record of your car's performance, and you'll save yourself the hours—even days—of inconvenience that accompany unexpected major car problems. Keep a small spiral-bound notebook in your glove compartment. Each time you buy gas, jot down the number of gallons purchased and the miles driven since the last fill-up. Also note the date and amount whenever you add oil or other fluids. Record the date and mileage for all oil changes and other maintenance services.

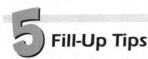

Fill-Up Tips

Ask for free fluids. Have your car's oil changed every 3,000 miles. It's good for the car, and as a loyal customer, you can request that the mechanic top off fluids for free as part of the service.

Fill up on time. Keep your gas tank at least one-quarter full so that there's enough fuel to keep the electric fuel pump lubricated. Driving near empty can cause this pricey pump to wear out faster than normal.

Don't pamper your car. Check your owner's manual to determine the best octane level for your car. It may perform perfectly well on the least expensive gas.

Avoid topping off the gas tank. Stop pumping gas as soon as you hear the first click on the nozzle, and you can save money by not having to replace the emissions canister, which can be damaged if you regularly overfill your tank.

Buy gasoline early or late. Gas pumps measure gasoline by volume, not density. You'll get the most fuel for your money if you fill up during the cool of the early morning or late evening, when gasoline is densest.

3 Time-Savers for Tire Changes

You never know when a flat tire may occur. Take these three simple steps in advance, and changing a flat tire will be much easier and less frustrating.

Change the wrench. Replace your car's wheel wrench with a cross-shaped wrench. The superior leverage provided by the cross-shaped wrench will allow you to remove the lug nuts with less muscle strain.

Throw in a wheel chock. Put a brick or a piece of wood about the same size in your trunk. It will come in handy as a brace for one of the wheels when you have to jack up your car.

Make a jack support. Look around your garage for a scrap of ½-inch-thick plywood. Cut it to about 2 by 2 feet and store it in your trunk. If you have to change your tire on unpaved ground, put the board underneath your jack to prevent it from sinking into the ground.

Jack

Jack support

Keeping records like these will help you notice quickly if your car is using extra oil or fluids, which could be a tip-off to a leak or other potential problem. Your notebook also will jog your memory that your car is overdue for an oil change, transmission service, or other important maintenance. And when it's time to sell or trade your car, providing a maintenance history can boost the car's resale value, because a used-car buyer likes to know what maintenance has been done and when. Used-car salespeople estimate that providing thorough car maintenance information to prospective buyers can net you up to several hundred dollars extra on the sale of your car.

Buddy, Can You Spare a Tire?

Have you joined the small-truck owner crowd? If so, take a tip from James Flynn of Crown Point, Indiana, who keeps his truck's spare tire in tip-top shape by storing it in the enclosed bed rather than mounted under the carriage. Stored in the bed, the tire is protected from extreme hot and cold temperatures and from the risk of damage from road debris. Plus, if you ever have a flat and need to use the spare, you'll find it much easier to pull it out of the bed than to worm your way under the truck to detach it from the carriage mounting.

A Simple Secret to Long-Lasting Brakes

James Flynn of Crown Point, Indiana, loves driving his truck, but he avoids jackrabbit starts and jamming on the brakes. He gives himself enough of a cushion between his truck and the vehicle ahead of him so he is able to brake steadily and gradually. His reward? "I've got more than sixty-seven thousand miles on my truck with the original brakes, and they are still in good condition," James says.

Use It or Lose It

Unless they routinely park on an incline, such as a sloped driveway or a hill, most folks just don't use their parking brakes very often. But that can cause problems because the cables that operate the parking brake, also known as the emergency brake, can rust in place from lack of use and fail to work when you really need them to. To save yourself a costly repair, not to mention a potential accident, apply the parking brake at least once a week as a preventive measure.

Milk It for All It's Worth

A blanket, gloves, a plastic gasoline container, a flashlight, batteries, an ice scraper, and extra dog leashes. What else is rolling around in your car's trunk? Keep your trunk perpetually organized with this trick from Carol Oddi of New Fairfield, Connecticut, who commutes daily to New Jersey for her job. Carol puts all her trunk items in a plastic milk crate and sets the milk crate in the trunk. She uses bungee cords to fasten the crate to the spare tire so that the crate never tips over or slides around.

Shop Smart, Shop Fast

6

Whether you shop to live or live to shop, there are ways to do the job faster and cheaper. From groceries and dry goods to clothing and cars, you'll find great shortcuts in this chapter for saving time and dollars by making a few smart changes in your shopping habits. We'll help you stick to your grocery budget, avoid impulse purchases, negotiate wisely for big-ticket items, have more fun at flea markets, and get the most out of online shopping opportunities.

GROCERY-GATHERING SHORTCUTS

Take Fridge Inventory First

Every now and then, there's a shortcut that's ridiculously simple, and this is one of them. But it's also a very effective technique for ensuring that you buy only what you need at the grocery store, and it doesn't take a second of extra time. Here's the idea: Clean out leftovers and clear space for new items in the refrigerator *before* you go grocery shopping instead of when you arrive home with food bags in tow.

The advantage of purging the fridge before you shop is that you'll know exactly how much space you have available for new purchases—and you may even find a few items already in stock that will trim your grocery list. You'll also cut down on return trips to the store because you can plainly see, for example, that the sandwich meat has disappeared or the olives you need for Thursday night's entrée have shriveled. One more benefit: The frozen foods you've just purchased won't defrost on the countertop while you're trying to find space in the freezer for them.

Computerize Your Shopping List

Lori MacDonald of Cumberland Foreside, Maine, has her computer help with the grocery list. Lori has created a master grocery list on the computer, covering all the items she buys in a given month. She posts this list on the refrigerator, and everyone in her family circles whatever they need. After a shopping trip, Lori prints out a new list and starts over. Her method beats the standard working-from-memory shopping list because it automatically reminds you to check on supplies of everything you might need from the store.

Coupons at Home Don't Count

Tired of arriving at the grocery store only to find that those carefully clipped coupons are still at home? In the future, keep your grocery list on the back of an envelope and store the appropriate coupons inside. That doubles your chances of remembering the coupons.

When Stores Compete, You Win

If you're one of those lucky people who live in close proximity to lots of grocery stores, shop at one that's located within a block of another. Having competition so close by encourages store management to offer more specials—even if the store is part of a chain. Plus, when a must-have item isn't in stock at your store, you won't have to choose a less desirable substitute. You can quickly stop and buy it at the neighboring grocery store on your way home.

Must-Have Household Items

When you run out of toilet paper, you've just got to go to the store—even if it means running to the convenience store at midnight and paying three times the usual price. To minimize costly trips like this (where you're also bound to pick up a few impulse items at inflated prices), stock up on any of the items below that are necessities in your home. Check your stockpile at least once a month to see whether you should add any items to your shopping list.

- Toilet paper
- Coffee
- Sweetener
- Pain reliever
- Feminine products
- Toothpaste
- Adhesive bandages
- Pet food
- Poster board for school projects
- Dishwasher detergent or dishwashing liquid

$ Store Neighbors Save $$$

Here's a money-saving strategy: Seek out a grocery store that's located in the same strip mall as a dollar store. That way, you can buy all your food and household supplies during one shopping trip. Start at the dollar store and pick up over-the-counter medicines and cleaning and laundry supplies. These items cost as much as 40 percent less at a dollar store than at a grocery store. When you're done at the dollar store, go to the grocery store and buy your food.

Be a Big Supermarket Spender

One easy way to cut your overall food budget is to *increase* your grocery shopping budget. That's because the cost of food at the grocery store is almost always lower than the cost of food at other outlets, such as take-out restaurants, fast-food joints, and convenience stores. For example, you may think that buying a canister of gourmet coffee mix that costs $6 for 12 servings is a big splurge, but compare that to paying $2.50 for a single caffe latte at the coffee shop. And spending $12 for a package of frozen lasagna that will feed the whole family *is* outrageous—until you consider that it costs twice as much to feed four folks greasy burgers and fries from the burger place.

**Shop Smart,
Shop Fast**

So spend more at the grocery store, and less on eating out. You'll end up eating better food and enjoying those special treats guilt-free.

Spend Less Time in the Lot

Save a few minutes on every grocery shopping trip by parking strategically. Instead of driving up and down the aisles angling for a spot close to the front of the store, park as close as you can to the cart return. That way, you won't have to brave traffic or make a return trip to the store just to drop off the cart.

I Know My Credit Is Good

To avoid anxiety at the checkout counter, Rose Kennedy always checks her credit before she gets in line with her grocery cart. "Before I shop, I pause at the pay phone at the front of the store, dial my credit card company's toll-free number, and find out my up-to-the-minute available balance," says this working mom from Knoxville, Tennessee. "I use the auto-

My Favorite
Shortcut

The Grocery Store Grump's Strategy

An idea born out of dislike has yielded several money- and time-saving strategies for working mom Cindy Prince of Knoxville, Tennessee.

"I absolutely despise going to the store," Cindy says. "I'd much rather spend my precious time hanging out with my kids or working in the yard." So Cindy saves "a lot of time and anguish" by grocery shopping only once every two weeks. "I figure out all the main meals I'm going to cook ahead of time, and on one Saturday morning trip, I go to three stores,

including a fancy fresh market and a discount canned goods place."

Cindy, her husband, and their 11- and 14-year-old sons eat all the fresh produce within the first week; the second week they rely on canned and frozen fruits and vegetables. "I save money as well as time," Cindy says. "My family is much more willing to eat leftovers when they know this is all the food we have to choose from. And I don't have as much cupboard clutter as a lot of my friends; between grocery trips, my family eats all the food I buy."

mated system, and it takes only thirty seconds. In the long run, it saves time because I never have to fumble for my checkbook or another credit card if the machine makes that dreaded beeping sound."

Nix Grocery Store Gridlock

If you're a type A personality—or even if you're not but want to make a quick trip to the store—never go to the grocery store after work on a weekday (approximately 4 to 7 P.M.). This is the busiest time at all retail stores, but particularly grocery stores.

Do the Math

The quickest way to keep your food budget under control is to carry a calculator into the store and tally your purchases as you go. No need to pinch pennies—round to the nearest dollar, if you like. If it's a pain to hold a tiny calculator in your hand, buy a clipboard with a solar calculator at the top. This type of clipboard costs just a few dollars at a dollar or closeout store, and you can clip your list and coupons to it, too.

Park Your Cart

Keep impulse purchases from slipping into your cart by parking the cart at the end of the aisle. Carrying items back to the cart gives you a few seconds to think about whether you really need that bag of chips or carton of ice cream.

Enter, Then Entrées

Regardless of your store's layout, shop for dinner entrée ingredients first. You'll be more likely to stick to your budget if you select the most expensive items first. Just as important, if you give entrées short shrift because you run out of cart space (or time or energy), you're much more likely to return to the store for another round of shopping—and impulse purchases.

Case the Joint for Better Prices

Some supermarkets will act like cost clubs, if you let them. If you are willing to buy canned or boxed goods by the case (soda is an exception), many store managers will give you a bulk discount. Just ask at the customer service counter before you start your rounds.

Ways to Avoid Marketing Ploys

Grocery stores are in it to make money, and they have sophisticated tactics to entice you to buy more—and more expensive—stuff. It takes only a few seconds to avoid most of the snares if you keep these four strategies in mind.

Look up, look down. Clever marketers have learned to place the most expensive brands at eye level.

Sample, don't buy. Snack on those free samples if you'd like, but remember that the supermarket would never spend the money to provide samples if the product wasn't a big earner. Buy the item only if you want a treat or if you're sure that sample is a genuine sale item.

Substitute, don't add. If you decide to buy an item because of a special promotion, recheck your list and your cart. Does the new item replace something you already have or plan to buy? If it might, compare the two and choose one.

Pair for yourself. When stores place complementary items together, such as strawberries and whipped cream, they're playing on shoppers' impulsiveness. Chances are, the complementary item is a high-cost item. Don't pick it up on the spot. Instead, add it to your list and consider it again—with a cooler head—when you come across the item in its regular aisle.

Don't Multiply the Loaves

Those savvy grocery chain marketers have discovered that if they place the freshly baked bread and the packaged bread in two different sections of the store, many people will buy two loaves. Save money and waste by visiting one section or the other, not both.

Save with a Cereal Taste Test

Even when brand-name cereals are on sale, they tend to cost more than generics. Think you need to buy the famous brand despite the price difference? Try this quick test, which costs only a couple of bucks to set up but may save you hundreds in the long run. Ask a brand-loyal cereal eater to be your guinea pig. Blindfold him, then pour him a small bowl of brand-name cereal and a small bowl of generic. Have him taste both and ask him to guess which is the more expensive brand. He just may choose the generic.

Check the Organic Aisle

If you've been fitting in a special trip to the health food store to buy organic or vegetarian staples, try taking a detour down the organic aisle at a major supermarket instead. Nowadays, large supermarket chains sell lots of health-conscious food products. They order in bulk, which means you'll save some money as well as an extra trip.

Single-Serve Yourself

Prepackaged single servings of chips and cookies cost as much as three times more per ounce than their "big bag" counterparts. So why not bag your own and save? Just stop by the plastic goods aisle and pick up some small resealable plastic bags. A box of bags and an 8-ounce bag of crunchy stuff will not cost anywhere near as much as a bag of snack-size treats. Honestly, will it take more than 1 minute to bag your own single servings to stick in a lunch box or tote bag? The same savings hold true for those fancy cookie packets and variety packs of cereal.

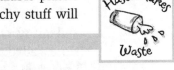

Taste Makes Waste

While you're bagging, go ahead and bag single servings of chips as well. Your effort will prevent chips from getting stale and provide the added benefit of cutting you off at a single serving. No more wondering, "Why do I have this empty one-pound bag of barbecue chips at my elbow?" after the evening news.

Sweeten the Checkout with Small Kids

Bypass the checkout aisle treats without suffering screaming toddlers—or angry glares from the people in line behind

Be Cautious about Bulk Buying

Buying food in bulk at a cost club cuts $50 or more a month from her food bill, says working mom and veteran cost club shopper Amy Witsil of Chapel Hill, North Carolina. But Amy has one hard-and-fast rule: "Never buy a giant quantity of any food from a price club unless you've tried a smaller container of it in the past." Enjoying a tasty 1/2-ounce sample of, say, coconut shrimp isn't proof that your family will use and enjoy 3 pounds of it before it goes bad. "When you buy in bulk, choose a product your family already loves—one that you have a hard time keeping in stock," says Amy.

you—by bringing your own treats from home. Choose a special toy or book that your child (or grandchild or neighbor's child) may play with only in the store, or bring a small sugary treat from a large bag at home. Make sure the child realizes that she'll receive the treat only if she cooperates while you check out.

Sweeten the Checkout, Step 2

Once you've succeeded with the strategy above, move to the advanced version: Let the child pick out next week's treat (from one of the cost-effective middle aisles of the store) during this week's shopping trip.

SMART SHOPPING STRATEGIES

Use the Phone to Get off the Hook

Carry your cell phone with you when you shop, and it may help you save money. Appliance dealers, computer centers, and many other types of retailers say they'll match another store's advertised prices. Carry your phone while you comparison shop. When you're close to making a purchase, call the competitor for a quote on the same item. That way, either store can give you the superior price on the spot—no second trip to bring back a competitor's advertisement and get a reimbursement. Phoning a competitor from the sales floor also can help you swing a better deal when negotiating with a high-pressure salesperson.

Forget the Phone, Bring the Book

Even if you don't carry a cell phone, carry an area telephone book in the car whenever you're shopping in a sprawling city or an out-of-the-way place. That way, you can check addresses and store names if you get lost, or find alternatives if one "out of stock" store leads to another.

Check the Beauty Supply Buys

If you live in a midsize city, chances are the local beauty parlors all buy the tools of their trade from a beauty supply store. You can buy the same items there at almost the same low prices (you might have to pay sales tax and a tiny markup since you aren't licensed for business). Beauty supply stores run sales just like any business, and you can pick up the same products sold by your hairstylist for a fraction of the price. Check makeup at beauty supply stores, too. You'll receive personalized attention, and you won't be rushed, because the salesclerks aren't on commission. Plus, there are plenty of test-size samples of all the latest products to try.

One Man's Lost Baggage . . .

If you can pack it to take on a plane, you can buy it at drastically reduced prices through the Unclaimed Baggage Center. That means jewelry, art, cameras, computers, and, of course, luggage of every description. You can visit the Unclaimed Baggage Center store in Scottsboro, Alabama, in person or shop on the Web, using the keywords unclaimed baggage center.

Test-Drive on Your Time

Do you dread spending hours on the weekend or after work shopping for a new car? Before you hit the lots, narrow your search to a couple of specific models by gathering information on the Internet. Find out all the facts in advance (safety, performance, price, features, and so on). When you're ready to climb behind the wheel to test-drive a particular model, make

 Ways to Win at Outlet Malls

The retail outlet malls so prevalent in some areas of the country can offer great bargains—or not. Here are four ways to increase your chances of success at an outlet mall.

Surf before you hit the turf. Most outlets have a Web site. Visit the site to learn about special sales and plan your visit accordingly.

Check your calendar. Managers tend to start new promotions on the first of the month, and that's also when they take deeper discounts on items already on sale.

Be a morning shopper. Shop when the outlets first open to get the best service (before the salesclerks have been on their feet for several hours).

Shop backward. The best bargains are usually located at the back of the store.

sure you schedule those rides during your lunch hour. This provides you with a definite time limit and a perfect exit line to give that high-pressure salesperson who's urging you to stay and buy. "Sorry, I need to get back to work," you can say. Take the guy's business card and tell him you will call him back. Away from the showroom sales pitch, you can decide at leisure whether you want to pursue that car.

Shop More, Wait Less

If you decide to take advantage of the gift-wrapping stations in department stores during the holidays, reduce the time you spend waiting while the gifts are being wrapped. Buy just a few gifts, drop them off at the wrapping station, and then return to your shopping. When it's time to drop off the second batch, the first group will be done, and your waiting time will be cut in half.

SHOPPING FOR YOUR HOME

Save with 6 Weeks' Notice

You could set your calendar by Susan Castle's home decor savings. As the owner of the Magnolia Lamp Shoppe in Chattanooga, Tennessee, Susan knows the "standard" that retailers follow when timing sales. So she waits precisely 6 weeks past the beginning of any sales season before making her purchases. "If it hasn't moved in six weeks, the store owners will slash the price," says Susan. To imitate her tactic, you can guesstimate or mark your calendar for the date 6 weeks from when you first see, for example, the bunny lamp display before Easter. Now that the Christmas season starts in October and the summer season in late April, you'll have plenty of time to display and enjoy seasonal items that you buy after the 6-week cutoff.

Bring Along Your Shopper's Guidebook

Fewer returns, less time spent at the store, and a better chance of choosing items that will match your home décor—those are the benefits when you buy a spiral-bound five-subject notebook that has pockets in the front and back. Dedicate one sec-

A personal shopper's guidebook complete with measuring tape, fabric swatches, and tons of ideas you've collected will help you shop successfully for furniture and home accessories.

tion of pages to each room or project you have in the works. Staple in paint samples, write down all-important measurements such as window dimensions, and paste in ads and magazine photos of the "look" you want for your home. The pockets at the front and back will hold a cloth measuring tape, fabric swatches, and project instructions. Tote your guidebook with you every time you go shopping or just for a drive. You never know when an interesting furniture shop or wood mill is waiting around the next bend.

Closeout Stores Open Doors

If you can buy it at a home furnishings boutique, odds are you can buy it cheaper at a closeout store. "I have not paid full price for a single home accessory since a friend told me about closeout store shopping," says Susan Castle. "I sell lamps, shades, and better home accessories, but I buy stuff for my own home at the stores that sell closeouts, such as T.J. Maxx and Tuesday Morning. Those stores sell the very same items that distributors sell to boutiques, but at the closeout stores, the merchandise is overstocks, which can be almost fifty percent cheaper."

GARAGE SALES AND FLEA MARKETS
Shop Like a Kangaroo with Triplets

Drag out your cargo pants or shorts before you set off for the flea market or several garage sales. Then you can stash small sums of money in different pockets, and you won't have to pull out a wad of bills when you pay for a small purchase. Word gets around a multifamily garage sale or flea market, and you don't want to undermine your credibility as a bargain hunter.

Act Interested

It's a myth that you should never show interest in a particular item at a garage sale or flea market, says Joanne Kennedy of Toano, Virginia. "If you play that game too much, you won't get the best price, because the seller won't know that you might be receptive to a better offer than the list price," she says. Instead, Joanne, who has been a "junk" shopper for more than 50 years, always tells the vendor or garage sale attendant what she's looking for. "An added benefit is that if the vendor doesn't have what you want, he may steer you to someone who does," she says.

Put the Seller in Charge

Lots of people lose bargains because they think put-downs and haggling work, says Joanne Kennedy's husband, Bob, a retired communications professor. He advises simply asking a vendor for her very best price. "Those words let the seller know she's in control of setting the price," Bob says. If the best price offered is still more than you can afford, let the vendor know that, without running down the merchandise. "I just say, 'Well, I'd love to have that, but the price doesn't fit into my budget,'" says Joanne. "That leaves the door open for her to offer you a better price."

Stay on the Wagon

Neighborhood garage sales can offer the best bargains—if you have the stamina to wade through all the stuff at several houses. To keep your hands free and save yourself the chore of toting heavy purchases to the car, dig out that old child's wagon from your garage (or buy one at a garage sale) to hold your treasures.

Lots of Dollar Bills Make Cents

Whenever you're shopping a sale with negotiable prices, bring along lots of one-dollar bills and at least a dollar's worth of change. That way, you'll never have to round up the price or lose a bargain because you don't have the proper change.

Things to Take to a Flea Market

Always avid "junk store" fans, Bob and Joanne Kennedy are now retired and can take all day Saturday to browse flea markets. According to them, these are essential items for success.

Two measuring tapes. Bring one soft and one made of metal. "You never know what you might need to measure, and you should measure your spaces for art and so forth before you leave the house," says Joanne.

A magnifying glass. "This is handy for checking jewelry, details on antiques, little electronics—it's my one must-have item," says Bob.

A notebook. Use it to write down specs on items you're considering, phone numbers, and the booth number of any vendor you might want to revisit.

Newspapers. "Sometimes vendors won't have any materials for wrapping a fragile item," says Joanne. "If I know for sure I'm looking for glassware, I might bring a box and some packing worms." Disposable diapers work as padding material, too.

Plastic or canvas bags. These are handy just in case a vendor runs out in the middle of a busy day.

A Built-In Measuring Tape

Even on those days when you've forgotten to bring your measuring tape on a shopping trip, you still have one on hand. Since ancient times, people have used their own bodies as measurement standards. For example, when you spread your hand, the length between the tip of your thumb and the tip of your pinkie is about 9 inches. The distance between the thumb and tip of the index finger is about 6 inches. The distance from your elbow to the tip of the longest finger of your outstretched hand is approximately 18 inches, called a cubit. And the width of an average finger is about ¾ inch, or a digit. Try measuring your own body to compare. You may discover that one of your knuckles is exactly 1 inch wide, for example.

Your hand is a handy on-the-spot tool for checking measurements in stores when you don't have a measuring tape at hand.

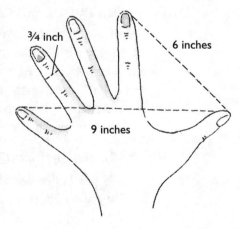
¾ inch
6 inches
9 inches

SHOPPING AT HOME

The All-Important Number

One rule of thumb will save you time with mail-order shopping, and it may even save the cost of replacing an item you've already paid for. "Always, always write down your order number," says Bostonian Cathy Steever, staffing supervisor for the Potpourri Group, a mail-order retail company. "And if you order online, print the confirmation out right away." With order number in hand, anytime you have occasion to call the company about your merchandise, it will take only seconds (rather than minutes) for the customer service representative to pull up your record. "And knowing that number gives you instant credibility with the people on the other end of the line," says Cathy. "They will definitely believe you when you tell them an order never showed up, even if their records are telling a different story."

Look for the Prepaid Label

Even though Cathy Steever works for a mail-order supplier, she occasionally orders things from other companies. And to save time, she simply assumes something will go wrong with the order. "I always try to buy from a company that offers prepaid mailing labels for returns," she says. "That way, you can just peel off the label and return the item with no hassle. There may be a nominal charge if you use the label, but that is so minor compared to what UPS or the post office would charge."

It Pays to Advertise

If you like the savings of buying used versus new but don't enjoy visiting flea markets and junk shops, try snagging that item you want by advertising in the Wanted section of your local newspaper, recommends writer and editor Kathryn Phelps of Katonah, New York. It's a shameless shortcut to finding just the right rug or piece of furniture at the right price.

Good Service Clocks in at Nine

To get better service from mail-order companies with absolutely no effort on your part, place your phone order between

9 A.M. and 2 P.M. The mail-order industry employs lots of working moms with school-age children, and the primary shift is during school hours. That's when the most knowledgeable, best trained order takers are working, and it's also when the customer service managers are available if you need questions answered or decisions made. Of course, if the only time that's convenient for you to call is late at night, you'll still get service, but the order takers may not know as much about a product or be able to answer your questions about size, color, and other details.

Know Who Keeps Company

If you're planning a large purchase from a mail-order supplier, consider making it even bigger. Almost any mail-order company will give you a 10 percent discount on orders over $1,000. Here's where a little research can really pay off. Most companies represent more than one catalog company, and they'll usually let you combine orders from the different catalogs to reach the $1,000 total. In preparation for a big purchase in the future, the next time you place a regular order, ask the phone representative what other catalog companies the

3 Ways to Save on Shipping

Catalog prices beat mall prices almost every time, but only when shipping and handling add-ons don't eat up the savings. Here are three ways to save on shipping charges when you shop by mail.

Combine and conquer. Lots of mail-order catalogs charge shipping fees based on the dollar amount of your order. Some even offer free shipping once you exceed a certain total. So unless you're buying clearance items, wait until you have several items and order them all at one time.

Take a spin on the Web. If you spot a product in a catalog, check the company's Web site before you call to order it. Some companies offer free shipping for Internet orders.

Keep it light. Consider buying statuary, pots and pans, comforters, and other heavy items in town, especially if the mail-order company sets shipping fees based on weight.

mail-order company represents. Or check online; that information is also available at the company's Web site.

Swear Off Bad Service

What's the quickest way to resolve problems with a catalog order? "Be pleasant but insistent," says mail catalog staffing supervisor Cathy Steever of Boston. "Never jump the chain of command. Try to solve the problem with the person on the phone. If you can't, pleasantly say, 'I know this isn't your problem, and I appreciate your help. Could I please speak to your manager now?' " Never shout or swear, says Cathy, or you may end up repeating the entire process of waiting for a representative and explaining the problem. "Any major mail catalog company gives its employees permission to hang up if you swear at them," says Cathy. "And if you're already shouting, a phone clerk may take liberties and say you swore, too."

Play Post Office at Home

If you want to do business with smaller mail-order companies or eBay "auctioneers" without spending lots of time at the post office, consider buying an inexpensive mechanical postal scale, which costs about $13 and is available at office supply or discount department stores. Then you can use ordinary stamps and your mailbox (or the mailroom at work if it's safer) to return items—no more paying to add an extra stamp, just in case. This tactic also will make you more likely to return an item that doesn't suit you, instead of rationalizing that it has its good points. If you'd like to invest in a pricier ($50 and up) digital postal scale, eBay is a great place to try to land one for a bargain price.

Put Your Computer on Author Alert

Are you addicted to Sue Grafton mystery novels? Tom Clancy techno-thrillers? If so, you simply must know the moment the writer's newest book is available. You can satisfy your need to know online, without even firing up a search engine. The big online booksellers such as Amazon.com (www. amazon.com) and Barnes & Noble (www.bn.com) will happily send you an electronic notice when your favorite author issues a new book. To sign up for this service, go to the bookseller's home page and click on a heading like Alerts. Fill in your e-mail address and the writer you want to track. When a new title is available, you'll get mail.

Gearing Down at Dinner and Day's End

7

The evening hours in an average American home are a frantic whirl of activity. In this chapter, we're going to de-frenzy the day's end with cunning shortcuts for preparing dinner, taking care of the kids, finishing unfinished daytime business, planning ahead, and then enjoying some relaxing activities that will prepare you for a good night's sleep.

EASY WEEKNIGHT DINNER IDEAS

The Two-Dinner Roast

When you know that you need a fast dinner on Wednesday, cook a roast on Tuesday. Choose a roast that's large enough to include enough leftovers to feed half your family. Cut the left-over meat into julienne strips (thin strips 1/4 to 1/2 inch wide), tuck them into a resealable plastic bag, and refrigerate. The following night, use the strips to whip up a meal in 15 minutes.

1. Pour half of a 15-ounce can (about 1 cup) of low-fat, low-sodium beef broth into a pan and stir-fry the meat strips for 5 minutes. Season with 2 crushed garlic cloves and/or 1 teaspoon thyme, sage, or soy sauce.

103

2. Top the meat with about 1½ cups baby carrots. Cover and steam for about 5 minutes on medium heat.

3. Add 2 cups fast-cooking chopped vegetables, such as broccoli, red bell peppers, and mushrooms. For ultimate speed, use a 1-pound bag of your favorite frozen combination—any mix without carrots. With the pan uncovered, stir to heat for 5 minutes. If needed, add ¼ cup more broth.

Serve this dish as is or over rice or pasta.

Score One for Speed

When carving the family roast takes too long and results in shredded hunks of meat, follow this advice from Northbrook, Illinois, butcher Ed Manacek: Always carve against the meat's natural grain. If the roast is tied, carve parallel to the string, since the string is placed against the grain. If the roast is not tied, ask the butcher to score shallow cut lines in the meat to guide you. Cook your roast as desired, then just place your carving knife in the scored grooves and slice.

Liven Up Leftovers

Transform leftovers into a fast, tasty meal by sandwiching them between two tortillas. The result is delicious quesadillas, and preparing them couldn't be easier. Coat a skillet with nonstick cooking spray and put it on the stove to heat. When the pan is warm, place a soft tortilla in it. On top of the tortilla, sprinkle about ¼ cup cooked fish, poultry, or beef. (Crumbled leftover hamburger or meat loaf also works fine.) Add ¼ cup cheese (shredded works best) and ¼ cup vegetables, such as sliced onion, cucumber, tomato, bell pepper, or zucchini. Place another tortilla on top. Cook over medium heat until the bottom tortilla is lightly browned. Flip and brown the other side. Transfer to a plate and cut into triangles. If you'd

Choose the Right Roast

Instead of eyeballing every roast at the store to try to pick one that guarantees leftovers, rely on this tip from Ed Manacek. Plan on approximately 8 ounces of meat per adult for a regular serving and 4 ounces per person for stir-fried leftovers. For a family of four, that comes out to a 3-pound (48-ounce) roast. By the way, for a second-night stir-fry, Ed recommends a tri-tip roast, also called a triangle roast.

like, serve sour cream, salsa, and/or your favorite salad dressing on the side for dipping.

Note: Tortillas vary in size, so you may need to adjust meat, vegetable, and cheese proportions accordingly.

An Egg-Cellent Dinner Idea

It's 5:30 P.M. You're hungry and you're staring into the refrigerator, but no candidates for tonight's dinner are in view. When this happens, "mix things up," says Monique Ryan, a nutrition counselor and lover of all healthy foods. "Appropriate dinner foods" are all in your mind, says Monique, so think outside the box. For example, eggs are an excellent dinner choice, and you almost always have a few on hand. Omelettes are great dinner options, but for something really different, here's a way to combine eggs with veggies for a fast, tasty, and nutritious dinner for four.

They Had NO Shame

1. Cook half of a 1-pound bag of frozen vegetables according to the package directions. Set the vegetables aside in a small bowl.
2. Scramble 8 eggs in a large nonstick frying pan.
3. Fold in the cooked vegetables with salt and pepper to taste. Or sprinkle on ¼ teaspoon garlic powder or 1 teaspoon lemon-herb seasoning mix.
4. At the last minute, top the eggs with about 1 cup of your favorite low-fat cheese. (Shredded is best, but thin slices also melt nicely.) Turn off the stove, set a lid on the pan, and let the cheese slowly melt as you prepare some toast to serve on the side.

Perk Up Frozen Pizza

When time is of the essence, a store-bought frozen pizza is certainly a

Dishwasher Fish

Stu Shryer of Glenview, Illinois, a retired advertising executive and active seeker of creative angles to anything, likes this fast recipe for poaching fish on a busy weeknight. It requires only about 5 minutes of prep time and no cleanup. In the middle of a large piece of aluminum foil, Stu places a fish fillet, a few lemon slices, and some sliced or chopped fresh vegetables. Tightly folding the foil shut, he places the packet in the top rack of his empty dishwasher and runs his dinner through the rinse cycle. (No soap, please!) When the cycle is complete, the fish is poached and the vegetables are steamed. No pans to clean, no basting needed, and while his fish is poaching, Stu is free to do whatever he likes.

We're Out of Mayonnaise?

You're cruising through preparation of a fast weeknight dinner, and you suddenly discover that you're out of a key ingredient like mayonnaise. Chances are, there's some other ingredient in your refrigerator or pantry that will work as a substitute. Check this list to see how you can adapt your plans on the spot. These substitutions are condensed from a list offered on BlueSuitMom.com by its owner and CEO, Maria Bailey.

Ingredient	Substitute
1 cup butter	1 cup margarine, or 7/8 cup shortening and 1/2 tsp salt
1 cup buttermilk	1 cup plain yogurt, or 1 cup whole milk and 1 tbsp lemon juice
1 cup heavy cream	3/4 cup milk and 1/3 cup butter or margarine (this works for cooking, not for your coffee)
1 cup light cream	3/4 cup milk and 3 tbsp butter or margarine (for cooking and baking), or 1 cup evaporated milk
1 cup mayonnaise	1 cup sour cream, or 1 cup cottage cheese pureed in a blender
1 cup sour cream	1 cup yogurt, or 3/4 cup milk, 3/4 tsp lemon juice, and 1/2 cup butter
1 cup plain yogurt	1 cup buttermilk, 1 cup sour cream, or 1 cup cottage cheese blended until smooth

• •

quick-and-easy choice. To make it a more nutritionally complete meal, add a layer of chopped fresh vegetables (onions, peppers, mushrooms, broccoli, and the like), then top the vegetables with a sprinkling of shredded mozzarella cheese. Cook according to the package directions. If needed, give the pizza a few extra minutes to ensure that the center is heated through.

Boost That Store-Bought Sauce

On a busy weeknight, cooking spaghetti sauce from scratch is a pipe dream. To give bottled spaghetti sauce a homemade flavor and a vitamin boost, simmer it for about 30 minutes with 1 or 2 minced garlic cloves and about 4 cups fresh vegetables, such as cubed zucchini, shredded carrots, sliced onion, and chopped tomatoes. Do not add any additional salt—most bottled sauces are high in sodium to start with.

Interesting Instant Rice

Quick-cooking rice is the thing to choose for hurry-up meals, and there's a very simple way to give it fantastic flavor. Instead of cooking the rice in water, use an equal amount of undiluted chicken or beef broth. Even better, use a seasoned canned broth, such as chicken broth flavored with roasted garlic or with roasted vegetables and herbs.

The Smart Chef's Salad

Think that a chef's salad is too much trouble for a weeknight meal? Think again. You can cut the preparation time to 20 minutes tops by choosing your ingredients carefully. At the deli counter of your supermarket, ask for 2 slices each of turkey, roast beef, and your favorite hard cheese cut ½ inch thick. Then swing by the produce department and buy a bag of salad-ready greens, a cucumber, and 2 tomatoes. In the spice aisle, pick up a container of Italian seasoning.

At home, wash the salad greens and let them dry. Meanwhile, slice the cucumber and tomatoes. Combine two parts olive oil and one part lemon juice or vinegar for a simple dressing. Put the salad greens, cucumber, and tomatoes in a pretty serving bowl. Add as much dressing as desired and toss the salad. Cut the meat and cheese into long, ¼-to-½-inch-wide strips. Arrange the strips on the salad and sprinkle the whole thing with Italian seasoning. Serve with some crusty bread and perhaps a glass of wine.

Condiments to the Rescue

When there's no time to plan a meal ahead, remember that you can work small miracles as long as you have a

The Second Time Around

Double-Duty Hot Water

One of the fastest dinners around is pasta and veggies with a drizzle of garlic-flavored olive oil. To make this dish even faster, Chicago writer and mother Donna Shryer uses one pot of boiling water to cook the pasta and veggies. First, she cooks sliced carrots, broccoli florets, and red bell pepper chunks in the water for 3 minutes. She uses a slotted spoon to remove the vegetables and sets them aside. Then she cooks the pasta in the vitamin-infused water, which returns to a boil in about 1 minute.

jar of salsa or a bottle of ranch dressing on hand. For example, cook some fish, eggs, or baked potatoes and served them topped with salsa. (Warm the salsa first in the microwave.) Or mix ranch dressing with tuna or hard-boiled eggs to make tasty tuna or egg salad. Ranch dressing also makes a good topping for baked potatoes and grilled chicken breasts.

Budget Gourmet

Amazingly, sprinkling pine nuts or sunflower seeds on an ordinary dish is enough to add a gourmet flair. Try this the next time you serve pasta with sauce, a simple fruit salad, or ordinary frozen vegetables. Nuts and seeds are perfect for adding a healthy crunch to a dinner salad (substitute them for those calorie-laden croutons), too. We bet your family will be impressed.

Share a Meal

If you're lucky enough to have a best friend living next door, make one night a week Neighbor Night. For example, on this week's designated night, she cooks dinner for her family and yours. Next week, you cook dinner for the two families. You can choose to share the meal together or simply run the spare casserole (or whatever) next door.

TAKE CHARGE OF TAKEOUT

Highlighting Helps

Ask everyone in your family to highlight and initial their favorite selections on each take-out menu that you keep on file. That way, when it's time to phone in an order but only half the family is home, you can order for the absentees with confidence.

Let Your Phone Call for Takeout

For the ultimate in speedy take-out ordering, enter the phone numbers of your favorite restaurants into the speed dial memory of your phone. This works best for restaurants with limited selections or a specific meal you always order—so you don't even need the menu in front of you when you call.

5 Ways to Keep Take-Out Menus Handy

Take-out food is a stress-relieving choice on a busy weeknight, but not if you spend 15 minutes searching for the menu. To ensure that take-out menus are always at your fingertips when your stomach is growling, try one of these approaches for keeping them handy.

In a slot. You know that cabinet in your kitchen that has vertical slots designed to hold serving trays? Save one slot to slide in menus.

In a binder. Get a three-ring binder or pocket folder and designate it for take-out menus. Keep your binder with your cookbooks. This is your anti-cookbook!

In a container. Buy a slim, trim plastic cereal container (available at any home store or discount store). Store your container, with menus inside, in a kitchen cabinet.

In the phone book. Tuck, staple, or clip menus inside your local city telephone directory. These big books are almost impossible to misplace, so your menus will always be traceable.

On a key ring. Stack your menus and use a hole puncher to punch a hole through the stack, about 3 inches in from a top corner. Slip a metal key ring through the hole and hang it on a hook next to your telephone.

Freebies Are Fine

If you have four menus from carryout pizza joints in your collection, reduce the clutter and confusion by tossing the menus that don't offer freebies. After all, if you're going for speed, you might as well go for economy as well. For example, many carryout pizza restaurants offer incentives, such as a free bottle of soda with any pizza order, free delivery if your total comes to a certain dollar amount (although you'll still want to tip the delivery boy), or free toppings if you order a large pizza.

Healthy Chinese?

Chinese food is an all-time favorite for take-out dinners, but the food can be surprisingly high in fat and calories. Follow these guidelines to quickly order a dinner that stays on the healthy side.

1. Skip over those deep-fried egg rolls and start with hot-and-sour soup, a flavorful way to take the edge off your appetite.

2. Stick with dishes that include lots of vegetables or selections based on bean curd (also called tofu). Shrimp or chicken with garlic sauce and Szechuan chicken or shrimp are generally lower in fat than many other Chinese dishes.

3. Choose steamed rice: It's a lower-calorie choice than any type of fried rice.

4. Remember to ask for chopsticks. Using them will slow you down a bit, so you'll eat less overall.

Double Rice Is Nice

Buy more Chinese take-out food than you can eat tonight to provide some fixings for a (mostly) homemade meal tomorrow. When you order, ask for a couple of extra containers of steamed rice. They cost only a buck or two and will simplify meal preparation the following day. For example, you can concentrate on whipping up chili or a stir-fry and just pop the rice in the microwave to accompany your homemade main dish. If the rice seems a little dry, add a teaspoon of water before you microwave it.

EASING KIDS THROUGH THE EVENING

Rely on Routine

Child psychologists agree that when kids are involved, evenings hum along more smoothly if parents set a routine. So does Chicago freelance writer Sue Bodmer, also known as Jane and Sam's mom. "After dinner, we read a story, the kids bathe, we sing a few songs, we sing one last song to Sam, and poof he's asleep," Sue says. "Then we sing one last song to Jane, and poof again, she's asleep. Some parents shy away from a routine because they think it's too boring, but kids love a nurturing routine."

Make Time for Games

Do you spend precious time worrying that your family spends too little time together in the evening? One family member is doing homework, another is practicing the violin, a third person is packing tomorrow's lunches, and no one's enjoying the fact that they're part of a wonderful family. To calm your anxiety, make a weekly or biweekly commitment to family game night. Evelyn Petersen, an early childhood consultant, reminds parents, "You get so very much for one hour of time, because as you play, the family becomes a team. It's a wonderful break from the usual parent-child roles." Evelyn adds that for multitasking fans, family game night accomplishes more than just fun: "Depending on the game, children are working on math, counting, vocabulary, spelling, deductive reasoning, problem solving, and money skills—without even knowing it." (If you need some game suggestions, visit Evelyn's Web site, www. askevelyn.com.) During family games, you're also encouraging children to develop skills such as cooperation, patience, honesty, and following rules. That's a lot accomplished in 60 minutes.

Gearing Down at Dinner and Day's End

Become a Basket Case

"Laundry baskets are my friends," says Kathy Kirrish, a mom from Kenilworth, Illinois. Kathy relies on laundry baskets to speed up before-bedtime cleanup, with a minimum of grumbling. Her two children have two laundry baskets each in their bedrooms. One is for laundry; the second is for gathering up toys quickly on nights when there's no time to put them away properly. Kathy also keeps one empty laundry basket in her bedroom. After she puts the kids to bed, she grabs the basket and tours the house, grabbing stray toys along her way to the basement playroom. After making her way down to the basement, Kathy works in reverse, using her laundry basket to gather items that belong upstairs.

The Argument for Procrastination

Lucky is the parent whose children are driven to come home from school and finish their homework immediately. But sometimes being too organized works against these kids. Professional organizer Kathy Paauw of Seattle has a client whose daughter likes to finish projects right away, even if she has a month to complete them. The problem: Occasionally, the teacher will fine-tune or outright change the assignment midway, which means that Kathy's daughter has to rework her project. Also, sometimes instructors teach concepts during the term of a project that should be incorporated into the assignment. If those concepts are missing from the project, the result may be a lower grade. Yes, organization is important, but so is timing.

The Bedtime Ponytail

To avoid spending precious morning minutes untangling little girls' curls, buy a package of inexpensive scrunchies and follow this before-bed routine recommended by Chicago mom Sue Bodmer and practiced by her 9-year-old, very longhaired daughter, Jane. First, brush the hair and gather it into a ponytail about 3 inches below the nape of the neck. Leaving some distance between the ponytail holder and the hairline is important to avoid putting undue tension on the hair, Sue says. Then use scrunchies spaced about 4 inches apart to contain the rest of the ponytail and keep it snarl-free while your child sleeps.

COPING WITH COMMUNICATION

All in Good Time

Jane Swanson-Nystrom, a working mother from Chicago, keeps her two teenage daughters on track in the evening by limiting phone time to 30 minutes on school nights and 60 minutes on weekends. "Once in a while, we set a phone moratorium for an entire evening—no calls at all," Jane says. "It's a battle, but you cannot believe how much gets accomplished." If the honor system doesn't work for your crew, you might extend Jane's idea by keeping a notepad next to the telephone, for logging in and out. If anyone goes over her time limit, she is penalized, such as by having to do the dinner dishes the next night.

You've Got Reminders

Rather than taking time to write every last personal detail into your office calendar, send reminders to your office e-mail address. For example, if you're eating breakfast and suddenly remember that today is your daughter's soccer practice, log on to the Internet from home and send an e-mail reminder to your desk. Or if your doctor mailed you a reminder card alerting you to the fact that it's time for that annual checkup, e-mail yourself a reminder to call the doctor's office and schedule the appointment.

Sing a Self-Reminder

If an e-mail reminder isn't enough to motivate you to follow up on important details, call your own answering machine and leave yourself a memorable voice message. To give the message special impact, tell a joke, talk in a funny voice, or even make up a little song, like this one (to the tune of "Happy Birthday to You"):

> *It's mom's birthday tomorrow,*
> *Buy a present, avoid sorrow,*
> *Get up early, order flowers,*
> *She'll be happy for hours.*

Post Popular Phone Numbers

Stop wasting time looking up telephone numbers that you call on a regular basis. With a computer (or even a pencil and paper), it's easy to create a family phone list and update it periodically. Print out a new version every month or so and post it by each phone in the house.

5 MINUTES A DAY

Foiling Telemarketers

It's easy to avoid annoying interruptions by telemarketers, says busy mom and business consultant Lori MacDonald of Cumberland Foreside, Maine. Save yourself a few minutes every day by following her tips.

- Use an answering machine to screen calls. If someone you know starts to leave a message, you can pick up the phone and take the call.

- Order caller ID from your telephone company so you can screen calls. If you don't recognize the name of the caller, don't answer.

- Listen carefully when you first pick up the phone. If there's dead space on the line for a few seconds, you've probably been called by an automatic dialer. Hang up quickly. If you accidentally hang up on a friend, she'll call you back.

- Be polite but firm if a telemarketer manages to penetrate all your defenses. Say "no thanks" and get off the phone immediately. Think of it this way: You're not being rude—you're just allowing the salesperson to quickly move on to the next, potentially more profitable, call.

113

Juggle Surf Time and Phone Time

If you enjoy surfing the Net in the evening but worry that you may be missing phone calls, forward your home calls to your cell phone while you're online. (Check your phone company's Web site for directions on how to do this.) Problem solved—except that you may be worried about using up all your cell phone minutes if a friend calls for a long chat. Explain that the call was forwarded to your cell phone and you'd like to call him back immediately from your home phone. Hang up, log off the Internet, and return the call.

Rotating News Bulletins

Are you part of a small group of friends, perhaps from your college days or a long-ago toddler play group, that's now spread all over the country? Instead of everyone writing individually, establish a rotating update schedule. In January, Mary writes a letter or e-mail message and sends it to the entire group. In February, Jennifer writes to the group, and so on. When it's your turn, feel free to respond to important news on behalf of the group. For example, if Mary wrote about the birth of her new granddaughter, congratulate her and offer her some grandmotherly advice—chances are that everyone in the group will enjoy your comments. And remember, you can also jot a handwritten addendum to each friend before stuffing the letters into envelopes for mailing.

PLANNING AHEAD TO SAVE TIME TOMORROW

Slow-Cook and Save Time

It's breakfast bliss: a hot and hearty bowl of oatmeal. But during the hustle and bustle of the morning, it's a challenge even to whip up a bowl of instant oatmeal. The trick to enjoying a hot oatmeal breakfast without stress is to cook it overnight.

Get out the old electric slow cooker, or Crock-Pot. Just before you go to bed, place rolled (not instant or quick) oats and water—along with raisins, peanut butter, or whatever else you like—in the pot. One cup of dry oats makes three to five servings; add about 2 cups of water for each cup of oats. (You may need a little extra liquid, about another ¼ cup, depending on how hot your pot cooks.) Set the control on low, and in the morning, your oatmeal will be nicely cooked, delightfully hot, and ready to dish out when you're ready to eat.

Prep Pancakes in the P.M.

Whole grain pancakes are another wholesome breakfast treat that we never seem to find time for during the week. If you mix the pancake batter the night before, though, you can surprise your family with a pancake breakfast any day of the week. Store the batter overnight in an airtight container in the refrigerator. In the morning, all you have to do is heat the griddle and flip a batch.

Package Some Leftover Lunches

Leftovers top the list of great microwaveable lunches. Take a few minutes right after dinner to prepare the leftovers. You'll appreciate it the next morning, when you can just grab a great lunch out of the refrigerator and head out the door.

Here are some easy ideas for assembling lunches the night before. You can package these meals in microwaveable containers or resealable plastic bags. Heating them for a minute or two on high power will produce a terrific hot lunch.

- To leftover meat, add 6 ounces frozen veggies and a can of drained black beans.
- Cook some jumbo pasta shells according to the package directions.

Let cool, then add leftover tuna salad, diced vegetables, or leftover meat with about a tablespoon of shredded cheese.

- If you have leftover baked potatoes, prepare a container of toppings such as salsa, cottage cheese with scallions, shredded cheese, or sour cream. Place a potato and the topping container in a lunch bag. At work, when you're ready for lunch, split the baked potato, reheat it, and then add the topping.
- Make sandwiches with leftover meat and a slice or two of cheese. At lunchtime, a 1-minute zap in the microwave will melt the cheese and heat the meat to perfection. Add tomatoes, lettuce, and condiments (bring these to work in separate containers) after heating your sandwich.

Pack for the Waiting Room

When tomorrow's schedule includes a doctor's appointment, think about your waiting room time. To use this boring period productively, assemble a waiting room kit tonight. Pack personal stationery or note cards (during the holiday season, pack your greeting cards), envelopes, a pen, your address book, and stamps. Throw in a bottle of water, a portable CD player with headset, or a novel you've been trying to read. Who knows, if your doctor is running really late, you may be able to finish that book.

Book Early and Smile

Hate to waste time in a dentist's office? When you're due for that twice-a-year checkup and cleaning, book the first appointment of the day. You'll be in and out in less than an hour and ready to flash that bright smile to coworkers on the job. Use this same shortcut strategy for routine physicals and other yearly medical exams.

Speaking of scheduling appointments, ask your dentist or doctor if you can schedule appointments online through a

3 Memory Boosters That Really Work

It's essential that you grab that plate of cupcakes in the refrigerator before heading out in the morning. Or perhaps you're going to meet your best friend for a birthday breakfast, and you mustn't forget her gift—a beautiful ivy plant that is sitting beside your living room window. If there's something you *must* do or grab before leaving the house, set out one of these reminders the night before.

The bold buzzer reminder. Set an alarm clock to go off at the time you usually leave the house and place the clock beside the front door. When the buzzer goes off, it will remind you that there's something you have to do.

The gold ribbon reminder. Tie a ribbon to the handle of your briefcase or purse. Use glittery gold holiday ribbon so you can't miss it.

The key note reminder. Write yourself a reminder note, punch a hole in it, slip a piece of string through the hole, and tie the note to your keys. You're not going anywhere without those keys, so you can't possibly leave home without spying your note.

Web site. If this service is available, you can schedule at your convenience, rather than trying to remember to call during office hours.

Display the Due Date

Can't remember when those videos are due? Well, you could take a long, involved class on how to boost memory skills, or you could simply do what Chicagoan Donna Shryer does. Donna bought a clear plastic envelope (available at office supply stores) and used a small nail to fasten the envelope to the inside of the cabinet door of her entertainment center. When she brings home a rented video, she places the rental receipt—which states the due date—inside the envelope.

Know What You'll Wear

Expert time manager Susan Fignar of Itasca, Illinois, suggests that before going to bed, you check your calendar to see what's up for tomorrow and pull out the appropriate clothing. As an added bonus, this ritual gives you an unhurried moment to check clothing for loose buttons, sagging hems, or previously unnoticed spaghetti stains. Either make the repair while you watch TV or choose another outfit.

Banish Wrinkles without Ironing

When you pull out tomorrow's outfit, hang it in the bathroom so that the steam from your morning shower can smooth out any wrinkles. Unless that cotton blouse was literally balled up in the back of some drawer, this should eliminate any need to pull out the iron. If you forget this handy trick, you can lightly mist a terry cloth towel with water and toss it along with your wrinkled clothes in the dryer. Set the dryer on air. After about 5 minutes, all the wrinkles should be gone.

WINDING DOWN

Breathe In over the Sink

As a marketing consultant for scientists and inventors, Amy Witsil of Chapel Hill, North Carolina, is no sucker for advertising schemes. But she does think that those "aromatherapy" dishwashing liquids on the market fulfill their marketing promises. "I don't get to relax in a bubble bath most nights, but I can relax while I do the dishes," she says with a laugh. Even though the pleasant scent only makes the dishwashing seem to go more quickly, it definitely encourages Amy to tackle pots and pans immediately after dinner, so they don't require as much soaking or scrubbing. And she really likes the stuff. "When I first bought some, I thought it was so great I was going to tell my engineer friends at work that my husband got it for me for Valentine's Day," Amy says. "But I was worried my joke would backfire and they'd all buy aromatherapy dish liquid for their wives next year."

A Stitch in Time

Tending to a few simple, mindless chores in the evening in front of the TV can be enjoyable and relaxing. Plus, when you take care of chores in the evening, you save yourself the irritation of doing them on the spot in the morning. Case in point: stitching a loose button or mending a sagging hem. You'll be most likely to take care of these repairs during TV time if you keep a little sewing kit at the ready. (For suggestions on what to put in the kit, see "Sewing Emergency Kit" on page 290.) And remember, when you're making a sewing kit for yourself, you don't need a fancy container. An empty oatmeal or powdered drink mix canister will do the job fine.

A Recipe for Relaxation

When four gorgeous chicken breasts are sitting in your fridge, properly thawed and waiting to be prepared, inspiration to try something different often strikes. But lack of time (where *did* you put that Greek chicken recipe?) and ingredients (who keeps leeks in the house?) drives you right back to the same old cooking method. Use that before-bedtime hour to search the Internet for a few new recipes. Many recipe Web sites offer a wealth of search options, such as preparation time, specific ingredient, course category, nutritional restrictions, or cooking method. When the hour is up, choose one recipe to try, print it out, and immediately add the ingredients you need to your shopping list.

5 Relaxing Evening Activities

Try these simple activities to unwind in the evening.

Sign up for shoe duty. Properly polish your shoes (you know, the ones you've been coloring with a black marker to cover the scuff marks).

Weed out recipes. Go through your stack of recipes torn from magazines and ask yourself, "Am I ever really going to make ratatouille?"

Sort through magazines. Go through that stack of old magazines and tear out the one recipe or article you want to save. Bag the magazines for recycling.

Do your nails. Give yourself a long, lazy manicure, including the soak in sudsy water that you rarely have time for.

Clean out that junk drawer. Pull the drawer out of the cabinet and put it on your lap or on a tray in front of you. Before you start, be sure the trash can is at your side.

Give Mom the Night Off

Every mom needs time away from the job, says Kathy Kirrish, who has a full time career as a stay-at-home wife and mother. "Knowing I have book club once a month helps make living through the rest easier," Kathy says. Think of the night out as a potential time- and money-saver—after all, buying a book once a month is cheaper than having a massage or seeing a therapist. Other low-cost stress relievers for overworked moms are a monthly movie group or Mom's Night Out. If you can't find an existing group, check with the mothers of other children in your child's class. Perhaps you can round up a bunch for a monthly dinner out at an inexpensive restaurant.

The Big Weeknight Date

Susan Allen, a busy mother and wife from Evanston, Illinois, plans a date with her husband at least once a week. With a little ingenuity, Susan has learned how to pull off an evening out with little effort and minimal babysitting expense. "Often our date follows something like a school parents association meeting," she says. "We've hired a sitter already, so after the meeting ends, we stop at a local restaurant for a quick bite." Susan

Gearing Down at Dinner and Day's End

also recommends bolting out the door with your spouse for a half-hour walk around the neighborhood whenever a relative stops by. The bonus? Special time together for the kids and that relative. Or Susan and her husband head for a shared workout at the gym, dropping off the kids at the gym's fully equipped, well-supervised babysitting room. Many exercise clubs offer this benefit, and if you have kids, it should be a deciding factor when you're shopping for a gym.

Take Time for Tea

The time you spend lying in bed trying to relax and fall asleep is surely time that would be better spent sleeping. To speed up the process of unwinding for sleep, brew yourself a cup of herbal tea before bedtime. There is some scientific evidence that certain herbs help induce sleep. Plus, drinking a cup of tea forces you to sit down and relax, lest you spill the hot liquid all over your pajamas. Three herbal teas recommended for bed-

Go Glam in 5 Minutes

Your friend calls at the last minute with the offer of a spare ticket to a local theater production. You have only 15 minutes to get out the door, so there's no time to take a shower and apply your evening face. Diane Ayala, owner of Ayala Maquillage in Chicago, offers these quick tips for revamping your daytime makeup for an evening out. The principle, Diane says, it to remember that by day we're in bright light, so we tone down makeup. On a night out, though, the lighting is often romantically dim, so it's best to apply slightly heavier makeup to keep your face from disappearing. (Be careful not to cross the line into clown academy!)

- Stroke and then smudge a dark eye shadow or eye pencil along the upper lash line and below the lower lash line. Diane likes deep plum-brown, since it complements almost every complexion and eye color and creates a soft, romantic look.

- Touch up your blush and apply iridescent powder lightly to the cheekbones, center of the forehead, chin, neck, shoulders, and décolletage.

- If by day you wear neutral peach or pink lip colors, choose a vivid red, romantic maroon, or rich terra-cotta lipstick for the evening.

- If dark colors are not your style, stick with your usual color of lipstick but add a matching lip pencil and shimmering gloss.

Try a Foot Massage

A before-bed foot massage can help you mellow out and fall asleep easily. Try this simple procedure with one foot, then the other. Keep in mind that every motion should be done gently.

1. Apply a dab of your favorite lotion to your palms. Sitting comfortably, place one foot on the opposite thigh. Use your thumbs to apply pressure to the sole of the foot, working from arch to big toe.

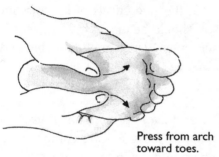

Press from arch toward toes.

2. One at a time, pull each toe out and away from the foot. Wiggle each toe. Using your middle or index finger, apply pressure between the toes.
3. Place the heel of your hand against the bottom of your toes and bend

the toes toward the top of your foot. Hold this stretch for 5 seconds. With the other hand, bend the toes down; hold for 5 seconds. This feels good, so 10 seconds is okay, too.

4. With the heel of your hand, make long strokes along the bones on top of the foot, from your ankle up to your toes. (Apply a little pressure as you do this.)

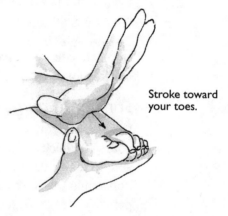

Stroke toward your toes.

5. Rub in a little more lotion, especially at the heel, and put on pure cotton socks.
6. Sleep tight.

time are chamomile, anise, and ginseng. Check the tea section in your grocery store or health food store; you'll often find teas that combine these herbs for ultimate benefit and flavor.

ACTIVITIES FOR NIGHT OWLS
Make Reservations at Midnight

When everyone else in the family is fast asleep and you're wide-awake, don't sit and do nothing. One activity that you can accomplish more quickly at night is scheduling airline reservations—especially those oh-so-time-consuming reservations that involve using earned miles. There is generally no wait to reach a phone representative when you call during the wee hours.

Primed for Nighttime

If catching your favorite prime-time comedy on TV is a wishful fantasy because of the frenzy of dinner cleanup, family chores, and preparing for the morrow, don't despair. Tape the show and watch it later in peace and quiet.

Check Prescriptions by Moonlight

Even some pharmacies are open 24 hours these days. If you have nagging questions about the side effects of one of your prescriptions or whether you should be taking it on an empty stomach, call your pharmacist after 10 P.M. You'll probably find her free for a lengthy, informative chat.

Surf Your Pharmacy

If you'd rather research answers to your prescription questions yourself, check your pharmacy's Web site. After completing a simple registration form, you will be able to request medication refills (delivered by mail or picked up in person), create personal health pages, research drugs, set up health records for easy access, and request e-mail reminders telling you when you need a refill.

PART 2

Chop a Chunk

out of Chores

8

In the Kitchen

Whether you're a shortcut chef or a gourmet cook, you can always appreciate tips that help you save time and effort in the kitchen. When you know how to cut the right corners, you can reduce time spent on kitchen chores and cooking without sacrificing taste, quality, or health standards. Read on for money- and timesaving ideas for keeping your kitchen clean, organizing your pantry and counters, cooking meals for your family, and preparing homemade baked goods. Use the time you save to enjoy other activities that let you leave the kitchen behind.

GETTING ORGANIZED

Color-Coordinate Your Pantry

Here's a quick way to organize your pantry or cupboard so that you can find ingredients more quickly and avoid the bother of accidentally buying duplicates of what you already have on hand. Group cans according to the color of the food inside: red foods on one shelf, green on another, and so on. Yes, that means the ketchup will be next to the cherries, which has no cooking logic, but you will always know where to find that ketchup. Another advantage of this method: Even a preschooler can help you put away the groceries.

Greet-and-Eat Recipe Cards

Still jotting down recipes on a napkin or the dog's vet bill, where they aren't seen for years? Correct that habit and take care of a clutter heap at the same time. Dig out that collection of greeting cards you've received over the years. Then cut the decorative front leaves off some of your favorites and use the blank back of each leaf to record a recipe. If you'd like, cut them down to whatever size fits your recipe file. Or collect some of the recipe cards you use most often, punch a hole in one corner of the cards, and thread them on a key chain. Hang the chain on the kitchen bulletin board or a cabinet doorknob.

If you're a food show junkie, make sure to keep a stack of blank greeting cards handy in a basket wherever you watch TV. Heck, if you get really good, you can match the card backs to the type of recipe—Christmas greetings for that famous fruitcake recipe, for example, or a birthday card with your niece's favorite birthday cake.

A Library of Spices

Kate Kearney finds that she saves time by alphabetizing her spices. "That way, I can find what I need easily when I'm cooking, and I know for sure what I don't have before I go shopping," says the young mother from Encino, California.

Rely on a Lid Bin

Storing pots, pans, and food storage containers in an organized way can be a challenge because there are so many shapes and sizes—not only of the pans and containers but also of the lids. Tracy Sebastian, a working mom from Beverly Hills, California, stacks what she can and tosses what she can't— into an inexpensive plastic bin (available at home supply stores). "I keep the lids in the bin, and that way all the pots and pans can be stacked nice and neat," Tracy says. "I use the same method for all my Tupperware—containers stacked and nested neatly, and the lids in a separate bin."

Whack the Wok

Tracy Sebastian is down on woks and other giant pans. "I never buy any pans, bowls, or small appliances that won't fit in the dishwasher," she says.

That policy keeps her kitchen purchases—and clutter—to a minimum, and she never has a sink full of large dishes waiting to be hand-washed.

Sort As You Go

The fewer times you have to handle recyclables, the better. Keep a separate trash can for cans and bottles in the kitchen. For a sort-as-you-go system for small items, attach two or three hooks to the inside edge of your recycling trash can, then hang plastic grocery bags on them. Toss batteries in one, small pieces of recyclable metal (such as can lids) in another, and other small items in another.

Can the Trash Bags

Never again will a roll of plastic trash bags unravel as you try to tear one free, nor will your mate and kids put coffee grounds in an unlined trash can because no one could find the trash bags. That's because you're going to use a 2-pound coffee can as a garbage bag dispenser and place it in plain view on the kitchen counter. Cut an X in the lid with a sharp knife and place the bags inside. Thread one bag through the slit and replace the lid. The X will act as a stopper so you can pull out just one bag at a time. If this shortcut works well for you and your family, spruce up the appearance of the can by covering it with wallpaper that matches your kitchen.

A coffee can in disguise hides a roll of kitchen trash bags in plain sight on your kitchen counter.

Lid

Roll of bags

127

Towel Tube Tuck-Aways

Leftover tubes from rolls of paper towels serve perfectly for storing empty plastic bread and produce bags (which are handy for wrapping up leftovers). Use your thumb and forefinger to poke bags into a tube. You can fit up to 10 bags per tube. Store the tube in a drawer alongside your boxes of plastic wrap and aluminum foil. It's easy to pinch a bag out of the tube whenever you need one.

Kick the Junk Habit

Every kitchen has a junk drawer—that repository of every odd item in the household that you don't want to throw away but don't know what to do with. Open the drawer, toss it in, and it's instantly lost. How about bringing order to the "cabinet of chaos" without spending a lot of money on special drawer organizers? It's easy. You probably throw out one or two mini-

Shop Rags to Kitchen Riches

Forget those homey embroidered dish towels, woven dishcloths, and, for that matter, cloth napkins, says Rose Kennedy of Knoxville, Tennessee. Why? "Everyone in my house uses the dainty little towels to wipe grease off their hands and leaves the wet dishrags in the sink until they stink," Rose says. "And I can never corral enough napkins for a matching set." So Rose has developed a substitute: mass quantities of unbleached shop towels. She can buy 75 towels for less than $10 at a wholesale club (or auto supply store).

In Rose's kitchen, the shop towels do triple duty. She uses them as dish towels and to wipe up messes on kitchen counters. Unlike thick dishcloths, shop towels dry quickly, long before they mildew. "We hang the wet ones on hooks and keep a whole bunch of dry ones in a deep drawer next to the sink. I've eliminated towel racks," she says.

Rose says she gets away with using shop towels as cloth napkins because the towels are buff-colored and her kitchen has a casual decor. "When people come over to eat, I put the shop towels in wooden napkin rings. No one knows I didn't pay the big bucks for them at a home store," she says.

containers a week, such as stationery boxes, paper clip boxes, bank check boxes, and more. Start stockpiling them instead, and in a few weeks, you'll have enough to create a grid of these open containers in the bottom of your junk drawer. Sort all the drawer's contents into these containers, suggests professional organizer Patty Bareford, owner of Wide Open Space in Concord, Massachusetts. You'll be able to find items quickly when you need them, and this container grid will keep the drawer's contents from sloshing forward when you open the drawer.

RETOOL YOUR REFRIGERATOR
Dry Up Some Shelf Space

Free up fridge space—and save money in the long term—with this hint from chef Rob Stanford of Tampa. Rob recommends discarding outdated jars and bottles of marinades, sauces, and salad dressings that are clattering around on the door of your refrigerator. Next, replace them with compact dry packets that you can mix up as needed—and in small portions. The packets will stay fresh much longer than refrigerated sauces and dressings containing oil or other ingredients that can spoil in a relatively short time.

Better Than a Bread Box

Nothing derails a quick lunch or snack like discovering that the bread is moldy at the very moment you've got the peanut butter out or the toaster waiting. Fortunately, there's an easy way to prevent bread from spoiling, and it saves counter space in the bargain. Throw out your bread box and store all your bread products, including bagels and muffins, in the freezer. Bread is one of the few products that you can freeze and defrost multiple times without harm. To defrost frozen bread, just pop it in the microwave. Or learn to love grilled cheese sandwiches or toasted bread, either of which you can make without bothering to defrost it. If you're going to store bagels in the freezer, request that your bagel shop slice them for you. Then remember to separate the bagel halves as you place them in the freezer bag, because you'd need the Jaws of Life to split a frozen bagel in half.

No More Moldy Messes

Leftover ingredients such as that half carton of ricotta cheese or a partial head of cauliflower clog up the refrigerator and usually end up going bad. To end the routine of tossing moldy leftover ingredients, buy only a small portion of limited-use ingredients from a deli or the pay-by-the-pound salad bar at your grocery store. If you stick with lightweight stuff, you'll probably pay less per pound than you would if you bought full containers of these ingredients. Here are a few ideas for making great meals from salad bar servings.

- Pizza toppings: Pepperoni slices to pineapple bits
- Pasta salad: Sliced olives and broccoli or cauliflower florets
- Potato salad: Celery sticks (to mince) and hard-boiled eggs (to chop)
- Nachos: Jalapeño chile pepper slices and shredded lettuce
- Omelettes: Green bell pepper rings (to chop) and julienned ham
- Casseroles: Onion slices (to dice), capers, and olives
- Soups: Crunchy Chinese noodles and grated cheese for garnishes
- Tossed salads: Croutons and alfalfa sprouts

Leaky Meat Is Yesterday's News

Anyone who's ever stored plastic-wrapped fresh meat in the refrigerator knows it has wily ways to leak and drip, which is annoying and can spread dangerous bacteria. Next time, deflect leakage by triple-wrapping. Leave the meat in its store wrappings, then fold several thicknesses of newspaper around the package. Not only will the paper catch any incidental drips, but the extra insulation will keep the meat super-fresh and juicy.

Chill Out with Brown Bags

Finally, there's a use for all those crumpled-but-intact brown paper lunch bags or fast-food bags—one that will save you a little time and trouble to boot. Use these bags to store ice cubes in your freezer instead of leaving the cubes in ice cube trays. Because the bags breathe, individual ice cubes stored in the bags won't stick together, and they won't pick up refrigerator odors.

Can Your Hamburger Patties

Pressing ground beef into patties before freezing saves time at the dinner hour (when you really need it), but a bag of frozen burgers is tough to stack in the freezer. The solution to this dilemma is to eat a sensible breakfast of old-fashioned oatmeal. That way, you'll have empty oatmeal canisters on hand to stack the patties in. When you stack the burgers, place a square of waxed paper between the patties for ease of separation later. The cardboard canister alone is fine if you're making the burgers only a day or two in advance. But if you're planning longer-term storage, place the canister in a resealable plastic bag before freezing.

KITCHEN CLEANUP

Keep Diamonds Out of the Drain

There's nothing more irritating than misplacing your rings and wristwatch when you take them off to tackle the dishes, or more heartbreaking than accidentally knocking a ring off the kitchen counter and down the drain. End these woes forever by taking a few seconds to screw a two-pronged hook onto the windowsill or the side of a cabinet that's close to the sink. Hang your rings and watch on the hook every time you do the dishes. Your valuables will always be safe and won't get lost. While you're at it, use Velcro squares to attach an extra eyeglass case to another surface nearby. That way, you can take off your glasses when you drain pasta or empty the hot dishwasher to avoid steamed-up lenses.

Spray It; Don't Soak It

Amy Witsil, a busy mom from Chapel Hill, North Carolina, picked up a dishwashing tip from a college friend's grandfather: "Grandpa Rosso always did the dishes, and he always had a spray bottle in hand, filled with one-third Joy liquid and two-thirds water." Thanks to his spray technique, Grandpa Rosso didn't have to fill the sink with soapy water in order to wash dishes, thus saving water and time. Instead, he would spot-spray trouble spots on dishes and let any with caked-on debris sit and soften before sponging them clean. He could

spray a wide area without using a handheld faucet spray attachment, which inevitably wastes water.

Dish Up Some Sparkling Glasses

Automatic dishwashers are top-rate timesaving appliances, but sometimes glassware washed in a dishwasher ends up spotted and dull. Without taking too much time or lowering your standards, you can give your stemware a nice sparkle. To do this, load the glassware in the top rack of the dishwasher. If you have a utensil basket on the bottom rack, place a cereal bowl inside the basket. If you don't, wedge a 2-cup rectangular plastic container firmly between two prongs on the bottom rack. Fill the bowl or container with 1$\frac{1}{2}$ cups chlorine bleach. Run the dishwasher to the start of the dry cycle, then shut it off and pour out any liquid that's in the bowl. Refill the bowl with 1$\frac{1}{2}$ cups white vinegar, put the bowl back in the dishwasher, and run the dishwasher again—this time through the full wash, rinse, and dry cycle. (The vinegar treatment neutralizes the bleach scent.) Repeat the process anytime your glassware needs a little extra attention.

Pay Less at the (Soap) Pump

That hand-pump soap dispenser next to the kitchen sink doles out more soap than anyone needs to wash his hands—which means time wasted rinsing off excess suds and more money spent on soap than need be. To make your soap dispenser stingier, wind a piece of twine or yarn around the stem of the pump attachment—enough to cover $\frac{1}{2}$ inch or so of the stem.

Wrap twine or yarn around the stem of the soap dispenser pump to save on soap.

Yarn

Red Film on Plastic Containers

Problem:

Tomato-based soups and sauces cling to the sides of plastic storage containers, and even intense scrubbing won't remove the unsightly residue.

Do This Now:

Before you store spaghetti, chili, or other tomato-based dishes in a plastic container, spray the inside of the container with nonstick cooking spray.

Do This for Good:

Buy some inexpensive black plastic containers with clear lids, such as GladWare. They're perfect for storing and microwaving leftovers, and the red residue will never show. Or look for the special red plastic containers that manufacturers tend to sell at Christmastime and use them year-round.

* * *

The yarn will stop the pump from depressing completely, and the result will be a smaller amount of soap.

Great, the Grater's Clean!

Pregrated cheese is convenient, but it's never as tasty as the cheese you grate yourself. You can enjoy freshly grated cheese without suffering through the nasty task of cleaning cheese debris stuck in those razor-sharp holes. Just remember to spray the grater with nonstick cooking spray before you start, and grater cleanup will be a breeze.

Blender, Clean Thyself

Rather than trying to mop out your blender while avoiding treacherous blades or struggling to dismantle the blender apparatus to run it through the dishwasher, encourage your blender to take care of its own mess. After you use it, pour out any contents that remain, then fill the blender halfway with water. Add a few drops of dishwashing liquid, put on the lid, and fire up the motor for about 30 seconds. Pour out the soapy solution and fill the blender halfway with plain water. Run it for 1 minute to rinse the blades. Pour out the water, replace the lid, and hit the blend button for 10 seconds to remove any remaining water from the blades.

Ways to Wash the Washer

When your dishwasher isn't working well, you waste time rewashing dishes that didn't come fully clean in the machine. To escape that onerous duty, try these "clean the cleaner" tactics.

Try a tangy trick. To clean the inside of the dishwasher, fill the detergent dispenser with 1 tablespoon orange-flavored powdered drink mix (such as Tang) or citric acid from the pharmacy. Then run a cycle with no dishes in the machine.

Clear the ports. If the water ports become clogged, use a pipe cleaner to clear the holes.

Deodorize it. To eliminate unpleasant smells inside, place a bowl of baking soda inside the utensil container and let it sit for 24 hours. Or if your utensil cleaner is on the dishwasher door, place a small plate of baking soda on the floor of the washer, under the bottom rack.

Loosen the crust. If a load of dirty dishes that's been left sitting develops a sour odor, sprinkle 1/4 cup baking soda on the bottom of the dishwasher before washing the dishes. The baking soda will also soften and loosen dried-on foods so they wash off more easily.

Beat the Pots-and-Pans Blues

Stainless steel pots and pans have a nasty way of turning a bit blue on the sides or bottoms as a result of heat damage. You can tackle these stains with little effort by letting the pot soak in a mixture of 1 part white vinegar and 10 parts warm water for 1 hour (or overnight for really entrenched stains). Or fix spaghetti tonight. Warm the spaghetti sauce in the heat-damaged pan, and the acid from the tomatoes will take care of the blue tinges.

Go Soak, You Stinky Sponge

It's hard to say whether it takes more time to go out and buy new supplies every time your cleaning sponges mildew or to resanitize the counters because you used an aromatic sponge without realizing it. Avoid both fates by periodically sniffing your cleaning sponges and disinfecting any that smell bad. Soak the bad-smelling sponges in a solution of 3/4 cup chlorine bleach and 1 gallon water.

Cut Board Odor with Mustard

It's nearly impossible to rid a cutting board of an onion smell using plain soap and water. Instead of repeated scrubbings with poor results, solve the problem in a minute or less. Just rub the board with a cut lemon, then rinse. And if you don't have a lemon handy, grab the dry mustard out of the spice rack. Rub a teaspoon of it into the board and rinse.

Keep the Drain Fresh and Free-Flowing

Whenever you fire up the kettle for tea, take care of a kitchen chore, too. Pour your cup of boiling water, then while your tea steeps, make a mixture of 1 cup baking soda, 1 cup salt, and ¼ cup cream of tartar. Pour one-quarter of the mixture into your kitchen drain, then chase the potion down the drain with the remaining hot water from the kettle. Save the rest of the mixture in an airtight container so you can repeat the process

The Second Time Around

Transform a Tent into a Floor Mat

Kitchen throw rugs get grimy fast, and tend to fall apart in the washer. A treated canvas floor mat, however, will wear well in high-traffic areas and can be wiped clean with a wet cloth or mop. You can save money by making your own long-lasting floor mat from a piece of that old canvas tent in the shed. Here's how.

1. Cut a piece of canvas from the tent that's about 20 percent larger than the finished size you need for the floor mat.

2. Wash and dry the canvas, iron it flat, and cut it to the precise size, leaving an extra 2 inches all around for the hem.

3. Iron down the 2-inch hem, then use a glue gun to fasten the hem in place. Use extra glue as needed to tack down bulky corners.

4. If you'd like, stamp a design on the canvas with acrylic paint, or paint it freehand.

5. Coat the entire cloth, front and back, with two coats of water-based polyurethane, following the manufacturer's instructions.

6. Let the cloth cure for a week or more before walking on it or rolling it up.

This floor mat can last for years. If necessary, place a nonskid mat under the floor mat.

once a week for 3 weeks. This is a lot quicker than trying to unclog a closed drain—and your drain will smell sweet, too.

Oranges Deodorize Oven Cleaners

Tired of fumes after you clean your oven? Don't spend the extra money for a self-cleaning oven yet. Instead, follow up the cleaning chore by putting your feet up—while you bake several orange peels in the oven at 350°F. By the time you've had a 20-minute break, their aroma will have erased that oven cleaner stench.

EASY, ECONOMICAL MEAL IDEAS

Speedy Spanish Meat Loaf

When you have a blue-plate-special appetite but a TV-dinner budget, get out the can opener. Open a 12-ounce can of Spanish rice, and you're well on your way to a homemade meat loaf. The canned rice substitutes for all the bread crumbs, seasonings, and such that usually go into a meat loaf. Use your hands to mix the undrained rice, 1 egg, and 1½ pounds of lean ground beef in a bowl. Then form the mixture into a loaf on a baking sheet and bake at 350°F for 50 minutes. Let the meat loaf rest for 10 minutes before slicing and serving.

Go Wild with Budget Rice

Packaged wild rice mix and rice pilaf are handy but can cost almost 50 cents a serving. With a few ingredients you probably already have on hand, you can make your own version for about 20 percent of the cost and still get 100 percent of the flavor, says Rose Kennedy, a food writer and mother from Knoxville, Tennessee. The secret ingredient: thyme. "You'd be amazed at how many of those rice mixes taste mostly of thyme," says Rose. "Open your jar of thyme and give it a whiff, and you'll see."

For her pseudo–wild rice concoction, Rose cooks ordinary long-grain white rice according to the package directions but adds 1 beef bouillon cube, 1 minced garlic clove, 1 tablespoon margarine, and 1 teaspoon dried thyme leaves. "Adding those few ingredients doesn't take any longer than opening the packets for one of the mixes," Rose says. If you're partial to **In the Kitchen** quick-cooking wild rice blends, try Rose's recipe using Minute rice but reduce the thyme to 1/2 teaspoon.

Doll Up Deli Chicken

When Beth Slate's husband, Jamie, was in graduate school, the couple cooked almost every meal at home and watched the food budget carefully. "At that time, I developed one recipe that tasted as good as lemon chicken from an Asian restaurant but was quick to cook and didn't destroy our budget," says Beth. In fact, the dish is still a favorite of this North Carolina family, even though it's no longer an economic necessity. The main ingredient is 3/4 pound of ready-to-eat, batter-fried chicken tenders, which are available in the deli department of large grocery stores. Beth cuts the tenders into 1-inch chunks

My Favorite Shortcut

Great Grilled Veggies

As a catering manager in Seattle, Kenny Heath works all day with great chefs, but he admits that he is no cook himself. So when Kenny comes across a foolproof food idea that tastes as fresh and good as the premier cuisine he tastes on the job, he snaps it up. "My wife, Leigh, and I use the gas grill all year long, and we also have two kids, so vegetables are real important to us," he says. "A year ago, we started making grilled vegetables that even the kids will eat. They're wonderful served hot, and they're great cold, too."

Kenny and Leigh cut onions (and sometimes mushrooms) into 1-inch chunks and bell peppers (any color) into 3-by-1/2-inch strips. They put the cut vegetables in a resealable plastic bag, adding 1 teaspoon seasoned salt, 2 teaspoons balsamic vinegar, and 2 teaspoons olive oil per 1/2 pound vegetables. "The bag is great because you can mix the whole thing without making a mess," Kenny says. "And you can leave it in the fridge, ready to grill, for several days if you'd like."

Kenny and Leigh grill the veggies over medium-hot coals until they're soft. "You can eat them right away, chill them to serve cold, or save them in the refrigerator for fajitas, omelettes, and quesadillas later in the week," Kenny says. "We've been cooking these a couple of times a month for a year and a half and haven't run out of possibilities yet."

and whips up a sauce by combining an undrained 10-ounce can of pineapple chunks with an 8-ounce bottle of sweet-and-sour sauce, then simmering the mixture until it's warmed through. She pours the warm sauce over the chicken. For extra color and flavor, she sometimes lightly steams a large handful of onion or green pepper chunks and adds them as well. Serve over rice.

Use Your Noodles Twice

Cheap, healthy, filling, and versatile, pasta is the ultimate homemade fast food—except for that long wait while a big pot of water comes to a boil. To maximize your efficiency, whenever you cook pasta, cook at least a full pound, even if you won't eat it all that day. Use what you need, then toss the remaining pasta with about a teaspoon of olive oil and store it in an airtight container in the refrigerator. Reheating cooked pasta in the microwave is a breeze. "The most important thing when you reheat pasta in the microwave is to put something on top—sauce or a little butter or cheese—so the noodles won't dry out," says Lucy Hall, a Knoxville, Tennessee, teenager who practically subsists on pasta dishes she creates for herself and her sister. Reheating refrigerated cooked pasta takes only about 30 seconds per serving on high power. Now *that's* fast food!

Fix It Fresh, Mediterranean Style

Rose Kennedy of Knoxville, Tennessee, cooks a pasta dish that's sophisticated enough for company but is easy on the budget and the dishwasher. Rose also appreciates the dish's simplicity and the flexibility of the ingredients list. "This is a friend's recipe from a year spent as an exchange student in Italy," Rose says.

To prepare this Mediterranean-style meal, preheat the oven to 250°F. Warm 2 tablespoons extra-virgin olive oil in the bottom of a large Pyrex bowl in the oven. While it heats, boil ½ pound pasta. Remove the bowl from the oven and add a diced fresh tomato and a drained 6-ounce can of tuna (albacore or imported Italian tuna are best, Rose notes). Use a fork to separate the tuna into chunks or flakes. Drain the pasta and add it to the

5 Ways to Be Spice Smart

Save money, space, and time by following these five spice strategies.

Buy ethnic. Dried herbs and spices from an Asian or Hispanic grocer almost always cost less than their supermarket counterparts.

Never choose the all-in-one. Handy as they look, you'll never use all the spices in those five-in-one shakers—or at least you'll never use them all before some lose their flavor and others have run out.

Say no to fresh oregano. A little goes a long way, so you're unlikely to use an entire bunch before it goes bad. Plus, any Greek or Italian cook will tell you that dried oregano tastes better and is what they use in the old country.

Steer clear of dried basil. If you can't get fresh basil or prefer not to pay for it, skip the dried version, too—it's tasteless. In pesto, there is no replacement, but if you're just spicing a sauce or veggies, try fresh mint or tarragon or dried thyme leaves in place of the basil.

Wrap herbs in a filter. Many recipes instruct you to tie herb sprigs in a cheesecloth bag before adding them to a stew or soup. If you don't have cheesecloth handy, use a coffee filter tied with a piece of white string instead.

• •

bowl. Add a pinch of salt and pepper and some grated Parmesan cheese to taste. Toss gently and serve right from the bowl.

The best part of the dish—aside from its taste—is that you can assemble it almost entirely from ingredients you keep stocked in your pantry. To vary the flavor, Rose suggests adding one of the following extras: a bit of fresh basil; 1/4 cup sliced black or green olives; 1 tablespoon capers, sun-dried tomatoes in oil, or garlic paste; or 1/2 cup canned chickpeas.

Pepper Lasagna with Pepperoni

No-boil lasagna noodles are a great time-saver when you're making homemade lasagna. But why not simplify further by skipping the fussy, messy step of browning the beef for the sauce? To do that, leave out the beef and instead flavor the sauce with a handful of pepperoni slices. (If the slices seem too large to blend in, cut them into strips.) They're consistent

3 Big Ideas for Chicken

Those giant-size packages of chicken in the grocery store can save you time and money if you know how to use them right. Try these tips.

Marinate and freeze. Make a batch of your favorite marinade, then freeze family-size portions of chicken plus marinade in plastic containers. The day before you plan to serve the chicken, transfer a container from freezer to refrigerator. The next day, you can grill or sauté the thawed, marinated chicken on the spot.

Do double duty. Cook twice as much chicken as your family will eat at one meal. Leftover grilled or sautéed chicken makes a quick-and-easy meal a day or so later, plus you'll be set for making chicken salad for sandwiches.

Have a wrapping party. Buy several giant-size packages at one time, especially if they're on sale. Buy a jumbo roll of aluminum foil, too. When you get home, set up an assembly line and trim, wash, and wrap all the chicken in family-size portions. Date each package and stow them in the freezer for future use. This saves kitchen cleanup time because there's only one meat packaging mess to clean up, but you'll have a ready-to-use chicken supply that will last for months.

* * *

with an Italian taste but don't need to be cooked—so no extra pan to clean later. To carry the pizza theme a step further, spread a few more pepperoni slices on top of the lasagna before baking.

Simple Chicken in a Skillet

Here's what guys like: a supper dish that tastes great and impresses the ladies but requires no great skill or sweat to make. Slow-cooked chicken may not sound like a shortcut, but, says "guy's guy" Michael Scherer of Louisville, Colorado, "It's no effort whatsoever." To make this dish, select a package of chicken thighs (one or two per person) at the grocery store, then swing by the produce section to pick up some fresh rosemary (unless the family gardener has planted some at home). Place the chicken thighs in a sturdy skillet with several sprigs of rosemary. Cover and cook on low. After 30 minutes, turn the pieces over. After another 30 minutes, they're ready to serve. Mmm-mmm good!

Fast, Framed Fried Eggs

Oh, the agony of breaking the yolk when you fry an egg. To prevent this tragedy, try "framing" fried eggs with fried toast. The cooking process will go more smoothly, and the end result is more attractive, too. Use a cookie or biscuit cutter, or the rim of a juice glass, to cut out a 3-inch circle from the center of a piece of bread (soft breads work best for this). Then melt a teaspoon of margarine in a nonstick frying pan over medium-high heat. Place the bread "frame" in the melted margarine and crack the egg into the hole in the center. Let the egg cook. When you're ready, use a spatula to flip the egg and bread as a unit. The yolk never breaks! And you don't have to time toast to coincide with the eggs either. (If you'd like, you can fry the 3-inch circle of bread in the pan at the same time or toast it in the toaster oven.)

Dressed-Up Biscuits Beat Fancy Rolls

Any homemade meal tastes better served with a hot roll, but some brands of refrigerated yeast rolls or croissants can cost more than your entrée. The low-cost solution is to dress up refrigerated biscuit dough, says Amy Witsil, an every-night home cook and mother of three school-age children in Chapel Hill, North Carolina. "Just stretch each round piece of biscuit dough into an oblong shape. Fold the ends over and pinch them together, shaping the dough like a croissant," Amy says. Set the shaped dough pieces in an ungreased baking pan, pour some melted margarine on top, sprinkle a few caraway seeds on them, and then bake as usual. "Four-packs of refrigerated biscuits cost eighty percent less than refrigerated hot loaves

Fool your dinner guests—and save money—by reshaping refrigerated biscuit dough to look like croissants.

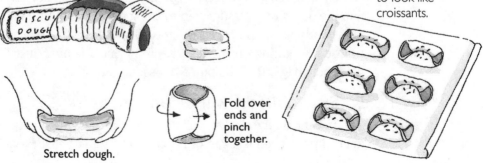

Stretch dough.

Fold over ends and pinch together.

and bread twists," Amy says. "Last year, I forgot to shop for bread for Thanksgiving dinner and had only biscuit dough on hand. My sister reminded me that we used to make these as kids, so that's what we did. I was amazed at how tasty they were. Even the adults were vying for the extras."

Fancy French Toast off the Shelf

Fancy flavorings for French toast are a treat, but with two "tweenage" children and a full-time job, Tracy Sebastian of Beverly Hills, California, doesn't have time to fuss with adding lots of special ingredients to French toast. So Tracy has whipped up a super-simple French toast recipe with a tasty flair. "I beat together six eggs and a quarter cup of flavored creamer from the dairy section of the grocery store—hazelnut is our favorite," Tracy says. "Then I dip pieces of regular white bread in the mix and cook them in margarine or nonstick spray over medium-high heat." The recipe makes 12 to 16 slices, depending on "how eggy you want it to be," she says. "But I always make lots of extras, and we reheat them in the toaster or microwave during the week."

CROCK-POT SHORTCUTS

A Cleaner Crock-Pot's in the Bag

Crock-Pots and other slow cookers are the perfect tools for busy folks. They allow you to plan ahead so that tasty food is ready at exactly your window of opportunity for mealtime. Cleaning a Crock-Pot can be a time-consuming chore, though. If you find yourself spending too much time scrubbing the baked-on mess, consider bagging it. No, not the Crock-Pot—its contents. When you prepare ingredients for a Crock-Pot meal, line the pot with a plastic oven-roasting bag before putting the ingredients in the pot. Fold the top edges of the bag over the rim before putting on the lid. When the meal is over, just lift the whole bag out of the pot. No fuss, no muss!

Perfect Pot Roast with Pepsi

For an amazingly tender, pull-apart pot roast with plenty of juice, all you need is a can of Pepsi. That's right, Pepsi (or any

brand of cola). Cook a 2-to-3-pound blade, round, or sirloin
roast in a Crock-Pot with half a can of cola and an envelope of
onion soup mix. You can also skip the time-consuming browning step if you cook the roast on high for the first hour, then
turn the heat to low and cook for 10 hours.

No-Bother Beans

Dried beans are a cooking staple and a good buy to boot. The
problem is, presoaking and precooking dried beans is an
involved process. Jim Slate, an avid outdoorsman and cook in
Winnsboro, South Carolina, offers this no-fail shortcut for
preparing dried beans in a slow cooker. "Wash a pound of dried
beans and throw them in the Crock-Pot with a hunk of salt pork
or a quarter pound of prosciutto and a couple of red pepper

My Favorite Shortcut

Three-Shortcut, One-Alarm Crock-Pot Chili

There's nothing better than dinner waiting when you get home, says Amy Witsil of Chapel Hill, North Carolina. And she should know: She has three school-age children, a husband who leaves work at 7 P.M., and a 45-minute commute. Amy has developed a three-shortcut technique for Crock-Pot chili that suits her busy lifestyle.

1. Amy's first shortcut is using half of a 1-quart jar of spaghetti sauce and half a can of light beer (the alcohol cooks out) instead of messing with cans of tomatoes and broth. "You could also use six ounces of wine or strong coffee in place of the beer," says Amy.

2. The second quick hit: "I just dice a cup or so of whatever vegetables are in the vegetable bin—carrots, onions, peppers, celery, zucchini," Amy explains. "I don't make any special trips to the store." Combine the spaghetti sauce, beer, and diced veggies in the Crock-Pot, along with a generous tablespoon of chili powder, a minced garlic clove (if you have it on hand), and two 15-ounce cans of drained and rinsed beans (black or red beans are Amy's favorites).

3. To finish the dish, Amy nestles several individually frozen skinless, boneless chicken tenders in the center of the chili—straight from the freezer, no defrosting. "If I put that on in the morning, the chicken is fully cooked and the chili is ready to serve by the time I get home," she says.

pods," Jim instructs. "Cover the beans with water and then cook them on low for ten to twelve hours." No soaking, no sticking, and no hanging around waiting for results. Jim's favorites are pinto beans. "I may add a jalapeño chile pepper and a diced tomato for those," he notes. Jim also likes cooking black beans, which he serves with sour cream and lime wedges.

COOKING SHORTCUTS

Soak Up Some News

Save some pennies on paper towels by draining your breakfast bacon on a section of newspaper—last week's, of course. Place a single paper towel on the newspaper to keep the bacon from touching the ink.

More Oval Cakes, Please

Round pancakes just don't fit well on a square or rectangular griddle. To squeeze in more pancakes at once, pour the batter on the griddle in an oval shape instead of a circle. Here's another advantage of oval cakes: You can stack them on one side of your plate, leaving more room for the rest of your breakfast.

Braising Beats Stewing

Old-fashioned stew is a favorite for many families, but cutting all the ingredients into 1-inch chunks is a time-consuming task that we'd rather not do. You can skip the chopping step if you slow-cook a large cut of meat (such as a shank or brisket) and whole vegetables instead. It's called braising, and many of us have forgotten this time-honored cooking method. Here's what you do.

First, brown the meat (whole) in a small amount of oil in a Dutch oven over medium-high heat. Then add

Better Store-Bought

With some foods, there's just not enough payoff in making them from scratch instead of buying them ready-made. Here are eight food items that cost a tad more store-bought but will free up your time without sacrificing quality.

- Salsa
- Sun-dried tomatoes in oil
- Piecrust (refrigerated)
- Biscuits (frozen)
- Meatballs (frozen)
- Pasta (buy fresh, not boxed)
- Egg rolls (frozen, refrigerated, or take-out)
- Brownies (buy a packaged mix)

some whole vegetables, such as carrots, potatoes, onions, and turnips. Add about 2 cups liquid (water, broth, or wine), pop the lid on, and set the Dutch oven to cook on low on the stove-top or in a 250°F oven. Then walk away and do what you like for 3 to 4 hours. When you return to the kitchen, check the meat. If it pulls away from the bone easily, the dish is ready to serve—and you can cut everything into bite-size chunks right on your plate with ease. An added benefit to braising is that it works wonders with tougher cuts of meat, turning them tender by virtue of the longer cooking time.

Frozen in Time

For best nutrition from your vegetables, don't cook fresh veggies; choose frozen instead. According to Dr. Jeanette Newton Keith, medical director of the New Beginnings Medical Weight Management Program at the University of Chicago, frozen vegetables are often just as nutritious as fresh vegetables and sometimes more so. Commercially frozen vegetables are often processed immediately after picking, and that locks in the vitamins. By contrast, fresh produce sometimes spends weeks in storage and transit before reaching the grocer's shelf. All that time between harvest and your home can ruin the food's nutritional value.

Quick Cooking Is Best

Good news for cooks in a hurry: When you're preparing vegetables, whether frozen or fresh, it's to your advantage to keep the cooking time short. Overcooking vegetables drains away vitamin content, says Dr. Jeanette Newton Keith.

Cut Onions the Corny Way

You can keep tears to a minimum if you cut an onion in two—from stem to root—and then turn the flat sides of each half facedown on a cutting board to slice or dice. Keep the onion smell off your fingers by using a corn holder. (Surely there's one in that kitchen drawer!) Pierce the side of one of the onion halves with the corn holder—at an angle and near the top—and hold the onion firmly in place with one hand while you slice with the other. Once you've sliced through half of the half, turn it around, resecure it with the corn holder, and finish slicing. Then repeat the procedure with the other half of the onion.

Bake a Batch of Potatoes

If you always seem to scorch your fingers while retrieving baked potatoes from the oven, stand the potatoes on end in a muffin pan to bake. The potatoes will cook faster, and when they're done, you can just grab the edge of the pan with an oven mitt to remove it from the oven.

The Mayo Mash

No one's ever going to mistake instant mashed potatoes for the real thing, says Volena Askew, the adult home economics supervisor in Knox County, Tennessee. "But you can avoid that out-of-the-box taste by whipping a tablespoon of real mayonnaise into a four-serving portion right before serving," she says.

3 Pots and Pans in a Pinch

If your kitchen is a little short in the pots-and-pans department, you may find yourself coming up short on those occasions when you want to try a special dish or baking project. Try one of these makeshift substitutes.

Double boiler. Use a clean, empty, 1-pound bimetal can (bimetal cans have a seam at the bottom as well as the top; aluminum cans have no bottom seam). Pour 2 to 3 inches of water into a saucepan, bring the water to a boil, and add a handful of clean marbles or glass beads. Place your ingredients in the can, then rest the can on the marbles. Be sure the can doesn't come in contact with the bottom of the saucepan.

Muffin pan. Use 6- or 8-ounce ceramic coffee mugs. Check the bottoms to make sure they're marked as microwave-safe. If so, they're also safe to bake in (not true of plastic mugs, of course).

Roasting rack. Use aluminum foil shaped into a curvy snake and set in the bottom of a roasting pan. Cut a long piece of 18-inch-wide heavy-duty aluminum foil. Roll the foil into a long, loose cylinder about 2 inches in diameter, then form it into an S shape in the pan. Rest the meat on top of the foil.

Measuring Up

The recipe calls for 2 cups of grated cheese. So you grate and measure, then you grate some more and measure some more. Here's a cheat sheet that lets you grab whole foods; chop, mince, or slice; and skip the measuring.

3 medium apples = 3½ cups sliced apples
1 pound hard cheese = 4 cups grated cheese
15 graham crackers = 1 cup graham cracker crumbs
1 cup heavy cream = 2 cups whipped cream
1 medium lemon or lime = approximately 3 tbsp juice
3 medium potatoes = 2 cups mashed potatoes
1 pound uncooked spaghetti = 7 cups cooked spaghetti

Batch—Don't Botch—Broccoli

Even the most organized among us has come across a big cluster of broccoli that has lost its luster in the fridge. With regret, we fish out the limp stalks and send the whole cluster to the compost pile. To avoid this scenario, spend a little more and buy fresh broccoli crowns or florets instead of whole clusters. Buy between ¾ and 1 pound at a time. Cook the broccoli soon after you get home from the store, all in one batch, steaming the florets until they're bright green. Plunge the hot florets into a bowl of ice water, then drain thoroughly. Split the broccoli into two batches in resealable plastic bags or airtight plastic containers. The packets will last in the fridge for up to 5 days, and you can pull one out anytime to serve on the spot. Just microwave for 30 seconds on high power for an instant veggie.

Emergency Salad Dressing

Dinner is 10 minutes away, and you suddenly realize that you're out of salad dressing. Put down those car keys and pick up the ketchup—that's right, ketchup. In a small bowl, whisk ⅓ cup ketchup, ⅓ cup extra-virgin olive oil, and 2 tablespoons vinegar (red wine, white, or balsamic). Add salt and pepper to taste and a shake of garlic powder (if you're so inclined), and you're ready to toss the salad.

3 High-Performing Kitchen Gadgets

Sometimes it's the little things that save the most time in the kitchen. Here are three simple, low-cost gadgets that will simplify your cooking life.

Over the sink and made of wood. Select a cutting board that fits over your sink. You'll preserve counter space for other tasks, and cleanup will be easier, too. Cost: $8 to $10.

Fun, funnel, funnest? Collect plastic and metal funnels in various sizes. They're handy for avoiding messes when you're pouring liquids from one container to another, such as tomato sauce from a pot into a canning jar or milk from a jug into a reusable plastic bottle. Small funnels are available at cooking or dollar stores; look for jumbo funnels at an auto supply store. Cleanup's a snap: just set the funnels in the top rack of your dishwasher. Cost: $1 to $4.

Not-just-for-baby-food grinder. Instead of an expensive food processor, buy a hand-cranked baby food grinder at a health food or natural food store. With it, you can puree vegetables for those trendy cream soups or fruit for sophisticated sauces. It's easy to use, and when dismantled, it takes up no more storage space than a couple of coffee cups. Cost: $5 to $6.

Start from the Bottom

Always open cans on the end that was resting on the shelf. The heavy contents of canned goods tend to settle to the bottom. When you open them bottom first, the contents come whooshing right out, and you won't have to spend time digging out that last spoonful of creamed corn or beef stew. Plus, if cans tend to sit for a while on the shelf in your kitchen, you won't get accumulated dust from the top on your fingers (or mixed in with your food).

Sandwich Bags Save on Messes

Robust cooks like to mix by hand, but it's messy work, and heaven forbid that the phone rings or you need to scratch your nose while you're working. Reduce the mess without cramping your style by taking the lead of workers in sandwich shops. They wear disposable plastic gloves to prepare food. But you don't need to buy special gloves. Just slip a plastic sandwich bag over your hand when you need to mix meat loaf, cut butter into pastry, squeeze the liquid from canned tomatoes, and so forth. Or if you really prefer the feel of food on your fingertips, work barehanded but keep a stash of sandwich bags handy. When you need to answer the phone or pick up another ingredient, you can just slip your hand into a bag while you perform the task, without taking time to wash and dry your hands.

BAKING SHORTCUTS
Halve Your Cake and Eat It, Too

Layer cakes are delicious, but they often go stale before you finish eating the whole thing. So follow the lead of Volena Askew, the adult home economics supervisor in Knox County, Tennessee, and bake half a layer cake at a time. You'll pay half as much, and you won't have a lot left over to go stale (or to tempt you to overindulge). Volena cooks a single-layer cake—using an 8-ounce box of mix instead of a 16-ounce box—in an 8-inch round pan. "I cut the cake in half, and stack the halves on top of each other to ice—which makes half a layer cake," she says. Volena cautions you not to try to ice the cut side of the cake, because the icing won't stick well and will become gummed up with crumbs. "The funny thing is," Volena notes, "I learned this trick as a newlywed. When I brought the half cake out to serve to my husband, he loved it, but he was convinced I'd already eaten the other half of the cake myself."

Cut cake in half.

Don't ice the cut edges.

Stack halves.

To save money and avoid waste, bake half a layer cake instead of a whole one.

Instant Ingredient Exchange

You're in the middle of baking and discover you're missing a key ingredient. Don't panic. Your masterpiece need not be ruined, nor do you need to fly to the store. Just consult this list of baking substitutions, which is condensed from a list presented on BlueSuitMom.com by its owner and CEO, Maria Bailey.

Ingredient	Substitute
1 tsp baking powder	⅓ tsp baking soda and ⅝ tsp cream of tartar
1 cup brown sugar	1 cup sugar plus 1 tsp molasses
1 ounce semisweet chocolate chips	1 square sweet cooking chocolate, chopped
6 ounces semisweet chocolate chips, melted	2 squares unsweetened chocolate, 2 tbsp shortening, and ½ cup sugar
1⅔ ounces semisweet baking chocolate	1 square unsweetened chocolate and 4 tsp sugar
1 square unsweetened chocolate	3 tbsp cocoa and 1 tbsp butter or margarine
1 cup all-purpose flour, sifted	1 cup plus 2 tbsp cake flour
1 cup cake flour, sifted	1 cup minus 2 tbsp all-purpose flour
1 cup self-rising flour	1 cup minus 2 tsp all-purpose flour, 1 ½ tsp baking powder, and ½ tsp salt

Do You Know the Muffin Mess?

Muffin batter often collects all over the muffin pan as you try to spoon the batter into the cups, and then there's the goop you get on your finger trying to guide it to its destination. Next time, keep clear of the mess by using an ice scream scoop to deliver the batter to the cups. This shortcut also helps you place an even amount of batter in each cup.

Cut the Fat

If you're trying to cut fat in your diet, you don't have to search around for special low-fat recipes. Just bake your favorites—but replace half the vegetable oil or shortening with applesauce. For example, in a bread or cookie recipe that calls for

½ cup vegetable oil, use ¼ cup applesauce and ¼ cup oil. **In the Kitchen** You can also substitute fruit butters, such as apple or peach butter, instead.

Better Quick Breads in Two Shakes

Time-pressed cooks definitely appreciate fruit or nut quick breads. They're delicious warm or cold, and they don't require yeast or kneading. The only problem is that all the "good stuff" tends to sink to the bottom of the loaf before it sets in the oven. To prevent this, shake the dried fruit or nuts in a bag with a little flour before adding them to the batter. They will stay evenly distributed throughout the batter, even during baking.

Filling Finesse Averts Spills

Unbaked custard and pumpkin pies are famous for spilling all over the oven floor. Believe it or not, that's the cook's fault, for filling the shells too full before putting them in the oven. Try a different strategy to save yourself a time-consuming cleanup. Fill the pie shell halfway, transfer it to the oven rack, and then add the rest of the filling, using a spouted measuring cup for precise delivery.

The Bag That Acts Like a Bowl

Reduce your dishwashing chores the next time you make cookies by mixing the dry ingredients inside a 1-gallon resealable plastic bag instead of a bowl. All it takes is a few shakes. Then pour the dry ingredients into your bowl of creamed sugar and butter. And as long as you don't include any sugar

Glorious Gizmos

Boil-in-Bag Chocolate Topping

A ribbon of chocolate is a delectable touch to add to boxed cookies, fresh strawberries, or frozen éclairs. Here's an incredibly easy way to create a device for spreading melted chocolate. Boil water in your teakettle and then pour the boiling water into a large bowl. Dunk an unopened 6-ounce bag of chocolate chips into the water to melt. After a minute, use tongs to remove the bag from the water. Wrap the bag in a dish towel (so you don't burn yourself), knead the bag to mix the chips, and then put the bag back in the water. Continue this until you have a pliable mass of chocolate in the bag. Then use scissors to cut off one corner of the bag (you want about a ¼-inch opening). Squeeze the bag gently to spread a ribbon of chocolate on a boxed cookie or other tidbit. If the chocolate resolidifies before you're done, clip the corner of the bag shut with a clothespin and put the bag back in the warm bath.

in the dry mix, you can fold the empty bag and store it in the flour canister to reuse next time.

A Sweet Deal

Decorating cookies with colored sugar is fun, but it's a pain to buy (and then store) containers of colored sugar when you use it only once or twice a year. Simplify things—and save money—by making your own on the spot when you need it. Just add a couple of drops of food coloring to 1/4 cup sugar, stir to mix, and spread the sugar on a piece of waxed paper to dry. Use any that's left over after baking to sweeten tomorrow's coffee. No need to save it—homemade colored sugar costs only 1 percent of the price of the commercially prepared stuff.

SNACK SHORTCUTS

No-Frills Nachos

Navy reservist Todd Allerton of Jacksonville, Florida, calls them no-frills nachos and is embarrassed to admit that his friends and young daughters consider the no-brainer snack his specialty. Instead of dicing jalapeño chile peppers, heating nacho sauce, and then distributing the peppers and sauce over heated tortilla chips, Todd plops half a bag of tortilla chips in an 8-by-8-inch baking pan. Then he grates a liberal portion of hot pepper Monterey Jack cheese on top and puts the pan in a 300°F oven until the cheese melts. "I sometimes even serve them from the same pan," he says. "Anyone who likes hot, spicy food will like these nachos, and afterward I have only the cheese grater and one pan to wash." From a budget standpoint, the pepper cheese costs less than buying cheese or cheese sauce and jalapeños separately. "And if you're out of chips, this recipes works just as well with Triscuits or dip-size Fritos," says Todd.

Turn Up the Heat on Chips

Next time you sit down with chips and salsa, make a plain-Jane snack special with little effort and no extra cost by pretending you're at a restaurant. The simple secret: Warm the chips. Of course, restaurant tortilla chips have probably just been pulled from a vat of hot oil, but you can get a similar effect by heating 6 ounces of chips in a single layer on a baking sheet. Start with 5 minutes at 250°F. If the chips are warm and toasty brown, take them out and serve. If not, leave them in the oven for a few more minutes.

Bargain Buffalo Wings

Always frugal, food writer Rose Kennedy of Knoxville, Tennessee, just despised paying what she calls "extortionist prices" for buffalo wings. "These tiny things with hardly a bit of meat on them cost seven or eight dollars a pound when you buy them frozen at the grocery store, much less at a restaurant," she says. "But my boyfriend just adored them." Everything changed when Rose learned that buffalo wings aren't difficult to make at home.

For her recipe, Rose uses chicken drumettes, which are chicken wings with the tips removed (they look like miniature chicken drumsticks). "You just place raw drumettes on a baking sheet and cook them at 400°F for thirty minutes," she says. No basting, no marinade? "You shouldn't even apply the sauce until the drumettes are out of the oven," Rose says. Then pour enough bottled "hot wing" sauce into a nonmetal bowl to cover the wings and add the cooked wings, turning to coat. After that, transfer the wings to a serving bowl or platter.

"I watch for the drumettes or chicken wings to go on sale and buy the hot sauce in bulk, so my wings cost about a fourth as much as store-bought or restaurant wings," she says.

Pocketful of Pita for Pennies

Seattle catering manager Kenny Heath, a big fan of grilled veggies, also grills his favorite snack. Kenny cuts ½-pound pita pockets into wedges, then combines 2 tablespoons olive oil, 1 teaspoon balsamic vinegar, and 1 teaspoon seasoned salt in a resealable plastic bag. He seals the bag and shakes it several times to mix the ingredients. He adds the pita wedges, shakes again, and leaves the wedges to marinate for an hour or so. Then he grills the wedges on a medium-hot gas grill, just until they're warm and a little crunchy. "My wife, Leigh, and I love to have these around to snack on, hot or cold—to eat plain or serve with hummus or dip, Kenny says. "They're relatively low-fat and also inexpensive, because we buy big packs of pitas at the local wholesale club."

Pureed Pizza Sauce—Pronto!

Jars and cans of pizza sauce fill grocers' shelves, promoted as a "quick hot snack solution." Although toasted English muffins, Boboli pizza crusts, or flour tortillas certainly make a tasty snack when topped with sauce and cheese, the sauce doesn't have to be that expensive (or that salty). Instead of buying sauce, brush the bread with olive oil, top with slivers of fresh garlic, and then slather on canned tomato puree before adding the topping of your choice. Store the unused puree in a jar in the refrigerator for up to 2 weeks. This "homemade" topping costs about one-third the price of commercial sauces.

Faux Cheese with a French Flair

The French garlic-herb cheese spreads that come in those tiny containers are delicious, but they cost almost $10 a pound. Instead of breaking your budget to enjoy this treat, make your own low-cost faux version in minutes. Cream 8 ounces cream cheese with 1 tablespoon softened butter and 1 tablespoon white wine (or chicken broth with a squeeze of lemon). Mix well with 2 minced garlic cloves, 1 teaspoon coarsely ground pepper, and 1 teaspoon dried thyme leaves. Refrigerate the spread for at least 1 hour so that the flavors can blend. Serve at room temperature.

I Scream for No Drips

Save a few dishes while you savor a childhood treat—ice cream cones. But don't make a mess while you're at it. Keep the tips of sugar cones from dripping by inserting a marshmallow in the bottom of the cone before you scoop the ice cream.

Living Room, Family Room, and Dining Room

9

Your living room, family room, and dining room are where your family gathers to eat, relax, and catch up on the day's events. Of course, you want these rooms to stay clean and look nice, but with all that furniture and carpeting, family heirlooms, and possibly a piano, you face a cleaning and decorating challenge. In this chapter, you'll discover clever shortcuts that will minimize problems such as scratches in the furniture and dents in the carpet. Plus, you'll learn how to have fun decorating and redecorating—without spending a fortune.

TAKING CARE OF YOUR FURNITURE

Make Tea for Your Furniture

Scratches in wood can make a piece of furniture look junky, even if it is an expensive heirloom. Fortunately, repairing scratches is as easy as brewing a cup of tea. Place a tea bag (use black tea, not herbal or green tea) in a mug and spoon a few tablespoons of hot water onto the bag. Let it steep for 2 to 3 minutes. The longer the tea steeps, the darker it will be, so

A Dented Tabletop

Problem:
You dropped a heavy object on a wooden tabletop, and it left a dent.

Do This Now:
Pour a little water on the dent. The water will swell the wood fibers, which will make the dent less noticeable.

Do This for Good:
Dampen a cotton towel and lay it on top of the dent. Then place a warm iron set to medium heat on top of the towel. Don't allow the iron to touch the wood directly. The combination of heat and steam will act to pull up the dent. Apply the iron for only a few minutes at a time, as the moist heat will affect the undamaged wood as well. Let the surface of the wood cool between treatments and repeat as needed until the dent disappears.

---

gauge steeping time to match the shade of the furniture that needs a fix. Dab the tea onto the scratches with a cotton swab, then quickly wipe away the excess with a paper towel to prevent the wood around the scratches from being stained. If the wood is a medium-dark color, you may need to apply the tea more than once.

Furniture First Aid

Uh-oh. Someone just left a big scratch in your favorite dark-wood coffee table. Don't spend your hard-earned money hiring a professional refinisher. First aid for a scratch in dark wood is just like first aid for a scratched finger: Break out the iodine. Use a cotton swab to apply the iodine to the scratch. Use a paper towel to wipe away the excess so it doesn't stain the wood around the scratch.

Use a Coaster Next Time

It's inevitable. Someone carelessly set a glass on a table in your living room, and the moisture has left a white ring in the finish. What doesn't have to be inevitable is a time-consuming trip to the hardware store for a commercial concoction to repair the damage. Instead, moisten a paper towel with corn oil and rub it into the spot until the ring disappears. Then wipe with a clean paper towel to blot up any excess oil.

Erase That Stain

You've already spent a small fortune on that leather chair, so the last thing you want to do is pay dearly to have it cleaned. Lucky for you, there's a shamelessly simple tool you can use to make minor spills and stains on leather upholstery disappear: an art gum eraser. (If you don't have one, you can buy one anywhere stationery supplies are sold.) Just give smudges and stains a rub with the eraser, and they should vanish.

PAMPERING YOUR PIANO

Polish with Paste Wax

"Aerosol furniture polish can damage a piano's casing," says Rob Ambrosino, a piano tuner and technician from Katy, Texas. Rob notes that such cleaners contain alcohol, which can dissolve the lacquer and varnish on a piano with a high-gloss finish, leading to an expensive repair. Instead, he says, "polish your piano cabinet with paste wax, which buffs up to a hard, glossy finish." Be sure to dust the cabinet with a feather duster first. Polishing a dusty piano might actually scratch the finish.

They Had NO Shame

Treat It Like a Rolls

It's a waste of time to polish the high-gloss finish on your piano's cabinet if all it needs is a light cleaning. However, it could be an even bigger waste of time—not to mention a painful expense—if you used with the wrong cleaner and ended up having to refinish the whole cabinet. To clean your piano, wipe it down occasionally with a damp rag. Clean one full surface at a time (the top or side, for instance) and then immediately wipe it with a dry, soft cloth until it's completely dry.

A Piano Washout

"It's okay to use a little water when cleaning the cabinet of a piano, but don't drown it," says Rob Ambrosino. "I actually visited a client who was outside washing his truck *and* spraying his piano lightly with the hose at the same time. He wanted me to wipe down the piano with him. I was there all day trying to get all the water out, fix the piano, and tune it. True story!"

Your goal is to avoid letting any surface stay wet for more than a minute or so. The wiping cloths should be very clean. Even the smallest grit—such as a little dust from the bottom of a rag storage box—can scratch your piano permanently. So clean your piano as though you were cleaning a Rolls-Royce.

Regulate the Weather

A piano—whether it's a baby grand or an upright—is a big investment that's worth protecting. Pianos do best if the humidity remains relatively constant year-round. As much as possible, maintain the humidity in the room that contains your piano in the range of 45 to 65 percent, says Rob Ambrosino, a piano tuner and technician from Katy, Texas. He advises all piano owners to invest in a humidifier and a dehumidifier, if needed, to meet these conditions. The money you spend on these two appliances can save you hundreds (or even thousands) of dollars in piano restoration work down the road. Run the humidifier in the room during the winter if your heating system tends to dry out the air, then switch to the dehumidifier during the muggy summer months.

SHINING THE SILVERWARE

Boil Away Tarnish

Cleaning silver flatware doesn't have to mean hours of scrubbing and polishing. In fact, you can clean a small load of silverware in as little as 10 minutes. Just place the tarnished silverware in a large saucepan lined with aluminum foil. Add enough warm water to cover the flatware, 1 teaspoon baking soda, and 1 teaspoon salt, then bring the mixture to a gentle boil. Let the solution work on the silverware for 2 to 3 minutes. Remove the pan from the heat and rinse the silverware under cool water. Dry and buff the pieces with a soft cloth.

Silver Polish That'll Make You Smile

Skip shopping for silver polish. You have the ingredients for a terrific polish right in your own medicine cabinet. Don your cotton gloves and grab a tube of toothpaste (not the gel type). To remove tarnish, coat the silver with toothpaste, then run it under warm water. Work the paste into a foam and then rinse it off. For stubborn stains or to clean silver with intricate patterns, use an old soft-bristle toothbrush.

Sunday Dinner Stops Tarnish

The best approach to polishing silver is to keep it from becoming tarnished in the first place, says Connie Hatch of New York City. She's had her family's silverware for more than 35 years. "The very best way I've found to keep my grandmother's silver from tarnishing is to use it," says Connie. "I never understood the point of pulling out the good silver just for special occasions." "My husband and I use it every Sunday when we have dinner. When we're done eating, I wash it, dry it well, and put it away."

Check Gloves before You Polish

When you want to polish your silverware, you'll probably also want to protect your hands from the polish. But don't reach for the rubber gloves—wearing them is a mistake that might force you to redo the whole job. Instead, wear cotton gloves. Polishing silver while wearing rubber gloves promotes tarnish, because rubber reacts with silver. In fact, contact with rubber can cause damage only a silversmith can repair. This applies to storing your silverware as well. When you put away your silver, make sure the drawer is lined with a cotton flannel or felt mat, not a rubber mat.

WINDOWS AND WINDOW TREATMENTS

Hang Curtains High

When it's window-cleaning day, there's no need to spend time taking down the curtains in preparation. Instead, hang a clothes hanger at each end of the curtain rod, to the outside of the curtains. Loop the curtains up and through the hangers. Voilà—no curtains blocking your strokes as you wipe the windows.

Tackle Panes with a Paintbrush

If you're lucky enough to have one or more multipaned picture windows in your home, you know what a chore it can be to clean around the edges of the mullions—the wooden slats that hold the glass panes in place. Speed up the process by investing a few dollars in two 2-to-4-inch foam paintbrushes from the hardware store. As the first step in cleaning a window that has mullions, dampen one of the brushes with your favorite window-cleaning solution and run the wet brush around the edges of each pane. Hold the brush flat against the glass, as though you were actually painting the edge of the glass where it meets the mullion. Next, follow up with the dry brush, in the same manner. Now go ahead and clean the panes as you normally would, but don't fuss with working the paper towel into the corners.

Give Blinds the Glove Treatment

Venetian blinds can be dust magnets. Try this shortcut for dusting blinds on the fly. Open the blinds, put on an old pair of cotton gloves, and spray the gloves with just a bit of dusting spray. Lightly grab a slat with your gloved hand and slide your hand along the length of the slat.

Glorious Gizmos

Blinded by the Shine

If you have venetian blinds or other window treatments with slats, you know how difficult and time-consuming it can be to clean them, especially if you have to take them down and put them back up again. A quick trip to the dollar store will solve that problem forever. Here's what's on your shopping list: a pair of toaster or salad tongs (the cheapest you can find), a household sponge, and superglue. (Of course, you may already have some or all of these items at home already.) Cut the sponge in half widthwise and then glue one half to the inside end of each arm of the tongs. You have the perfect tool to clean the blind slats individually without having to take down the whole

shebang. Just open the blinds so that the slats are horizontal, dampen the sponges with sudsy water and squeeze

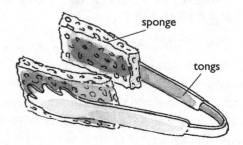

out, and grasp a slat at one end. Sandwich the slat between the tongs and run the tongs along the length of the slat. If the slats aren't too dirty and need just a quick wipe, place an old sock over each sponge instead of wetting the sponges.

Shortcut Shade Cleaning

You don't need to take down those window shades for cleaning. When you have your vacuum cleaner out, but before you vacuum the floors, give the shades a quick vacuuming, using the brush attachment.

Wash the Car, Wash the Blinds

"My mother is a neat freak," says New Yorker Lori Baird, managing editor of Healthy Living Books. "She was also a nut about saving time by doing two things at once whenever it was possible. One of her most clever shortcuts was washing the venetian blinds at the same time my dad washed the car in the driveway. She would lay the blinds out on an old plastic shower curtain liner, and then my dad would soap them up at the same time he soaped up the car. While he scrubbed the car, Mom sponged off the blinds. Then my dad would hose them off before he hosed off the car. It was a perfect system."

FLOOR AND CARPET CARE

Use a Custom Dirt Catcher

Nothing wears down the finish on a hardwood floor like the dirt and grit brought in on the treads of your shoes. Reduce the grit—and save on vacuuming time and the ultimate cost of floor refinishing—by taking one simple precaution: Use a doormat. But, says Lisa Bellistracci, a neatnik who lives in Astoria, New York, "don't just buy one of those cheap rubber welcome mats. They're ugly. You can get a better—and better-looking—mat at a local carpet store." Lisa found a nice remnant at a carpet store near her home. It cost only a few dollars, and the store also cut the mat to size and finished the edges with binding. Keep in mind that a long mat is better than a short one. After all, the longer the mat, the more steps you need to take to cross it, so the more grit it will trap.

Bind It Yourself

If your carpet source won't bind the edges of a remnant as part of the deal, you can do it yourself with some adhesive-backed fabric mending tape. Apply the tape along the edges of

Dents in the Carpet

Problem:

Deep dents show where furniture has compressed your carpeting.

Do This Now:

Gently scrape and fluff the dented fibers with the edge of a coin, a spoon, or a butter knife. If that doesn't remove the dent, spray the area with a little water and then dry it with a blow dryer set on low, while continuing to fluff with the coin.

Do This for Good:

Use caster cups, which distribute the weight of furniture over a wider area, helping to prevent dents. Also, once a month, shift furniture to the left or right an inch or two. This gives compressed areas a chance to spring back.

- -

the remnant, allowing half the width of the tape to extend out from the edges. Then fold that half of the tape down over the edges and underneath the remnant.

Ditch Your Shoes at the Door

Vacuuming, mopping, shampooing, refinishing—those are all time-consuming chores that most of us want to avoid. To do so, you need to keep dirt out of your house, and there's one absolutely free way to accomplish that. Take a tip from the Japanese and ask everyone to remove their shoes before they enter your home. Keep a few pairs of slippers near the entranceway—enough for each member of the family, as well as any regular visitors such as your next-door neighbor or the babysitter. If you think that your friends might be uncomfortable removing their shoes, have them wear disposable shoe covers instead. Some painters and construction workers wear these papery overshoes over their boots while they're working indoors. Buy the shoe covers in bulk at paint stores that cater to the construction trade and at home centers.

Buff Up on Floor Care

Maintaining the finish on a wood floor is expensive and time-consuming, right? On the contrary, maintaining the shine can be quite quick and easy, and you don't need a professional buffing machine to do it. Instead, just wrap an old cotton towel around the business end of a dry mop. Use a rubber band to secure the towel around the mop handle. Spray the towel with a little furniture polish (but just a little; you don't want to make the floor too slippery) and buff the floor along the length of the wood's grain. This task takes only a few minutes.

Make Scuff Marks Scat

When Johnny comes marching through the living room and leaves scuff marks on the wood floor, don't waste time or money searching for commercial cleaning products. Instead, just grab a pencil and use the eraser to eliminate the marks lickety-split.

Shortening Wipes Out Sap

Everybody loves the fresh evergreen scent that a live Christmas tree brings to the house, but nobody likes the sap it leaves on the living room floor. Luckily, there is a quick, easy, and free way to get rid of it. Apply a little vegetable shortening to a cloth and rub it on the sap. Then wipe the area with a paper towel. The sap should come right off. If you don't have any vegetable shortening, dampen a cloth with a little rubbing alcohol and try that for sap removal. (Don't try this on carpet.)

CLEANING SHORTCUTS

Get in a Cleaning Groove

Let's face it, cleaning the large living areas of your house takes time, but you've gotta do what you've gotta do. At least make the process as enjoyable as possible. Tune the radio to your favorite station or pop in your favorite CD. If music's not your thing, slip a tape-recorded book into your Walkman and listen to an exciting mystery or sappy romance. Put on some comfy clothes and pop open a soda to sip. If you make yourself as comfortable as possible and give yourself a few treats, cleaning will seem to go more quickly.

One caveat: Don't choose the "reward" of turning on the TV while you clean. Inevitably, you'll be distracted by *Dr. Phil* or *The Pet Psychic*. What a waste of time, especially if you're in

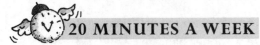

TV Time Cleaning

With self-discipline and some advance planning, you *can* combine cleaning and TV, which opens up some non-TV time each week that you'd otherwise spend cleaning. The trick is to plan to clean during the commercial breaks of your favorite TV show, when you know you'll be in your living room or family room (wherever the TV is) for a solid hour. Before the program starts, pull out your vacuum cleaner or dust cloth. During a 1-hour TV show, there are usually four commercial breaks that last 3 to 4 minutes each. If you jump up and clean during the opening credits and every commercial break, you'll have accomplished 20 minutes of cleaning without missing a minute of your show.

a hurry. If your plan is to clean up fast, turn off the TV. (If you really need to know whether Faith killed Benny, set the VCR and watch your soap opera after you finish cleaning.)

Pocket Your Tools

Nothing wastes more time when you're cleaning than retracing your steps from living room to dining room or family room (or vice versa) to retrieve a cleaning tool that you left behind. To avoid this time waster, wear an apron. If you're too manly for a kitchen apron, buy one in the woodworking department of your local home center. Be sure the apron has deep pockets so you carry your supplies with you from room to room as you work.

Panic-Free Pickup

Company's coming, and the living room and family room need a quick pickup. Some folks would hastily pick up all the stuff on the floor and toss it into miscellaneous drawers and closets. That's a mistake, because by the time your company leaves, you may not remember that you tossed the TV remote in the junk drawer and your knitting in the toy box. Here's a way to clean up fast, but without panic: Keep one of those over-the-door shoe holders inside the entry closet, but don't put shoes in it. Instead, leave it free as a last-minute place to stash small items such as toys, hobby materials, magazines, catalogs, and even the TV remote and cordless phone. Then, when your company leaves, you'll know exactly where all those items are.

When Smear Tactics Won't Do

Where there's a wall repair being done, there's plaster dust. And that excruciatingly fine coating of powder all over your living room presents quite a dilemma. If you attack plaster dust with a wet cleaning cloth, the dust will turn into a thin film of wet plaster smeared all over your floor, baseboards, and furniture. If you use a dry cloth, it will take three or more cleanings to remove all the dust. The solution: Wipe the plaster dust up in no time with electrostatic cloths such as those made by Swiffer and its competitors, suggests Mikal Watson, director of sales for Miracle Maids in Brooklyn. These disposable, charged cloths attract dust and dirt without moisture. Some are even designed to fit on the end of a mop handle. Others are separate wipes meant for dusting furniture and other surfaces by hand.

Say So Long to Soot

When the brick outer surfaces of your fireplace need cleaning, escape paying the hefty fee that a professional would charge by using some cleaning ingredients that you already have in your kitchen. First, don a pair of rubber gloves to protect your hands, then lay some newspaper on the floor at the base of the fireplace. In a small bucket, mix equal amounts of dishwashing liquid and table salt (start with about $\frac{1}{2}$ cup each). Add enough water to the mixture to create a creamy paste. Use an old cloth to apply the mixture to the brick or stone, rubbing it in well. Let the mixture dry for about 20 minutes (depending on how humid the day is), then brush it off with a scrub brush onto the newspaper. The soot will come right off. When you're finished, gather up the soot-covered paper and dispose of it in your outdoor trash can.

A Brass-Cleaning Concoction

Cleaning lacquered brass—the most common type of brass found in homes—is a breeze. This type of brass, used in modern lamp fixtures and doorknobs, has a protective coating, so you can just wipe it down with a damp cloth. If you need a little more dirt-defying power, use a touch of mild detergent. But unlacquered brass that's turning a little dingy (such as that old set of candlesticks) calls for a more powerful approach. Dr. Sarah Kirby, an associate professor of family and consumer sciences at North Carolina State University in

Raleigh, recommends this homemade concoction. Combine some lemon juice and baking soda until the mixture has the consistency of toothpaste. Rub the paste onto the brass with a soft cleaning cloth, rinse with water, and then dry with another cloth. The acid in the lemon juice and the cleaning action of the baking soda make this an easy task. You'll need sunglasses to protect your eyes from the shine.

Spit-Polish Your Paintings

Oil and acrylic paintings can get dirty just hanging around, especially if they're hung near your kitchen or in a dining area. You can send soiled paintings to a professional art restorer, but you'll pay a pretty penny. If the paintings aren't too grimy, or too delicate, try this tip from Barry Schrager, a professional artist and art installer in New York City. "If I need to clean a small area of a painting, I just wet a cotton swab with saliva and gently dab the painting," Barry says. The saliva is strong enough to dissolve household dirt or built-up grease, but it won't harm the paint itself. "You can clean an entire painting this way," says Barry, "but make sure you drink lots of water!" Also, keep track of which end of the swab you've already put in your mouth and don't "double dip."

MANAGING CLUTTER

Recycle before You Read

The best shortcut we can recommend for dealing with paper clutter is to prevent it from building up in the first place. For example, consider the Sunday paper, with all those news sections and advertising supplements. Once it's in your house, it seems to spread by its own volition, covering all available surfaces. To avoid this, when you return home from the newsstand or receive your Sunday delivery, keep that paper firmly in hand and march to the recycling bin. Drop the entire newspaper right in the bin. Then pull out the few sections you want to read and leave the rest behind. With this system, those parts of the paper you never read will never end up cluttering your house.

Catalog Your Catalogs

Browsing through mail-order catalogs is a nice pastime for a rainy day, but between those leisurely review sessions, a mountain of catalogs can pile up in the living room and family room. Here's a clever shortcut for maintaining a manageable catalog pile, courtesy of inveterate catalog shopper Jane Fleming of West Burlington, New York. "First, gather all the catalogs and decide which ones you don't want," Jane says. "Then call the toll-free customer service number of those companies and ask to be removed from the mailing list. Get rid of those

The Second Time Around

Newspaper "Logs"

Here's a crafty shortcut that accomplishes three tasks. First, it reuses old newspapers. Second, it provides you with free logs for your fireplace. Third, it's a great rainy day activity for kids, which will keep them busy and leave you free to catch up on other tasks. It's a win-win-win situation!

1. Gather lots of old newspapers (no glossy supplements), spray bottles (clean), and twine. Fill the spray bottles with warm water and add a drop or two of dishwashing liquid to each bottle.

2. Place a drop cloth or an old plastic shower curtain over a table or on the floor. Lay a few sheets of newspaper on the drop cloth and spray them until they're wet but not sopping.

3. Roll up the stack very tightly and secure it with twine. (If kids are old enough to use scissors safely, they can cut the twine themselves. For young children, precut a supply of short pieces of twine and then put away the scissors.)

4. Repeat this process, wrapping more sheets of wet newspaper around the roll until it's about 3 inches in diameter.

5. Keep rolling logs until you run out of newspaper.

The logs need to be completely dry before you use them. (Let them air-dry in the attic or garage.) Dry, tightly wrapped logs will burn steadily and put out about the same intensity of heat as lightweight wood.

Warning: This can be a messy project. For easy cleanup afterward, you may want to have your kids wear old clothes and latex gloves while they're making the logs.

catalogs, then alphabetize the ones you do want." Jane keeps her catalogs in a wicker basket in the living room—stacked in alphabetical order. "When I receive a new catalog, I go right to my basket, replace the old catalog with the new one, and pitch the old one," she says.

Subdivide Subscriptions

Newsweek, Time, the *New Yorker*—we love weekly magazines like these. They're chock-full of good information, but let's face it, few of us read them in a timely manner. In fact, you probably have several months' worth of old news lying around your living room and family room. Here's a shortcut that will save you money and clutter. Divide up subscriptions to favorite magazines among several like-minded friends. For example, you subscribe to *Newsweek,* a friend subscribes to *Time,* and another friend subscribes to the *New Yorker.* Once a week, you all swap magazines. If you don't find time to read the issue in hand before the next swap, it's no great loss. And if a particular article title in a magazine intrigues you, your friends will let you keep the issue another week. You gain two ways: reducing magazine clutter by two-thirds and spending only one-third of what you would have for three yearly subscriptions.

Match Container to Clutter

Each room in a house seems to suffer from a particular clutter problem. Thus the first step to controlling the problem is to decide what's causing clutter in any one room. Perhaps magazines are the cause of clutter in your living room, while you're forever tripping over toys in the family room. The second step to controlling clutter is to find baskets or containers that are well-suited to hold mass quantities of the clutter-causing items that prevail in each room. For example, you may need a capacious magazine holder in the living room. A large wicker basket may be just what's called for to corral toys in the family room. Once those convenient containers for stashing stuff are in place, you can de-clutter whenever you have a spare moment.

Cat Box Cozy

Tom Cavalieri of Long Island City, New York, has a simple solution for camouflaging the cats' litter box when friends visit. "My wife and I share a small apartment with our cats, and unfortunately, their litter box is in the living room," Tom says. "We keep it immaculate, so there's no problem with the smell. But still, it's not the prettiest sight. I designed a canvas cover that fits over the box, with a flap in the front so the cats can still get in. Anytime we have company, I pull the cover over the box. And since it's made of cotton, the cover can be laundered."

A pretty pillow-case serves as a discreet cover for a cat litter box when company comes.

If you're not handy with a sewing machine, use an old decorative pillowcase instead of canvas to fashion a cover. Cut the pillowcase open along the side seams and drape it over the top of the box. Tie a ribbon or a piece of string or yarn around the top of the box so that the cover won't fall off when Kitty pushes aside the material to get in.

DEFT DECORATING SHORTCUTS

A New Look for Free

New York City interior designer Susan Hager knows some clever shortcuts for changing the look of a room. "One of the simplest things you can do is move your furniture," she says. "It doesn't cost a cent, it doesn't take long, and when you're done, it's like you've completely redecorated."

Chart Your Course

Susan Hager also offers a shortcut to her own shortcut. "Instead of moving all the furniture around three or four times and deciding what works by trial and error, use some graph paper to diagram the room," she says. Set a scale so that each square on the paper equals 1 square foot. Draw in the furniture (don't forget to note where the windows are) and experiment with placement before you move a thing.

Two for the Price of One

Why buy two pieces of furniture when one will do? It's what former professional shopper Andrea Crawford of New York City calls double-duty furniture. "If you're already shopping for new furniture, try to choose pieces that serve two functions, like a big hassock that can double as a coffee table, or a window seat that has a removable top to store stuff in," Andrea advises. It's the ultimate decorating shortcut, and if

Decorating with Fancy Frames

Eileen Fitzmaurice of Woodbridge, New Jersey, is a sucker for yard sales and crafts. "My husband and I just bought a house, so we're pretty much tapped out," Eileen says. "That means I have to be pretty frugal when it comes to decorating." Eileen's favorite buys are old picture frames: "They're cheap, and I can almost always make them look great by gluing something to the front." All it takes, says Eileen, is "a hot glue gun and some imagination."

Frame laid upside down on fabric

Fabric

One of Eileen's favorite techniques is to decorate frames with scraps of fabric. She chooses plain frames without molding or carving. She lays a frame facedown on the wrong side of the fabric and cuts the fabric as shown above. Then she turns the frame faceup and applies glue to the front of the frame. She presses the wrong side of the fabric onto the frame and waits for the glue to dry. She then flips the frame over and glues down the flaps.

Eileen also enjoys decorating frames with other items that she can glue into place. Here are just a few examples of odds and ends that work well as frame adornments: old game pieces (such as Scrabble pieces), seashells, yarn (coiled or in random patterns), buttons, and beads and stones from old costume jewelry. Dig through your junk drawers and jewelry boxes, or look for finds at a flea market. Customize each frame to suit its surroundings or the subject of the picture it contains.

you have a small home or apartment, this strategy will help you use space as efficiently as possible, too.

Rely On Off-White

Dirty walls, peeling paint, or just an ugly paint color can ruin your daily enjoyment of your living room. If you don't have the time, energy, or money for a full-scale makeover, try a simpler approach instead. Scrape off the loose paint and then cover the walls and woodwork with one coat of off-white paint. (If the walls are painted a dark color, they may need a second coat.) The brighter, cleaner look will carry you through in good spirits until the day when you can really redecorate.

Combine Chips for Color Confidence

If you think painting a room off-white is boring, you need to pick a more exciting color for your walls. The trouble is, when you want to choose colors, those tiny paint chips from the paint store aren't much help. When your sample is only 1 inch square, it's difficult to imagine what the color will look like across the expanse of a wall. The solution is simple. Instead of relying on just one sample chip, grab 8 or 10 chips and tape them together. Then tape the megachip on the wall to gauge how well the color will work.

One Wonderful Wall

Here's a dramatic redecorating technique that you can complete in 1 day and that won't set you back a fortune. Choose just one wall in a room and paint it a different color. Painting one wall costs less than painting an entire room and takes only about one-fourth the time to complete. It requires less setup and clean-up time, too. A final advantage: If you decide after the fact that you hate the color, it takes that much less time and money to undo.

Accentuate Accessories

Redecorating a room does not have to involve a long, drawn-out process. In fact, says New York City interior designer Susan Hager, "you can redo a whole room just by changing a

Fast Chair Recovery

Redecorating a room doesn't have to cost a fortune or take months to accomplish. For example, changing the fabric on padded dining room chairs can instantly liven up a tired-looking room, and it doesn't take a professional upholsterer to do it. All you need is a screwdriver, some new (or old) fabric, some newspaper, and a staple gun (or a few thumbtacks and a hammer). Here's what to do.

1. Turn over a chair, remove the screws that fasten the seat to the chair frame, and lift off the seat. As long as the old fabric and padding aren't in horrible shape, you can leave them intact.

2. Place the seat faceup on a large piece of newspaper. Trace around the seat, adding about 8 inches all the way around. This is your pattern for the new seat cover.

3. Now it's time to visit the fabric store or rummage through your own fabric stash. Choose fabric that can stand up to spills and occasional use of the chair as a stepladder.

4. Spread out the fabric and use your newspaper pattern as a guide to cut out the new seat covers.

5. Place a piece of fabric over each chair seat, then use the staple gun or hammer and thumbtacks to secure the fabric to the underside of the seat.

6. Screw the seats back onto the chair frames, and you have a new dining room set.

- -

couple of accessories." Change the covers on the sofa pillows. Place a colorful throw on a chair. Try some new (inexpensive) curtains. With a little imagination, you can "redecorate" without spending more than a couple of dollars.

Slipcover Solution

"I love sofa slipcovers," says Myrsini Stephanides of Astoria, New York. "They're inexpensive, so I can change them more often than I could possibly afford to change my sofa. And putting on a new slipcover makes it look like I totally redecorated the living room." Myrsini would love to change her slipcover every 6 months, but that would be too pricey. Instead, she found a shortcut that works almost as well as a new slipcover. "Fold a throw cover in half and lay it across the back of the sofa," she says. "My slipcover is plain, kind of a tan color. To make it brighter, I switch between putting a bright red and a deep green throw on the back. Since throws are even cheaper than slipcovers, I *can* change the look of my sofa every six months."

Just the Shades

By now you know that the smartest decorating shortcut is to update your accessories. Well, that goes for lamp shades, too. "They're the one accessory that many people tend to forget about," says professional art installer Barry Schrager. "I live in New York City, where there's a store for everything," he says. "In fact, there's a store here that sells just lamp shades and it's called Just Shades. Really." Luckily, you don't have to live in New York to change your shades. Your favorite furniture store will probably have a good selection of inexpensive lamp shades.

Avoid a Crease Crisis

When guests come for dinner, spreading a special tablecloth is a quick way to dress up your dining room. But tablecloths stored folded in a linen closet develop creases that take forever to iron away. To keep your "company" tablecloth crease-free, use this strategy from housewife Benedicte Whitworth of Raleigh, North Carolina: Hang the tablecloth on a coat hanger and store it in a closet, covered by a large plastic bag from the dry cleaner. To do this, you'll need to start with a crease-free tablecloth (which may mean one last ironing session). Fold the tablecloth in half lengthwise, then fold it in half

The Second Time Around

5 Hang-Ups You Already Have

Finding items to adorn your walls doesn't have to be expensive or time-consuming. In fact, we'd bet that you already have the materials on hand to create several works of art. Any of the following items would add a lovely accent to your living room, family room, or dining room.

Children's artwork. Frame several drawings or paintings and hang them in an informal arrangement on one wall.

Maps and nautical charts. Frame and hang maps and charts of your favorite destinations.

Postcards. Display a record of your travels.

Seed packets. Arrange several on a mat board and then frame it for a country look.

Sporting event tickets. Frame these to show everyone what team you support and how lucky you were to be there when they won.

again lengthwise and slide it over the hanger. The tablecloth will be crease-free when you retrieve it for your next big dinner party.

Get Flower Power

One simple shortcut you can use to brighten any room is to add a vase of fresh flowers. Expensive, you say? Not at all, says Tom Donnelly of Flushing, New York. Tom is the business manager of a funeral home. Funeral homes always have extra flower arrangements on hand. "At times, people get too many arrangements to take to the cemetery and have to leave some behind," Tom says. "We throw out thousands of dollars' worth of fresh flowers every year. It's a real waste." Tom takes fresh flowers home to his wife almost every night. "I know some people might think it's creepy, but I feel good that the flowers aren't going into the Dumpster," he says. Tom also encourages his friends and family to "rescue" flowers from funeral homes near where they live: "The funeral homes are usually happy to let neighborhood folks take flowers. They won't charge a cent, and most funeral homes will actually be grateful to you for taking them."

10

Bedrooms

A bedroom can be an oasis of calm—your last stronghold of serenity in a busy life. You'll certainly want to set up your bedroom to meet your needs and comfort, but that doesn't mean style has to go. Check out the shortcuts in this chapter to learn how to organize your clothing and closet, control clutter, add style without spending a bundle, and prepare for a peaceful bedtime hour. Plus, you'll find clever shortcuts for improving kids' bedrooms (even some ways to make homework fun).

THE BEDROOM CLOSET

Avoid a Door Jam

In a crowded bedroom, this is an all-too-frequent occurrence: You swing open your closet door and end up whacking a nearby piece of furniture. There's a quick fix for this problem. Replace your standard door with a bifold model. Opening and closing your closet will be smooth and collision-free. Plus, a bifold door is lightweight, and when open it allows access to the whole closet. Pick one up at any home center; it's easy to put it in yourself. All you need is a drill and a screwdriver for installing the floor plate and frame track. It's smooth entry from then on.

Hooked on the Past

Take a cue from your grandmother's attic: Ease the space crunch in your closet by adding a few well-placed hooks. Install them on the end walls on either side of the clothes rod and along the front wall of the closet. Handbags, neckties, ball caps, and maybe a jacket or two—the storage possibilities are limitless with this idea from the past.

Dresser Up Your Closet

Shave dollars and steps off a closet renovation by moving an old dresser into it, says fashion reporter Sharon Edelson from Woodcliff Lake, New Jersey. Make sure the dresser is short enough to fit neatly under clothing hanging from the rod. You'll find it's a great addition for storing extra blankets and bed linens, as well as kids' sports uniforms. If appearance counts, paint it to match the closet walls.

Shelving: A Space Odyssey

Flexibility is important in a bedroom closet, because as your lifestyle changes, so do the things you keep in your closet. Including movable—and removable—shelves ensures that you'll be prepared for new dimensions to your life, such as taking up the saxophone or starting a new collection. One system that earns high marks for versatility uses ready-made brackets that fit into notched metal tracks so that you can move shelves up or down as often as needed. Most home centers sell these brackets fairly inexpensively. You can pair the brackets with laminated shelves or spend less by making your own from standard lumber, such as 1-by-12s cut to length. (Lumberyards and home centers will cut boards for you at little or no cost.) Just be sure to fasten the metal tracks into wall studs, and they'll be able to handle the heaviest loads. Install shelves at just one end of your closet; you'll still have most of the space available for hanging clothing.

Hang 'Em High . . . And Low

If a large portion of your wardrobe consists of shirts and trousers, you can double your usable closet space by borrowing a trick from the pros. Add your own short rod under a portion of the long rod. First, determine how much of your closet space you'd like to convert to double-hung clothes (as shown in the illustration at right). Next, head to your hardware store and pick up two 46-inch lengths of medium-gauge chrome chain; a piece of 1-inch-diameter galvanized conduit pipe, cut to length; two 1-inch-diameter rubber cane tips; and two S hooks (big enough to slip over your closet rod). The chain and pipe can be cut by the hardware store at no extra cost. Now you're ready to make your add-on clothing rod.

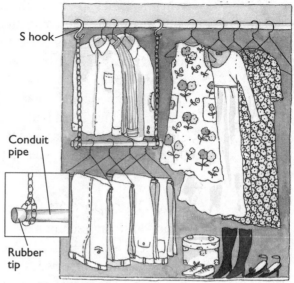

S hook

Conduit pipe

Rubber tip

1. Use a pair of pliers and a screwdriver to pry open the bottom link on each length of chain.
2. Wrap the end of one length of chain around the conduit pipe and hook the opened link into another link, forming a loop encircling the pipe.
3. Using pliers, crimp the opened link closed.
4. Repeat steps 2 and 3 with the other chain at the other end of the pipe.
5. Cover the open ends of the pipe with the rubber cane tips.
6. Hang the S hooks from your closet rod and link the free ends of the chains into the hooks.

Now you can hang shirts and trousers from both the main rod and the second-tier short rod. Use the remaining length of the main rod for dresses, your bathrobe, and other long items of clothing.

Note: If you're a very tall person, you may need to have the chains cut longer than 46 inches so that your clothing will fit. Try measuring the length of one of your shirts or a pair of your folded pants. Add the height of the hanger, plus an extra 9 inches; the total is the correct length of the chains.

CLOTHING CARE AND STORAGE

Chop the Clothes Swap

When it comes to drudgery, nothing is worse than swapping your seasonally stored clothing. For a never-unpack-again solution, buy two sets of see-through stacking boxes—one set for each season. Fill one set with fall/winter pants, shirts, sweaters, and other foldables and the second set with spring/summer items. This system is shamelessly efficient for exchanging attic-bound off-season clothing for more appropriate attire. Stack the retrieved boxes on shelves (or on the floor) in your closet, where you can see what's in them for quick wardrobe selections.

How Transparent!

A simple storage solution for out-of-season clothing, blankets, and linens is right in front of your eyes at your local supermarket: a box of clear plastic "recycling" bags (look in the trash bag aisle). The cost is only pennies per bag. Slip folded items into bags and secure them with a twist tie for dust- and moth-proof storage. Stack the bags on a closet shelf. You'll be able to see at a glance just what's stored where.

Patchwork Guilt

"Some people just weren't cut out for sewing," says medical office assistant and homemaker Marge Baldi of Oakdale, New York. When Marge finally faced up to being all thumbs with a needle and thread, she remembered a shortcut her mother used to extend the life of favorite pairs of pants: those old-fashioned iron-on patches. Fabric and discount stores sell them, several to a package for around $2. These patches come in many colors and can mend a multitude of tears and ravels for the sewing-challenged.

Stuck-On Buttons

Here's a tip that will save you hours of time and aggravation. Mother, grandmother, and power sewer Jane Ann Ellis of Columbus, Ohio, suggests that when you bring a new blouse or other garment home from the store, you put a drop of Fray Check

Clothing That Needs Mending

Problem:

Setting up your portable sewing machine each time a single item is in need of a fix doesn't seem worth the effort.

Do This Now:

Throw all shirts and pillowcases with frayed seams, dresses with unraveling hems, and other clothing that needs repair into a special hamper.

Do This for Good:

When the hamper is full, spend a couple of hours mending a number of articles at once. Or, if you're not handy with a sewing machine, take the whole lot to a professional seamstress.

⋯⋯⋯

(available at fabric stores and craft stores) on the thread that holds each button. This will keep the thread from unraveling and hold the buttons securely to the blouse—no more resewing buttons on a brand-new blouse or buying a whole new set of buttons when just one falls off and you can't find a match.

It's Better for the Sweater

Some knits, such as delicate sweaters, don't fare well when crammed into drawers, even if you take the time and effort to fold them neatly first. Hang them on padded hangers, "to keep them wrinkle-free for the morning rush," recommends fashion reporter Sharon Edelson of Woodcliff Lake, New Jersey.

Support Your Hose

Sheer pairs of panty hose are too expensive to risk ruining with snags—especially when you're not even wearing them. Store delicates such as hosiery and silk scarves in resealable plastic bags, which can be tucked easily into dresser drawers. The bags protect hose from getting snagged on rough drawer interiors. You can organize them by colors to save time coordinating outfits in the morning.

Get More Mileage from Ties

A few ties that go with everything are an important wardrobe component for men, particularly those who spend more time

Make Your Shoes Stretch

Who needs a closet-choking shoe collection? Men can manage very well with a pair of soft-soled, leather lace-up shoes for work and play. Women can follow their lead and give shameless shoe pileups the boot. Use these shortcuts to selecting shoes that cover all the bases, and you'll spare yourself clutter—and money.

■ For versatility, stick with dark shoes (brown or black shoes are most versatile), but have a light neutral color, such as bone, on hand for very light colored outfits.

■ Red, sometimes called the other neutral, coordinates with most outfits, and it has pizzazz.

■ For a go-with-anything style, choose a low-heeled pump, a dressy loafer, or, in hot weather, a closed-toe sandal such as a huarache or even a clog with a tapered toe.

hopping onto planes than shopping. Computer specialist Chaz Macdonald of Center Valley, Pennsylvania, who travels for his job, has two favorite all-purpose ties: a small paisley-patterned multicolored tie and a burgundy solid-colored tie. Chaz says the paisley tie is suitable for most occasions and, as a bonus, the pattern hides accidental food spills. He likes the way the burgundy tie sets off suits, be they navy, black, gray, or brown.

Fast, Free, and Fantastic Shoe Storage

You can make shoe storage boxes like those sold at mass merchandisers and in mail-order catalogs for free. Just take a trip to the local wine shop and pick up some empty bottle boxes, which come with compartments just the right size for stashing shoes or other small items. Stack as many of these boxes as needed to hold your shoes. As you buy more shoes, add more boxes. Such boxes are especially budget-friendly additions to a teenager's closet. Spray-paint the boxes or cover them with wallpaper or contact paper to give them a professional appearance. The best part is that you can toss the boxes when they're no longer needed.

ACCESSIBLE ACCESSORIES
Crafty Cases

How about hanging your earrings on a dressed-up sheet of plastic needlepoint canvas? Sue Gartner, a senior center activities director and homemaker from Hopewell Junction, New York, concocted this crafty idea from her needlepoint projects with the seniors. Hook the earrings through the large perforations in the canvas or, in the case of post earrings, push the posts through the perforations and attach the backs from behind. Then thread a colorful ribbon through perforations near the top and hang the whole piece from a wall hook. Plastic canvas can be found at craft supply stores in a choice of appealing colors for about 15 cents a sheet.

Spice Things Up

Hang on to that spice chest that served you so well before you updated your kitchen. Its tiny drawers are perfect for all those little rings, earrings, and pins that can get separated in large jewelry boxes. If it has a natural wood finish, it's bound to blend well with your bedroom furniture. Or paint it to coordinate with bedding and accessories.

Pearls of Wisdom from a Pro

Collect baskets for their looks but make them work for their space, as does Ceil Meredith, a jewelry designer from New York City. Baskets are great for storing jewelry, but expensive jewels need extra care. For instance, pearls and precious gemstones (which can get damaged easily if they are jostled

Nifty Accessory Organizers

Ties, belts, scarves, and jewelry seem to get tangled whenever you're not looking. Try one of these strategies for keeping accessories under control.

Tie one on. Store necklaces on closet hangers designed for ties or belts. You can either place the hanger on the back of your closet door or hang it on the wall by your dresser in lieu of a framed picture.

Girlie stuff. For your daughter's room, freshen up an old nightstand with a quick coat of paint and use the drawers to store bracelets, headbands, necklaces, and all the other accessories that girls love to collect. Reserve the top of the nightstand for jewelry boxes to hold rings and special jewelry items.

Easy to tackle. A small tackle box or hardware organizer has lots of compartments that are ideal for storing pairs of earrings. These boxes may not be fancy, but they'll do the trick, and you can count on finding them at most discount and hardware stores for only a few dollars.

around) should be kept separate from one another. A variety of pouches and little Chinese envelope bags can serve as interesting containers for gems and also are fun to collect. But basic plastic sandwich bags will do the trick, and you can see instantly what's in the bags.

Low-Tech Tie Rack

Spare yourself the expense of buying a specialized tie rack. Instead, use clothespins to secure several ties to a standard wire clothes hanger.

CLUTTER CONTROL

Tin Types

Use old flour, sugar, coffee, and tea canisters to store personal items in your vanity, says writer Alexandra Greenwood of Mahopac, New York. Fill them with cotton balls, cotton swabs, nail files, and polish. Besides being unusual, these collectibles are available for next to nothing in thrift shops.

Borrowed Time . . . And Space

One short-term storage area you might not have tapped into is the space under your bed. Try this shameless sorting method devised by Mira G. Dessy of Sherman, Connecticut. This busy wife, mother of three, and business manager for an online research firm uses dedicated under-bed drawers to keep bedroom clutter out of sight. One is for suddenly mateless socks, another is for items that need mending, and a third is for those miscellaneous papers whose future is yet to be determined. Mira stashes until a drawer fills up, then sets aside an hour to deal with the contents.

Freewheeling Storage

Store an awkwardly shaped or heavy object under a bed on an inexpensive, wheeled plant dolly, which you can buy at any garden center. These sturdy caddies are designed to hold up to 200 pounds. They make it nearly effortless to pull out, for example, that guitar case for playing your favorite song or boxes of dumbbells for pumping iron.

Net Profits

Stuffed animals can take over a preschooler's bedroom. Rather than have these critters bury the bed or occupy valuable shelf space, try this trick from Laura Warshawsky, a mother and financial analyst from Brooklyn, New York. Hang some netting in a corner along the upper reaches of the walls, using one sturdy hook on one wall and another on the adjacent wall. (Screw the hooks into studs.) Stash a portion of the stuffed animal collection in the net, where your little one will still be able to see them through the netting. Keep a step stool handy so that you can rotate stuffed toys in and out of the net.

Wall-to-Wall Friends

Here's a highly decorative way to store all those "semiretired" dolls and stuffed animals your child just can't part with. Doting aunt JoAnn Marra of West Bay Shore, New York, suggests installing a wall-to-wall shelf 15 to 18 inches from the ceiling.

 Strategies for Clothing-Free Floors

Can you see the floor in your child's room, or is it completely hidden by stray clothing? Uncover the floor with one of these clothing control policies.

Lock it up. Put a school locker in your child's room for stashing sports uniforms, raincoats, and other bulky items. A locker is inexpensive and indestructible, and you can find one at building salvage companies, flea markets, or home centers. Paint the locker to match the decor or let your child personalize it with stickers and posters.

Rack 'em up. One item that's withstood the test of time for keeping stray clothing in check is a coat rack—umbrella stand unit, says Laura Warshawsky. Laura uses a large coat rack to control "the daily eyesore" of her husband's discarded sweatshirts, T-shirts, and other clothes.

Slam-dunk it. You'll save countless thankless minutes of picking up your son's dirty clothes with this sporting idea. Tie a mesh laundry bag to a basketball hoop and mount the hoop on the bedroom wall within easy reach (a minimum of 4½ feet from the floor), using strong anchors and screws. In no time, he'll be practicing hoop shots with every pair of dirty socks he takes off.

The shelf can be supported by standard brackets or a decorative crown molding that is at least 8 inches deep. (The molding costs a little more but looks more finished than brackets.) A lineup of loyal friends, tucked out of the way but clearly visible, should please kids and moms alike.

A Doorful of Toys

Children will be more motivated to pick up their toys if they can see the results of their labor. So give new life to an over-the-door shoe holder as a stash-it bag for your child's favorite things. Hang the bag on the outside of your kid's closet door. It's ideal for stashing small stuffed toys and other items.

Keep a Lid on Toys

To avoid having toys become dust collectors, organize building blocks, musical instruments, crayons, markers, and other items in individual boxes with lids. Moms can label each box with the contents. For very young kids who can not yet read, use containers with see-through lids.

Don't Agonize over Art

The Second Time Around

Children's drawings and paintings can accumulate at a stunning pace. After all, what mother can bear to part with her little Picasso's creative output? But all that artwork eventually turns into bedroom clutter that will require half a day to organize. Here's a shortcut suggested by Lori Baird, editor of *Cut the Clutter and Stow the Stuff.* "Let your children decide what to keep and what to get rid of," Lori advises. "They're sure to be less sentimental than you are about their artwork and will probably want to throw out more than they want to keep." With your kids making the decisions, you can get rid of items knowing that you're not breaking any little hearts. (And if your own breaks a little, that's part of parenting.)

From Cookie Jar to Toy Jar

Hang on to those large, clear-plastic jars from animal crackers, pretzels, and other snacks—the kind that you buy at the warehouse store. Business manager and homemaker Mira G. Dessy of Sherman, Connecticut, says they make terrific, unbreakable storage containers for assorted small items, such as doll accessories and Legos.

BEDTIME TIPS

Your Warm Bed Beckons

Want a toasty bed to climb into? Head for the laundry room with your comforter in hand. So says Oakland, California, psychotherapist Paula Yurkewecz, who learned this cozy trick during cold winters back east, when she was growing up on a dairy farm. Simply throw your comforter into the dryer for 5 minutes, then remove it and run back to bed with it. The warmed comforter will stop those shivers as you wait for your body's natural heat to take over.

Heat the Feet for Free

Long before mail-order catalogs started cashing in on the idea, independent-spirited 80-something retiree Marie Devlin of Stamford, Connecticut, made her own microwaveable "husk sack" to warm her cold feet in bed. To make yours, start with some soft flannel material. Fold it over and sew seams to create a sack the size of a travel pillow. Fill it with old dried beans, hand-stitch the final seam, and it's ready to heat (30 seconds on half power) for whatever needs warming up in bed.

Bedspreads Beat Comforter Covers

Flannel comforter covers are delightfully soft, but they add weight and warmth to a large comforter, which might not suit you, especially if you're a woman experiencing the hot flashes and night sweats of menopause. It also takes extra time and energy to remove these covers for laundering. To save time and give yourself more options,

What Every Nightstand Needs

Here are 12 items that everyday experts consider indispensable to keep on top of their nightstands or in the drawer.

- Small flashlight (for middle-of-the-night rummaging or emergency power outages)
- Small phone book (with emergency phone numbers and doctors' numbers)
- Nail clippers and file
- Pencil and notepad (for capturing those late-night thoughts)
- Small reference book (for nighttime reading—famous quotes, Bible passages, hints and tips)
- Small sewing kit
- Tissues
- Earplugs
- Antacid and headache remedy
- Bottled spring water
- Eye masks
- Battery-operated light that goes on and off automatically when you open the drawer

just spread a bedspread on top of a bare comforter. At night, you can use the bedspread for added warmth or fold it down until morning if you feel too warm with it pulled up. Also, when you make your bed, the coverlet often will lie more smoothly than a comforter cover.

Slather Shamelessly, Dress, and Go . . . To Sleep

Keep a pair of old socks on hand and use them at night to cover your feet after you slather them with lotion or arthritis cream, recommends Stamford, Connecticut, retiree Marie Devlin. Putting the socks on will keep your feet warm and your sheets dry and clean and will allow the lotion to soak into your skin. Wear a pair of white cotton gloves to protect lotion-covered hands.

Easy-Sew Bed Caddy Sack

When you're snug in bed in the evening, it's often a stretch to reach your bedtime reading, eyeglasses, tissue box, or water, even if your nightstand is nearby. With this easy-sew solution, you can whip up a bedside caddy sack in under 30 minutes. All you need is a spare pillowcase of your choice:

1. Fold the case in half widthwise. On one side, use a piece of chalk or a pencil to draw a line lightly about three-quarters of the way along the fold, centered.

Turn a pillowcase into a bedside caddy for items you like to have at hand when you're in bed.

2. Cut a slit along the line on that side only and finish the cut edge by sewing a contrasting color of seam tape (available at a fabric store) around the cut edges.

3. Sew the open end of the pillowcase shut.

4. Tuck one short edge of the pillowcase between your mattress and box spring, leaving the new opening exposed.

5. Tuck your book, glasses, bottled water, and other bedside items in the caddy, and you'll be all ready to tuck yourself in for a good read.

Safety First: Throw Out the Throws

Forgo throw rugs in the bedroom, and you won't have to worry about slipping or tripping over them in the dark. Also, set a chair beside the bed to use to steady yourself as you get up for nighttime forays.

No-Nonsense Nursery

Save precious minutes of sleep with this speedy nursery setup. Add a small microwave oven and dorm-size fridge stocked with formula to the nursery for fast nighttime feedings. In one stop, you can grab a bottle, warm it up, and feed baby.

EASY BEDROOM MAKEOVERS

Bored with Your Headboard?

Transform that old wooden headboard with this inexpensive trick. All you need is a staple gun, scissors, quilt batting, and a designer bedsheet or thin bedspread. Start by covering the front and sides of the headboard with several layers of quilt batting, enough to achieve a padded look. Pull the batting around the sides and, using the staple gun, fasten it to the back of the headboard. Then cover the front of the headboard with the fabric, pulling it around the sides and stapling it over the batting on the back. For a more finished look, take additional fabric (cut to fit), fold over the edges, and staple it over the back of the headboard after completing the front. To give the headboard a tufted look, staple the front of the headboard at regular intervals and sew or hot-glue buttons over the staples. Voilà—a custom-upholstered design that will change the way you feel about your bedroom.

Curtain Call

Retirement affords people the time, at long last, to enjoy redecorating their homes, but not always the income to do so. Kat Butler, a recently retired magazine editor from Kearny, New Jersey, offers this shortcut for sprucing up a bedroom on a fixed income. Buy coordinating sheets on sale and make your own custom curtains. It's cheaper than buying cotton by the yard, and there's enough fabric for long panels, if desired.

Bamboo for the Bedroom

If you're setting up house, don't get hung up on spending big bucks on simple items such as curtain rods. Newlyweds Charlie and Dana McGimsey of Elizabethtown, Kentucky, decided to limit themselves to a few fairly primitive purchases in order to stay within their budget, and they ended up with a perfectly wild decor. Try their scheme in a bedroom you'd like to redecorate cheaply. Buy 6-foot-long bamboo garden stakes, balls of thick jute twine, and several yards of cotton blend, leopard print fabric. (You could substitute an ivy or wildflower print to complement a woodland or garden theme.) For the curtain rods, use the twine to tie bunches of bamboo (cut to window width using pruning shears) together, then throw in decorative knots as embellishments. Use the fabric to make simple curtains and a bedspread. Save the remaining fabric to cover an old bench or stool, then add twine contrast piping and macramé corner tassels. You'll have a bedroom decor wild enough for Tarzan—and you'll be wild about the savings.

Romantic Fabrications

Add romance to your bedroom by using this sensual shortcut from former antiques dealer Suzanne Flynn of Elizabethtown, Kentucky. Pick up several yards of inexpensive tulle netting and drape swaths of it above your headboard. Attach it to the wall and headboard discreetly with straight pins, a staple gun, or stick-on Velcro tabs. To enhance the draping, make some tulle rosettes by first cutting the tulle into 8-inch-diameter circles. Layer several circles on top of one another and drape them over your index finger. Gather them together and secure them with a tight-fitting rubber band. Repeat to make several rosettes. Pin the rosettes to the gathered points of your wall draping. Spray on some magic with gold glitter fabric paint.

A Benchmark of Convenience

A small chair-height vanity bench at the foot of the bed is much easier to use than the bed itself for putting on shoes and socks. It also affords an aging pet a midway point for jumping from the floor to the bed.

A No-Sew, Low-Cost Valance

In less than 2 hours, you can fashion a professional-looking, no-sew window valance to match your bedding and save the hundreds of dollars a drapery expert would charge. You'll need a twin-size bed skirt that coordinates with your sheets, a small bag of polyester quilt batting, a 1-by-12-inch board cut to the width of your window, two 6-inch L brackets, screws and wall anchors, scissors, and a staple gun. To make the valance, follow these steps.

1. Attach the L brackets to the bottom of the board, flush with one edge and 4 inches from each end.
2. Wrap one layer of batting around all sides of the board to soften its edges, tuck it around the brackets, and secure it to the board with staples.
3. Cut a piece out of the bed skirt ruffle. Include enough of the white core fabric to cover the top of the board. Cut the piece to the length of the board, including both ends, plus 2 inches.
4. Line up the ruffle with the front edge of the board so that only the patterned fabric shows; wrap the white core fabric over the top of the board. Staple the white fabric to the back of the board and tuck staples into the top edge of the ruffle (where they won't show) to secure it along the front edge. Fold and tuck the ruffle around the ends, turning the cut edges under for a finished look, and staple.
5. Hold the valance unit in position above the window and use a pencil to mark the wall through the holes in the brackets. (Have a friend help with this step.) Drill holes at the marks, using a bit slightly larger than the screws, and insert the wall anchors. Then screw the brackets into the anchors.

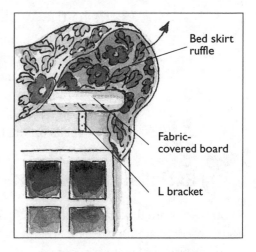

Bed skirt ruffle

Fabric-covered board

L bracket

ESPECIALLY FOR KIDS
Chalk It Up to Learning

It's never too early to encourage a child's efforts to study and learn. Since most children love to draw with chalk, you can motivate them to develop their creativity, solve mathematical problems, or practice making their letters and also "decorate" their room with an original mural all at the same time. Simply paint the lower 3 feet of one wall with blackboard paint (green or black blackboard paint is available at home centers and paint stores), then attach a chair rail where the "blackboard" meets the upper wall. (Most lumberyards and home centers will cut such trim boards to length at little or no charge.) Use the chair rail as a chalk and eraser shelf and encourage your children to create the mural of their dreams.

Words to the Wise

Make learning a game. One great shortcut in spelling and vocabulary development is the board game Scrabble. Be sure your child has the game in his room and offer to drop in to play it with him now and then. For added incentive, offer extra points for any school vocabulary words or current events words he spells on the board.

 Excellent Items for Kids' Rooms

If you have more than one child in the house, chances are they're all fond of having furnishings for their exclusive use, especially if they are the same gender. Mira G. Dessy of Sherman, Connecticut, the mother of three girls, provides these fairly inexpensive items in each of her daughters' rooms to help them feel special.

Bulletin board. Kids love to display all those souvenir movie tickets, photos, funny notes from their friends, and small doodles. A bulletin board spares the walls from the effects of adhesive tape and pushpins.

File cabinet. It's great for the budding artist or writer who needs to organize a growing body of work.

Full-length mirror. This ended the competition and bickering when it was time to primp before going out (and that helped Mira feel better, too).

Homeroom-Style Discipline Helps

To help children develop a positive homework routine, try this stress-relieving way of focusing their attention on the task at hand. Set up a designated study area in each child's room, such as a small table or desk and chair. Provide a desk lamp for reading and set it on an electric timer, so that it turns on at the same time each evening to gently remind your child that it is study time.

Customized Pencil Holder

Empty 1-pound coffee cans make great, cheap desktop pencil and marker holders for your kids, says Mira G. Dessy. Have each child use Con-Tact paper or construction paper to customize the can to suit her personality.

Blue Jeans Beds

Who can't relate to denim and its forgiving nature? As a comforter cover, denim can stand up to wear and tear from shoes, books, coloring projects, and more. If you like to sew, you can spare yourself the search for one in the store, as well as the expense. For a girl's room, try a soft blue faded denim with a contrasting dark denim bed skirt. For a boy's room, use dark denim and coordinate it with sheets and curtains that have a western or sports theme. And for a small child, sew on a few pockets from old jeans to stash treasures such as stuffed animals. If you quilt, collect denim or chambray work shirts from thrift shops to cut quilt pieces from.

Form a Picket Line

Give clever detailing to kids' bedroom walls using picket fencing. Inexpensive prefabricated fencing from a home improvement store lends itself to quirky, fun wainscoting for one wall. With a few modest purchases from a

My Favorite Shortcut

Clip Art for Kids

Alexandra Greenwood, a writer and mother from Mahopac, New York, suggests this cute idea to keep girls' hair clips and barrettes ready and waiting without the need to rummage. Using heavy, 1-inch-wide ribbon that matches the decor of your child's room, tie a big bow with long tail ends. Attach strips of stick-on Velcro to the back of the bow and the bedroom door and hang the bow on the door. Clip barrettes and hairpins right onto the bow.

3 Artful Approaches to Kids' Decor

Your kids can teach you a lot about art—and bedroom decorating. Eileen Herman-Haase, dance teacher, homemaker, and mother from Medford, Massachusetts, discovered this from her creative 11-year-old, Haylee. Eileen suggests these simple, fun activities to foster artistic development in your child.

Wallpapering. Let your child use posters and his own drawings to cover a wall of his room from top to bottom. If you're worried about ruining the wall's surface, cover it first with a neutral-patterned strippable wallpaper (for savings, check the discount bin at a wallpaper store) before turning him loose with the glue pot.

A magnetic wall. Attach a piece of galvanized sheeting to a wall. (First cover the edges with soft, splinterless polystyrene molding for safety.) Encourage small children to display their paper artwork using colorful magnets. Galvanized sheeting and white polystyrene molding are sold at home centers and lumberyards, most of which will cut them to size at little or no cost.

Beaded curtains. Tell your daughter she can fashion her own unique café-style window curtain using strings of beads tied to a pressure rod. She can string her own beads, using those collected from thrift store jewelry or purchased from a craft supply shop. Or you can buy finished beaded fringe by the foot at craft and fabric stores.

craft supply store, you can add interesting special effects, such as stenciled or stapled-on silk flowers above the fence, or a painted pastoral scene complete with horses or barnyard animals. Or try stenciling baseball bats "propped" against the fence and hang baseball caps on the pickets. A matching gate makes a great headboard.

Camouflage Detail

Diana dos Santos, a New York City homemaker and mom, made an army-themed bedspread for her teenage son, Tiago. To whip up a similar spread for your teenagers, buy some camouflage cloth at a local fabric store and sew it together with just a few seams. As an added bonus, piece some scrap material together for a simply stitched coordinating curtain. At ease, son!

The Home Office

11

The home office is usually the smallest room in the house and the room you least want to enter—it's the scene for bill paying, tax preparation, and, for some people, day-to-day work. But these chores become a lot more manageable, if not actually pleasurable, when your office is well-organized and your financial routines are efficient. From painless bill paying and tax preparation shortcuts to no-brainer computer tips and Internet savvy, this chapter will help take the sting out of life's necessary evils.

ORDER FROM CHAOS
You Put That Where?

When two or more people file documents in the same file cabinet, the result can be multiplying folders and misfiled papers—after all, file management philosophies abound. To avoid time-wasting searches, choose a designated filer for each class of documents, such as insurance, investments, and home repairs. (Only the insurance filer should file insurance papers, for example.) You can also avoid confusion about important documents by color-coding your files. Use different-colored folders (or labels) for different classes of documents—green for taxes, yellow for investments, red for insurance, and so on—and tape a color key to the side of the file cabinet.

Are You a Front Filer?

File folders can quickly become jammed with random mutual fund statements, medical bills, and the like, but there's a simple way to keep documents like these organized chronologically. Look through your existing files and analyze your filing style. Do you tend to put new documents in the front of the file folder or the back when you drop them in? If it's the front, *always* put new documents in front of the old ones; if it's the back, *always* stick new documents at the back. Mount a reminder message on the front of your file cabinet: Write New in Front or New in Back on a piece of paper and use a magnetic photo frame to affix it to the file cabinet. Follow the rule, and you'll never again have to sort through a huge folder to find that statement you need from June 2001.

What to Save for the Tax Man

In general, the IRS has only 3 years to audit a return, but the agency can challenge a return for up to 6 years if it suspects underreporting of income or other problems. Most tax professionals recommend saving tax-related documents for 7 years. Always file such papers by year and not by category. For example, you should maintain a 2003 home expenses folder, not separate folders with repair bills and mortgage statements for the past 7 years. That way, it will be easy to purge a given year's documents once the statute of limitations is up.

These are the documents you should save for 7 years: W-2s, 1099s, dividend and interest statements, medical bills (if you deduct medical expenses), annual mortgage statements, bank statements and checks related to tax deductions, credit card statements reflecting tax deductions, and any other tax-related receipts.

Make Many Offices in One

Most homes have space for only one office, so spouses (and even kids) must share the office desk and computer. To avoid scrambled files and misplaced homework, adopt the philosophy "to each his own." Each user of the office space should have his own in box, file drawers, and bookshelves, which are off-limits to other family members. Most computers can be set up to require a personal log-in, so each person can access only certain software and see his own documents, e-mail messages, and the like. (A very useful program for logging in children this way is KidDesk Family Edition, which costs about $25.) Even digital answering machines and voice mail can be programmed with separate mailboxes, so callers can leave private messages for a specific person.

The Overflowing In Box

Everyone's heard of the one-touch rule for office paperwork. But for most people, it's practically impossible to pick up a piece of mail or a magazine article only once. Some things just need consideration. Here's how to apply the rule in a way that works for the average procrastinator. Keep two in boxes in your home office: one for "action" items and the other for "I really want to look that over someday" materials. Whenever new paper comes into the office—mail, bills, computer downloads—make your one-touch decision on where to toss the paper: the action box, the think-about-it box, or the recycling bin. You won't solve your procrastination problem completely, but at least the must-do items won't get lost amid the recipes and book recommendations.

Save These Forever

There's no way around it: some things just have to stay in your files forever—or nearly forever. They include:

- Tax returns. These hold all of your basic financial history.
- Major appliance receipts. Keep them as long as you own the item, for insurance and warranty claims.
- Home improvement bills. Tax laws on home ownership are always changing. You may need to document your major home expenses someday.
- Retirement plans. Keep records of any investment purchases until you retire or close an account—and then keep them for another 7 years for tax purposes.
- Diaries. Even if you never refer to them, someday your grandkids may enjoy them.

Give Paper Clips the Slip

Paper clips are not the essential office supplies you think they are. In fact, they can actually contribute to confusion in your filing system because they can easily be pushed loose as you move documents in and out of a file cabinet. To stave off file

 Things You Don't Need to Keep

Efficiency in a home office is as much a product of what you don't keep in your files and bookshelves as what you do. Commonly collected paperwork that you can toss includes the following:

Gasoline receipts. Unless you deduct actual expenses for operating a car for tax purposes (most taxpayers use the mileage rate), you don't need to document gasoline purchases. However, gas purchases when you *rent* a car are deductible as appropriate business, educational, or charitable expenses.

Meal receipts. Unless you're reporting meal expenses to an employer, don't bother keeping receipts for tax purposes. Most self-employed business travelers opt for an IRS per diem (daily allowance) deduction, which is easier to use and often more generous than the tab from the meals you're eating at McDonald's.

Quarterly investment statements. If you're a long-term investor, there's no need to save every report from your mutual funds. The annual statements contain all the information you need.

Pay stubs. Keep your year-end paycheck to compare with your W-2 form for taxes. Dump all the rest after you check them for accuracy.

Old insurance policies. No need to keep them.

Magazines and newspapers. Don't save entire magazines for one article you might read. Instead, clip out the article and keep it in a folder of related stories, such as travel ideas or books to read.

Photos. Take a tip from professional photographers and edit your photos ruthlessly as soon as you pick up the prints or slides from the store. Toss out any that are out of focus, poorly composed, or duplicates. Your photo collection will be much more useful and entertaining—as well as easier to store and maintain—if you keep only the most compelling photos.

Medical bills. Once they've received insurance reimbursements, most healthy people don't need to save every medical receipt, because they're unlikely to meet the IRS threshold for deducting medical expenses.

cabinet chaos, stow the paper clips and staple all multipage documents you intend to file.

Wait and See

Here's one timesaving suggestion that runs counter to all the efficiency experts' advice: Do nothing. Many office organization efforts bog down because you can't decide whether something should be filed or thrown away. Rather than puzzle too long over the decision, put the wait-and-see items in a pile and don't touch them for at least a month. Time has a way of clarifying such decisions: When you re-sort the pile, you'll find that as many as 90 percent of the papers in it can be thrown away.

Don't Drown in Digital Photos

Digital cameras are a savings boon to people who take a lot of snapshots because they no longer have to buy film and pay processing costs. But how can you keep track of all those digital images? Professional photographer Corey Rich of Sacramento, California, recommends a software program called ACDSee for organizing digital photos on your PC. (A similar program called Photo Mechanic is designed for Macintosh computers.) With these programs, it's quick and easy to view digital images, attach keywords to them, and sort them for storing, printing, or other uses.

Keep a Card Cache

Twice a year, make a trip to a card store and stock up on thank-you notes and generic message cards. Keep the cards, along with a sheet of postage stamps, in your desk. Whenever you

5 MINUTES A DAY

Systematize with Storage in Mind

To keep file cabinets from collapsing under the burden of a mass of paperwork, purge them of expired and seldom-used files each year. But picking through individual documents in every folder would take forever.

Pave a shortcut for the annual purge by organizing your file folders by year. Create a new folder each year for bank statements, tax returns, mutual fund reports, and the like.

At the end of the year, pull out all the file folders that are two years old or older and stick them in a cardboard file storage box. Label the box with the appropriate year(s) and stash it in a closet or the attic. The hour or two per year you spend on this culling process will save you precious minutes every time you consult your files.

hear of a happy—or sad—occurrence among family or friends, you'll be prepared. If you don't have to make a special trip to pick up a card, you'll be much more likely to respond on the spur of the moment to a relative or friend who deserves a kind note.

If Only I Had the Manual

Can't figure out how to program your VCR, and the manual has vanished? Solve the problem forever by using an alphabetized accordion folder to hold all your instruction manuals and warranties. As soon as you buy a new appliance, drop the manual into the appropriate place in the folder. If you still manage to lose a manual or you want to preserve storage

They Had NO Shame

Why Buy Supplies?

Working as a hand-to-mouth freelance writer, Dougald MacDonald of Louisville, Colorado, learned early in his career to scrimp on office supplies. He stands by the environmentalist's (and cheapskate's) three R's: reduce, reuse, and recycle. "I still use notepads from a job I left in 1994," Dougald says. "It wasn't really pilfering, because they had been printed with my name on them so no one else could use them. And I'm still working through a box of envelopes I took from a company when it relocated. I've also never purchased a pen. The ones in the mug on my desk came from a Holiday Inn, an insurance salesman, a Westin hotel conference room, and a friend's law office." Dougald reuses printer paper until every surface is covered, and when he finishes a job and empties out file folders, he simply folds the folders over and labels them on the other side for a new project.

Dougald also recommends refilling black ink cartridges for ink-jet printers. To do this, you must buy a refill kit, but the savings compared to buying new cartridges are dramatic. You can order the kits online (search under "ink cartridge refills"). A refill of black ink for his printer averages about $5.50, while the best price for a new cartridge is over $25, Dougald says. Follow the refill kit instructions precisely, and always run the printer's self-cleaning program once or twice after installing a refilled cartridge.

space, check for the manual online. Many consumer goods companies keep updated manuals on their Web sites. These Web sites also often post frequently asked questions (FAQs) about their products, and the problems other people have experienced may lead to a solution for you.

Office Tupperware

Photographer Mike Landkroon of Stony Creek, Ontario, uses plastic sandwich containers to store small office supplies such as paper clips, staples, and tape. "I have no desk drawers—other than file drawers, which hold my files—and these containers are stackable and see-through, so it's easy to find what I need," Mike says.

Cut a Custom Desk

In jam-packed homes, the home office may be only a desk crammed into a guest bedroom or den. Finding furniture to fit the space available can be a problem. Solve the problem by doing what corporate trainer Jonna Lemes of Red Cliff, Colorado, did: Build your own. "I used furniture-grade, three-quarter-inch plywood and a power saw to cut the plywood to the exact shape," Jonna explains. "I finished it with three coats of polyurethane and placed the plywood on top of a couple of two-drawer file cabinets. The desktop cost almost nothing, and it fits the space perfectly."

Don't have the tools to cut plywood yourself? Trace the space on a large sheet of paper and take the sketch to a lumberyard that will cut the wood for you. When you set up your desk, be sure to position the file cabinets so that the desktop is well-balanced, taking into account the weight of your computer, books, and other items.

Cut plywood to fit an available spot in your home and prop the plywood up on file cabinets. Instant office!

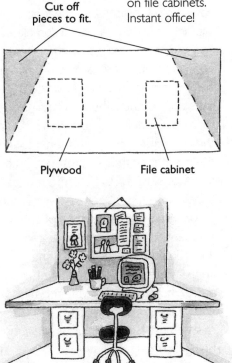

Cut off pieces to fit.

Plywood — File cabinet

The Office That Follows You Around

No space in your home for a proper office? Find yourself conducting business on the dining room table and periodically wandering the house in search of supplies? There's a solution to your dilemma at an office supply store near you. It's a wheeled office organizer (lovingly called R2-D2 by some), which has space designed for holding files and sundry supplies. When you're working, it's there at your side dispensing pens and paper clips. When you're done, wheel it into a corner of the room or a storage area.

Glorious Gizmos

The Low-Tech Reminder System

Fancy calendars and computerized planners are fine, but they don't work for everyone in a family, and they can't easily hold the notes, newspaper clippings, and letters that accumulate. For a family-accessible planner, use an accordion file to create a family tickler file. Ticklers are used by journalists, salespeople, and others to remind them of an idea or lead months down the line. Label your accordion file with the months of the year, reserving the first four slots for the current month. Label those four Week 1, Week 2, and so on. Place articles about upcoming events, phone messages, and school and community schedules in the appropriate months. When a new month comes up, divide it into the appropriate weeks. Nobody will ever miss a must-see event or whine about being bored again.

Strategic Office Shopping

Don't pay the full retail price for office supplies, advises computer programmer Kevin Frederick of Boulder, Colorado. "You can pick up home office and computer supplies for pennies on the dollar if you purchase everything together, at just the right time," Kevin explains. "The trick is to combine mail-in rebates, instant rebates, and online coupon codes to generate a large initial purchase."

For example, Kevin cites a recent online order from OfficeMax. He ordered four pieces of software, some compact discs, CDs, and other items, with a combined retail price of $146.33, including sales tax. Kevin used a coupon for free shipping, a $25 discount for large online orders, and mail-in rebates totaling more than $100 to reduce his net purchase price to just over $20.

Always check the fine print on rebate offers, Kevin warns, because they have a way of expiring just as you're about to use them.

PAYING THE BILLS

Black and Blue Checkbooks

If your family maintains two or more checking accounts, order the checkbook covers and checks in contrasting colors. That way, you'll always grab the right checkbook when you're rushing out the door.

Divide and Conquer

In many families, one person handles all the family finances. But why not hold each spouse responsible for half of the financial chores? The trick is to play to each person's strengths. For example, says efficiency expert Lori MacDonald of Cumberland Foreside, Maine, "I pay all the bills, revise the budget annually, and track expenses. My husband is in charge of preparing the taxes and long-term investing." In other words, she adds, "I make sure we have money to put aside, and he makes sure it multiplies!" On a more serious note, sharing responsibility for finances is wise in case one spouse should suffer a serious illness or injury. The healthy spouse can more easily take charge of financial matters because he or she is already familiar with at least part of the family's financial situation.

Sharing a Checkbook in Peace

The joint checking account lies at the root of many marriage disputes. Although it may be impossible to avoid arguments over the shamelessly high cost of a new dress or fishing reel, it is possible to prevent the clashes that occur when one spouse faithfully records purchases in the checkbook and the other does not. Interior designer Susan Steele of Longmont, Colorado, has come up with an easy solution that works for her and her husband, Dan. "We leave the checkbook on the kitchen counter, and instead of writing checks, each of us uses an ATM or debit card to access the money," Susan says. "When we get home, all we have to do is stick a receipt in the checkbook." When Susan balances the checkbook, there's no problem with missing entries—the receipts tell the story. In other families, one spouse carries the checkbook and the other

Just Charge It

Professional photographer Mike Landkroon of Stoney Creek, Ontario, pays all his bills by credit card. Because he maintains separate bank accounts and charge cards for personal and business use, he can track his expenses easily. Charging everything saves Mike time and money in several ways, as he explains.

■ "As long as I'm diligent in using the right card for purchases and the right bank account to pay the credit card bills, my accounting is done by my bank and credit card statements."

■ "I collect air miles on both credit cards and rack up significant points."

■ "I have all my bills automatically charged to my credit cards. I have no monthly bill payments, and when I'm away, things take care of themselves."

■ "Using my credit card consolidates all of my spending and makes it easy to stay on budget."

Of course, charging everything requires discipline, and it won't work for everyone. And there's one rule you *must* follow, says Mike: "I always pay my credit card balance in full each month."

• •

a debit card. If you do this, just train the debit card holder to keep receipts and put them consistently in one place—perhaps a covered basket or crock on the kitchen counter or in the home office.

Highlight It

Save time at tax season by keeping a highlighter handy when you pay your bills. Each time you write a check for a tax-related item (charitable donation, educational expense, and the like), highlight that line in the register with the marker. The same goes for tax-related payments by credit card—when you pay the bill, quickly scan the statement and highlight anything that's tax-related. When it's time to prepare your taxes, you'll find deductible items easily.

MANAGING YOUR FINANCES

Home (Yawn!) Insurance Movies

Home insurers recommend that you prepare a detailed inventory of the contents of your house so that you'll be ready to prepare a claim in case of a calamity. But who has time to list every book, print, necklace, and collectible in the house? Instead, shortcut the inventory process by making a movie of your entire home. Using your video camera, pan slowly across every shelf and through every closet, describing particularly valuable items as you go. Keep the tape in a safe-deposit box or at a relative's house. If you don't own a video camera, photographs of individual rooms are better than nothing. They'll help you remember possessions and thus claim more for insurance and tax deductions. Making a video or taking photos is also a good way to document the move-in condition of a rental when you arrive.

Unorthodox Insurance Savings

Everyone knows that a clean driving record reduces auto insurance premiums. But how about a clean ashtray? Many insurers offer premium discounts based on such little-known qualifications as not smoking, parking inside a garage, carpooling, or being married. You won't know until you ask.

Pay It Down

It might seem crazy, but adding a little extra to your mortgage payment each month can actually save you money—a lot of money—in the long run, says public relations consultant Paige Boucher of Steamboat Springs, Colorado. Over the years, such payments dramatically shorten the life of a loan. For example, if you hold a 30-year mortgage of $100,000 at 7 percent interest, adding just $50 a month to the principal and interest payment of $665 a month will shorten the loan period to 24 years and save you more than $31,000 in total interest payments. (You'll also earn much more equity in the house sooner, a benefit if you sell earlier.) Make sure your lender doesn't charge prepayment penalties (most don't) and check with a financial planner to determine whether that $50 might be better spent each month on traditional investments.

Do Without Long Distance

Save money on telephone calls by dropping your long-distance service at home, suggests publisher Chris McNamara of Mill Valley, California. Chris isn't suggesting that you give up calling your family and friends who live far away, though. "I use a pre-paid phone card instead of long distance," Chris says. "It's usually cheaper per minute, and you don't pay any monthly service charge." Another alternative is to find a mobile phone plan that includes free long distance. Often such calls are cheaper than making long-distance calls from your regular phone.

Speedy Refunds

If you're expecting a tax refund, file your return electronically. The IRS says refunds are processed at least twice as quickly for electronic returns as they are for paper returns. Moreover, the software used to prepare electronic returns "remembers" much of your information from the previous year, saving you from reinputting the same data year after year. Here's another plus: Electronic returns are about 10 times more accurate than handwritten paper returns, according to the IRS, because the computer does the calculating for you. File electronically through online tax return services or tax preparation software, or ask a tax preparer to file electronically for you.

 Shortcuts to Wealth

Books such as *The Millionaire Next Door,* by Thomas J. Stanley and William D. Danko, have debunked the myth that wealth is always generated by high-powered investments or convoluted real estate deals. Most millionaires get rich by spending conservatively and saving aggressively. Here are five short-cuts to high net worth.

Save as much as possible. Start a monthly savings plan and stick to it faithfully.

Pay off credit cards every month. Even in the strongest bull market, it's tough to find an investment that earns as much as you pay out each month for interest on credit card balances.

Defer taxes. Contribute as much as you can afford to tax-deferred savings plans such as 401(k) plans and individual retirement accounts (IRAs).

Own your home and other property. Don't rent or lease. Most wealth is built in fixed assets such as real estate.

Buy only what you need. It may not be as much fun as *Lifestyles of the Rich and Famous,* but living simply is how most millionaires make a mint.

The Simplest Way to Play the Market

Those personal finance magazines that promise "10 Best Mutual Funds for the New Year" rarely mention one of the simplest and most effective fund strategies: Stick with index funds. Index funds are mutual funds that don't try to beat the market. Rather, they buy the stocks of one of the major market indexes, usually the Standard & Poor's (S&P) 500, and try to match that performance. Boring, yes, but effective. During the bull market of the 1990s, such index funds outperformed more than 90 percent of actively managed mutual funds. The core reason is simple: Index funds are much cheaper to manage than actively managed funds, and the mutual fund companies pass the savings on to their investors. So instead of moving money from one fad fund to another, stick to an index fund and save hassle and money.

COPING WITH COMPUTERS

Easy Keyboard Cleaning

Loose bits of food, hair, and pencil shavings that fall between the keys can cause your computer keyboard to begn wrtng lke ths. To eliminate frustrating jams, buy a can of compressed air at a computer or photo supply store and use it frequently to clean your keyboard. Disconnect the keyboard from the computer, hold it upside down, aim the can's nozzle between the keys, and spray air into the keyboard, working your way up and down the rows. (Never turn a can of compressed air upside down, or it could spray freezing propellant into your keyboard.) If a particular key isn't working, pop it off with a screwdriver, spray around the area or wipe it with a cotton swab, and snap the key back into place. To keep your keyboard functioning smoothly, never eat or drink near your computer. If you can't resist, keep a dish towel or paper towel nearby to spread over the keyboard while you enjoy your desk-side picnic.

Control Cables with a Twist

Once you set up that home computer, you'll have to contend with all those cords and cables snaking all over the place.

They're unsightly and could be a tripping hazard. You could go to the computer shop and buy those expensive cord tubes, but who has time for that? Instead, just reach for that box of plastic trash bags and grab a few twist ties out of the box. They're great for wrapping around coils of long wires to prevent tangles. Join two or three ties together to make extra-long ones, if needed. Also use twist ties to secure cables and power cords to the leg of a table, which will eliminate the possibility of folks tripping over those cords.

Keep a Clean Mouse

When a mechanical mouse—the kind with the little rubber ball that rolls around underneath—gets gunked up with grime,

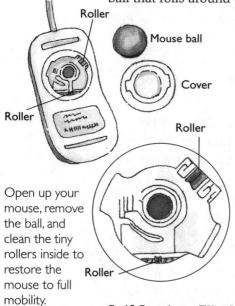

Roller

Mouse ball

Cover

Roller

Roller

Open up your mouse, remove the ball, and clean the tiny rollers inside to restore the mouse to full mobility.

it doesn't work well. But there's no need to endure the frustration of erratic mouse function and no need to buy a new mouse. Just take a few minutes to clean the mouse ball. Unplug the mouse and twist off the plastic lid that holds the ball in place. Remove the ball and wipe it off with a dampened cloth or premoistened towelette. Clean the tiny rollers inside the mouse, against which the ball rotates, with a toothpick and rubbing alcohol. Finish the job with a blast of compressed air. Reassemble, and the mouse should respond perfectly to your touch.

Self-Sorting File Names

Ralph Erenzo of Gardiner, New York, juggles several small businesses on his home computer. To keep all his electronic files straight, he has learned to name each document systematically. Ralph starts the name of a document with the date, but instead of typing it as month-date-year (mm-dd-yy), as most people would, he types year-month-date (yy-mm-dd). The result is that his computer always lists his documents in exact chronological order. To complete the name of a file,

Balky Computers

Problem:

A personal computer acts strangely or freezes up.

Do This Now:

Restart the computer. Computers have built-in diagnostic and repair functions that go to work every time you start them up. Often this is all it takes to solve a problem.

Do This for Good:

Learn the simple steps to maintain a personal computer.

1. Install a utilities program, such as the Norton series, and set it up to inspect and repair your hard drive automatically at least once a month.

2. Install an antivirus program on your computer and maintain it with updates, which your program can download automatically from the Internet.

3. Clean out unused files and software programs periodically.

4. Learn to dump the cache for your Internet browser. The cache stores Web pages and photos to help frequently used Web sites load faster on your computer, but it's a big memory hog. Look at the Preferences or Options section of your browser to find the controls for the cache.

Ralph follows the date with a word that describes the document, such as *letter* or *invoice*. For example, Ralph would name a letter written June 22, 2003, to the soda pop supplier for his country store as 03-06-22.letter. An invoice dated July 10, 2003, would be named "03-07-10.invoice." He stores his files in folders according to the vendor or the name of the particular business. "It doesn't seem complicated till you try to describe it," says Ralph. "I do it automatically, and it's extremely helpful."

Respect Those Error Messages

When your computer develops a problem, it may require hours on the phone with a technical support person or an expensive visit to a computer shop to find the solution. But you can cut the time and cost of such repairs dramatically by taking careful notes about the problem before you call a tech-

10 Timesaving Keyboard Shortcuts

Many casual computer users always wield the mouse to operate their computers. But experts use keyboard commands that are much quicker and easier on the hands and wrists.

Key commands speed common tasks such as printing and cutting and pasting text. These commands work with most software, and, amazingly for the computer industry, they are the same for PCs and Macs.

Here are the 10 most useful key commands for everyday computer usage. (With Macs, press the Apple instead of the CTRL key in the combinations.)

Keyboard Combination	Command
CTRL + S	Save.
CTRL + O	Open existing document.
CTRL + N	Create new document.
CTRL + P	Print.
CTRL + A	Select (highlight) everything in a document.
CTRL + C	Copy selected items.
CTRL + X	Cut selected items to move them.
CTRL + V	Paste selected item that you just cut or copied in a new location.
CTRL + Z	Undo previous action.
CTRL + Home	Go to top of the page.

• •

nician. It's especially important to write down any error messages or symbols that appear on your screen, along with the circumstances that led up to the message. These clues inevitably lead to a much speedier repair job.

Preserve Precious Packaging

Packing and shipping a computer or monitor for repair is time-consuming and risks further damage to the equipment—unless you saved the boxes and packing material your equipment came in. If you have the storage space, always save these specially designed boxes, at least until the equipment's warranty expires.

Backing Up Simplified

Mention backing up data to many home computer users, and images of room-size machines with whirring tape drives come to mind. But backing up essential data is easy if your computer has a compact disc (CD) writer. A single CD will hold all of the word processing documents, spreadsheets, e-mail messages, and addresses on the average computer. The key to simple, speedy backups is to organize your data files so that they all are contained in a single folder. (Both PC and Macintosh systems allow you to create a single folder called My Documents or Documents.) Don't worry about your software applications—they're too large and complicated to back up, and if your computer suffers a major crash, you should reinstall the software anyway. Just copy and "burn" your documents folder onto a CD every few weeks or months, depending on how often you create new documents.

When E-Mail Is Not the Right Call

E-mail can be a great time-saver, but there are times when the telephone or an old-fashioned letter is still the best way to communicate. For example, when you need an answer right away, use the phone. Making a phone call is also the right choice when you're not sure what you're looking for. No matter how well it's designed, a Web site can't anticipate your needs or react to your questions as well as a live person can. The other time to avoid e-mail is when you're dealing with a touchy subject. E-mail is abrupt; the recipient can't hear the inflection in your voice. E-mail messages also tend to be banged out without enough thought, and misunderstandings are all too common. Use the phone or carefully craft a letter to break bad news or explain a delicate problem.

Create a Password Cheat Sheet

It would be great if you could use the same password at every Web site you visit, but that's not the way it works. If you have trouble remembering all your passwords, make a list of them and keep the list in a low-profile place in your home office. Such a list will save you endless time and frustration on seldom-visited Web sites, and there's little security risk in your home.

Block That Spam!

Spam is junk e-mail sent by companies that "harvest" e-mail addresses by the thousands from the Internet and send out their obtrusive—and often offensive—promotions. Wading through the spam in your e-mail in box wastes valuable time—especially if you pay for online service by the hour. Here are some tips from efficiency expert Lori MacDonald of Cumberland Foreside, Maine, to help you minimize spam.

- Don't give your e-mail address to anyone you don't know.
- Open a second e-mail account at a free provider such as Hotmail (www.hotmail.com). "I keep this account for when I need to give my e-mail address in order to sign up for a freebie," Lori explains.
- Never reply to spam, even if it's only to remove your name or opt out of future offers. If you do, the spammers will collect your e-mail information and resell it. Instead, delete spam immediately.
- Use the filtering functions of your e-mail program to block unwanted mail. Most of them can be set, for example, to delete any message from an address that's not in your address book or to place such messages in a junk mail folder. "I breeze through the junk mail once every few days, and after taking care of a few that need my attention, I can usually delete the rest by pressing one button," Lori says.
- Forward offensive spam to your Internet service provider, which can attempt to block any future e-mails from that source.

Speed the Search

Computer search engines are great tools for looking up just about anything. But they can be frustrating, too. Each search site uses keywords and codes differently, so one way to save time is to stick with one search engine. You'll become more efficient if you learn one system really well. Keep in mind that being precise in your choice of search words can help. If you're looking for information on insects that attack fruit trees, for example, try searching under "preventing insect damage in fruit trees" instead of just "tree pests." But don't go overboard. If you try something too specific, such as "flat-headed apple tree borers in Vermont," you may miss a broader reference that could be helpful. Also, vary your search words. For example, if "automobile" isn't yielding what you want, try "automobiles" or "cars." If "U.S." isn't working, try "United States." If "bicycle" isn't working, try "bicycling."

Filling Out Forms Automatically

If you fill out lots of forms on Web sites, check to see whether your Internet browser has a function that will automatically complete your name, address, and other vital information when you start typing a form.

Printing in Black Pays Off

Color printers and copiers are cheap to buy but expensive and slow to operate. For cheaper, speedier printing, choose black-and-white printing unless you really need something in color. With most printer software, you can easily set your printer to use only black ink unless you specifically need color. Also, set your printer's default settings to draft mode, which triggers the printer to print in lighter tones, thus conserving ink.

This Side Up

Can't remember which way is up for printing letterhead? Tape a sample of your letterhead in the correct orientation by your printer. You'll never get it wrong again.

 FIX IT FAST • FIX IT FOREVER

E-Mail Out of Control

Problem:
Your computer is full of old e-mail messages.

Do This Now:
Set your e-mail program's Options or Preferences to save the messages you receive for 1 week or 1 month, then delete them automatically. This will reduce the contents of your e-mail in box by one-half.

Do This for Good:
To manage incoming messages, create e-mail folders organized by subject. For example, you might set up folders for Family Correspondence, Investment Club, and Church Newsletter. After you read each new message, either delete it immediately or move it into a folder. Your main in box should be empty at the end of each e-mail session.

Make Your Own Letterhead

Most word processing programs allow you to create and save templates for frequently used documents, such as letterhead or invoices. Create a look you like and save it for all your letters.

Paper-Saving Printing

When you're printing documents for your own archives, save paper by printing two to four pages on one sheet of paper, advises database manager Jo Johnson of Boulder, Colorado. "I check a box in my printer software before printing and it prints every other page, then prompts me how and when to put sheets back in to print the other pages, so I get perfect two-sided pages," she explains. "I can also print two pages on the same side. Printing two pages to a side saves paper and is less to store. If it needs to look nice, I print on both sides."

Worth the Price

A handheld electronic organizer may seem like an expensive toy, but here's one great reason to own one: If you lose your electronic organizer but have backed up the same address information on your computer, replacing those lost addresses is a 10-minute exercise. However, if you lose your plain-paper address book or personal organizer, how long will it take to replace all of the lost information? Days? Weeks?

The Second Time Around

Scrap Paper with a Purpose

Put an empty office paper box near your printer and use it to hold paper from those botched printing jobs. Turned over, this paper can be used for draft and file copies. If you do a lot of printing on scrap paper, it may be worth buying a second paper tray for your printer. Keep one loaded with scrap paper and the other with the good stuff.

Just Fax It!

Once you decide to buy a home fax machine, you'll be amazed how much you use it. Fax machines are cheap—many sell for less than $100—and faxing documents can eliminate time-consuming trips to schools, accountants, doctors, and the like to pick up or deliver documents. Faxing also saves mailing time and postage.

Bathrooms and Laundry Room

12

Bathrooms and laundry rooms are all about keeping things clean and orderly—your body, your medical supplies and toiletries, and your clothes. Swabbing out the bathtub, fixing a clogged drain, and ironing your shirts may not be your favorite tasks. All the better, then, that you're armed with this collection of shortcuts.

CLEANING THE BATHROOM

Wax Your Bathtub

Think of your bathtub as an inside-out car, and you'll understand why Lyle Jones, the owner of American Porcelain and Fiberglass in Richmond, Virginia, likes to put a finish of car wax on the inside of his tub. Dirt just rolls off the waxed sides of Lyle's tub and down the drain, leaving him with a minimal cleanup job. Any car wax can be used to reduce bathroom-cleaning chores, says Lyle. And car wax works not only on bathtubs but also on sinks, shower walls, kitchen appliances, and patio furniture. (One important warning about the tub: Don't wax the bottom—that would be too slippery.)

Applying a paste car wax and buffing to a shine requires more elbow grease than applying a spray wax, but a paste wax finish lasts twice as long, Lyle says. To clean your waxed bathtub, use a gentle dishwashing liquid mixed with water or, of course, a car-washing detergent. Avoid strong household cleaners, which will destroy the wax finish.

Wipe Out Deposits in Advance

That milky, smudgy film covering your shower stall is known as hard-water deposit, and cleaning it is one of the most daunting tasks in the bathroom. Why not just nip it in the bud? Jo Benwell, a former food and nutrition lecturer at Farnham College in Surrey, England, wipes the excess water off the shower wall after every use to prevent this crusty buildup. A small bathroom squeegee will do the job in seconds. An alternative: Just give the walls a quick wipe with the same bath towel you used to dry your body.

Spray It Away

Another way to banish hard-water deposit from your shower is to keep a bottle of Clean Shower spray in the stall, says Natalie Salatto, sales supervisor at Emerson Supply in Guilford, Connecticut. This product works well on grime, hard-water deposit, and mildew. After each shower, spray a little Clean Shower on the walls and let it stay there—no wiping. The next time you take a shower, all that crud will disappear down the drain.

Prevent Buildup with Baby Oil

Here's another easy way to prevent the buildup of hard-water deposit on your shower door. Apply a thin coating of baby oil or mineral oil to the inside of the door every couple of weeks, says Judy Brown, an organizing consultant in Yale, British Columbia. The water will roll right off and never leave a residue.

A Cleaner Curtain without Scrubbing

Don't waste your time squirting and scrubbing a filmy shower curtain. Just pull it down off its rings and toss it in the washer with a few towels, which will do the scrubbing for you. Stop the washer before the spin cycle and hang the curtain back in place to drip-dry.

Go Soft on That Shower Curtain

Look in your laundry room to find a fabulous shower curtain cleaner, says Judy Brown. Fabric softener will clean up soap residue in a jiffy. Dab some liquid fabric softener on a cleaning cloth and wipe down your plastic or vinyl shower curtain. Or put a couple of teaspoons of fabric softener in a spray bottle and fill the bottle with warm water. Squirt the shower curtain all over with the solution and wipe. Rinse with the shower hose. If you don't have a shower hose, remove the curtain from the rod and take it outside—you can use your garden hose to rinse it. Still another alternative: Use fabric softener sheets to attack that soap scum. Just dampen a sheet, wipe the curtain, and rinse. This also works well on shower doors. It even works with sheets you've already used in the dryer.

3 Low-Cost Toilet Bowl Cleaners

Why should you spend good money on a toilet bowl cleaner? It's expensive, and there's only one place in the house where you can use it. Dr. Sarah Kirby, associate professor of family and consumer sciences at North Carolina State University in Raleigh, offers three ways to clean toilets using common household materials. You can whip up these solutions in seconds—for mere pennies.

Lemon juice and borax. Combine lemon juice and borax until the mixture is about the consistency of toothpaste. Flush the toilet to get the sides wet. Rub the paste into the ring around your toilet bowl and let it sit for 2 hours, then scrub with a toilet brush.

Baking soda and vinegar. Sprinkle some baking soda in the toilet, pour in some vinegar, and scrub with a toilet brush.

Bleach. Pour ½ cup chlorine bleach into the toilet. Let it sit for up to 45 minutes, then scrub with a toilet brush. (*Caution:* For safety, never mix bleach with vinegar, toilet bowl cleaner, or ammonia.)

4 Clever Remodeling Hints

It's not every day that you have the luxury of tearing out your old bathroom and building a new one. But if you ever do, some clever design touches will save you a lot of time and aggravation.

Double up. Install his-and-her showerheads with separate controls, suggests Natalie Salatto, sales supervisor at Emerson Supply in Guilford, Connecticut. You and your spouse will be able to get through your hectic morning routines with no waiting.

Counter intelligence. Likewise, his-and-her vanities will let you and your spouse come and go as you please, without bumping heads, says Tim Koehler, president of Koehler Kitchen & Bath in Greensboro, North Carolina.

Hear ye, hear ye. Include a radio or mini-TV in your new bathroom, and you'll be briefed on the day's news before you even get your clothes on.

Close for comfort. Position your water heater as close to the bathroom as possible, suggests Tim Koehler. The shorter your hot-water line is, the less water—and time—you'll waste as you wait for the hot stuff to arrive.

Get Militant with Mildew

Mildew is tenacious, moisture-loving stuff, especially in the shower, where it flourishes in the grout, in the corners around the tub, or on the shower curtain. When you have to fight mildew, try the favorite weapon of Barbara Webster, president of Nice N Clean Maid Service in Miami: chlorine bleach mixed with water. Combine the ingredients in a bottle with an adjustable spray. When you apply this cleaning solution, use the direct spray (rather than the fan-shaped spray), because chlorine bleach is caustic stuff and you want to be sure you know exactly where it's going. The concentration of bleach you need depends on how heavy the mildew is. For general cleaning, 2 tablespoons of bleach per 1 gallon of water ought to do it. For tougher jobs, increase the amount of bleach to as much as 1/2 cup.

Caution: Never use more than one cleaner at a time. Mixing chlorine bleach and ammonia creates a deadly gas.

Rub the Mar Out of the Marble

Scratched that marble counter in your bathroom? Not to worry. Just pop open the medicine cabinet and pull out your denture cream toothpaste. This mild abrasive will smooth out little scratches in marble and make them invisible. Squirt some onto a dry rag or an old toothbrush and rub it into the scratched area. Then wipe up the paste thoroughly with a damp sponge.

Rout That Grungy Grout

It doesn't take long: Just a few weeks of neglect can transform your bathroom's cement tile grout from a sparkling white grid into a dingy mess of hard-water deposit and mildew. To tackle these tough problems, pull out the big guns. Start with orange oil or lemon oil cleaner, which you can buy at dollar stores, hardware stores, and home stores, says Anthony LoGiurato, owner of Anthony the Tileman in Upper Darby, Pennsylvania. Spray the cleaner on, let it sit for 2 minutes, and then wipe it off with a rag or sponge. (If you let it sit too long, it will dry out, and you'll have to start all over again.) An alternative: Dip a sponge into a bowl of white vinegar and give the tile a scrubbing.

Want yet another technique? Denture cream toothpaste (assuming you still have some left after rubbing that scratch out of your marble counter) will have the extra bite you need. Squirt a bit of this mild abrasive onto your sponge and scrub. Denture cream toothpaste is quite sticky, so be sure to rinse thoroughly. Otherwise, it will attract dirt. Avoid the temptation to use a Brillo pad, since that could dig into the grout.

Clear Out Bathroom Clutter

Being a practical person, you hate throwing out perfectly useful items. There's a downside to that admirable quality though: This unconscious accumulation of stuff creates clutter and

The Second Time Around

Keep Backup Bags

Plastic grocery bags make perfect liners for those little wastebaskets that people put in the bathroom. Keep a few stashed in the cabinet under the sink so you won't have to go searching for a new liner when you notice that the basket is full.

stress. One key to stopping this runaway clutter is to be intentional about every item you keep. For each item, ask yourself, "Should I have this? Do I need it?" Get into the "good steward" habit—pass along items you don't need to friends, nonprofit organizations, or charities. The local animal shelter, for instance, would probably love a stack of old towels to use for bedding or washing. And that 20-year collection of hotel soaps would be welcome in a homeless shelter. If nothing else, hold a yard sale and price your extraneous goods so low that they're sure to find a new home. You'll spend less time hunting through the clutter for the items you really need day in and day out.

Have Your Reading Ready

You may be accustomed to reading while you're, well, on the throne. Rather than wandering around the house looking for something to read every time nature calls, keep a small book in a convenient drawer of the bathroom and reserve it for bathroom reading only.

The Oreo Organizer

Vanity drawers in the bathroom typically become a jumble of free samples, contact lens equipment, nail tools, and bottles of shampoo. There's no need to spend 10 minutes pawing through this clutter every time you need to find an emery board or nail clippers, says organizing consultant Judy Brown of Yale, British Columbia. The solution lies just down the hall in your kitchen. Many brands of packaged cookies come protected in a rigid plastic casing with three or more compartments. After you finish the cookies, wash and dry the casing and slide it into your vanity drawer: instant organizer! What's more, if your organizer gets grungy after several months, just toss it in the trash and procure a new one from the cookie shelf.

MANAGING THE MEDICINE SHELF
A Is for Aspirin, B Is for Benadryl

A cluttered medicine shelf is a waste of time and materials. (How many times have you bought a new tube of antibiotic ointment because you had no idea what happened to the last one?) To de-clutter a medicine cabinet, start by weeding out unneeded items. Sort through the bottles, tubes, and boxes and flush down the toilet any medicine that has passed its expiration date, has changed color, smells funny, or is missing its label. Alphabetize all medicines and swear a solemn oath to put them back in their proper places. (Other family members will need a little schooling in this.) Write the name of each family member on a resealable plastic bag and put personal medicines in the appropriate bags. Store the bags in a small box in a closet near the bathroom.

Even Pill Bottles Prefer a Dry Climate

Sure, they call that box behind the mirror in your bathroom a medicine cabinet, but that doesn't mean you have to store your medicines there. In fact, says John Beckna, director of Ukrop's Pharmacy in Richmond, Virginia, your medicines will last longer if you store them away from the heat and humidity of your bathroom. That hall closet just around the corner is a good location—on a high shelf preferably, out of the reach of kids. With your medicines staying potent longer, you'll prevent some of those expensive trips to the pharmacy. To make the best use of the newly opened space in your medicine cabinet, pluck the four or five most-used items out of that junky vanity drawer (dental floss, cotton swabs, tweezers, nail clippers, and contact lens case, for instance) and give them the prime real estate behind the mirror.

First Aid to Go

Keep first aid items in a lidded plastic box on your medicine shelf, suggests Lillian Martin, school nurse at All Saints' Episcopal School in Vicksburg, Mississippi. This would include bandages, medical tape, 4-by-4-inch gauze pads, cotton balls, hydrocortisone cream, and insect bite swabs. No more hunting around the house when you need these items fast. In an emergency, or when you're headed out the door on a trip, you can just grab the box and go.

The Kitchen Medicine Cabinet

Keep a container of often used medicines in a Tupperware container right in the kitchen, says Donnica Moore, M.D., a women's health expert based in Neshanic Station, New Jersey. The kitchen is the most frequented living area in a home, so it's likely to be a convenient place for treating children's boo-boos and meeting other medical needs. Also, many medicines are supposed to be taken with food, so why not store them next to the Cheerios? Be sure to put the container on a shelf out of the reach of kids and away from the stove. In her own mini first aid station, Dr. Moore keeps cough and cold medicines, acetaminophen, ibuprofen, adhesive bandages, hydrocortisone cream, tweezers for removing splinters, burn medicine, and vitamins. She keeps a duplicate cache upstairs for quick access, too.

Clean the Cleaning Tools

You probably switch to a new toothbrush every 6 months, using the freebie from your dentist. But toothbrushes, as well as the cup you rinse your mouth with in the bathroom, can become germ-laden much more quickly than that, especially if you've had a cold. The simple solution? Toss your toothbrush and cup into the dishwasher every once in a while to sanitize them, says organizing consultant Judy Brown of Yale, British Columbia.

The Bathroom Spoon

Having a spoon in the bathroom is useful for taking some medicines. Rather than traipsing to the kitchen every time you need one or losing your spoon in one of the vanity drawers, just hang a spoon in an unused slot of your toothbrush holder.

TAKING CARE OF CAULK
Beginners, Start Small

If you're new to the caulking game, rest assured that you'll have innumerable opportunities to make a big mess. One easy way to keep that mess to a minimum is to be cautious when you snip the tip of the caulk cylinder. You see, caulk comes in a plastic cylinder, which is set into a metal caulking gun, a device with a trigger handle that you squeeze to drive the caulk out of the pointed tip of the cylinder. You open up a new cylinder of caulk by clipping off part of this pointed tip. Expert tile installer Anthony LoGiurato of Upper Darby, Pennsylvania, advises beginners to snip near the tip, so that only a very fine bead of caulk flows out when you apply pressure with the trigger handle. This will give you better control. And remember, if the bead is coming out too small, you can always reclip the tip to make it larger—but you can't make a large bead smaller again.

Use the Vinegar Treatment

Anthony LoGiurato knows the secret of a long-lasting grouting or caulking job. It all depends on how well you prepare the surface before you apply the grout or caulk—it has to be clean, clean, clean. Anthony's cleaning secret is white vinegar. Dampen a cloth with vinegar and wipe it all over the tiles and gaps where the grout or caulk will be applied. Let it dry thoroughly before proceeding. With properly prepared surfaces, your job will last years longer.

Turn Up the Heat

Water will dilute and weaken caulk and grout, says Anthony LoGiurato. So it's very important that all surfaces you plan to caulk or grout be perfectly dry before you do the job. Anthony uses a blow dryer to thoroughly dry the area

The Second Time Around

Caulking Precaution: Bag It

Unfortunately, the caulk in your bathroom is not a permanent thing—it needs to be redone every 2 years or so, says John Alldredge, senior technical service manager for Custom Building Products in Seal Beach, California. If you're going to have to haul out the caulking gun that often, it pays to learn how to use it with a minimum of mess. The basic technique calls for you to squirt out a bead of caulk along the gap that you're sealing, press the caulk into the gap by running your finger along it, and then wipe up the excess with a damp sponge. Of course, this leaves you with some pretty messy and sticky fingers. To solve this problem, put your finger inside a plastic grocery bag and use that to press on the bead of caulk. Bonus: The plastic leaves a nice, smooth finish on the caulk. When you're done, toss the bag in the trash and give yourself a little applause—you've saved yourself a tough hand-cleaning job.

for about 5 minutes. This not only dries the surfaces but also heats them up. When you apply the caulk or grout, it will melt and become sticky, making it adhere amazingly well, which means that your work will last longer, too.

Tape to the Rescue

As careful as you may be, caulking can sometimes turn into a smeary mess along the joint you're trying to seal, especially if the caulk slops over into nearby tile grout. So take a tip from painters, suggests John Alldredge, senior technical service manager for Custom Building Products in Seal Beach, California. Edge the joint you're caulking with blue, low-tack painter's tape, then apply the bead of caulk and press it in place. Inevitably, some of the caulk will smear onto the tape. No problem—just pull up the tape when the job is done, leaving a nice straight line of caulk. (Avoid using regular masking tape for this. Masking tape can pull up paint and wallpaper.)

The Caulk Screw Shortcut

Old, half-full cylinders of caulk present a quandary. It's a shame to throw out so much usable caulk, but inevitably the caulk left in the nozzle has solidified into a hard plug. What to do? Make like a wine connoisseur. First, clip off a little more of the plastic tip. Then find a long, thin screw with a wide thread (drywall screws are great for this). Drive the screw into the opening of the nozzle, through the hardened caulk. Pull out the screw (use pliers if necessary), and the dried-up caulk will come with it. You've saved yourself some pocket money, plus a trip to the hardware store for new caulk.

Nail Your Caulk Closed

As fun as it is to open up an old container of caulk like a wine bottle, save yourself the bother in the future. The next time you store a partially used cylinder of caulk, push a nail down into the nozzle and then cover the tip with plastic wrap, secured with a rubber band or twist tie. Your caulk will be fresh and flowing whenever you need it.

KIDS IN THE BATHROOM

Wipe One Cleaning Chore off Your List

Baby wipes are terrific bathroom-cleaning tools that are easy for kids to use, says organizing consultant Judy Brown of Yale, British Columbia. For example, let children use them to shine the bathroom tap. (When the wipes are all gone, the plastic boxes they come in make great storage containers.)

Pocket the Tub Toys

Keep toys under control by storing them in an over-the-door shoe holder hung above the tub. You can suspend it from a towel rack or use suction-cup hangers. The pockets are ideal for holding kids' bath toys. Poke a hole in the bottom of each pocket for drainage.

Tub toys fit fine in the pockets of a plastic shoe holder.

Containing the Storm Waters

When an older child gets done in the shower, the bathroom floor typically looks like a scene from *The Perfect Storm*. Keeping the shower water in the tub is a simple matter, says organizing consultant Judy Brown of Yale, British Columbia. Buy Velcro strips with sticky backing at your local home store. Stick three or four pieces on the bottom of the shower curtain, then stick their companion halves on the inside wall of the tub. Ask your children to make sure each piece of Velcro is in place before the next storm rages.

Cast a Net for Those Toys

Bath toys can clutter up a bathroom fast. A mesh bag (the type that onions come in) can solve the problem, freeing up precious bathroom space while making the bath toys available to the little tykes, says Judy Brown. Thread yarn, twine, or some old shoelaces through each little hole surrounding the opening, creating a drawstring. Make sure you leave enough excess string for hanging the bag from the showerhead or shower door. With all the bath toys in the bag, youngsters can get their own toys out and pick up after themselves at the end of rub-a-dub-dub time. Since the wet toys will drip right down into the tub, there's no mess for you to mop up later.

BATHROOM REPAIRS

A Closet Auger Conquers Clogs

Chances are, you already own and know how to use a toilet plunger. But what happens when your toilet is *really* clogged—no matter how many times you pump the plunger up and down? You could call a plumber, who will fix it in 2 minutes—and hand you a whopper of a bill. Or you can buy a handy little device called a closet auger, which is available in hardware stores and plumbing supply shops. A closet auger, also known as a toilet auger, will pay for itself the first time you need it, says Chuck Schoen, owner of 24-7 Plumbing in Tucson. The auger has a long handle that reaches down into the toilet, plus a spiral cable that reaches farther down into the drain. When you turn a crank on the handle, the cable bores into the blockage and pulls it free. If a hard object is creating the blockage (you'll hear it rattling around down there), you'll probably need to call a plumber to remove the toilet and pull it out. (We know one plumber who recovered a set of false teeth for an embarrassed customer.)

Give It the Hose Treatment

You've tried all the tools at your disposal—a plumber's helper, even an auger—and still that tub drain is clogged. Ready to call the plumber? Try one more tool—your garden hose. Remove the drain cover and insert a hose as far as it will go. Pack rags into the drain around the hose to create a seal. Press down on the rags to keep the pressure from dislodging them and have an assistant turn the water on (full blast) and off several times. The pressure will shove the blockage out of the way.

Note: Don't try a technique like this if someone has poured caustic drain-opening chemicals into the pipe.

Plumbing Worries Down the Drain

A sluggish bathtub drain can make your heart rate soar as visions of plumber's bills dance in your head. Reduce your anxiety by keeping those drains wide-open with a simple monthly routine. First pour ½ cup baking soda down the drain. Follow that with ½ cup white vinegar. Let the mixture bubble away for a while, then flush with cold water.

Showerhead Stopped Up? Sleep on It

Is your showerhead stopped up with hard-water deposit? Fix it the no-muss, no-fuss way. After the last shower of the evening, unscrew the showerhead from the pipe and set it in a bowl of white vinegar. When you get up in the morning, you'll have a like-new showerhead ready for action. (If you can't get the showerhead off, just fill a plastic bag with vinegar, pull the bag over the showerhead until it's submerged, and secure the bag in place with rubber bands.)

Give Your Toilet the Color Test

A leaky toilet can allow 5 to 10 gallons of fresh water to escape down the drain in just 1 hour, which is an environmental shame as well as a blow to your pocketbook. Checking for a toilet leak is easy, says Judy Brown, an organizing consultant in Yale, British Columbia. Put a few drops of food coloring into the tank at the back of the toilet and let the toilet stand without flushing for 15 minutes. If the water in the toilet bowl ends up colored, you have a leak that needs to be repaired right away. (The most common source of a toilet leak, by the way, is a worn flapper valve.)

LAUNDRY LOGISTICS
Put Your Clothes in a Lineup

Your mother told you decades ago that laundry has to be sorted into distinct piles—darks, colors, lights, and whites. The problem is, many clothes do not fit neatly into any category. What do you do with a white rugby shirt with navy blue sleeves, for instance? The solution is to sort your clothes in a continuum instead of into piles. Sort them in a line across the laundry room floor: clothes that are overall the darkest go at one end, and clothes that are overall the lightest go at the other end. Just promise yourself that you won't fret over how to categorize them—the mental agony isn't worth it. No piece of clothing gets more than a split second's thought. When you're ready to load the clothes washer, grab up everything from one end of the line until the washer is full.

Note: You'll probably need to wash your true whites separately. (Turn to "Keeping Up with the Laundry" on page 35 for more shameless ideas for minimizing the chore of sorting the wash.)

Glycerin Beats Ink

It's one of the most frightful stains in the laundry room: ballpoint pen ink, smeared across a shirtsleeve. Your best bet: Pour a few drops of glycerin (available in drugstores) onto the stain, rub it in with a clean cloth, then launder as usual.

Freezin' and Heatin' Beats Wax

Candle wax stains typically appear on a tablecloth, of course, but they're not unheard-of on shirtsleeves or other garments.

It's horrifying to see the wax seep into the fabric and solidify. But picking and scraping at the goo will take forever and could damage the fabric. There's a quicker, surefire way to remove the wax. If the fabric is washable, you'll beat that drippy mess with extreme temperatures, says Dr. Herb Barndt, an expert on stain removal at Philadelphia University in Philadelphia, Pennsylvania. First, throw the garment into the freezer (no kidding), and put a kettle of water on to boil. When the wax on your garment has turned brittle, take the garment out of the freezer. Most of the wax will snap right off. Then stretch the wax-marred area of fabric over a bowl and pour boiling water through the spot. The remaining wax will flush right out. If there's any remaining stain from the wax, treat the spot with chlorine bleach (if appropriate) and wash the garment as usual.

No Sense Wining about It

Red wine dribbled on your white shirt—groan! There's no need to leave the party or restaurant to seek a change of clothes. Just grab that bottle of club soda behind the bar and retire to the restroom for a minute. Splash a bit of the club soda onto the stain and blot it up with a towel. Spend a couple of minutes in front of a hair dryer or hand dryer, and you're good as new. White vinegar also will do the job.

Lend Those Greasy Pants a Hand

Grease spots on your clothing can easily turn into a permanent fixture if the stain isn't treated quickly. Judy Brown takes a tip from gardeners and mechanics to rout grease stains from clothing. Her secret is a waterless hand cleaner, such as Citra-Scrub, which is sold in automotive stores. To treat a grease stain, remove some of the waterless cleaner from the container with your fingers and rub it into the

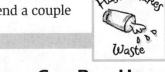

Haste Makes Waste

Sneakers Can Run Up a Repair Bill

Your sneakers get caked with mud, so—no problem—you toss them into the washer and then the dryer. Well, you may actually *cause* a problem, warns Ruben Masas, manager of Maid of Honor cleaning service in Fort Lauderdale. Sneakers in a dryer often take violent bounces, which can break the dryer's heating element. Better to give your sneaks a day to dry outside, near a radiator, or near a heating vent.

fabric. Then toss the garment right in the wash. (Don't let it sit, because the cleaner could damage the fabric.)

Baking Soda Kills Smoking Odors

You had a delightful night on the town, but now your jacket smells like a half-smoked Cuban cigar. Sure, you could drive to the dry cleaner's, pay several dollars, and lose the use of your jacket for several days. But there's a simpler way to freshen up that jacket. Hang it inside a heavy plastic bag and put an open box of baking soda in the bottom—just as you would do to kill odors in your refrigerator—suggests Dr. Herb Barndt of Philadelphia University in Philadelphia, Pennsylvania. In a day or two, your jacket should be smoke-free and ready for action again.

Use Your Dryer for Dust Removal

Curtains don't collect dirt and grime the way carpets do, but curtains do gather dust. You may be able to wash your curtains, or they may have to go to the dry cleaner—neither of which is high on anyone's list of fun things to do. But chances are, those curtains don't need laundering at all. Just take them down, pop them in the dryer, and set the dryer on air. Your dryer will dust them off like one big vacuum cleaner.

Delightfully De-Linted

To get rid of lint in your clothes, wash them the way you regularly do but add ½ cup white vinegar to the rinse cycle. (*Caution:* Never combine vinegar and chlorine bleach.)

With Dryers, Less Is More

Tumbling your clothing in the dryer until it's bone-dry actually damages the fabric. So when you throw a load in the dryer, use the less dry setting regularly and hang up your clothes to finish drying in the open air. Your

The Second Time Around

A New Use for Orphaned Socks

When socks become irretrievably separated from their mates despite your best efforts, put the orphans to good use. Make a nifty cleaning tool for those hard-to-reach places by slipping an orphan sock over the end of a yardstick and securing it with a rubber band. Use it to dust under your stove and refrigerator and to reach those high corners where the spiders are holding a convention.

clothes will last longer, they'll have fewer wrinkles, you'll get through laundry cycles more quickly, and your electric bills will be lower.

End the Sock Drawer Jumble

All of us who dress in semidarkness may wear mismatched socks now and then. To avoid this embarrassment, use a simple folding trick to keep all your family's socks properly paired up until the moment they get slipped on. When you're folding the laundry, hold two properly paired socks side by side. Slide your thumbs into the top of one of the socks and turn about 4 inches of the sock inside out, folding it over the top of the second sock. This forms a clever little knot that will keep the socks paired until you're ready to wear them.

My Favorite Shortcut

Don't Hang Wash on Water Pipes

You're down in the basement laundry room, slipping hangers into clean shirts. Now where can you hang them? How about on those handy little copper pipes overhead?

Not so fast, says Ed DuBois, owner of Hire a Hubby in Hartford, Vermont. He's had customers with this brilliant idea who learned the hard way. Adding weight to your home's water pipes can put too much stress on soldered or welded joints, causing them to crack. So buy a laundry rack for your laundry room and leave the pipes to their water-carrying duties.

Get the Little Ones on a Roll

You'll get more help in the laundry room if you devise some kid-friendly tasks, organizing consultant Judy Brown of Yale, British Columbia, suggests. For

Wetter Is Better

Most people think of ironing linen as a dreary chore, says Joseph Dever Larmor, president and managing director of the Ulster Linen Company in New York City. But it's actually a breeze if you get your timing right. The secret is to take your linen out of the dryer or off the clothes line while it's still damp and iron it right away. You'll skate through the task in no time. Use spray starch, if you'd like, and put your iron on a medium (for blends) or high (for pure linen) setting. Iron only until you have the fabric smooth, not totally dry, and then hang it to dry the rest of the way. (Trying to steam-iron dry linen will not produce the same speedy effect. Household irons just can't create enough steam.)

Welcome This Technique into the Fold

It doesn't take long to fold a knit shirt, but if you could fold those shirts faster, the time saved could really add up.

Stand near your folding table (the top of your dryer will do). Grip the knit shirt by the shoulders, hanging it in front of you so you're facing the front of the shirt. Your little fingers should be touching the shoulder seams, your thumbs should be a few inches from the edge of the collar, and your palms should be facing away from you. Now, twist both of your forearms around so that your palms face toward you, folding each side of the shirt vertically. Lower the shirt onto the folding surface until the bottom half of the shirt is lying facedown and you're holding the other half up. Then drop the top half of the shirt into place, collar to shirttail. Practice it a few times, and you'll be able to fold shirts in one quick motion, cutting minutes off the time required to fold a load of wash. The technique works well with T-shirts, sweatshirts, and sweaters, too.

Twist to fold vertically.

Lower to finish folding.

instance, folding towels is a cumbersome chore for some youngsters. But folding towels once lengthwise and then rolling them is a snap for kids. So why not change the way you store towels in the closet? Rolled towels take up less room anyway.

Bored with Folding? Use the Board

If you're looking for a way to speed up your laundry folding, a little mechanized help may be in order. Barbara Zagnoni, education director for Rowenta, a maker of high-end irons, swears by a folding board for zipping the process along and actually making it fun. Barbara's board is made of black vinyl and measures about 24 by 9 inches. It consists of three hinged panels. You lay your garment across the board, flip the panels

230

closed, and presto—the garment is folded neatly and wrinkle-free. If you're trying to get your children involved in the laundry chores, they'll be fighting over who gets to use the folding board first. Barbara bought hers from QVC (www.qvc.com), but they're also available at some mass merchandisers and drugstores. They cost around $15.

Check Your Board's Padding

Good equipment means you can iron faster, says Barbara Zagnoni. Cotton padding under the ironing surface is best, so there is good ventilation for the steam from your iron. Foam padding, she says, disintegrates quickly, so you'll have to waste time and money replacing it. So if your ironing board cover has foam padding, replace it with one with cotton padding. Ironing board covers with cotton padding are available at mass merchandisers for $10 to $15.

Stop That Slippery Zipper

No one appreciates a zipper that slides open all on its own. Sure, you could replace the offending zipper, but doing so is a major sewing project. It's much easier to slow down the zipper's sliding action by spraying on some hair spray. If you have the opposite problem—that is, if your zipper sticks too much—grease the skids with soap.

Who Needs the Static?

Fabric softener sheets are miracle workers even outside the laundry room. Sometimes when you slide out of the car seat or slip off your overcoat, you generate enough static electricity to spark your own personal lightning storm. Your hair takes on a life of its own, and your hose and skirt cling together immodestly. Dispense with

They Had NO Shame

A Customer of Note

Take a tip from the stick-em notes lady. One way to get excellent service out of your dry cleaner is to give the counter attendant as much information as possible on how you have stained your clothes. This helps the dry cleaner decide which method is best for stain removal. One cleaning expert tells of a woman who always brought in her clothes festooned with stick-on notes. She had a note with an arrow pointing to each spot on her garments, plus a complete written history of the stain—what made it, how long it had been on the garment, and what methods she had tried to remove it. The dry cleaner loved receiving this useful information and always gave her great service.

the problem in seconds by wiping a fabric softener sheet over your head and panty hose. Your hair will calm down, and your skirt will hang freely. So the next time you're in the laundry room, slip a couple of those sheets into your purse, and you're good to go.

Winning the Soapbox Derby

Those large cardboard containers that laundry detergent comes in present a vexing disposal problem. Toss one of those monsters into a standard-size trash bin, and there's room for nothing else. And smashing them flat isn't easy—unless you have a pet elephant. But Benedicte Whitworth, a Raleigh, North Carolina, homemaker, has the solution: Don't throw the carton in the trash can; use it *as* a trash can. When a carton is empty, set it in a corner of your laundry room and toss your dryer lint and other trash into it. When the carton is full, tape it closed and place it in your garbage can outside.

Ship It in Lint

If you think of dryer lint as merely a troublesome by-product of the laundry process, think again. Dryer lint is a great packing material, says organizing consultant Judy Brown of Yale, British Columbia. Stuff dryer lint into old bread bags or newspaper bags and use it as padding when you box up items to mail.

Lint-Filled Fire Starters

Another way to use lint is as part of a homemade fire starter for your fireplace or a campfire, suggests Judy Brown. Pack lint into each section of a cardboard (not plastic foam) egg carton. Melt candle stubs and pour the wax over the lint in each section. Allow it to cool completely before handling. When you're building a fire in your home fireplace or outdoors on a camping trip, break off sections of the carton as needed and place them among the kindling. Your fire will start fine every time.

Note: Lint is quite flammable, which is why you should not use it as stuffing in pillows.

Garage and Home Workshop

13

Great tools, handy gadgets, and a bit of organization go a long way toward making every job go more smoothly, whether you enjoy spending time fine-tuning cars in the garage or just using your workshop for essential home repairs. In this chapter, you'll find great shortcuts to speed up all sorts of projects from setup to cleanup. Plus, you'll find ingenious ideas for putting ordinary items such as wire ties, duct tape, and old worn-out hoses to good use, as well as easy, fast ways to organize everything from electric cords to nuts and bolts.

TOOLS AND EQUIPMENT

Great Grippers

Hate having to keep track of nails as you climb up and down a ladder? Worse yet, who hasn't dropped a nail and wasted time on hands and knees searching for it? To make sure nails will be there when you need them, wrap several rubber bands tightly around the end of your hammer, then stick the nails under the rubber bands. They'll stay right where you want them. Rubber bands make a great handgrip around the base of a screwdriver, too.

A Little Dab Will Do

Tired of searching through box after box looking for a nail or screw that will fill the bill for a particular project? Home handyman Paul Veri of Columbus, Ohio, just dabs a bit of glue on the front of the box and attaches a sample. That way, he can see at a glance what's inside the box.

Screws Simplified

For everyday jobs such as hanging Peg-Board and hooks or fastening boards together, don't spend time worrying about all the different kinds of screws you can buy. Just use drywall screws. According to home handyman Peter Evans of Berks County, Pennsylvania, these black screws are self-setting because they have such sharp tips. You can easily screw them into most surfaces without having to drill pilot holes first.

Pick It Up!

Metal objects such as screws, tools, or even kitchen cutlery are a cinch to pick up if you keep a magnetic pickup tool on hand. Pickup tools contain a strong magnet that's shielded on the sides so it doesn't attach to everything as you fish for a lost object. You can find these nifty devices at home centers and hardware stores. Sears offers a pen-size model that costs just a few dollars and telescopes out to about 22 inches. Models that telescope to 30 inches also are available.

Easy Rubber Band Clamp

Need a third hand in the workshop? Instead of waiting around for a family member with a bit of free time, use a pair of needle-nose pliers and some

A Second Life for Sponges

Worn-out sponges make fine no-slip tool handles. Just wrap them around the handle, secure them with a rubber band, and grip away. The sponges will cushion your hands, help prevent blisters, and help reduce slipping if your hands perspire. (If the sponge is greasy or grimy, run it through the dishwasher before you use it to cushion a tool handle.)

7 Wire Tie Solutions

Originally designed to hold bundles of electrical wires in place, plastic wire or cable ties have zillions of other uses. Buy a package in various sizes so you'll have them whenever and wherever you need them. (You'll find them at home centers and hardware stores; a bag of 100 ties costs less than $5.) Wire ties are easy to use, and you can remove them by cutting them with clippers or wire cutters. Try using wire ties around your garage and workshop as follows.

Extension cord holder. Temporarily suspend an extension cord over a doorway or other walkway and keep it out of the way while you work on a project.

Wood clamp. When you're working with wood, use wire ties to hold pieces of wood together while the glue dries.

Plant stake surround. Fasten bundles of plant stakes together in fall for easy, clutter-free winter storage.

Christmas light keeper. Tie up strings of Christmas tree lights to keep them neat and untangled in storage.

Fastener organizer. Link similar-size pipe fittings, nuts, or washers together to keep them organized.

Trailer insurance. Loop wire ties through linchpins on trailers or car carriers as an extra precaution to ensure that the pins won't work loose.

Key ring. To use a wire tie as a temporary key ring, slip the keys on the wire and pull one end through the other, but don't tighten the wire all the way.

* * *

rubber bands as your assistant. For example, if you need to hold a small nail in place until you pound it in, position the nail, clamp the jaws of the pliers around the nail, and then wrap some rubber bands around the pliers handles. The rubber bands will hold the jaws tightly shut. This trick also works to hold two pieces of metal together while you are soldering. In addition, the banded pliers can serve as a miniclamp for items that are being glued.

Old Hoses Never Die

Old garden hoses can get too torn up to transport water well, but there's no need to throw them away. Instead, cut some short lengths off the hose, slit them down one side, and use them as blade guards for all manner of sharp-edged tools. They're great for protecting the teeth on a handsaw, for example.

Plain and Practical Pry Bar

It's not pretty or fancy, but a pry bar is a multipurpose tool for tons of home projects, says Barbara Ellis, a writer who is renovating her second old home in eastern Pennsylvania. Not to be confused with a crowbar, a pry bar is a flat bar of thick steel with a scraper blade on one end and a flat, bladelike hook, also sharp, on the other. A pry bar has a diamond-shaped hole toward the hooked end that is perfect for pulling nails. What else is a pry bar good for? It's great for loosening stuck windows, scraping paint off woodwork or walls, gouging paint out of cracks and other hard-to-reach places, smoothing out bumps in plaster or drywall seams, and prying open paint cans. It also makes a handy lever and, in a pinch, a screwdriver or lightweight hammer. All this from a tool that costs about $10!

A Pry Bar That Measures Up

Since you'll be using your pry bar frequently, make it even more useful by adding marks for inches and half inches along one side—either with nail polish or gouged with a drill. Now you've got a handy measuring tool, too.

Bucket Brigade

Here's an easy system for sorting tools and making sure you always have exactly what you need for the job at hand. Start with several 5-gallon buckets—the kind you can get for free at a deli or doughnut shop. Empty drywall buckets work fine, too. Either use the buckets as is or buy canvas bucket organizers that fit over the top and have pockets around the inside and outside. Fill the buckets with tools sorted by the type of job—electrical, automotive, and general household repair, for example. In some cases, you'll probably want to buy duplicate tools, so you can have a pair of pliers in each bucket, for example. When you have a household chore to tackle, pick up the appropriate bucket, drop in any special tools (such as a drill) that you might need, and you're on your way.

Let There Be Light

Tired of wasting time trying to drill in a tight, dark spot? Aiming a light and holding a tool is difficult at best, especially in a small space. You can eliminate this problem in a jiffy with a small penlight and a bit of self-sticking Velcro tape. Just figure out where the penlight needs to be positioned on your tool. (This will vary, depending on the tool's shape.) Attach the "loop" side of the Velcro tape to the tool and the "hook" side to the penlight, then stick the penlight in place. Turn it on, and you're no longer working in the dark. Add a piece of "loop" Velcro tape to an electric screwdriver or other tool, and you can move the penlight from place to place as needed.

Velcro tape

Light up dark spaces when you're working with your portable drill by using Velcro tape to attach a penlight to the drill.

Put Your Tools on Wheels

Tools weigh a ton, and if lugging them to a home repair job is bad, getting them back to your workshop is worse. Well, lug no more! Toolmakers have come out with toolboxes designed like carry-on luggage, with wheels and a waist-high handle that makes them easy to transport. Several models are available.

Easy Tool Cleanup

To keep garden tools as clean as a whistle in less than 5 minutes a day, fill a 5-gallon bucket about three-quarters full of builder's sand. Add a quart of vegetable oil and mix. When you come in from working in the garden, use a trowel or a squirt of water from your hose to remove big clods of soil from tools. Then jam each tool into the sand and work it up and down several times. The oily sand will clean the

The Second Time Around

Tool Cord Roundup

It seems as if electrical cords on tools get tangled into a mess as soon as you turn your back. Instead of fighting with the cord every time he reaches for a tool, home handyman Doug Liston from Worthington, Ohio, recycles toilet paper tubes to keep his cords on the straight and narrow. He loosely folds the cord and sticks the folds into a tube. Try it yourself. The cord will still be neat and tidy the next time you use it.

tool's surface and oil the blade in the process. Replace the sand when it gets too dirty.

ORGANIZING YOUR GARAGE

Get Ducky with Duct Tape

Sharp corners abound in garages and workshops, whether it's a metal corner on a shelf or tool or a piece of pipe that sticks out at an odd angle. To take the edge off these corners quickly, pull out a roll of duct tape. Cushion those sharp corners by covering them with a few layers of tape. To make bumpers that will cushion the sharpest edge, grab some spare pieces of foam rubber, fit them over the offending area, and then use duct tape to fasten them securely in place. Look beyond the workshop and garage for places to use these handy bumpers, too. They work just as well to soften the metal corners of a bed frame (the ones you whack your shins on) as they do to cover up a sharp workbench edge.

A Simple String Caddy

There's no doubt that string has a zillion uses, but the leftover pieces—a quarter of a ball here, 20 feet there—junk up drawers in a jiffy. It's also impossible to find spare pieces when you need them. Home handyman Doug Liston from central Ohio suggests making a simple string caddy so you'll never need to search for string again. You'll need a large (32-ounce) yogurt container or a small (1-pound) coffee can. Gather your extra pieces of string together and put them in the container. Using a hole punch or an awl, punch a round hole with a slit attached—something like an old-fashioned keyhole—in the plastic lid of your container. Thread the end of one length of string up through the hole and catch it in the slit. When that piece is used up, thread the next one through. You could also punch holes on both sides of the lid and use them for two different types of string. Empty baby wipe containers work well as string caddies, too.

Grommet and Grab It

Weekends almost always find Wade Slate of Knoxville, Tennessee, tinkering with a car or building some contraption in his garage. To make sure he has plenty of clean shop rags on hand, Wade invested in a $4 grommet kit from a family camping supply store. He punches one ³/₈-inch brass grommet into each shop rag so that he can hang it on a hook on the wall or a cabinet door. "The grommets go right through the wash, and I have no excuse for piles of oily rags on the floor," he says. "I try to put the hook right at eye level so I don't have to stoop."

Rolling Trash Collection

Have a broken shop vacuum sitting around just taking up space? Turn the canister, which has wheels on the bottom, into a rolling wastebasket. It's generally the right size for a plastic grocery bag liner, and you can easily roll it anywhere you need it. The canister won't mind being kicked into position either.

FIX IT FAST • FIX IT FOREVER

Perennially Misplaced Tools

Problem:

You can never find your garden tools because they're piled up all over the garage.

Do This Now:

Buy a cheap metal or plastic garbage can and put all long-handled tools in the can. Procure one or two 5-gallon plastic buckets (often available for free from delis and bakeries) and corral all your hand tools in the buckets.

Do This for Good:

Create a custom storage system for your tools along a garage wall, as garden writer Barbara Ellis of Berks County, Pennsylvania, did. "Line up all your hand tools—small and large—against a wall and arrange them so they use space efficiently," Barbara says. "Put two shorter tools between rakes with wide-spreading tines, for example. My tools are stored high on a garage wall, so there is room for a stack of kindling and recyclables underneath them." For really sturdy hooks to hang your tools, mount a 2-by-4 along the top of the storage wall (affixed to the studs) and insert tool hangers into that. You also may want to add a section of Peg-Board so it's easy to hang smaller tools such as pruners and saws. Plant staking systems, such as linking stakes and support rings, are easy to group and store on Peg-Board as well.

A Snug Equipment Cover

Garages just won't hold all the equipment we want to stuff in them. If you need to store some equipment outside, such as a lawn mower or small boat, you can buy a fancy protective cover for it, or you can make your own for a lot less money. All you need is a tarp, a piece of rope, and a fish tape (a tool used for stringing electrical wire through walls). Here's what to do.

1. Use scissors or a utility knife to cut semicircular "bites" (5 to 6 inches across) at intervals around the edge of the tarp.

2. Insert the fish tape into the hem along the edge of the tarp and feed the tape all the way around it.

3. Attach a thin rope to one end of the tape, then pull the tape, with rope attached, back through the hem.

4. When the end of the rope emerges from the hem at the point where you started to feed, untie it from the fish tape and tie the rope to itself, forming a continuous rope handle around the edge of the tarp.

You'll be able to grab the rope wherever it emerges from the cutouts for a handhold or to tie down the tarp. Reinforce the edges of the tarp as needed with duct tape. To use the tarp as a cover, cinch up the rope to cover the equipment being protected. If needed, tie the cover to tent pegs nailed into the ground around the equipment.

You can also use this tarp as a leaf collector in the fall. Just rake the leaves onto the tarp, then fold it up and pull it by the handles to the curb or your compost pile.

Mark Your Mower's Territory

Wade Slate of Knoxville, Tennessee, has even more garage clutter than most folks: His space doubles as storage for his lawn care business. "I really hate it when I fit everything in and then come back and find that someone has plunked a wagon where the rolling trash can belongs," Wade says. To stake out his territory, Wade drew everyone in the family a picture—with electrical tape. "I marked off the spot where the mower, trash can, and all the other big stuff belongs," he says. "That way, even the spaciest of our teenage daughters can see where everything belongs."

Suspend Some Supersize Stuff

Need some floor space in a garage that's jam-packed with stuff? Setting up temporary shelves—even the board-and-cement-block kind—is a fast and easy way to get organized. For oversize but lightweight items such as sleds, ladders, and canoes, look up to the rafters for handy storage. Hang pulleys in the rafters to make it easy to shift the equipment up and down. You'll need at least two pulleys for each item—one at the front and one at the back. Arrange tie-down straps to make a sling for each item, then attach the ends of the straps to the ropes that run through the pulleys. Also install a sturdy cleat on the wall of the garage at about shoulder height to tie off each rope after you've pulled an item up into the rafters.

ORGANIZING YOUR WORKBENCH

Extension Cord Roll-Up

Long extension cords wreak havoc in a drawer or on a workbench, getting snarled and looping around a dozen different items. They also take forever to untangle and use. For somewhat easier storage, bundle them up like rope. Just loop lengths from your hand to your elbow, then wrap the ends around the entire bundle of loops and plug one end of the cord into the other.

For an even handier cord storage system, visit your local hardware store. You can buy cord reels, or ask the store to save some of the reels that rope, wire, or chain are sold on. To make a cord holder out of one of these reels, cut two slots the thickness of the cord in the outer rim of the reel. Then measure off about a yard on the male end of the cord and stick that length through one slot. Wind the rest of the cord around the reel and stick the female end in the other slot. That way, you can plug in the cord, roll out as much as you need, and use it without having to unroll it all the way.

A homemade extension cord holder ends the hassle of tangled cords for good.

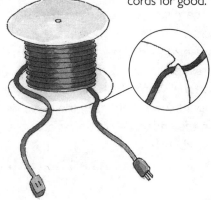

Keep Extra Caps Handy

If you're forever searching for the caps to bottles of glue, keep a supply of screw-on wire caps (used to splice electrical wires) on hand. They make good replacement caps that are easy to open and close. Keep a container of assorted sizes on your workbench.

Bag It!

An old over-the-door shoe holder makes a handy storage catchall in a workshop. Either hang it over a door or mount it on a wall. Bottles of glue, solvents, and other items fit nicely in the pockets and won't tip over. You can also use the pockets for storing larger items such as extension cords or jars of screws or other hardware.

My Favorite Shortcut

Speedy Storage Solution

Keeping nuts, bolts, and a host of other fasteners right at hand used to be a hassle for Ethel Ondra, an amateur woodworker from Pennsylvania. Now, however, she just uses a simple organizer her uncle gave her. It consists of a round piece of plywood (rectangular would work well, too) that hangs overhead in her workshop. Twenty or so jar lids are attached to the plywood with screws, with the threaded side of the lids facing down. Nuts, bolts, and whatnot are stored in clear glass jars that screw into the attached lids. The organizer hangs low enough that the jars are easy to reach but high enough so Ethel won't clonk her head. You can mount several jar lids in the same way on the underside of shelves above a workbench.

Peg It Up

A Peg-Board, some coat hangers, and a permanent magic marker are all you need to organize your workbench forever. Put up the Peg-Board and hang your tools on it in the ideal arrangement. If you would like to hang an oddly shaped item that won't hang well from conventional hooks, use plastic-covered coat hangers to make custom hooks. Untwist or cut a hanger at the top. With the object lying flat on your workbench, bend the hanger to conform to the object's shape. Once you have the overall shape right, bend the tips of the wire so they'll stick in the holes of the Peg-Board. Once you have all your tools on the Peg-Board, use the marker to draw the outline of each tool on the board. Now you have a permanent record of that ideal arrangement, and you can tell at a glance what's missing.

The Eyes Have It

If you need glasses to read, you need glasses in your workshop. The catch is, you can never find those glasses. Home and car repair expert Peter Evans from Berks County, Pennsylvania, finally thought up a shortcut to save himself from those frustrating searches: He bought enough extra pairs of glasses so that he can always put his hands on one in an instant. There's a pair hung on the Peg-Board above his workbench, one in the glove compartment of his car, another in his briefcase, and so forth. All these glasses didn't cost much—they're available at discount stores in packs of three or five. They're also available for a buck apiece at dollar stores. If you don't know your prescription, call your optometrist and check before you buy. It's best for your eyes not to buy a pair that is stronger than you need.

Hose Bumpers

Still have some worn-out garden hose left? Cushion sharp corners on your workbench with it. You can slit the hose open or leave it whole. Use a staple gun to fasten it around the corner, forming a cushioned bumper.

A Handy Sink Hose

That last 5 to 10 feet of old hose, the part that still has the female connector end attached, is handy to keep on hand by your work sink. Attach it to the faucet and use it to fill buckets—no need to lift the buckets up and over the edge of the sink. Short pieces also make washing the dog easier.

Under-the-Bench Storage

Look to the area under your workbench if you need more storage space in your workshop. An old chest of drawers might just fit there. And if part of the space under your bench is taken up by shelves, there's probably still room for some under-the-bed boxes. The kind with wheels are especially handy, since they are easy to pull out and push in, making everything stored in them easy to reach. If you have a large piece of equipment to store, such as a heavy toolbox, set it on

Wall-to-Wall Remnants

Ordinary carpet remnants can help you save time and effort in the workshop. With almost any project you tackle, there's a reason to keep a carpet nearby.

- A square of carpet on top of your workbench acts like a trap when you set down screws, screwdrivers, and other small items that roll. No more time wasted looking for essential parts that have rolled onto the floor.
- Need a cutting surface that prevents tools from cutting into your work surface (and also keeps blades sharp)? Use a carpet remnant!

- A piece of carpet is a handy cushion that helps prevent damage to tools that commonly lie on a hard workbench.
- To cushion your feet and relieve stress on your back and legs while you work, add a large carpet remnant on the floor of your workshop. For added padding, buy a piece that's twice the size and fold it in half. (You'll have to stamp down or cut the fold so the carpet will lie flat.)

However you use your remnants, when they get too dirty or are cut to shreds, toss them out and get some more.

a three-wheel dolly (or two) so you can pull it around and position it with ease.

The Workshop File Cabinet

According to Peter Evans, a car and power-equipment enthusiast from Berks County, Pennsylvania, one of the handiest tools in his home workshop is an old two-drawer metal file cabinet. It became too small for his home office, but it's just the ticket for filing all the instruction booklets, warranty information, and service manuals from vehicles and power equipment—everything from cars and motorcycles to drills, lawn tractors, and string trimmers. That way, instead of having books spread all over the garage and house, they're easy to find if he has a question about scheduled maintenance or needs to use the troubleshooting feature for a niggling problem. There's no more traipsing through the house (and undoubtedly tracking mud) looking for the right book, so this simple system saves on cleaning time, too. Since the books take up only one drawer, he uses the second drawer for power tool storage.

HOUSEHOLD REPAIRS

Left High and Dry?

Disaster! The outside pipe connecting your house to the water main has broken. Take quick action by shutting off the water supply both at your home's primary valve and at the water main by the street. Then call the repair folks. Now you need to figure out what to do until the repair is made.

With help from your neighbors, you can be fully supplied with water without hauling buckets, says Scott Campbell, owner of 1st Choice Plumbing in Everett, Washington. Ask a neighbor if you can tap into her water supply temporarily. Hook two garden hoses together with a female-to-female coupler (available at home stores and hardware stores). Fasten one end of this super-hose to your neighbor's outside spigot and the other end to your own outside spigot. Open both spigots, and your home will have a brand-new water source as water flows through the hose and into your plumbing system.

Note: Some outdoor spigots have a gizmo called a hose bib vacuum breaker attached. This prevents the backflow of water from your hose into your plumbing system. You can remove it in 30 seconds with a pair of pliers. Just loosen the set screw on the side, then twist the cylindrical vacuum breaker off.

Hose That Pipe

Sections of old garden hose come in handy for quick pipe repair. Cut off a small section of hose (about 4 inches long for a small hole) and slit it along its length. Slip the hose over the leaky pipe so that the leak is covered by the middle of the unslit side. Place a

A No-Brainer Guide

Susan Liston, a working mother of two from Columbus, Ohio, isn't particularly handy when it comes to home repairs, but she does know that it's hard to find someone with a cool head during a plumbing crisis. After surviving one emergency when it took an extra few minutes to figure out how to turn off the main water valve, she vowed never to repeat the experience. She cut off the bottom of an old bleach bottle and cut a hole in the center of it so she could hang it over the water shut-off valve. Then she used a permanent marker to draw and label arrows that indicate on and off before hanging it there permanently. No more questions in a crisis!

C-clamp directly over the hole and tighten it until the water stops leaking.

Clamp Down on Leaks

A leaky water pipe spraying in your basement is an emergency that needs attention fast. The surest solution, of course, is to find the pipe's nearest shutoff valve and cut off the source of the water. But sometimes you just can't live without water—for example, when dinner guests are on the way and you're in the midst of cooking. Save the day with compression clamps, which will stop or minimize the leak until the plumber comes, says Justin Majors, owner of Majors Residential Design and Construction in Oakland, California. Compression clamps are inexpensive ringlike devices, some of which work in conjunction with a rubber sleeve. Just slip the compression clamp around the leak, tighten it with a screwdriver, turn the water back on, and get back to that pasta primavera in the kitchen.

Duct Tape Does the Job

A backup plan for doctoring a leaky pipe is to wrap the leak with duct tape, says Ed DuBois, owner of Hire a Hubby in Hartford, Vermont. Use several layers at least—the more the better. To take a little pressure off the pipe, find the water shutoff valve that controls the pipe and turn it partway off. This will allow some water—at a lower pressure—to the fixture that the pipe feeds.

Soda Softens Rust

If you need to remove a bolt that has rusted and won't budge, try pouring a carbonated beverage on it. This really works!

Assemble by Number

Ever taken a faucet or other thingamajig apart and had trouble figuring out how to put it back together—or ended up with a leftover piece when you reassembled it? According to Peter Evans, who repairs all manner of gadgets on his small farm in Pennsylvania, all you need is a plastic ice cube tray or Styrofoam egg carton, and you'll never mess up again. Use a permanent marker to number the indentations in the ice cube tray or egg carton. As you take the item apart, put each part in a numbered holder. If a part is too big to fit, set it alongside the organizer and skip one indentation. To reassemble, just follow the numbers.

Water Management

One of the best accessories you can buy for your car is WeatherTech floor mats, says Peter Evans. These are heavy-duty rubber trays with deep grooves that catch and hold water or melting snow rather than letting it soak into carpets, where it can foster the growth of smelly mold and mildew—not to mention rust. These floor mats also catch spilled coffee or soft drinks, saving you a time-consuming carpet cleanup. Buy mats that fit your particular model car. They're available for both front and back seat areas, as well as the cargo area in SUVs and station wagons.

PAINTING AND WALLPAPERING

Whiter, Brighter Spackle

When you need to fill two or three nail holes in a wall before painting, don't buy an entire can of Spackle that will dry out on the shelf before you can use it up. A dab of toothpaste, spread into the hole like Spackle, will work just fine, says woodworker Keith Gotschall of Salida, Colorado.

Mix It Up

If you're planning on painting tomorrow, turn the paint can(s) upside down tonight. (Be sure the lid is pounded on tight first.) This will make the paint easier to mix in the morning.

Prep Before You Pay for Paint

Cut clutter, save money, and save the environment by doing the dirty work before you buy paint, says Bob Grimac of Knoxville, Tennessee, an environmentalist and elementary school fine arts instructor. "Never buy paint until you've cleared out the area you intend to paint and prepped the windows and walls for painting," says Bob. "So many times people do the fun part of painting—choosing the colors—and then they never get around to the grunge work." Unused paint takes up valuable space in the garage and sometimes even gets thrown away.

Bargain-Basement Paint

Julie Garrison of Boulder, Colorado, suggests looking for half-empty paint containers at your local recycling center or hazardous waste drop-off. "They [probably] won't be Martha Stewart colors, but they're fine for low-visibility paint jobs or priming," Julie says.

Rubber-Coated Hardware

When painting hinged doors or other items with attached hardware, first coat the hinges or handles with rubber cement. Let the cement dry, then paint. After the paint is dry, you can rub off the cement with your fingers. This trick sure beats taking off all the hardware or covering it with masking tape.

My Favorite Shortcut

Drip-Proof Paint Cans

When you open a new can of paint, before you pour any paint out into a tray or dip in your brush, take a tip from Ohio home handyman Doug Liston and drip-proof the can. "This doesn't save painting time," says Doug, "but it does make cleanup a lot easier. Just take a hammer and nail and poke holes in the inner slot of the rim of the can. You'll need to poke about three holes around the edge. That way, any paint that lands between the two beads of the lip will drip back into the can. You'll save a bit of paint in the process, too."

Bag Your Paint Tray

To cut paint tray cleanup time down to zero, put the entire tray in a plastic grocery bag, then pour the paint into the tray. When you're done, all you need to do is turn the bag inside out and throw it away. The tray is clean and ready for another day of painting.

Soak Brushes before You Paint

To make cleanup really easy, try this trick before you start. Soak a new brush for oil paint in linseed oil for 24 hours before using it. For latex paint, wet the brush thoroughly with water—to the base of the bristles—before painting. This helps keep paint down toward the tip of the brush. Both techniques make brushes easier to clean.

Add Paint to Primer for Perfect Results

To ensure that a coat of dark, richly colored paint goes on quickly and evenly over a coat of primer, add a bit of the final color to the white primer before you start painting. Just pour ¾ to 1 cup of the dark paint into a gallon of white primer and stir.

May I Cut In?

Cutting in around the edges of doors, window frames, and the like can be frustrating. When you're cutting in, put a rubber band around the bristles of your paintbrush. It helps hold the bristles together—especially those frustrating strays that stick out at odd angles—which makes painting in tight places easier. Don't put the rubber band on too tight, though; it should gently hold the bristles together but not squeeze them and change the shape of the brush.

Paper the Panes for Painting Ease

Taping a window frame before painting is a good practice, but there's an easier way to protect glass when you paint frames. Uses pieces of damp newspaper instead of tape. The newspaper will stick right to the window. Cut the newspaper to the size of the window panes. Use a wallpaper tray to soak the newspaper. Be sure to let the paper finish dripping before putting it up on the window, or the drips will wet the wood at the bottom of the frame. If the newspaper gets too dry before you're finished painting, remoisten it with a barely damp sponge. When you're done painting, just bundle up the newspaper, toss it out, and move on to the next window.

No-Brush Touch-Ups

If you notice a few missed spots after painting a room, get out the cotton swabs for a quick touch-up. Dip them in the paint, dab away, and then toss them when you're done—no cleanup required. Cotton swabs come in handy for fixing small scrapes and chips, too.

Handy Hidden Records

Want to know the easiest, most foolproof place to keep track of how much paint or how many rolls of wallpaper you used to redecorate a room? You can jot down the information on index cards or keep it in your computer, but who can find notes like that when the time comes to paint or wallpaper again? Instead, write the information on the back of the light switch plate by the doorway—either directly on the plate or on a sticky computer label that you attach to the plate. You'll need to remove the switch plates anyway when you paint or paper again.

Paper Plate Drip Preventer

Eliminate cleanup headaches when you're painting a ceiling by sticking the handle of the paintbrush through a paper plate before you start. This cuts down on drips and spatters that may land on you.

Part Fast with Extra Paint

If you end up with extra paint, cut clutter by donating the paint to a worthy cause immediately, says Bob Grimac of Knoxville, Tennessee, an environmentalist and elementary school fine arts instructor. "Any group—from the local Habitat

Wallpaper Wisdom

Wallpapering is really much easier than it looks. Follow this advice, and you'll create a stylish room with a minimum investment in time and money.

- Especially if you're a beginner, choose wallpaper that has a small pattern—one that repeats every 2 inches or so. That makes lining up sheets easier.

- Avoid plaids or patterns with stripes or lines that have to be lined up. It's easier to match patterns that have blank space between elements in the design. In older houses, where corners are far from square, plaids can be downright frustrating to match.

- Start off with plenty of new razor blades so you can make each cut cleanly and quickly.

- Use a chalk or plumb line in the center of a wall to position the first piece of wallpaper. Corners are seldom plumb and square, and starting from a vertical line in the center is the easiest, fastest way to get wallpaper lined up straight.

- Use a fabric-backed vinyl wallpaper whenever possible, because it is by far the easiest to remove. This will be important down the road if you want to change your decor.

for Humanity to a high school theater group or day care center—might be happy to have your leftovers," says Bob. "Unless you're sure you're going to use it, why have it take up space and eventually end up in a landfill, when someone else could use it now?"

Flip the Lid on Leftovers

Whether you're storing leftover paint for a few days until you can pass it along to a local nonprofit or storing it for your own projects down the road, you can extend the shelf life quite a bit with very little effort. "Cover the paint can opening with a piece of plastic wrap," says Bob Grimac. "Then securely replace the lid and store the can upside down. That way, the paint creates a tight seal around the lid, keeping it fresh for as long as three or four years."

Chilling Beats Cleaning

Some painting projects stretch out over weeks. Instead of cleaning your brushes at the end of each stint, save time and fuss by putting each brush in a plastic bag. Wrap the bag tightly around the brush and store the brushes in the refrigerator. This works well as long as you'll be using the brush again within a few days. If you want to store dirty brushes for several weeks, pop them in the freezer instead of the refrigerator.

Paint Can Cover-Up

Before banging the lid of a paint can back in place at the end of a day's work, drape a sheet of newspaper or a rag over the top, which will keep the paint from shooting out in all directions and save you additional cleanup.

Dip, Don't Drip

As a Web site editor for the Home and Garden Television Network, Ralph Davis knows quite a few remodeling experts. But he learned this paint cleanup tip by trial and error. "I use a large plastic measuring cup to dip paint out of the can and pour it into the paint tray," he says. "That really cuts down on splashing and drips down the side of the can, and I can just rinse the cup with water at the end—which is not true of the paint can."

WEATHERPROOFING PROJECTS

A Strip in Time Stops Drafts

If you need a fast fix for a drafty door, use a staple gun to install weather stripping around the frame so that the door closes against the weather stripping. Also install the weather stripping along the top and side edges of the door. This will tide you over until you can either fix the door or replace it altogether.

Airy Indicators

Have a drafty, unfinished basement or crawl space that leaks cold air? To save on heating bills and increase your comfort, it's a good idea to block the leaks—but first you have to find them. To do this, pick up a flashlight and look for spiderwebs in the basement or crawl space. Since drafts bring in insects that the spiders feed on, their webs are nearly always located in the path of a draft. Once you find a web, look for the source of the draft, then plug it up with weather stripping or insulation.

As the Flame Flickers

A lighted candle is another tool you can use to search out places where cold breezes seep into your house. Watch the flame as you carry a candle around a room—it will flicker as you move it into a draft. Move the candle around windows and doors especially, but also use it to look for other sources of drafts, such as poorly sealed joints in corners or between walls and floor. Poorly insulated electrical outlets also can let in a lot of cold air. If you feel a breeze from an outlet, turn off the electricity, take off the switch plate, and fill the space with fireproof insulation.

CAR CLEANING AND MAINTENANCE

Supersoft Wash

Soft rags are a must for washing your car—it's far too easy to scratch the paint. Old flannel sheets make fabulous car-washing rags. Just tear them into usable size. Wash the rags between uses to remove any paint-scratching grit that gets stuck in the fibers.

Oil Away Dirt

The next time you wash your car, add a few drops of ordinary vegetable oil to the bucket and stir it up. The oil will help carry dirt away from the paint as you wash.

Say So Long to Streaks

It can be really hard to get a streak-free windshield, but luckily there's a nearly free, super-easy solution. Don't use rags or paper towels to wash car windows. Instead, use a good window cleaner and sheets of newspaper. They'll leave your windows streak-free the first time.

Park It in the Shade

Whether you're waxing a car or a recreational vehicle, you can make the entire process easier with one simple step: Park the vehicle in the shade. The sun will dry the wax too fast, making it harder to polish. Apply wax to one panel of the car or one section of the camper, let it dry to a dull haze, then buff with a clean terry cloth towel before moving on to the next section.

Crayons to the Rescue

A tube of touch-up paint works great for a quick-and-easy scratch repair. If you don't have touch-up paint, look through a giant box of crayons and pick one that matches the color of your car. Then work the crayon into the scratch to prevent rust.

Watch That Pressure

Keeping a eye on the air pressure in your tires not only saves you money on gas, but it also prevents tires from

My Favorite Shortcut

Perfect Parking

To avoid that sickening sensation of feeling your car bumper hit the shelves on the garage wall, rely on a tennis ball, says Ralph Davis of Halls, Tennessee. Ralph whizzes his car right into the garage every day and always stops in the perfect place. That's because Ralph, in addition to helping edit a Web site for the Home and Garden Television Network, plays tennis. Really, there is a connection. "With a pocketknife, I cut a little X at the top and bottom of an old tennis ball, then threaded a long string through it and tied off the end," Ralph says. "I parked the car in the garage perfectly, then tied the string on a rafter above the car so the tennis ball dangled at precisely the point where it touched the top of the windshield of my parked car. Now as I pull in, I know to stop just as the tennis ball appears at the top of my windshield."

wearing out too soon or wearing unevenly. Ideally, you should check your tire pressure every month. Instead of wasting time stopping at a gas station, keep a good-quality pressure gauge in your glove compartment so that you can check the tire pressure easily and quickly. Remember to check the pressure in the spare, too. To find the correct tire pressure for your vehicle, look in the owner's manual, on the driver's side door panel, or on the gas tank lid. (The pressure listed on your tires is the maximum pressure for the brand of tires you have, not the correct pressure for your car.) Always check your tire pressure when the tires are cold (before you've driven more than about a mile), because air pressure changes from 1 to 2 pounds for every 10 degrees of temperature change.

A Penny for Your Thoughts

All you need is a penny to check the tread depth of your tires. Place the penny in the tread, and if part of Lincoln's head is covered by the tread, your tires are okay. If you can see his whole head, you need new tires. While you're looking, check for spots where the tires have worn unevenly. Consult a tire dealer if you notice any uneven wear.

Put the Brakes on Old Fluid

"If you're hanging on to car wax or brake fluid that's more than a year old, toss it," says Tommy Goodman, a lube technician in a quick-stop shop in Knoxville, Tennessee. "It's no good after that time and it just takes up space." Next time, buy a smaller size or share a container with your neighbors.

Around the Yard

14

Is there ever enough time to relax in our own backyards? All our work and family responsibilities often leave us too little time, money, or energy to enjoy outdoor time. Yet the yard is exactly the place most people crave for unwinding. In this chapter, you'll learn how to minimize the time you spend on yard chores, whether it's taking care of your deck, patio, or pool; mowing your lawn; or cleaning the gutters. Plus, you'll find some great ideas for simple landscaping projects that will make your yard a more beautiful place to be.

COOKING OUTDOORS

Paul Newman's Latest?

Save yourself an emergency trip to the store when you run out of charcoal lighter fluid: Ignite your coals with salad oil. Any vegetable oil will burn well enough to light charcoal (although none is as good as lighter fluid), so use the cheapest type of vegetable oil you have on hand.

The Chimney Starter

For a quick, hot charcoal fire, use a chimney starter. This low-tech tool looks like an overgrown coffee can with a handle on the outside and a grillwork platform inside. To use a chimney starter, place a few pieces of crumpled newspaper under the starter, fill the top portion with charcoal, light the newspaper, and wait 10 to 15 minutes. The chimney generates a strong updraft that quickly turns briquettes into hot coals. Using tongs or an oven mitt, grab the handle and dump the coals into the grill. You're ready to cook.

You can make your own chimney starter from a 10-to-12-inch length of stovepipe. Use a hammer and a sharp spike (a large nail) to punch vent holes in the bottom 2 to 3 inches of the pipe. (You may need to brace the inside of the pipe with a chunk of wood as you punch these holes.) Using a smaller nail, punch holes at 1-inch intervals all the way around the pipe, just above the vent holes. Weave galvanized wire (available at any hardware store) through these holes to form a grid to hold the charcoal. (*Caution:* Since it has no handle, you'll need tongs or pliers to move the hot stovepipe.)

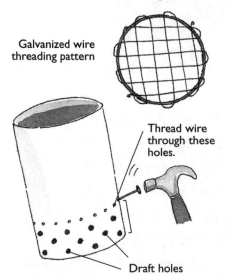

Galvanized wire threading pattern

Thread wire through these holes.

Draft holes

A piece of stovepipe with a lattice of strong wire to hold the charcoal will serve as a chimney starter.

Recycled Charcoal

Don't throw out those partially burned charcoal briquettes. Grillmeister Michael Scherer of Louisville, Colorado, says, "Half-used charcoal lights easily and burns well." When you clean the ashes out of your grill, shake it aggressively to knock the loose bits and ash off the old briquettes. Then, using a pair of tongs, place them on top of the new briquettes before lighting. You'll save money, and the fire will heat up more quickly.

Disaster Preparedness

Keep a spare tank of propane at your house (stored outside, away from the grill) in case you run out of gas just as guests arrive for a cookout.

Spare the Sauce

Baked-on tomato sauce is the toughest mess to clean off a grill. If you cook with tomato-based sauces, apply them at the last minute, right before taking your food off the grill. This will minimize messy spattering.

How (Not) to Clean a Grill

It may be quick, but scraping the burnt remnants from the previous cooking session off your grill with a spatula can ruin that expensive protective porcelain coating, making it susceptible to rust and that much more difficult to clean the next time. Here's how to clean your grill the right way.

1. Immediately after grilling, brush off the stuck food bits with a soft, brass-bristle grill brush.

2. After the grill cools, brush it lightly with cooking oil. This will keep food from sticking the next time you use the grill. (If you forget this step because you're busy eating by the time the grill cools, brush on the oil before you light the grill next time.)

3. Every 3 or 4 weeks during busy grilling season, turn the grill to high after you're done cooking and leave it on for a few minutes. This will burn off any remaining scraps of food. Don't do this after every barbecue, though, because it puts a lot of stress on the grill.

PATIOS AND DECKS

Sunscreen for Deck Furniture

Too much sun can be just as harmful to deck furniture as it is to people. To protect your outdoor wooden furniture from sunburn and avoid messy and time-consuming refinishing jobs, apply a quick coat of penetrating finish each year, recommends master woodworker Keith Gotschall of Salida, Colorado. (Keith

---

20 MINUTES A WEEK

Year-Round Grilling

A conveniently located propane grill may be the greatest labor-saver for home cooks since the microwave oven. Chris Blackmon of Louisville, Colorado, grills at least twice a week, even in the winter. Grilled meat or fish is quicker to make and healthier than fried or sautéed fare, and there are no pots or roasting pans to wash. Chris estimates that she saves at least 10 minutes in prep and cleanup time each time she grills. Her keys to year-round grilling? She located her grill on a deck just outside the kitchen door and under a good light, covers the grill when it's not in use, and maintains a snow-free path to the grill.

likes Thompson's Water Seal, but there are many others.) These finishes are easy to wipe on with a paint pad or rags. Avoid film finishes, such as spar varnish or lacquer, says Keith. They look good at first, but they soon blister, whiten, and peel in the sun, requiring heavy-duty sanding and refinishing.

Clean It at the Car Wash

The patio furniture, grill, and other large objects loitering on your deck can accumulate a grimy coating over the years. It looks awful, but it would take half a day with a bucket of soapy water and a scrubber sponge to expunge the grime. Fear not—there's a quicker way. Toss all the dirty items into the trunk or backseat (protected with a plastic tarp) of your car and drive to the nearest self-service car wash. Set out the items in the drive-thru bay and hose them down with the pressure wand. You'll be done in minutes! Even faster: Set up all your backyard gear in the back of a pickup truck and pressure-spray without unloading it. Got teenagers? They'll think this sounds like fun and do the job for you without griping.

Spick-and-Span Decks

Haste Makes Waste

Sanding and refinishing a worn and dirty wooden deck is a huge job. It can require more than 8 hours of work, spread over several days. Instead of struggling with this task, try one of the chemical wood cleaners available at home improvement stores. Look for a non-bleach cleaner, which will remove dirt and nail stains without affecting the wood's natural color or harming neighboring grass and shrubs. Cover all the nearby aluminum and glass, sweep the deck completely, and keep it wet with a light spray from a hose while you apply the cleaner. Follow the product's mixing instructions and use a long-handled brush or roller to apply; extra-dirty spots will require

Paint Is No Shortcut

You may be tempted to paint your deck, because paint seems to require less maintenance than stain or oil. But paint will quickly chip and peel on heavily traveled decks, and it blocks the proper flow of water vapor from the wood. Choose a penetrating oil or stain finish instead. Also, never paint or stain a new deck until it has weathered for 6 months to a year.

Pop-Up Nails

Problem:
Nail heads often pop out of wooden decks, which looks ugly and can be a hazard.

Do This Now:
Use a nail set to hammer the nails a bit deeper into the underlying joists, where they can bite into more wood.

Do This for Good:
Pull out all of the nails that have popped up and replace them with longer nails driven at a slight angle. For an even better solution (but also more expensive and time-consuming), replace common nails with spiral-shank nails or deck screws.

· ·

hand-brushing. (Wear rubber gloves while you work to protect your hands.)

After the deck has soaked for 20 to 30 minutes, hose it off thoroughly. Cleaning a medium-size deck this way takes about 2 hours. In some cases, especially with redwood or cedar decks, you'll get the best results by following up with an application of wood brightener, which is also available in various brands.

AROUND THE DRIVEWAY

Home Oil Slicks

Here's the simplest way to remove oil and other fluids from your driveway or garage floor. Sprinkle cat box filler on a pool of oil to absorb the fluid. For stains, scrub the litter and oil with a small block of wood. For stains that don't respond to this tactic, look for a household product—whitewall brightener, dishwasher detergent, or wood cleaner—that contains trisodium phosphate or sodium metasilicate. Dilute this cleaner (1/2 cup in 1 gallon of water), pour a little on the stain, and use a scrub brush to work at removing the stain.

Hold the Line against Weeds

Some people will tell you to pour boiling water on weeds that poke up through the bricks or concrete cracks in a patio or

Cracks in Your Driveway

Problem:

Blacktop or concrete driveways often dry out and crack over time, and as water penetrates the surface and expands when it freezes, the cracks will only get worse.

Do This Now:

Fill ¼-inch or smaller cracks with liquid crack filler, which is available at any hardware or home improvement store. Depending on the mix, you pour the filler into the cracks or apply it with a caulking gun. Larger cracks or craters must be filled with a patching mix that's spread on with a trowel.

Do This for Good:

Once the crack filler or patches have cured for at least 30 days, prevent future cracks by sealing the driveway with a sealer recommended by your local hardware store. (Bring a sample of your driveway material for the best match.) Clean the surface thoroughly (chemical cleaners may be needed for gasoline and oil residues), then use a paint roller with a long handle to apply the sealer.

• •

walkway. That's certainly quick. But Steve Shadel, a manager at McGuckin Hardware in Boulder, Colorado, says boiling water only temporarily wipes out weeds, because it doesn't kill their roots. Instead, for weed control in walks, trying filling a spray bottle or hand pump with white vinegar. Applied to the leaves and crowns of young weeds, vinegar is an effective natural herbicide.

Steve also cautions against using those thin-bladed tools designed to root out weeds in flagstone and brick walkways. They work, he says, but sometimes too well, tearing up the landscaping fabric that is laid under walkways to—you guessed it—control weeds.

Secure Your Can

Raccoons, roving dogs, and other critters always seem to find your garbage cans just after you've filled them with the remnants of a messy lobster dinner. Cleaning up after the critters is a real pain. To keep trash can lids on tight during an animal assault, find bungee cords, with hooks on both ends, that are the right length to strap securely over the top. Drill a small hole in one side of the can so that one end of the bungee hooks into it permanently. That way, the cord won't disappear between the times you use it.

PLAY PLACES

It's a Sandbox, Not a Litter Box

A child's sandbox must be covered, or it will quickly become the neighborhood litter box. If your sandbox doesn't have a cover, make one that's easy for kids to move aside when they want to play in the sand. Cut 1-by-6-inch planks to the length of your sandbox. Lay the boards side by side on top of the box, with about a 2-inch gap between them. Cut enough boards to cover the entire box. Using a heavy-duty staple gun or hammered brads, fasten five or six strips of 3/4-to-1-inch-wide nylon webbing across the boards to hold them together. Use at least three staples or brads to fasten the webbing to each board. Voilà—you have a lid. When it's time to use the sandbox, your kids will find it much easier to roll up this cover than to lift off a heavy-framed lid. Don't fool yourself, though—you'll be the one putting it back in place!

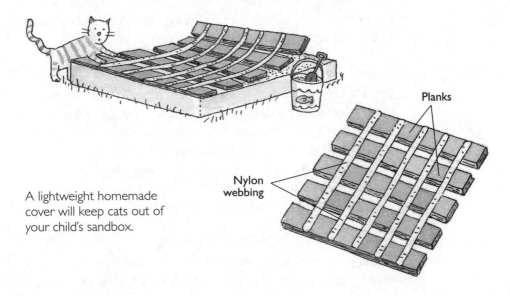

A lightweight homemade cover will keep cats out of your child's sandbox.

Planks

Nylon webbing

Keep Swinging

When you install a swing set in your yard, take time to lay a bed of 3 to 4 inches of sand or pea gravel instead of setting it up on the grass, recommends Pat Neff, owner of Swingset Corral in Oxnard, California. The couple of hours you spend on this will save many frustrating hours of trying to maintain grass in the play area. Plus, says Pat, sand or gravel provides a softer landing for errant swingers, and it makes the swing set easier to keep level. That's important because a level set won't experience as much torque as one placed on bumpy ground, and therefore the parts will last longer. Check your swing set every year for loose nuts and bolts, and if it's made of wood, wipe on an oil-based penetrating finish whenever the wood starts to look weather-beaten.

Keep It Cool

Even a small change in the thermostat setting on your pool or hot tub can cut energy usage dramatically. Try lowering the temperature by 1 or 2 degrees. The savings will really add up, because every 1-degree reduction in temperature cuts energy usage by 5 to 10 percent, according to statistics from the U.S. Department of Energy. A cooler pool also is cheaper to keep clean, because cool water is less conducive to bacteria and algae, and thus requires less filtering and chemicals. Retain heat by using a pool cover when the pool is not in use.

Timing Is Everything

To save time on spring-cleaning, close and cover your pool in the fall before the autumn leaves start dropping into the water but after daytime temperatures fall into the 60s or below. Why? Close the pool too early, and you could find an algae bloom in the warm water under the cover—and then you'll have to reopen and clean the pool. Close it too late, and your pool will be filled with dead leaves come spring.

Double Coverage for Hot Tubs

A low-cost way to cut energy bills for a hot tub is to buy a floating cover, says Ann Davis Helke of Mr. Pool in Boulder,

3 Water-Wise Pool Tips

With water becoming an ever scarcer resource, every pool owner should be concerned about water conservation. Here are three water-wise recommendations for pool owners from Ann Davis Helke.

Keep the pool filled year-round. Even in the harshest climates, you don't have to drain a pool and refill it. Be sure that during the off-season, the pool is drained below its skimmers, the pipes to and from the pool are drained and filled with antifreeze, the filter is drained and covered, and the pool is properly covered. A full pool is actually more resistant to damage from shifting soils (from freezing and thawing) than an empty one.

Cover the pool whenever feasible. To reduce evaporation, cover your pool in the summer whenever it won't be used for a while. If you have an electric or crank-operated cover, you can close it anytime you won't be using the pool for the day. If you must cover your pool by hand, you probably won't want to cover it that often, but do cover it whenever you're going away for a week or more.

Install a cartridge filter system. A cartridge filter system uses much less water than a traditional sand filter system, because it doesn't require frequent backwashing for cleaning. Also, a cartridge filter system requires less maintenance during pool season.

* * *

Colorado. Ranging from about $12 to $75, depending on the material, these covers float atop the water in the tub and provide an extra layer of insulation. They also reduce chemical condensation on the tub's main cover, which means the cover will last longer.

HOME LANDSCAPE DESIGN SHORTCUTS
Mark Twice, Dig Once

Professionals use computer software to create landscape designs, but if you're designing your home landscape yourself, you'll need a less costly way to visualize the outlines of paths, beds, walls, or water gardens. Peg Giermek, owner of Nature Calls Landscaping in East Aurora, New York, recommends this: "Start with some clothesline or colorful rope, which is lightweight and bends easily. Lay out the lines of your beds or

paths. Then go to the vantage point you think is most important—your window, deck, or maybe the street. Keep adjusting
the lines, going back and forth to your viewing spot, until you
like what you see." Peg notes that it's helpful to have a patient
helper participate in this process. Once you're satisfied with
the layout, mark the lines using washable spray paint or
marker paint (the type used on athletic fields). Dot the paint
4 inches inside the hose lines, every foot or two. Recheck the
lines once more from your vantage point, and as long as
you're satisfied, paint solid lines. Now you're ready to follow
the lines to lay the path or dig the bed or water garden, knowing you'll end up with just the shape you want.

Finding a Focal Point Fast

Deciding whether you've found the right spot in your yard for
that statue, birdbath, or trellis you bought at the garden center
yesterday can be a challenge. Make the choice quickly and
confidently by following these steps recommended by Master
Gardener Babbidean Huber of Amherst, New York, who
teaches landscape design.

1. Decide on the primary vantage point from which you'll
   want to view your treasure. Is it the kitchen window, or perhaps the street for the viewing pleasure of passersby?
2. Stand at the vantage point and look over your yard. Search
   for a spot that is not at the dead center of the view, but
   where your piece would fit in well. (Dead center is not usually effective, as it sets up a strict symmetrical design.)
3. Put your art object in the spot.
4. Return to your vantage point and see how things look.

Repeat steps 3 and 4 as many times as needed until your piece
is perfectly situated. Now you can add plantings or other
design features around your focal point. Just remember, if you
add too much, it will become a jumble. A little goes a long way.

Take Advantage of Natural Beauty

Sometimes Mother Nature offers the best landscaping ideas for
free, says Pennsylvania organic farmer Melanie DeVault.
"Everyone who enters our back porch on Pheasant Hill Farm

immediately comments on the beautiful vine that winds its way up across the porch roof," she says. When they ask what it is, we tell them, 'It's Virginia creeper, and it planted itself!' " Melanie says that birds love building nests in the vine—the family once counted nine nesters. She cuts the vine back when it starts to grow downward too heavily or tries to take over the roof. Keep an eye open for natural opportunities like this around your yard.

Puddle Plants on a Slant

A sloping area of lawn can be dangerous to mow, so converting slopes to a planting of trees, shrubs, or perennials is a landscaping choice that makes sense. However, planting on a slope becomes non-sense if the plants don't survive. Landscape designer and Master Gardener Peg Giermek of East Aurora, New York, says, "On a slope, the soil dries out faster than in ground-level plantings." To counteract this tendency and prevent plants from dying of thirst, notch a shallow concave planting basin in the slope for each plant. The basin will catch and direct rainwater or irrigation water and funnel it to the plant's roots. This advice applies whether you're planting a small perennial or a large tree. Peg adds, "Shape an outer rim two to three inches high to form a little pond, with an outer lip like a smiley face. All those smiles make it much more likely that you will be smiling as you look at living plants a year later."

Let Your Landscape Rock

Digging out rocks can be the most backbreaking part of a home landscaping project. Well, here's some good news: There's no need to remove rocks. Farmers have always had to dig

Haste Makes Waste

Weed before You Weep

"It's no shortcut to bypass bed preparation," says Cornell Cooperative Extension educator Sally Cunningham of East Aurora, New York. "If you ever ran a timed comparison, you would find that corrective weeding—pulling out weeds after a planting becomes established—takes at least four times the hours as removing weeds before planting the bed." How do you clear weeds before planting? Sally says to keep it simple: Pull or dig out the weeds, roots and all. Then, after planting, mulch the bare soil around the plants to prevent new weeds from sprouting up.

rocks out of their fields to protect their farm equipment from damage, and perhaps that's where we got the idea that rocks must go. Unless you plan to plow your landscape beds, however, it's fine to leave rocks where they lie. In fact, they serve a useful purpose. In the soil, stones and small rocks contribute to drainage, provide pockets for roots, and contribute micronutrients as they very slowly decay.

If you come across an attractive large rock when you're digging a bed, you may want to use a crowbar to shift it partially above soil level. The rock will add an interesting feature to the landscape bed, especially if you plant ground covers or low-growing perennials with finely textured leaves beside it.

Rechannel Difficult Drainage

When your yard has a perpetually soggy spot because of poor drainage, don't fight nature—go with the flow. Follow the lead of garden lecturer Mike Shadrack, who divides his time between London, England, and East Aurora, New York. Mike looked at his fiancée's garden one rainy April, when small sailboats were actually floating around the irises, and said, "Let's make a stone creek!"

Mike dug a trench about 2 feet wide and 8 inches deep meandering through the poorly drained area, thus solving the drainage problem. If you follow his lead, make sure the sides taper gently away from the center; this is a stream, not a ditch. Collect rocks and stones from your garden and from friends' yards to line the trench. Choose rounded stones to create a natural effect. Place larger stones in the bottom of the creek bed and smaller stones up the sides. When it rains, the stream will run full, and when it's dry, your yard will feature a picturesque Japanese-style dry stream.

Limb Up the Losers

Overgrown shrubs are commonplace in front of houses all over the United States and Canada, and it can be backbreaking or expensive to remove them. Cornell University home-grounds/community horticulture extension leader Charlie Mazza says, "Make it easy on yourself and turn a loser into a wonderful plant, the way professionals do in some of the best arboretums." The trick is called limbing up: You use a lopper or pruning saw to cut off the side branches up the trunk or main stems. (Cut outside the branch collar—the ridge where the branch meets the main stem.) Try it with those sprawling junipers and yews that are blocking the windows. "You'll be amazed at the beautiful texture on the trunks," Charlie says. "Suddenly, you have an attractive four-season plant instead of an eyesore." Plus, limbing up lets more light reach ground level, so a wider range of perennials and groundcovers can thrive at the base of the shrub.

The Sprinkle-Down Method

Here's another low-effort method for watering trees. Peg Giermek, owner of Nature Calls Landscaping in western New York, says, "I like the upside-down sprinkler method." Buy a doughnut- or ring-type sprinkler and invert it over the tip of a conifer or a high branch of a deciduous tree. You can run the sprinkler for hours; adjust it so there is just a slow trickle dripping through the branches."

Tall Perennials Save Bucks

Putting up a fence or planting a shrub hedge is a fast fix when you want privacy or to block an ugly view, but it can cost you $500 and up. Take a tip from perennial garden design expert Sharon Webber of Buffalo and plant a hedge of tall, wide perennials instead. Some perennial hedges serve only in the summer, but others are more permanent, such as ornamental grasses, which continue to stand tall through

Getting Gallons to Thirsty Landscapes

Newly planted trees and shrubs need more than 8 gallons of water per week during the summer while they're getting established. "Everybody underestimates how much water trees really need," says Tom Harris, an advisor to the East Aurora (New York) Tree Board. Tom recommends making a garbage can irrigation system for supplying water to new trees and shrubs. To do this, you need a 10-gallon plastic garbage can for each plant or a 30-to-40-gallon can for a cluster of new plants. Use a portable drill with a ¼-inch bit to drill 2 or 3 holes in the bottom of each can. Place the can under the dripline of the tree (not against the trunk or right on the rootball). Check the soil weekly, and whenever it is dry to a depth of 4 inches, fill the can with water. It will take hours for the water in the can to penetrate the tree's root area.

the winter. Good perennial hedge choices include butterfly bush (*Buddleia* spp.), goatsbeard *(Aruncus dioicus)*, plume poppy *(Macleaya cordata)*, and large ornamental grasses such as feather reed grass (*Calamagrostis acutiflora*) and maiden grass (*Miscanthus sinensis*). The cost of planting a dense hedge of perennials or grasses can be as little as $150.

Disguise Your Compost Pile

Compost is the best soil improver around. And although there are plenty of inexpensive choices for making a backyard compost bin—pallets, snow fencing, cinderblocks, or trash cans—none of these look exactly lovely. To beautify your composting structure, heap up materials inside it (ideally in the spring), then put a tabletop over the bin. You can often find discarded plastic picnic table tops, or just use a piece of plywood. The tabletop can serve as a place to summer your houseplants outdoors or to show off container gardens. If you include some vines or annuals that drape over the sides, nobody will know what practical matters are concealed underneath. When fall comes, you can remove the tabletop and spread the compost in your garden.

Prepare to Be Stumped

If you must have a dead tree removed, leave the stump intact. It may save you part of the cost, and you can turn the stump into a landscape feature. Ask the arborist to cut the trunk off flat 10 feet above ground level and put a birdhouse there. Or have the stump cut to 6 feet to serve as the base for a tray-style bird feeder. A 3-foot stump is a great platform for a large planter, pot, urn, or statue. Cut the stump off at 1 or 2 feet and use it as a planter: Hollow out the center, add some compost and soil, and plant annuals or perennials.

Fallen Logs

A fallen log in your yard can be a treasure, too. Use it as a garden seat, either as is or by attaching some boards to provide a level bench. If you know someone who is handy with a power saw, ask him to flatten the top for your sitting comfort. To create a more natural look, add woodland plants such as ferns or dogtooth violets around the log. They'll benefit from the humus as the wood decays.

QUICK-AND-EASY LANDSCAPE PROJECTS
Dot and Dash through Path Design

Landscape designer Peg Giermek of East Aurora, New York, reveals her secret for the professional-looking grass paths that wind through her planting beds. She marks out the paths first, making sure they are of even width, and lets them direct the bed shapes.

Peg also has a secret for quickly laying out paths that are precisely uniform in width. To use her technique, you'll need marker paint (used to mark baseball diamonds) and a piece of a 2-by-2 about 2 inches shorter than the desired width of your path. (For example, if you want paths that are 3 feet wide, cut the 2-by-2 to 34 inches.) Make a mark at the center of the piece of wood.

Walk along the route of the path, and every 3 feet place the piece of wood on the ground in front of you, with the center

---

Add Plants, Not Work

We asked veteran gardeners how they continue to buy and collect new plants for their yards without creating more and more yard work for themselves. Here's what they said.

- When you plant a new shrub or tree, append it to an existing island or bed rather than isolating it in its own spot, which would be more work to mow around.

- When you bring home something new, get rid of something you don't like or have too much of (just like in your clothes closet).

- Never buy more plants than you have places for.

- Never buy a plant until you have planted everything you bought the previous weekend.

- Don't buy a shrub or tree just for the flowers. Be sure you like its appearance in the nonflowering seasons—because that's how it looks most of the year.

- Choose plants realistically for the soil and site you have rather than adjusting the site for the plants.

- Research the mature height and spread of a tree or shrub before you buy it. If the plant overgrows its site, fixing the problem will be costly, difficult work.

mark directly in front of your body. At each end of the wood, spray a mark on the ground. When you're done, go back along the route and use the marker to connect the dots, forming continuous edges for the route of the path.

Set Rocks on Sand

If you are adding rocks as part of a landscaping project, dig out the area for each rock and pour an inch of sand into the hole before you roll the rock into place, says landscape designer Peg Giermek of East Aurora, New York. Then, if you need to adjust the rock, you don't have to lift the rock out of the hole to dig out or add more soil; you can just roll the rock or lift one side of it and scoop out or add more sand.

The Sink-and-Rotate Landscape

Adding flowering plants or ground covers under deciduous trees is difficult, especially if the trees have shallow root systems (maples, for example). If you undertake this project, follow the advice of longtime Master Gardener Flo Zack of Elma, New York. Dig individual holes wherever you can among the

My Favorite Shortcut

The Collapsible Trellis

Putting up a trellis against a wall of your house can be expensive and tricky to do right. Also, it's tough to paint behind a trellis. Nurseryman Skip Murray of Orchard Park, New York, has devised his own trellising system for vines that's inexpensive and easy to work with.

He fashions a trellis from a 4-to-5-foot-wide section of chain-link fence that extends from ground level to just below the gutters. Skip screws two large screw hooks just under the gutters. The hooks need to be large enough to hold the top crosspiece of the chain-link fence. Then he sets the fence on the hooks—the bottom crosspiece rests on the ground.

"Plant the vine at least eighteen inches from the house, outside the fence," Skip says. "During the growing season, when you want to do work on your house or prune the vine, you can simply unhook the fence from the top and lay the whole vine down on the ground. You and the vine will never get in each other's way again."

tree roots without a struggle. Sink large, heavy plastic pots into these holes and fill them with rocks or wood chips to keep them in place. You're "planting" these pots permanently, because they'll maintain open spots for plants that are relatively free from competition by the tree roots. (This job is even easier if you can plan ahead and dig these "pot holes" when the tree is young.) "I don't quite have the strength to dig them in, but I like to see bulbs in the spring, impatiens and 'Wave' petunias in the summer, and mums in the fall," says Flo. "This trick makes it simple." When you're ready to plant, just remove the rocks or chips from the sunken pots and insert potted plants, pot and all. Plant rotation is a breeze! When you're tired of one look, just lift out the pots and substitute something else.

The Door to Nowhere

Space is at a premium in small backyards in a town or city. There's no shortcut to make a small yard bigger, but there is a simple way to create the illusion of more space, says landscape designer Sharon Webber of Buffalo. On trash day in her neighborhood, Sharon watches for old doors set out at the curb. "A door in the landscape adds a sense of mystery about what's on the other side. A door pulls people toward it," Sharon says. She positions the door at the far end of a yard, where it creates the illusion of a much deeper yard or another garden "room" beyond—even if nothing is there. Brace a door to stand upright by pounding 2-by-4s solidly into the ground on each side of it or by fastening it to upright posts. Sharon likes wooden doors with faded paint, panels, or carving. You can plant tall perennials to flank the door and even leave it slightly ajar to make it more enticing to peek through.

HASSLE-FREE LAWN CARE

Create Islands in Your Lawn

Individual trees and shrubs in your yard create an obstacle course for the lawn mower. To reduce the time spent mowing, "get rid of the sharp turns, small circles, and zigzags," says Jim Pavel, who organizes beautification and cleanup projects for the city of Buffalo. "Give the lawn-mowing person a

Mowing Takes Too Long

Problem:

You can't find an efficient way to mow your lawn. Finishing off all the odd spots and missed patches adds an hour to a process you don't enjoy to start with.

Do This Now:

Mow in a concentric circular or oval pattern. It's the fastest way to mow because there's no turning or backing—you just keep pushing.

Do This for Good:

The nooks and crannies of your lawn—where you have to push the mower forward and pull it back again and again—are the parts that really eat up your time. Eliminate these spots by rounding out the edges of your flowerbeds and foundation beds so that you can mow all of your lawn using a circular or oval pattern. In the spring, devote 1 hour to replacing grass in awkward mowing spots with low-maintenance groundcovers such as pachysandra. It's easy to do. Simply cover the grass with 8 to 10 layers of wet newspaper, making sure to overlap the edges. As you work, cover the newspaper with a layer of shredded bark to hide it and keep it from blowing away. Then dig holes down through the mulch and the paper and plant the groundcovers. One hour of planting can save you 15 minutes each time you mow your lawn, and that adds up to more than 5 hours of saved mowing time over the course of a year.

straight path or a long curve." One helpful approach is to eliminate the lawn between individual trees and shrubs to create a mulched island with a clean, simple outline. Cover the lawn between the plants with two-to-four-ply black plastic and cover the plastic with wood chips. (The grass underneath will die.) Creating islands around trees and shrubs has a secondary benefit, too: It reduces the risk that the plants will be accidentally gashed by the lawn mower.

Don't Sit on Your Lawn

Leaving lawn furniture or a picnic table and benches on the lawn also adds time to the weekly chore of lawn mowing, as the person doing the mowing has to move the furniture and then put it back in place. Be kind to the designated lawn mower in your family and keep the lawn furniture on the patio. If you don't have a paved patio, create a mulched island for the furniture, using the same technique as described in the previous tip.

Embellish Your Lawn Ornaments

Mowing a tight circle around a birdbath, statue, or planter set in the lawn is a time-consuming job. Make the job easier—and enhance the look of that lawn ornament—by creating a small planting bed around it, planted with an easy-care groundcover such as heather, lamb's ears (*Stachys byzantina*), or rock spray cotoneaster (*Cotoneaster horizontalis*).

Mow What You Sow

If you love the look of your nice green lawn but resent the time you spend mowing it, try changing the type of grass you grow. "Plant a low-maintenance grass, such as certain fescues or bermudagrass in our area," says Wade Slate, a self-employed lawn care professional in Knoxville, Tennessee. (Your turf grass selection will vary in other regions, but the principle remains the same.) "They're still green, but they grow very slowly, and you won't need to mow nearly as often." Ironically, Wade won't plant such grass in the 50 or more yards he maintains. "That kind of grass would put me out of business," he says.

Let the Fertilizing Wait

When the lawn starts to turn green in the spring, most people think it's time to fertilize the grass to help it along. But most lawns are better off without early fertilizing at the beginning of the growing season (which is at the end of the winter in most parts of the country). In the Northeast, for example, lawns begin to grow in March or April, but experts at Cornell University's Turfgrass Program recommend waiting until the end of May to fertilize the lawn. In more southern zones, the same advice applies, just earlier in the calendar year. To get the most from the time and money you spend on lawn care, check with your local Cooperative Extension Service on the ideal time to fertilize your lawn.

Around the Yard

Let the Lawn Brown

Watering your lawn during the summer is hard work and tough on the water bill or well. And worse yet, if you water your lawn the wrong way, you're doing it more harm than good. Research at Cornell University has shown that irregular watering—a little every once in a while—stresses the lawn more than allowing it go dormant during a dry spell. So when summer turns hot and dry, stop watering and simply let the lawn go dry for up to 6 weeks. The grass will turn brown, but it will not die as long as there is as little as ¼ inch of rain during that period. When the fall rains arrive, that lawn will grow green again, and you can gloat over all the water you saved and all the work you avoided.

A Watering Can for the Lawn

"Many people water the lawn somewhat foolishly," says Rochelle Smith, a Niagara Community College instructor and landscape designer. "It's human nature to underestimate how long it takes to apply the amount of water a lawn needs, which is an inch of water per week." Use the cat-food-can trick to make sure you're applying enough water to benefit the grass. "A cat food or tuna can is about an inch deep," Rochelle says. "So when you water the lawn, whether by hand or with a sprinkler, set out a few cans here and there on the lawn." When the cans have filled up, you can stop watering.

Stop Mowing; Make a Meadow

If you live in the country or have a private suburban backyard, cut back on lawn care by giving your lawn a new name—a meadow. Decide which parts of your lawn you want to keep as traditional lawn and continue to mow those portions. Let the rest grow. As

Waste Makes Waste

Meadow in a Can

If you decide to plant an open area as a meadow, heed the warning of wildflower experts and beware of "instant meadow" wildflower mixes: They're not easy and certainly not instant! Plus, they may contain seeds of invasive plants that will take over your meadow, then move on to take over your yard. If you want to plant a meadow, follow a recommended plan from a horticulturist or Cooperative Extension Service specialist.

274

the grasses (and weeds) stretch tall, some wildflowers will creep in, and wildlife may begin to show up. If you'd like, mow a few paths through your meadow so that you can enjoy the flowers and observe the wildlife. Plant some native wildflowers, bulbs, or grasses along the paths, too. Mow the meadow once a year to prevent woody or invasive plants from taking over. Mow in the fall so that you won't disturb ground-nesting birds or small mammals.

FALL CLEANUP

Bag It for the Long Haul

Cornell Cooperative Extension educator Sally Cunningham always stops to pick up leaves left on the curb in her town of East Aurora, New York. "To avoid making a mess of my car or myself, I always carry a box of the best four-ply garbage bags in my car," Sally says. That way, she can bag loose leaves on the spot and double-bag leaves that have been stuffed into thin bags, which split open easily.

Back at home, Sally piles bags near the foundation of her house to block drafts and hold in some heat. She also uses bagged leaves as a windbreak along a fence at the end of a perennial bed. In areas where she intends to dig new garden beds in the spring, Sally sets bags of leaves on top of the grass. She uses a screwdriver or knife to poke holes in the bags so the contents don't become smelly. "In the spring, I spread the contents as mulch right where they are stored," Sally says. When she empties intact bags of leaves onto the compost pile in the spring, she saves the bags for reuse in the fall, after turning them inside out and allowing them to dry well in the sun.

The Lazy Raker Gets the Early Bird

Always looking for a reason to cut leaf-raking chores short in the fall? Go ahead and skip raking the leaves from under shrubs and bushes. Sure, your sore muscles will benefit, but so will the bushes and birds. A layer of leaves will create a moisture barrier that helps retain water for the roots of your shrubs and also draws all kinds of fascinating worms and bugs—just what ground-feeding birds such as robins enjoy

If you're one of those people who dreads leaf drop, try one of these low-effort, free (or cheap) alternatives.

Wait for the wind. Depending on the lay of the land in your neighborhood, a few good windstorms will do most of the work for you.

Spread a leaf catcher. Most leaves drop in a very short period of time in the fall. Prepare for the big drop by spreading sheets and tarps on the lawn under your trees. (Use rocks or boards as anchors so the wind doesn't blow your leaf catchers away.) After the leaves drop, gather the corners of the sheets and drag the leaves to your compost pile or holding place for mulch, or to the curb for collection.

Start an island bed. Grass does not grow well under leafy tree canopies, and it steals nutrients from the trees. So before the leaves fall, outline an island bed under your trees with rope or a hose. Let the leaves lie inside the outline, and that should reduce your leaf-raking chores significantly. The fallen leaves will become the first layer of mulch for your island-to-be.

most. So you subtract a few minutes of hard labor and add hours of potential bird-watching fun.

Go Fishing in Your Downspout

A device called a fish tape—used to pull electrical or phone wires through a wall—is just the tool for cleaning a clogged downspout. Just push the tape (which is actually a stiff, flexible steel wire) up the downspout.

All-in-One Ladder Work

Whenever you clean your gutters, take care of other routine roof maintenance while you're up on the ladder. You'll save time and reduce the amount of work needed next time around. For example, trim back any tree branches that grow near your roof. A gap of at least 1 foot between the nearest branches and the roof minimizes shingle-tearing scrapes during windstorms. Trimming branches also reduces the leaf and needle litter that must be cleaned from your gutters. If snow and ice haven't jammed your gutters when holiday season rolls around, you can clean your gutters and hang your Christmas lights at the same time. Most outdoor lights attach to the eaves on or near the gutters. As you move the ladder along and clip on those lights, clean out the accumulated leaves and debris and drop them to the ground, where they can be raked up. You also should hand-sweep the nearby shingles. When it's time to take down the lights after the holidays, clean the gutters again. With luck, you won't have to touch them again until fall.

Gutter Blowout

Hardware store manager Steve Shadel of Boulder, Colorado, uses a lightweight electric leaf blower to blast leaves and pine needles out of his gutters. With this tool, he can clean an entire length of gutter with just one or two trips up the ladder. Safely back on the ground, he then rakes up the accumulated leaves. For compacted leaves or mucky dirt, attach a high-pressure nozzle to your garden hose and fire a cleansing stream down the gutter. Steve points out that this muck all flows to the downspout, which then must be cleaned thoroughly with the hose—a good practice once a year anyway. This is also a good time to check that your gutters are oriented correctly. The water should move steadily toward the downspout. If it pools anywhere, the gutter needs to be repositioned.

WINTER CHORES

Gummy Gutters

Fixing a gutter in winter is difficult and can be dangerous. If a small leak develops during the winter, make a temporary fix by chewing some bubble gum until it's soft and pliable, then working it into the hole to fill it completely. The gum will quickly harden and stay in place until spring, when you can make a permanent repair.

Light Rails

No matter which method you use to hang Christmas lights along the eaves of your house—gutter clips, shingle tabs, staples, or nails—you'll have a much easier time of it each year if you permanently place anchor points at each corner of your roof. The simplest are screw-in eye hooks. As you string the

lights, tie a half hitch in the strand around each hook you pass. This will keep the lights straight and true.

Point 'Em Down

You'll replace fewer bulbs on your outdoor lights if you orient them downward. Moisture can seep into the sockets of upward-facing bulbs and short them out. Waterproof connections between strands by wrapping them in plastic bags and sealing them with electrical tape.

Ready, Set, Go!

Save money and hassle by putting all your outdoor Christmas lights on timers. Plug-in timers are available wherever holiday lights are sold; buy one for each side of the house. Once these are set, you won't have to march out into the cold night before bed to turn off your lights. If your outlets are outdoors, make sure you buy a timer rated for outdoor use.

The Sun Is Your Friend

It's tough to get all the snow off your walk or driveway when you shovel. But the sun can do some of your snow removal work for you—if you help it along. Shovel or brush deep snow before the sun comes out, and even a cold winter sun will finish the job. Trim bushes and move patio furniture or cars that shade key footpaths. Even if you expose just a little blacktop or concrete, melting will speed up considerably, because the sun warms the pavement and melts snow and ice from underneath. Try shoveling your driveway in strips. Work to expose bare concrete on about one-third of the drive; just scrape off the surface snow on the rest. The melting will spread outward from the carefully shoveled strips.

Hold the Salt

Don't use rock salt or salt-based products to melt the ice on your brick or masonry patio or walk. It will melt the ice quickly but also speed up deterioration of mortar and concrete. Moreover, salt that runs off a walk or driveway can damage nearby plants. Instead, use sand or cat box filler to increase traction.

Outdoor Uses for Christmas Trees

When the Christmas season ends, don't discard your Christmas tree. Instead, put it to good use in your yard.

Decorate your front yard. Place your tree (still in its stand) in an attractive position in front of the house. It's the shrub you never had. Bury the stand in snow to support the tree. If there's no snow, weight the tree by filling the stand with stones, or use boards to brace it.

Set up a windbreak. Ask your neighbors if you can have their trees, too. In snowy climates, set a line of trees in the snow, and they will often freeze in an upright position for a long time.

Feed the birds. Set your tree out in your yard (where you can see it from inside the house). Make suet cakes, cranberry strings, and other bird treats and hang them on the tree. Add new treats weekly and enjoy the show.

Create a wildlife hideaway. Lean a few Christmas trees up against the trunk of a large, limbed-up tree to make a wonderful winter hideaway for pheasants and small animals.

Shelter the birds. Line up a few trees so they will block your bird feeder from winter winds and offer the birds a warm perch. (The birds will congregate on sun-warmed needles, which hold more warmth than hard surfaces.)

Mulch your perennials. Cut off some tree limbs and lay them over perennial beds to protect the beds against frost heaves.

No-Stick Shoveling

Spray your snow shovel with a nonstick cooking spray such as Pam before you use it. Wet and icy snow will slide easily off a greased shovel and into the snowbank where you want it, sparing you from hefting excess weight. Also, store your shovel outside or in a cold shed or garage. Snow won't stick to a cold shovel.

Sweep It Up

Use a janitor's push broom instead of a snow shovel to clear light snowfalls from your walk and deck. The broom is much lighter and easier to maneuver than a shovel. Plus, it won't snag on cracks in the pavement, and it won't chip paint on a deck or porch the way a shovel will.

Ice Dams

Problem:

Some houses are susceptible to ice dams on the eaves. These dams form when melting water runs off a roof and freezes around the eaves, forcing water back under the shingles and down into the house.

Do This Now:

Use a long-handled rake to clear the snow and ice off your eaves right away. If you can make a quick trip to a home center or hardware store, buy a roof rake for this job. A roof rake has an extendable handle and dull tines, which are less likely to damage shingles than a garden rake. A typical roof rake costs about $50.

Do This for Good:

Ice dams usually form because the roof is too warm, while the eaves are too cold. To keep the roof from overheating, improve the insulation in the attic. Seal any openings in the floor, including gaps for electrical wiring and plumbing, and lay fiberglass insulation between and over the floor joists. However, make sure you don't block the vents near the eaves or the channels leading from those vents into the rafters. These allow cool air to ventilate the attic. If ice dams persist, you may need to hire a contractor to install metal flashing or electric heat tracing (which can be turned on to melt ice buildups) along the eaves.

Toboggans for Trash

In snow country, sledding and tobogganing are not just for the kids. Garbage cans like sledding, too! In places where the snow piles up and stays around for weeks or months, getting the garbage out to the street for pickup is a real problem—there's no way to maneuver your garbage cans through the drifts to the road. That's where sleds and toboggans come in. Take a rectangular cardboard carton about the same width as your sled or toboggan. Put the carton on the sled and the trash bags in the carton. Or if you spot a child out sledding, ask for his help. Invite him to ride on the sled, steadying your box, can, or bag of garbage as you pull it to the road. A round saucer-type sled also works well for hauling a garbage bag to the curb.

PART 3

Special Shortcuts for

Weekends and Holidays

Ingenious Gift and Craft Ideas

15

H omemade gifts come from the heart—that's why they're always appreciated. Fortunately, you don't need to wear your fingers to the bone or spend hours in the kitchen to make gifts your friends and family will love. The shortcuts in this chapter offer a host of ideas for whipping up gifts in a jiffy and helping your kids with presents they really *can* make themselves. You'll also find ideas for keeping all your craft and sewing equipment organized, so that you spend your time crafting, not searching for supplies.

GIFTS FROM THE KITCHEN
Double Your Potential

If you're cooking up something for your family that also would make a nice gift, why not double the recipe? It doesn't take any more time to make two loaves of bread instead of one. When all's said and done, you'll have a special gift on hand that you can give away immediately or keep in the freezer until needed.

The Big Chill

Homemade cookies are a great gift for many occasions. Although store-bought refrigerated cookie dough is convenient, it just doesn't produce the same results as cookie dough made from scratch. Instead, build up a stash of homemade frozen cookie dough and produce baked-from-scratch cookies quickly and easily whenever you need them. It takes almost no extra time, and your friends and family will be dazzled by your seemingly magical ability to whip up a plateful of assorted homemade cookies in a flash. Whenever you make cookie dough, double the recipe. Bake half for now. With the rest, form walnut-size balls of dough, set the balls on cookie sheets, and put them in the freezer until they're frozen solid (at least 1 hour). Then transfer the uncooked balls to resealable plastic bags. (Label them with the date and type of cookie.) Do this every time you bake, and you'll soon have several bags of various cookie dough balls in your freezer. When you need a gift on short notice, select a few balls from each bag, place them on a cookie sheet, and allow them to defrost for about 45 minutes. After that, just preheat the oven and bake.

Homemade Apple Butter without the Hot Stove

Here's a cool, no-fuss way to make an old-fashioned treat you'll love to have on hand for gifts, especially around the holidays. Start with 4 pounds of apples you have picked yourself, bought at a roadside stand, or picked up at the grocery store. A mix of apples is best, but be sure to include some tart, flavorful baking apples such as Granny Smith. Peel and core the apples, then put them in a food processor. Add 2 cans of frozen apple juice concentrate, then puree. (Do this in two batches if your food processor isn't large enough.) Pour the mixture into a slow cooker such as a Crock-Pot, cover, and cook on high for 8 to 10 hours. Taste the apple butter occasionally as it cooks, adding a teaspoon or two of sugar and cinnamon, if needed. Check the flavor between additions—you don't want to overdo either of these ingredients. After 8 to 10 hours, adjust the taste one final time, then cook on high until the apple butter is very thick—the time will depend on the type of apples you use and how hot your cooker gets. Spoon the apple butter into sterilized pint canning jars (running jars and lids through the dishwasher is an easy way to sterilize them) and cover. Put a bow on each jar, and you have gifts all set to go. Store in the refrigerator for up to 2 months. You can also freeze the apple butter or process it in a canner.

A Gift of Chocolate

An unforgettable gift of luscious chocolate sauce—if you can bear to give it away—is easier to make than you might imagine. Just melt 4 squares of unsweetened chocolate in the microwave. (Heat it on high power in short bursts of about 30

FIX IT FAST • FIX IT FOREVER

Lack of Wrapping Supplies

Problem:
You need a wrapped gift in a hurry, but you don't have anything to wrap it in.

Do This Now:
The Sunday comics make great emergency wrapping paper, and so do colorful magazine pages (match the photos to the theme of the gift). Another quick choice is a clean, neatly folded paper bag—perhaps with a design stamped on it if you have a stamp pad and ink handy. If not, borrow some of your children's crayons or markers. Even a plastic grocery bag with a big bow makes fine wrapping paper in a pinch for all kinds of gifts, especially ones from the kitchen.

Do This for Good:
Build up a supply of containers for spur-of-the-moment gifts. For gifts from your kitchen, canning jars are perfect for items such as preserves or chutney, but they're also great for nuts, dried herb mixes, and even nonkitchen items such as glitter or beads. Also stockpile wrapping paper, labels, ribbon, bows, and sturdy resealable plastic bags. Aluminum foil is great for wrapping bread—fold the ends just as you would a package and add a bright ribbon and bow. A roll of plastic wrap or cellophane also comes in handy. (For more great gift-wrapping ideas, see "Gift-Wrapping Shortcuts" on page 359.)

seconds each so you don't burn the chocolate.) Pour the melted chocolate into a blender and add 1 cup sugar, 6 tablespoons warm coffee or milk, and 1 teaspoon vanilla extract. Blend until smooth and silky. Pour the sauce into small jars (half-pint or pint canning jars are perfect) and refrigerate for up to 10 days—although it won't last that long if your family has anything to say about it! This sauce has the texture of icing when chilled and can be used to frost cakes. Or warm it slightly in the microwave and pour it over ice cream.

Custom Labels for Home Preserves

Instead of buying fancy labels for canning jars, create custom labels on your computer. It's easy to do but makes your gifts extra special. Blank labels come in standard sizes—1 by 2½ inches, 2 by 4 inches, and 3½ by 4 inches are typical. Or buy full-page 8½-by-11-inch labels and let your creativity take over as you design and cut out any shapes that you like. Dress up any size label with clip art or a photo. You can even include the name of the recipient right on the label ("Strawberry jam made especially for Aunt Mary—Love, Susan"). If you don't need an entire sheet of gift labels, print the extras with your own name and address to create a handy stash of return address labels.

Dip Up a Hostess Gift

Chocolate-dipped pretzels are a quick-and-easy hostess gift. To make them, you'll need a bag of pretzels and 8 to 16 ounces of chocolate bark coating or candy-making chocolate (available at craft supply stores or gourmet stores) or sweet cooking chocolate. Melt the chocolate in a microwave oven or double boiler. (This is a treat even kids can make, but supervise them carefully, and also make sure the chocolate doesn't burn.) Use hooks made of wire to dip regular pretzels or tongs to dip pretzel sticks in the melted chocolate. Spread the pretzels on waxed paper and immediately sprinkle with jimmies to decorate. Refrigerate the coated pretzels for at least 30 minutes. After the chocolate is firm to the touch, wrap in cellophane or plastic bags tied with ribbon.

GIFTS FROM NATURE AND THE GARDEN

Perfectly Easy Drying

To dry flowers in record time, make small bunches of 5 to 10 stems. Large bunches are easier to make, but the flowers won't dry as fast or as well, and the stems may be attacked by mold. Flowers that dry quickly also tend to have brighter colors. To make bunches in a hurry, use rubber bands rather than string. Not only can you slip a rubber band around a bunch in a jiffy, but the band also will hold the bunch together as the stems shrink. Hang bunches in a dark, well-ventilated place such as an attic or garage.

Bought Bouquets Boost the Supply

At the end of the summer, if your own supply of dried flowers doesn't include all the colors or bloom sizes you need for that perfect project, don't hesitate to buy a bouquet or two. Combine purchased strawflowers, dried chile peppers, or even

Pick 'Em While You've Got 'Em

As you work in your garden, keep an eye out for plants that would dry nicely and could be used to make gifts. Picking a bunch of flowers here and a few stems there isn't much extra work, and watching your stockpile grow is really fun. Here are some great, easy-to-grow perennials that are easy as pie to dry. Unless otherwise noted, cut the flower stems, then strip off the leaves before bundling and hanging to dry.

- Baby's breath (*Gypsophila paniculata*): Make small bunches of flowering stems and pull them apart gently when dried, as they are brittle.
- Bee balm (*Monarda didyma*)
- Blazing star (*Liatris* spp.)

- Blue false indigo (*Baptisia australis*): Harvest stems of blue-black seedpods.
- Chinese lantern (*Physalis alkekengi*): Cut the seedpods and hang to dry.
- Delphinium (*Delphinium* × *elatum*)
- Globe thistle (*Echinops ritro*)
- Lavender (*Lavandula angustifolia*): Dry both flowers and foliage.
- Sea holly (*Eryngium* spp.)
- Sea lavender (*Limonium latifolium*)
- Sedum (*Sedum* 'Autumn Joy'): Set flower heads in a vase with 1 inch of water in it. Don't replace the water, and the heads will dry nicely.
- Yarrow (*Achillea* spp.): Dry these the same way you would sedum.

dried sunflowers with your own materials to add pizzazz to a wreath or bouquet.

Make Lots of Hang-Ups

Attics and garages are prime places for drying flowers, but space can be a big problem. For a tidy, space-efficient drying area, hang an old ladder from the ceiling and use wire hooks made from clothes hangers to hang bunches. An old clothes-drying rack hung in the same manner works well, too.

Give a Garden

Want to skip shopping altogether but still come up with a tremendous gift for a friend who has a new home or wants to start a garden? Give plants! Lifelong gardener and garden writer Barbara Ellis suggests potting up divisions or rooting cuttings of your favorites. Choose plants that will grow best in the conditions your friend's garden has to offer—sun or shade, moist or dry soil—and gather up a garden to give. Three or four 2-quart pots look great in a new bushel basket, or fill a flat or basket with smaller pots. (Make sure you include labels.) If you want a gift a new gardener will never forget, Barbara suggests filling your car with new plants, then spending a few hours helping your friend plant them.

Note: Make sure you're giving your best plants—not just the ones you have the most of. Invasive plants are one problem you don't want to pass on to a friend.

Market Pack Gift Basket

A pretty basket of flowers doesn't have to cost an arm and a leg. You can save more than half the cost of what you'd pay at a florist if you design your own flower baskets. Market packs of annuals such as Johnny-jump-ups, pansies,

The Second Time Around

Keep On Potting

Whenever you're gardening, scout for plants that you can dig up and pot—self-sown seedlings, offsets on the edge of a clump, or perennials that need full-scale dividing. Pot up these bonus plants, label them with the name of the plant and its growing requirements, and keep them in a protected, semishady spot, such as along the north side of the house. Also, whenever you visit dollar stores and flea markets, watch for decorative pot sleeves or baskets. You'll soon have a stockpile of gift plants, and all you need to do to prepare a gift is to pop one of your potted finds in a basket.

Give Simple Herbal Vinegars

These flavorful brews make wonderful gifts from both garden and kitchen, and making them is as simple as can be. You need fresh herbs, a bottle of high-quality white or red wine vinegar, a glass jar with a plastic lid, a plastic spoon, coffee filters, a plastic funnel, and glass jars for the finished vinegars. Don't use metal spoons, lids, or other equipment, because metal reacts with vinegar and will spoil the taste.

1. Wash all the equipment in hot soapy water and rinse in hot water.

2. Put 1 cup fresh herbs and 2 cups vinegar in the steeping jar. Try a mix of herbs such as basil, parsley, and garlic. (Keep notes so you can duplicate the recipe later.)

3. Close the jar and set it in a dark, cool place to steep. Shake or stir occasionally.

4. Taste the vinegar in a week. For robust flavor, most vinegars should steep for about a month.

5. When the flavor suits your taste, use a coffee filter and funnel to filter out the herbs as you fill clean glass jars with the mixture. Add a fresh herb sprig; cap the jar with a glass, plastic, or ceramic lid; and label it.

• •

or marigolds make great gifts if you dress them up a bit. These inexpensive packs of annuals are available everywhere, from garden centers to grocery stores. A single pack fits in a basket with an inside measurement of $5\frac{1}{4}$ by $3\frac{1}{2}$ inches, two packs fit in a basket that measures $6\frac{3}{4}$ by $5\frac{1}{4}$ inches. Look for decorative baskets at your local dollar store, at flea markets, or in your basement, and keep a supply on hand. Line a basket with plastic, drop in a market pack, and you're good to go. Want to color-coordinate? Individual plants pop out of their cells easily, so buy packs in two colors, then mix and match. Or buy market packs of several types of basil, parsley, and other herbs, then switch plants around so you have herb gardens to give. (Make sure you label the plants.) Whether you give them as hostess, housewarming, or thank-you gifts, these pretty baskets are perfect for enjoying indoors or planting out in the garden.

Give a Little Project

Sometimes a gift that involves a little creative input by the recipient can be just the ticket, says lifelong gardener and garden writer Barbara Ellis of Berks County, Pennsylvania. One of the best gifts she ever sent her grandmother, who lived in Florida and missed the flowers of a northern spring, was a huge bunch of forsythia stems in the dead of winter. When the package of forsythia arrived, her grandmother had a wonderful time arranging them and sharing extras with friends. Anticipation was the best part of the gift, though, as she watched the buds swell and the flowers open. Although this is a great gift for someone who lives in a frost-free climate, it's also suitable for anyone who doesn't have a large yard or who lives in an apartment or nursing home. Other stems, such as apples and cherries, can be forced, but forsythia is a good choice because it's absolutely foolproof.

Ride the Posy Express

Homegrown posies, whether presented in a jelly jar or a brand-new vase, make an excellent, inexpensive gift. All you need to start your own posy express is a few packets of annual seeds—zinnias and cosmos are good choices. Sow a row or two in the vegetable garden or plant patches in flowerbeds. Keep them watered and fed, and keep the flowers picked, because that encourages the plants to grow more. You'll be cutting and giving away bunches all summer long.

Packin' Posies

Need an easy, no-fail way to transport a vase of flowers in your car? Place the jar or vase in a box and cram newspaper around it. This will prevent the jar from tipping over as you wind your way through traffic.

SEWING AND CRAFTS
Sewing Emergency Kit

A box outfitted for emergency sewing repairs makes a thoughtful gift. (While you're at it, make an extra one for yourself.) Start with an attractive box or basket that has a lid, then fill it with thread in various colors, needles, and pins, along with a pincushion, seam ripper, needle threader, scissors, and an assortment of buttons. Add a small screwdriver, an awl, and a

Sew-Simple Napkins

You don't need any sewing skills at all to make a set of dinner napkins for a gift or for yourself. Start by taking a trip to a fabric store and picking some fabric in a pretty print, gingham, or solid color. A polyester and cotton mix is best to eliminate ironing. Most fabrics are sold in 45-to-48-inch widths. Dinner napkins measure 18 by 18 to 20 by 20 inches, so buy about 1¾ yards of fabric to make six napkins or 3½ yards to make a dozen. Once you get the fabric home, here's how to turn it into napkins without sewing a stitch.

1. Preshrink the fabric by running it through the washer and dryer.

2. Spread the fabric on a table with the right side facedown.

3. Use a measuring tape and a sliver of soap to mark cutting lines for the napkins. (The soap will wash out easily afterward.)

4. Cut out the napkins.

5. Create long-lasting frayed edges by pulling out a dozen or so threads on all four sides.

6. Fold each napkin in fourths, then roll it up and tie it with a pretty ribbon.

Note: If you have leftover fabric and also have a friend who's a quilter, you've got an instant bonus gift. Quilters always appreciate fabric!

pair of needle-nose pliers for other simple repairs. Keep your own emergency sewing kit by the TV for on-the-spot fixes while you watch the news or your favorite show.

Instant Color Themes

Whether you're sewing a pillow, decorating a box, or painting a picture frame, settling on a color scheme can be a real headache. What colors will look best? Will this one look okay with that? For an easy answer, pick a piece of fabric, a rug, or even an article of clothing with a color scheme you like, then use those colors in your project.

Button, Button, Where's the Right Button?

There's a cigar box or cookie tin in your sewing room that's brimming with thousands of buttons. (Some of them have been awaiting a needy shirt or jacket for a few decades.) Finding precisely the button **you need** is probably an hour's task—unless you're as well **organized** as Benedicte Whitworth, a housewife in Raleigh, North Carolina. Benedicte saves old jam jars and sorts her buttons into them according to color. Since you're likely to have many more white buttons than any other color, sort the white buttons according to the number of holes as well. Now you'll be able to find the right button in seconds.

Shaded Supplies

Tired of looking at shelves of fabric and other sewing supplies? Mount a roll-up window shade on the top shelf. When you pull it down, the problem disappears. A simple pair of curtains over the front of a bookcase works just as well.

All That Glitters Is a Gift

The inexpensive papier-mâché boxes available at craft supply stores make great gifts that you can decorate in a jiffy. Vary the decorations to suit the occasion—a Valentine's Day or Mother's Day gift, or an extra-special box to contain a Christmas treasure. All you need is white craft glue and decorations such as felt or wood cutouts, stick-on jewels, glitter, or other items that can be applied with glue. You can paint the boxes first or leave them plain. To decorate with glitter, you'll need a deep-sided cookie sheet, jelly roll pan, or cardboard box lid lined with newspaper. Here's what to do.

1. Use glue to draw shapes or patterns on the box.
2. Set the box in the middle of the tray and sprinkle glitter generously on the glue. (Shaker applicators work best for this.)
3. Dump the excess glitter off the box and into the tray. The remaining glitter will stick to the glue. Recycle the glitter as needed by doubling up the newspaper and pouring the glitter back into the applicator.

Decorated boxes are a great gift for kids to make, too. Children as young as 2 can make them, says Diane Thomas, a mother of three and child care provider in Alburtis, Pennsylvania. Really little tykes will need to be supervised so they don't eat the glue or decorations, though.

Drawn-Out Gifts

When you need a half hour free from interruptions by your kids, here's an ideal diversion that also produces a useful gift.

Any kid who can wield a crayon or marker can make hand-decorated stationery or note cards. Once you set up the supplies, you can just let the kids work. Naturalist Janet Ellis of Helena, Montana, says the stationery her son, Daniel, drew was one of the nicest presents she ever received from him. (Daniel drew lots of flowers at the top of each piece of stationery and on the back flap of each envelope.) Note cards with matching envelopes are available in craft supply stores, and these can be decorated in a similar fashion. Ideally, find a box in which you can give or keep this original artwork—the recipient may or may not be able to part with a single sheet.

Wrapping Paper, Kid Style

If you're pressed for time, why not have your kids make wrapping paper for you? They can create wrappings for their own gifts as well as yours. (You'll probably want to help out—this is loads of fun.) All they need is sheets of butcher paper (which is sold at craft supply stores) and art supplies for printing. Old sponges cut into shapes or even potatoes that are past their prime for cooking make wonderful stamps. Just spread a bit of poster paint in a shallow plastic foam tray (like the ones meat comes in). Press the sponge or potato into the paint, then print away. Kids can easily add to their designs with crayons or markers. Every sheet of paper will be a piece of original artwork.

Beaded Beauty

Pipe cleaner decorations are a perfect project to occupy kids on a rainy afternoon. All you need to have on hand are pipe cleaners and packages of plastic beads. Choose fairly large beads that are easy to work with. (Supervise very young kids so they don't put the

Glorious Gizmos

Handy Sewing for All Situations

Even if you don't have a regular sewing machine, you'll find plenty of uses for a handheld model. (These machines are advertised on TV and available at fabric stores.) A handheld sewing machine is the perfect tool for spot repairs where you need to fasten two seams together. Use it to hem or repair curtains while they are still hanging, mend canvas items or duffel bags, or even hem a coat in an emergency. Since such machines sew a chain stitch, they're also useful for tacking up a hem for a fitting or holding together a Halloween costume.

Beyond Cross-Stitch Kits

You'll love these tips for making cross-stitch pictures. They're so simple, even a child can do them—in fact, they're recommendations from a child. Teenager Jenny Liston of Columbus, Ohio, likes making cross-stitch pictures for friends and relatives. She suggests the following:

■ Instead of buying kits, which cost more and take all the creativity out of selecting pictures and picking colors, she and her mom visit the library and find patterns in cross-stitch books.

■ Using the grid system in each pattern book, figure out the thread count of the fabric and the final size of the design. (Start new cross-stitchers on 8-count fabric, then move toward 12- or 14-count fabric once they get the hang of it.)

■ Jenny enjoys stitching quotations surrounded by borders, and since she likes to give finished, mounted projects, she plans her pieces to fit in a standard picture frame (usually 4 by 5 inches). That way, they're easy to mount by wrapping the edges of the fabric over a piece of cardboard and setting it in the frame.

■ Small cross-stitch projects are never overwhelming to finish, and they're very portable. Pack them in resealable plastic bags along with essentials such as scissors and thread, then carry them anywhere.

beads in their mouths.) Show the kids how to twist a small circle at the base of a pipe cleaner so the beads won't fall off the bottom, then let them string away. Diane Thomas, a mother of three and child care provider, suggests using red and white beads to make candy canes, green and red ones to make wreaths, or all red for hearts. Once the pipe cleaners are covered with beads, twist a circle in the other end of the pipe cleaner to secure the beads. Then bend the pipe cleaner into the desired shape. Voilà—easy gifts for family, friends, and teachers that kids can really make themselves. For older children who want more "professional-looking" results and think pipe cleaners are just for little kids, substitute wire for the pipe cleaners.

Paint a Pot

Another great craft activity for kids is decorating empty terra-cotta pots. (Find the extras in your garden shed and clean them up before giving them to the kids.) Kids can paint the pots or use pictures from magazines for a decoupage effect. Use the pots to organize desk clutter, such as pens and pencils, rulers, and scissors.

Stylish Shoe Boxes

Kids and grown-ups can all enjoy decorating a shoe box with Con-Tact paper, construction paper, or old scraps of wallpaper. The finished product is perfect for holding everything from recipe cards to the seashell collection your grandchildren brought back from the shore. Label the box fronts so you'll always know what's inside.

Got Milk? Make Building Blocks

Montana second-grader Daniel Hanson and his mother, Janet Ellis, dreamed up a great way to recycle half-gallon cardboard milk containers. They make them into gigantic, lightweight blocks. Just cut the top off each carton and wash it really well. Then take two cartons and jam one into the other as far as it will go. Daniel builds forts and walls from his recycled blocks, and they're sturdy enough to crash into, says Janet. Even if one gets smashed now and again, it's not a tragedy, and they won't damage floors or furniture like wooden blocks do. Several other families in Daniel's hometown have made sets of milk carton blocks and pass them from house to house as kids get older.

Simple Storage Solution

Craft supplies can take up space, and if they're spread all over the house, you're likely to spend more time looking for them than actually crafting. Katherine Scott, a mother of twins

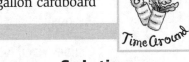
The Second Time Around

Showery Solution

Glitter, paint, and glue can all be pretty messy to use, and certainly they're a pain to clean up—especially if the only place you have to make crafts is the dining room table. What to do? Hold on to those old plastic shower curtains. They can be used to cover the table, spread on the floor, or even drape over chairs to protect against spills. You can even make a paint-proof poncho by cutting out a square of shower curtain that's as wide as the wearer's arm span. In the center of the square, cut a hole that's slightly larger than the wearer's neck; also cut a slit so the poncho can slip over the head. Then use duct tape to close up the sides.

from Westerville, Ohio, has a simple solution to the storage headache. She has two inexpensive metal shelving units in the basement. Craft materials are sorted into clear plastic boxes by type—paint supplies, knitting and crochet supplies, and so forth. She also has a special box of remnants from a variety of sewing projects, because she knows that scraps of fabric or pieces of yarn always come in handy.

Craft Cartons

Save empty egg cartons for times when you or your children or grandchildren are working on a project that requires keeping track of and separating lots of small parts. If you have clear plastic egg containers, you'll be able to see what's inside even when the lid is closed. As a bonus, egg cartons are perfect for holding small quantities of tempera paints. When the kids are done with the project, you can simply toss the egg cartons in the trash.

Cube Your Craft Drawer

Most folks have at least one extra ice cube tray hanging around the kitchen, attic, or basement. These trays come in handy for organizing a drawer of craft items, such as buttons and snaps, knitting needle tip protectors and stitch markers, safety pins, and thimbles.

Put Ideas in Their Place

How many times have you lost a magazine or newspaper article with a great gift idea or wasted time looking for the directions to make a special craft? Instead of tucking ideas all over the place, make an idea file folder for your household file cabinet. Whether you label it Craft Ideas, Gift Ideas, or just Ideas, designate the folder as the only place where you'll stash magazine articles, newspaper clippings, pictures of projects that look interesting, notes jotted down at a craft fair, directions for making paint or play dough for your kids—any gift or craft idea that's interesting and ingenious to you. You don't have to keep them in any particular order, because paging through them can be fun in and of itself.

A Junk-Clogged Craft Drawer

Problem:

Your craft drawer is so clogged with project pieces, tools, ribbon, and other flotsam that you can't find anything.

Do This Now:

Buy a box of 2-gallon resealable plastic bags. First, pull out all the pieces of yarn, ribbon, string, and wire in the drawer. Put them in one bag—two if you can pull them apart fairly easily. Put hand tools such as pliers and tweezers in another bag, half-finished projects in a third, the glue gun and supplies in a fourth, and so on. Use a pancake turner to pick up all the buttons, beads, glitter, and whatnot from the bottom of the drawer. Now at least you have items in the drawer somewhat sorted, and the tangle won't get any worse.

Do This for Good:

Instead of cramming craft supplies in a mishmash of bags and boxes, measure your drawer(s) and survey the items you want to store there. Then buy clear plastic boxes in suitable sizes. Shallow boxes divided into lots of compartments are perfect for buttons, beads, and other small items, while a larger box may be just right for holding a glue gun and accessories. If you need to, arrange the boxes you're thinking of buying right there in the store. Measure and then adjust your choices so that the boxes will fill every available space in the drawer. Once you bring the boxes home, sort all your stuff into them—a good job to tackle while watching TV.

A Crafty Closet Overhaul

If your clothes closet is the only available storage space you have, organize your clothes, and you just may find extra space for craft supplies. Move dresses and coats to one end, skirts and blouses to the other, and you'll have space for a small chest of drawers or rolling file cabinet under the blouses and skirts—especially if you raise the bar to 6½ feet. If you have the room, hang two bars in one section, one above the other. (See "Hang 'Em High . . . And Low" on page 177 for instructions on hanging a second bar.) Fill this section with skirts and blouses, then divide the rest of the closet into space for longer garments and storage space for craft supplies. Hanging shelves, which you can suspend from the clothes bar (available from suppliers such as Hold Everything), may be just the ticket for a wide variety of supplies.

COLLECTIONS AND MEMORABILIA
An Easy, Ever-Changing Display

Whether you have art of your own to display or projects from your child's classroom, a giant-size display wall is what you need. Start with a sheet of Homasote—a gray, 1/2-inch-thick paperboard product that comes in 4-by-8-foot sheets. Available at lumberyards, it can be cut to any size you like right at the store. You'll also need a staple gun, 60-inch-wide fabric to match your room, ribbon that complements the fabric, upholstery tacks, and heavy-duty fasteners to attach the Homasote to the wall (ask at the lumberyard for suggestions). Cover the Homasote with the fabric, using staples to hold it in place. Then crisscross the fabric with pieces of ribbon. (Craft ribbon is fine for this; real ribbon is more attractive but also more expensive.) Staple the ribbon at each end on the back, and use upholstery tacks to fasten the pieces down where they cross in some spots. Hang the fabric-covered board securely, ideally fastening it to wall studs at the top and bottom. To display works of art, just tuck the ends under the ribbon—no tape or tacks required.

A homemade display board is the perfect showcase for art projects. There's no need for tape or tacks that can ruin your artwork or end up underfoot (ouch!) on the floor.

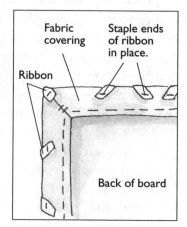

Fabric covering

Staple ends of ribbon in place.

Ribbon

Back of board

Talk It Up

Scrapbooks and photo albums don't have to be gigantic affairs. In fact, small photo albums—the kind with one picture per page—are perfect for summing up the highlights of a vacation or a holiday visit with your family. They're perfect for times when you're visiting with a friend and want to catch up on family news. Katherine Scott, an Ohio mother of twins, makes small photo albums containing about 15 pictures that represent activities her daughters have participated in over the past 6 months. These "talk books" include shots of everything from vacations and birthday parties to visits from friends and new pets. When adult visitors ask what they have been doing recently, Katherine's daughters pull out their talk book and explain the pictures. According to Katherine, this has replaced shy silence and shrugs with a productive conversation. Her daughters have learned how to relate to adults in a positive way—a valuable boost to their confidence and communication skills. Talk books also help adults relate right back.

Custom Calendars from the Computer

A custom family calendar is one of the best gifts Janet Ellis of Helena, Montana, ever gave to her parents, grandparents, and siblings—and the beauty of the gift is that, by using the family computer, Janet had to design only one calendar and then print a copy for each recipient. She selected two pictures for each month—mostly cute pictures of her and her siblings as kids—and had multiple copies made, then glued them in place and drew up the calendar pages, noting family birthdays and holidays. "I tried to pick appropriate pictures for each month— a Halloween picture in October or birthday pictures of the person who

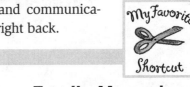

Copy Family Memories

A mixture of old-fashioned sentimentality and modern technology allows Jane Ann Ellis, an Ohio homemaker and grandmother, to share memories of trips and family events in super-efficient style. She makes scrapbook pages with photographs taken on a trip or during an event, then adds captions along with decorations such as glued-on confetti or stickers. She takes the scrapbook pages to the local copy center and has high-quality color copies made. That way, she can easily share the memories with everyone who was there.

was having a birthday that month," Janet says. Computers make custom calendars an especially easy gift, because you can scan in pictures or use digital images, then draw up the calendar pages with standard software.

Cut the Clutter, Keep the Memory

Children's artwork can clutter up a house fast, but home-maker Katherine Scott of Westerville, Ohio, has a foolproof art storage system that couldn't be easier to use. She buys an artist's portfolio for each child each year—the kind that has a handle and sides and is made of fairly lightweight yet strong cardboard. She writes the child's name and grade level on the flap at the top, then stores it under the child's bed. After art-work or other school projects have been displayed and appre-ciated in the family room, they get filed in these portfolios. Eventually, Katherine will sort through it all, but for now it's safely stored and yet right at hand.

Great Garden Shortcuts

Our gardens are a great escape from the high-tech haze of the 21st century. Raising vegetables and herbs and tending a beautiful bed of flowers are stress-relieving pleasures that we seldom have enough time to enjoy. With the tips in this chapter, you'll learn how to make the most of your gardening sessions by planting more efficiently, reducing time spent on routine maintenance, and solving animal and insect pest problems. You'll also find plenty of money-saving ideas for container gardens, trellises, and even a low-cost greenhouse.

SEED STARTING AND PLANTING
Baste Your Seedlings
Watering seedlings can be a time-consuming job, especially if you have pots or flats of seedlings tucked under lights indoors. Specialty flower grower Linda Essert-Kuchar of Emmaus, Pennsylvania, finds that using a turkey baster speeds the job of watering delicate seedlings. With the baster, she notes, you

can extend your reach into tight corners. Also, you can direct water right at the soil surface and thus avoid shocking the foliage of the tender seedlings with a spray of water.

Store Seeds Safely

It's a shame to throw away opened packets of seeds. But if you've tried storing seeds in paper packets through the winter, you've probably discovered that sometimes the seeds leak out or spill. Or perhaps you've had the unpleasant surprise of finding that mice have chewed their way into your stored seeds. To protect your seed supply from both of these hazards, transfer the seeds from opened packets into empty plastic film canisters or pill bottles. Use a permanent marker to write the variety name on the lid of the container or attach a stick-on label.

Put Parsley on the Fast Track

Fresh parsley from the garden is a treat, but it's tough to grow parsley from seeds, which can take up to a month to germinate. But Master Gardener Christine Bailey of Germansville, Pennsylvania, knows the secret for persuading parsley seeds to germinate in less than 1 week. Instead of planting seeds dry or soaking them for 1 day, as is often recommended, Christine says that she lets the seed soak for three full days, changing the water once during that time. By the time the third day of soaking arrives, the seeds look "plumped up," she explains. "I drain the seeds and sow them in seed-starting mix in a container. I cover the container with plastic wrap, then put it on a windowsill where it will receive strong afternoon sun, but where the temperature is a little chilly." Each night, Christine moves the container to the top of a radiator by her window. (The top of a refrigerator or another warm spot will work, too.) Within 6 days, the first of the seedlings emerge.

The Second Time Around

The Ladder of Seeding Success

Skip the task of marking out areas for sowing lettuce, carrots, dill, and other crops that you seed by broadcasting. You can set up a symmetrical planting grid in an instant by laying an old wooden ladder across a garden bed. You may have an old ladder that's too unstable to climb tucked away in your garage or shed. Or watch for one at garage or farm sales.

3 Free Seeding Tools

"Some of our favorite tools for working with seedlings aren't available in glitzy garden catalogs," say Pennsylvania market gardeners George and Melanie DeVault. Odds are, you already have their favorite tools around your house.

Yardstick row maker. "To make planting rows quickly in seed flats, we use a yardstick, cut to just shy of the length and width of the flat," says Melanie. Press quickly and lightly into the potting mix to form a straight row.

Fork seedling lifter. When transplanting seedlings after the first true leaves have emerged, Melanie uses a plastic fork (the kind you get with take-out meals). Melanie removes the outer tines of the fork, leaving just two tines intact. The remaining two tines help gently lift the seedlings.

Measuring tape spacing guide. When seeding or transplanting vegetables in a garden row, George brings along a wind-up measuring tape. He stretches the tape along the length of the row and refers to the inch marks to plant seeds or transplants at exactly the proper spacing.

Forget Seed Tapes

Making seed tapes sounds like an ideal time-saver: vegetable seeds sown on a strip, spaced perfectly, ready to be laid in a seed furrow and quickly covered up. But in the real world, gardens have rocks and lumps and bumps. Creating that perfectly straight furrow for the seed tape is as much work as planting a packet of seeds. Melanie and George DeVault tried seed tapes as a project when they were gardening with their young children but found that the kids always got frustrated by twisted and broken tapes. So instead, Melanie and George sowed vegetable seeds the old-fashioned way with their kids: by hand.

VEGETABLES AND HERBS

For Best Beans, Pick Early

Last summer, Melanie and George DeVault accidentally discovered that harvesting their bean crop early was a brilliant idea. The couple needed some beans to sell at their farm market, but the beans on their bush bean plants were only 2 inches long. George decided to harvest some anyway. On tasting the baby beans, George and Melanie were delighted—the flavor was terrific. They packaged the beans in half-pint containers and labeled them as gourmet beans, and the crop was a big hit with their customers. You can harvest baby gourmet beans from your home garden, too. A bonus of this early-picking method is that your plants will be stimulated to produce more flowers and bean pods, so you can reap a second and third harvest.

4 Secrets for Summer Lettuce Success

Gardeners, even market gardeners, often shy away from growing lettuce in the scorching summer months, because they're worried that their crop will be bitter or bolt before it's ready to harvest. But growing lettuce during hot weather is a breeze if you know these strategic shortcuts.

Choose a heat-tolerant variety. There are plenty to choose from, such as 'Nevada', 'Magenta', and 'Jericho'. Catalogs will tell you which varieties are heat-tolerant. Even discount stores and home stores offer a good selection of lettuce seeds, so you can pick up a packet or two on a regular shopping trip.

Set up some shade. If you live in an area with extreme heat (lots of 90°F days), set up shade cloth over the lettuce patch. Pound in four 4-to-5-foot-long tomato stakes, one at each corner of the patch. Use a staple gun to fasten a piece of shade cloth (available at garden centers) to the top of each stake.

Plant in furrows. Don't scatter seeds over the surface of the bed as you might in the spring. Instead, use your fingers or a wooden stake to open shallow furrows 6 inches apart. Sprinkle in the seeds thickly and cover them lightly with soil. For a continuous supply, plant one short row every 2 to 3 weeks.

Use a soaker hose. Moisture is essential in hot weather. Snake a soaker hose between the rows and water daily for 1 hour if there's no rain.

Follow these guidelines, and you'll be cutting baby lettuce about 28 days after you first sow seeds. Use scissors to cut the plants about 1/2 inch above the base, and they will keep growing. Harvest lettuce in the cool of the morning or evening.

An Easy-Weave Tomato Trellis

Tomato cages work well for supporting large tomato plants, but if you don't have time to make tomato cages, money to buy them, or space to store them, you need an alternative. Try this easy, low-cost trellising method from Pennsylvania market gardener Aimee Kocis. The only materials you'll need are several sturdy 5-to-6-foot-long posts and a ball of twine.

1. Plant a row of tomato plants, spacing them 2 feet apart.
2. Pound in a stake at each end of the row and also at about 5-foot intervals along the row. (Set them equidistant from neighboring plants.)
3. Allow the plants to grow, watching for signs of floppiness. If they look ready to flop, or when they reach about 2 feet tall, tie one end of the ball of twine to the end post, 12 to 18 inches above ground level.
4. Stretch the twine past the tomato plants to the next post. Wrap the twine around the post and pull tight. Repeat this to the end of the row.
5. Wrap the twine around the end post, pull tight, and continue unrolling the twine down the other side of the row, wrapping it around the posts as you go. Tie off the twine at the end post.

Continue this process of adding twine every 12 inches until the plants either reach the top of the stakes or stop growing.

Aboveground Vegetables

If you have problem soil, the easiest way for you to grow vegetables may be in containers above ground level. "Peppers, eggplants, and tomatoes are great container plants for me," says Pennsylvania home gardener extraordinaire Janon Johnson. Janon grows peppers and eggplants in 10-, 14-, and 18-inch pots and heirloom tomatoes in 20-inch or larger pots. She kept her costs low by shopping for the pots at garage sales. Janon has created a container garden by spreading newspaper thickly (up to 1 inch thick) over the soil near her patio and topping the paper with 1 to 2 inches of wood chips. She nestles the pots into the wood chips. The chips provide good drainage, and the newspaper below prevents any weed growth. With a system like this one, a container vegetable garden stays looking great all season, and you never have to contend with digging up rocky soil, fighting tough weeds, or worrying about growing food plants in contaminated soil.

The Benefits of Borage

Borage, a tasty herb for salads and seasoning, also can help you cut short weeding chores. The trick is to use borage as a living mulch in your vegetable garden. Pennsylvania Master Gardener Christine Bailey says, "I let borage reseed throughout my vegetable garden wherever it wants to from year to year." If borage seedlings have popped up in an area where she wants to plant seeds, Christine removes them, but elsewhere she allows the plants to flourish. "By the middle of summer, each borage plant spreads out and covers the soil to keep moisture in and weeds down," she says. "Also, the flowers attract beneficial insects all summer long." Borage plants bear

They Had NO Shame

Spuds in the Bathtub

A friend of Pennsylvania market gardener Melanie DeVault saw a treasure in an old, cracked cast-iron bathtub abandoned by a creek bed. "She conned her husband into bringing it home, much to his dismay," Melanie recalls. He was pleasantly surprised with the results, however, because his effort provided the family with copious quantities of potatoes. Melanie's friend scrubbed and disinfected the old tub and set it on cinder blocks at the side of her suburban home. She filled the tub partway with a mixture of organic compost, a little sand, leaf compost, a little organic mushroom soil, and regular garden soil. The resourceful gardener then bought some organic pota-

toes from a health food store, ate the nicest ones, and left the others to sprout. At planting time (April in Pennsylvania), she cut the sprouted potatoes in half, let them sit a day to heal, and planted them in three rows in the tub. As the plants grew, she added more soil and ended up harvesting 2 bushels of potatoes. To disguise the nature of her potato production center, she planted some other containers of climbing flowers and vegetables in front of the tub.

Note: If you want to try this method for growing your own potatoes, you don't *have* to use a bathtub. Any tub or large container with bottom drainage will do.

tiny blue and pink flowers that are a gourmet treat. Remove and discard the middle from the star-shaped flowers, then float them in summer drinks or punch bowls. Add young borage leaves to salads, mix them with vegetables, or add them to soups for a mild cucumber taste.

Another Borage Benefit

Not only is encouraging borage volunteers an easy, no-cost way to mulch, but Christine Bailey says that it's also a technique for building up organic matter. At the end of the season, the borage plants will die back, and you can dig them into the soil as you clean up your garden in the fall.

Fight Weeds the Easy Way

If you think that planting a cover crop is too much work, think again. Here's a planting scheme for a cover crop for northern gardens that is truly easy. The time you invest in planting will be more than repaid by the time you save on weeding the following year.

1. In September or early October, remove the remains of the vegetable plants and any weeds from your garden.
2. Rough up the soil surface and sprinkle annual sweet white clover seeds over the ground (about 2 cups of seeds per 100 square feet).
3. Rake in the seeds lightly or just walk over the seeded area a few times.
4. If conditions are dry, water the bed well. After that, you can forget about it.

   Annual sweet white clover will grow more than a foot tall before it dies, forming a great mulch to cover the soil through the winter. In the spring, you can plant right in the mat of dead clover; just scoot the dead plants aside enough to open planting rows or hills. If you prefer, you can till the plants under. Whichever way you choose, you've added nitrogen to your soil and kept the weeds at bay.

Crimson and Clover

If you miss your chance in the fall to plant a cover crop, spring into action in the spring instead. Plant crimson clover in early spring (use the same planting technique as in the previous tip), and it will keep spring weeds from sprouting and build soil quality. You will need to cut back the crimson clover occasionally because it will keep growing through the summer. When you're ready to plant your garden, run your lawn mower over it. Dig up small areas as needed to plant seeds or transplants. If you have a large garden area, leave pathways of crimson clover between rows of vegetables or flowers wide enough for your mower, and mow occasionally. Bag the clippings, and you have instant nitrogen-rich mulch. At the end of the season, dig or till the clover in for a great nitrogen boost.

Herbs That Do Double Duty

Fresh basil and dill are the perfect accents for many favorite recipes. It's best to harvest young leaves frequently. Sometimes, though, the plants get away from you and go to flower. If that happens, don't abandon them. Just cut the flowering stems and use them in flower arrangements and bouquets. Their wonderful scent is a nice addition to an indoor arrangement. Be sure to remove the lower leaves from the stems before you put them in water.

Hint: When you cut flower stems from your dill plants, leave a couple of the flowers to set seeds. The seeds will drop and sprout quickly, producing a second crop later in the season. Other easy-to-grow double-duty herbs include Greek oregano, chives, and mint.

Manageable Mint

A sprig of mint spruces up a summer meal, a handful makes a great tea, and the smell of fresh mint seems to lessen the heat on a sultry afternoon. But mint has a well-deserved reputation for spreading. A single plant can take over your garden, and trying to control it can drive you crazy. Fear not—there's a surefire shortcut that allows you to keep both your mint and your sanity: Grow mint in a tub or large container right on your patio. Most garden centers sell a good selection of popular mints, such as peppermint, spearmint, and apple mint. Buy two or three small plants in 4-inch pots, and they'll quickly fill your container.

Homegrown Greenhouse

Minigreenhouses like the kind shown in mail-order catalogs are a gardener's dream—an expensive one. Save hundreds of dollars by making your own instead. You will need rebar, polyvinyl chloride (PVC) pipe, electrical tape, and a sheet of heavy-duty clear plastic (with a UV inhibitor).

1. Cut six 18-inch lengths of rebar, three 10-foot sections of ¾-inch PVC pipe, and one section of ¾-inch PVC pipe slightly more than 6 feet long.

2. Mark out a garden bed measuring 4 by 6 feet. Pound the rebar 12 inches into the ground at each corner and also at the midpoint of each long side of the bed.

3. Insert one end of a 10-foot piece of PVC pipe over one rebar stake. Bend the PVC pipe across the bed and fit the other end over the rebar stake on the opposite side. Repeat this with the other two 10-foot pieces of PVC pipe.

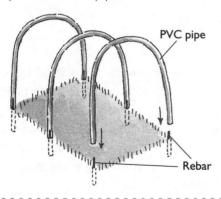

PVC pipe

Rebar

4. Place the 6-foot section of PVC pipe over the three hoops, taping each joint well with electrical tape. Cover the ends of the pipe with tape, too, so they won't poke a hole in the plastic.

5. Cut the plastic to the size you need, leaving at least 1 foot extra all around.

6. Cover the hoops with the plastic. Open a furrow along one side and one end of the frame and bury the edges of the plastic in the furrows. Use rocks to weigh down the edges of the plastic on the other side and end, for easy access when you want to go inside.

Rocks hold down plastic.

Use your greenhouse to extend the season in both spring and fall. Move your started seedlings into the greenhouse in spring, and sow some crops directly in the ground in late summer for fall harvest. If you live in an area with heavy snowfall, remove the plastic before winter sets in, or you're likely to find your greenhouse flattened come spring.

Herbs at Your Fingertips

When you're cooking dinner and the dish needs a little piz-zazz, fresh herbs are the answer. But it often seems like too much trouble to run out to the herb garden when you're in the midst of cooking. The solution is to grow herbs within reach of your fingertips while you're at the stove—on your kitchen windowsill. Plant a minigarden in the spring, and it will last for months with little care. (Your kitchen windowsill must receive direct sun, though.) You'll need a few small pots, a small bag of organic potting mix, a small container of liquid fish emulsion fertilizer, and a few herbs. Plan on one herb plant per pot, or if you prefer an all-in-one planter, visit a garden center and look for a larger oval pot that will fit on your windowsill.

Check the plants every couple of days and water them whenever the top inch of the soil seems dry. (Clay pots will dry out more quickly and need to be checked more often than plastic pots.) Apply a shot of liquid fish emulsion fertilizer once every couple of weeks to keep the herbs healthy. (Follow the label directions for applying the fertilizer.)

An Herb Planter Layout

One planter combination that will cover many of your season-ing needs is two compact 'Genovese' or 'Spicy Globe' basil plants, placed at the center of the planter, with one Greek oregano plant, two curled parsley plants, and one thyme plant set around the outside.

FLOWER GARDENING

Draw Me a Picture

Before you head off for the local nursery to buy plants, dig out your colored pencils and make a rough drawing of your plant-ing area. "You're always way ahead if you sketch out the area you're trying to fill, or even bring a photo," says Knoxville, Tennessee, landscaper Wade Slate. "If the nursery worker can't visualize the space you're working with, his recommen-dations of plants will be a shot in the dark."

Grow Forth and Multiply

Most 2- to 4-inch pots weigh only a few ounces and often represent the best deal when you're buying herbs, vegetable transplants, plants for pots on the patio, and bedding plants. "You can pay twice the price for six-inch pots or two or three times more for the gallon size, but the small plants will quickly catch up to the big ones within a few weeks of planting," says Wade Slate. "Save your budget for the times when you really need the bigger size, such as when you're buying slow-growing perennials or shrubs."

Grow Flowers, Not Weeds

Flowers don't like weeds any more than you do. To prevent weeds from competing with your flowers, do what the big flower growers do: Grow your beauties in a bed covered with black plastic or landscape fabric (a synthetic fabric that allows air and water to pass through but suppresses weeds). Whether you have a 3-foot patch or a 30-foot strip, you'll find that your flowers will thrive without the competition from weeds. Before laying the fabric or plastic, till or hoe the area well, pull out any big rocks that might rip the plastic, and water well. Lay the plastic or fabric over the bed, pull it tight, and bury the ends in the soil. To plant, just use a dibble to poke holes through the plastic or use scissors to cut planting Xs in the fabric. In a short time, the flowers will be resplendent, and you won't even notice the fabric or plastic at ground level. Some weed barrier landscape fabrics will last more than one season, but remove the black plastic at the end of each season. After all, it's much easier to pull up some plastic than to pull out a bed full of weeds.

Squeeze in Small Sunflowers

Sunflowers are beautiful, but growing giant sunflowers takes a lot of space. Enjoy sunflowers on a smaller scale by planting a small-flowered variety such as 'Sunbright' or 'Sunrich'. Start the seeds indoors in small pots or peat pots. Transplant them outdoors as close as 2 to 4 inches apart. They'll yield plenty of small blooms that are terrific for bouquets and arrangements.

An old wicker chair rescued from the trash can become a sturdy and attractive garden trellis for roses and flowering vines.

Turn Trash into Treasure

You see them alongside the road on trash day, or especially on "big item" pickup days—old wicker chairs with broken seats, backs, or armrests. Gardener Janon Johnson of Emmaus, Pennsylvania, says that a cast-off chair makes a beautiful, useful, and (dare we say) cheap garden decoration. Janon took advantage of just such a find. She removed the remaining wicker from the broken seat, set the chair in a garden bed, and planted a rosebush in the center of the seat. "I plant morning glories around the chair legs, and I train them to grow up the arms and back of the chair each year," Janon says. "It's beautiful! The rosebush uses the support of the chair." Janon says that she has also made a basket "cage" out of chicken wire to fit in the broken seat frame to hold a container of annuals.

Thin Those Blooming Zinnias

Zinnias are easy to grow, but Kansas market gardener Lynn Byczynski, author of *The Flower Farmer*, has discovered a shortcut that makes growing them even easier. After the last spring frost, plant a row or bed of zinnia seeds rather thickly. The seeds are big and easy to work with, so your children or grandchildren can help you plant. Lynn says not to bother with thinning the closely planted zinnias at the seedling stage. Instead, let the plants grow and flower. Then comes Lynn's shortcut. "I cut the first blooms off right at the ground," she says. By doing so, she combines thinning and harvesting the first round of blooms into one step, opening up space in the bed for more plants to bloom.

Be Prudent about Gift Plants

Before you accept free gift plants from neighbors or acquaintances, be sure you know that the plant giver is really your friend and that you know what plants you're being given. Many "easy" perennials—such as black-eyed Susans (*Rudbeckia* spp.), 'Silver King' artemisia, bellflowers (*Campanula* spp.), and yarrows—are perfectly good plants if you have the right place for them. However, they also can take over a home landscape or smother precious specimen plants. If that's the case, over time your "easy" perennial will become the one that takes the most time—digging it out!

Raise Camels for Low Maintenance

Garden "camels"—drought-resistant succulents, hardy creepers, and leathery-leaved plants such as sedums and lavenders—are great choices for a quick-and-easy perennial garden, says New Jersey garden writer Cass Peterson Doolittle. For a dramatic border, mix Russian sage (*Perovskia atriplicifolia*) and an artemisia such as 'Powis Castle' with sedum 'Autumn Joy', Cass suggests. For a tidy low border, use hardy ice plant (*Delosperma* spp.) and any of dozens of varieties of low-growing dianthus and creeping sedum. "How easy are they? In the

5 Free Bouquet Fillers

Weeds have no place in flower arrangements, right? Wrong. Some highly popular bouquet fillers that professional florists like to use are nothing more than common weeds. You can find them for free in fields or ditches near you. These fillers add depth to floral arrangements and have a long vase life. Here are a few worth searching for.

Foxtail. The fuzzy flower spikes of this weed are a long-lasting addition that give bouquets a natural look.

Johnsongrass. Although it's a noxious weed, if you cut the stems just

as the seedheads emerge from the sheath, you'll have a nice filler that holds up well in arrangements.

Ironweed. Cut the flowering stems when they're at the bud stage, before the purple flowers open.

Queen Anne's lace. The delicate, lacy white flowers of this weed (which some people call a wildflower) are borne on strong stems that have a long vase life.

Goldenrod. The yellow flowers of this weed light up roadsides and vacant fields and can bring a ho-hum flower arrangement to life, too.

spring, top-dress the bed with some compost and let the rain wash it in," Cass says. "And in the fall, when a hard freeze causes the foliage to turn black and crisp, do cleanup chores with a string trimmer or lawn mower set on its highest setting." End of chore list! To reduce maintenance even more, you can let the plants stand over the winter, then combine cleanup and fertilizing in one early-spring session before new growth starts.

Mulching a Potted Garden

Mulching around newly planted perennials can be a tedious task, but landscaper Gary Campbell of Coopersburg, Pennsylvania, has figured out a shortcut that speeds the work of mulching. When Gary plants a bed of perennials, he plants the large ones first. As he goes, he inverts the nursery pot that each one came in over the top of the plant (unless the plant is too large). Then he quickly shovels mulch over the bed, without worrying about messing up the foliage. After mulching, he removes the protective pots. If Gary has any plants in small pots, he saves those for planting after mulching. He just pulls a small amount of mulch aside at the desired spot, opens a small hole in the soil, and drops in the plant.

Corral Flowers with Tomato Cages

Use tomato cages to support gladioli, peonies, and other tall perennials that tend to flop, says Linda Essert-Kuchar, specialty flower grower from Emmaus, Pennsylvania. They're much more economical than the specialty garden hoops sold to hold up flowering plants.

Politics Aside . . .

You know all those election signs stuck on wire frames in medians all over town? After the election, those wire frames make great stakes for plants or to hold up perennials—and they're free!

Trim More Than Hedges

Hedge shears make quick work of other garden jobs besides trimming hedges. For example, rather than struggling to pull

Secrets for Fabulous Cut Flowers

Ever wonder how flower farmers and florists make their bouquets last so long, when the flower bunches you cut seem to wither overnight? Here are a few secrets to save you money and lengthen the life of beautiful homegrown bouquets.

■ Choose flowers that have a long vase life. Zinnias, snapdragons, sunflowers, yarrows, butterfly weed, China asters, and many others are good bets. Consult flower catalogs to learn which flower varieties are good for cutting if you aren't sure.

■ In most cases, cut flowers when they are just beginning to open. Fully open flowers look impressive, but they won't last.

■ Cut flower stems cleanly with a sharp knife or scissors, taking as long a stem as you can. Remove the leaves from the bottom third of the stems and plunge the stems into water in a clean container. Don't allow any leaves to contact the water. They'll decay, increasing bacteria and mold, which will make the flowers die faster.

■ After you cut flowers, move them out of the sun and into a cool place as quickly as possible. Once you're in a cool, shady location, you can take your time arranging the flowers in a vase, recutting the stems as you work.

■ Change the water daily, or at least every other day.

■ Try adding a homemade floral preservative. Add 1 crushed aspirin tablet, 1 tablespoon sugar, and 1 teaspoon vinegar to 3 cups water.

sunflower stalks out of the garden, use the shears to slice through the stalks near ground level. Hedge shears are also a great tool for cutting thick, tough ornamental grass foliage.

Try This Tool Caddy

Having the right tools at hand when you're gardening can prevent little jobs from turning into big problems, according to New Jersey garden writer Cass Peterson Doolittle. For example, says Cass, if you don't have your pruning shears at the ready when you notice a small pruning job, the small job can mushroom into a big chore. Or that leaning perennial may topple flat if you don't have stakes and string with you at the moment you first notice it. Cass has discovered a simple solution that allows her to carry all her tools to all parts of her yard: an old golf bag mounted on a hand-pulled cart. Cass says that instead of woods and irons, the bag holds a rake, a garden fork, a hoe, long-handled pruning shears, and bamboo stakes. All those neat zippered pockets hold twine, plastic markers and a marking pen, a notebook and pencil, a bottle of soap-spray solution, and more. "It's taken innumerable strokes off my gardening game," Cass says. If you don't have an old golf bag and cart in the attic, look for one at area garage sales.

GARDENING IN CONTAINERS
They're the Berries

Planting a bed of strawberries is a big job, but there's an easier way to have fresh strawberries all summer long. Grow alpine strawberries in several containers right on your patio. One- and 2-gallon nursery pots and large plastic hanging baskets work fine for growing alpine strawberries. You probably have some leftover nursery pots and baskets stashed in your garage, or ask your neighbor whether she has any.

Buy cell packs of alpine strawberries at a local garden center. The plants will grow well in a mixture of regular potting soil and compost or mushroom soil. Give them full sun and water them regularly. Fertilizing them with liquid fish emulsion every few weeks will help keep them productive, too. Alpine strawberry plants produce berries that are much smaller than the large berries sold in the grocery store, but the supply will be steady throughout the summer.

Bonus Berries

Don't throw out those baskets of alpine strawberries when fall rolls around. Store them in a protected location over the winter and bring them out the following spring for another year's crop. You can dig and divide 2- and 3-year-old clumps, too, to start a second generation of container plants.

A Bushel, a Basket

That old farmer's friend the bushel basket is also the container gardener's friend. A bushel basket is a great inexpensive container for patio plants. Line the basket with a plastic garbage bag (33-gallon size), punch some holes in the bottom of the liner for drainage, and fold the ends down below the top of the basket so the bag doesn't show. A lined basket will last for 2 or 3 years. If the basket you're planting has slats that are close together, you can simply fill the unlined basket with potting soil. An unlined basket will last only a year or two.

If you're going to place the basket on a wooden deck or concrete patio, elevate the basket on some flat stones or bricks. This will help prolong the life of the basket and prevent it from staining the deck or patio surface.

Foliage Baskets Flourish

Did you ever spend some hard-earned cash for a beautiful hanging basket of flowers, only to have it droop and die after about 2 weeks? It's just plain hard to keep hanging baskets thriving through the dog days of summer. But Master Gardener Christine Bailey of Germansville, Pennsylvania, has a fix that can save you money and also achieve a great decorative

Waste Makes Waste

Watch Out for Wind

Pennsylvania gardener Pamela Heckman loves filling containers with seasonal flowers. She uses large aluminum tubs and big plastic pots around her suburban home and patio. Since Pamela likes to be able to move the containers from place to place, she substitutes lightweight packing peanuts for soil in the bottom half of the containers, then tops the peanuts with 6 to 8 inches of soil—plenty for growing annuals. One year, Pamela was so eager to plant her flowers that she didn't notice the strong wind blowing. "When I poured the peanuts in the tub, they blew all over the yard," she says. When she picked up the mess, she came up short on peanuts. Pamela decided that there must be a better lightweight filler than peanuts, and she found one. "I put a couple of clean, empty plastic milk jugs, with the tops on, in the bottom of the containers first," Pamela says. "Then I put the peanuts around the jugs—when the wind died down." The experiment was a success, and that's how Pamela has set up her containers ever since. She puts a piece of aluminum or plastic screening on top of the peanuts and jugs so that she can easily remove the soil at the end of the season without having it become mixed in with the peanuts.

effect: Choose foliage plants, not flowering plants, for hanging baskets. "I love to pot up several variegated vincas and a couple of purple annual sweet potato vines in a large hanging pot," Christine says. "The color from the foliage and the long, lush growth look lovely all summer and into slightly cooler weather." If she wants an accent of flowers, she nestles one or two small zonal geraniums—which can tolerate hot weather—between the vines.

Bigger Can Be Better

Planting and maintaining large hanging baskets may seem like more work than planting smaller ones, but the opposite is true. "I find that the larger the hanging container I use, the more successful I am at keeping the plant looking fresh during hot weather, because there's more soil mass to hold moisture," says Pennsylvania Master Gardener Christine Bailey. She has a simple tip to help you determine when that basket needs to be

Soda Bottle Waterer

Hanging baskets planted with cascading geraniums, petunias, or sweet potato vines add a lovely touch to your yard, whether you hang them from a tree limb or from hooks on the front porch. Watering those baskets can be messy business, though, and sometimes you end up as wet as the plants do.

Master Gardener Ray Nowak of Lackawanna, New York, ended his watering woes by crafting a simple overhead watering device that's great for watering hanging baskets, as well as seedling trays on top shelves. It costs about a dollar to make. Visit your local hardware store and buy some 1/4-inch-diameter plumber's tubing. Back home, take any size soda bottle, clean it well, and use a portable drill to drill a 1/4-inch hole in the bottle cap. Cut a 6-inch length of the tubing and insert it in the cap, pushing about 1/8 inch of the tubing to the inside of the cap. To ensure a tight seal, Ray uses a small soldering iron and just touches the heat to the cap (not the tube) around the edges of the hole. This melts the plastic of the cap a little, sealing the connection with the tube. Fill the bottle with water, screw on the cap, and you're ready to go. And it's a great drinking-water bottle, too!

watered, too. "Moisten the basket thoroughly, then push up on the bottom to see how heavy it feels," she says. Use the same test daily, and when you notice that the basket feels lighter, that means it needs watering. "I've also found that when a hanging plant is very dry, the soilless mix pulls away from the sides," Christine says. "When you add water, it runs right down the sides. To rehydrate a container like that, soak the whole thing in a tub of water until it's saturated again."

Gel Is Swell

Christine Bailey notes that adding a polymer gel product such as DriWater to the soil mix in her hanging baskets helps reduce her watering chores. The water-retaining gel helps keep the plants moister longer.

PEST CONTROL SHORTCUTS

Alliums Repel Rodents

Chipmunks, squirrels, mice, and voles love to nibble on your prized tulip bulbs. An easy way to stop them is to interplant members of the genus *Allium* (which includes onions, garlic, and chives, among others) with your tulips and other bulbs that are enticing to rodents. Try ornamental onion bulbs known for their cut flower potential, such as drumstick chives (*Allium sphaerocephalon*).

Give Your Bulbs Onion Breath . . .

Here's another onion-related shortcut for foiling bulb-munching critters. Sprinkle a little onion juice in the hole as you plant your tulip bulbs. To make onion juice, just throw some onions in a blender with a little water and blend on high for several seconds. Onions that are past their prime for cooking are perfect for a batch of onion juice. Check your onion supply, or ask your local market gardener if he has any onions that have gone bad.

. . . Or Garlic Breath

Garlic planted with bulbs also tends to repel rodents. Try sticking some garlic cloves in the bed at the same time you plant bulbs in the fall. The garlic will sprout during the winter, so not only will this tactic repel rodents but it also will mark all the spots where you can expect to see bulbs pop up in the spring. Next spring, you can clip the garlic greens, chop them up, and eat them in salads or use them in stir-fries.

Make Critters Say Ah-Choo

Another way to protect your prized bulbs is to sprinkle crushed oyster shells or clamshells and a couple of teaspoons of cayenne pepper on top of the bulbs as you plant them. If you don't have access to a beach, visit a farm store or feed supplier to buy the crushed shells. Critters don't like the feel of the shells or the fiery kick of the cayenne.

Dispenser of Death (for Bean Beetles)

When yellow dots cover your bean plants, look more closely, and you'll probably see that the plants are infested with Mexican bean beetles and their larvae. To deal with these pests fast, you need a simple dispenser for hydrated lime, which is toxic to the beetles. Keith Crotz makes a lime dispenser from a 3-pound coffee can. Keith turns an empty coffee can upside down on his workbench and uses a ¹⁄₁₆-inch drill bit to drill several holes through the bottom of the can. Outside in the garden, put some hydrated lime in the can. Hold the can over your bean patch and tap the can with your hand to release a dusting of lime on the foliage. "The beetles chow down on the lime dust and die," says Keith.

Caution: Hydrated lime is somewhat caustic, so be careful not to get it on your skin. Wear gloves, long sleeves, and a dust mask when you work with it.

Blend Some Bug Juice

Japanese beetles can ruin your roses as well as many other landscape plants and vegetable crops. If your garden is infested with Japanese beetles, fight back fast by using the beetles as a weapon against themselves. Collect a cup or two of the beetles in a container. Put the beetles in an old blender (one you don't use for food preparation) with some water. Blend them well, then strain the resulting liquid through cheesecloth into a spray bottle. Add water to dilute the bug juice (four parts water and one part bug juice). Spray the mixture directly on the crops being devastated by the beetles.

Hose Your Squash

To stop squash vine borers almost without effort, try the panty hose technique used by Illinois gardener and

Slip panty hose section
over seedling.

Unroll panty hose as
plant grows.

Have your squash vine wear a section of old panty hose to prevent squash vine borer damage.

former biology professor Keith Crotz. "Cut a leg off a pair of panty hose at the ankle and thigh level," Keith says. "Roll it tightly and set the roll around the base of a plant once the first set of leaves form." Then let the vine grow for a week or two. After the vine has lengthened, unroll the hose along the vine, covering the cotyledons and bases of leaf stems as well as the main stem. Eventually, you'll extend the hose to protect the first 12 inches or so of the main stem. The barrier prevents vine borer moths from laying eggs at the base of the plant, which is the most vulnerable part. This technique works for squash, melons, pumpkins, and zucchini.

Hunt Slugs in Style

Mike Shadrack, a garden lecturer who divides his time between England and New York State, loves to inspire new hosta collectors. Unfortunately, slugs love to turn hosta leaves into a holey mess. Thus Mike offers his converts a well-refined method for killing slugs efficiently. He tells gardeners, "Just dress up for an evening out and catch the slimy fellows—or at least scare them." Mike's slug-catching outfit begins with a battery-powered headlamp (a headband or cap with a flashlight attached; available from sporting goods stores), which allows you to keep your hands free. Next, don rubber boots: They keep your feet dry, they're good for squishing slugs on the path, and they wash off easily afterward. The third element of the costume is barbecue tongs, which extend your

Low-Cost Deer Deterrents

Any gardener who lives at the edge of a wood knows that deer can be a real problem around the yard. How do you live with them rationally—and easily and inexpensively? Keep surprising them. Here are some simple surprise tactics for spooking deer.

■ Attach a plastic garbage bag to a stake. When the wind blows, the moving bag will scare the deer. Change the position of the stake occasionally to keep them guessing.

■ String clear fishing filament at several heights between two posts across a path where you see lots of deer tracks. Change the positioning of the posts and line every few weeks.

■ Stuff chunks of highly fragrant soap into old net bags or panty hose and tie it to a post or the branch of a tree. Change the soap when it loses its scent. (The small bars available in hotel rooms are the perfect size for this, so be sure to collect them when you travel.)

■ Plant a thick border of gladioli all around your vegetable garden. Deer usually won't try to push through this plant barrier.

reach for grabbing slugs off foliage. Once you're in gear, grab a plastic bag and head out to the garden to collect slugs. When the hunt is over, don't fuss with dumping the slugs into a bucket of soapy water to kill them. Instead, just seal the bag with a tight knot and put it in the garbage.

Screen Out Rodents

If voles or other rodents are digging in your garden, screen them out for good by installing a simple mesh barrier beneath a raised bed. You can buy a kit for framing a raised bed or fashion one yourself from scrap boards or landscape timbers. Clear the area where you plan to install the bed and spread rustproof wire mesh over the area. Then assemble the frame right on top of the wire mesh, using a staple gun to secure the edges of the mesh to the outside of the frame. Add 6 inches or more of soil and compost to the bed, and you're ready to plant. Once the initial work is done, you'll have years of successful gardening without any rodent problems. (This setup will not work for some root crops, such as longer carrot varieties.)

Worry-Free Weekend Trips

Whether you're getting away from it all for a day trip, an overnight, or a blessed long weekend, you want to make every minute count. So there's no need for shortcuts, right? Wrong. Check out this chapter for shameless shortcuts that will help you avoid the disappointments and delays that can suck time away from the activities you want to enjoy. From packing smart to negotiating airport security, and from sightseeing savvy and photography pointers to camping trip can-do, you'll find shortcuts that will heighten the fun of every trip and sometimes save you money to boot.

PACKING FAST AND EASY

Modernize That "Historic" Toilet Kit

Toilet kits are like time capsules—full of long-forgotten and neglected items. Before you set out on your next trip, perform an audit on your toilet kit. Whenever possible, pack the smallest available containers of toothpaste, shampoo, and other goods. Make sure all bottles are full. Replace old razors.

Change the batteries in electrical devices. And take out any items that you won't need on that particular trip. A 15-minute kit overhaul can insure you against a half-hour (or longer) emergency dash to a drugstore while you're away from home.

Take a Shower, Save Some Space

Buy shampoo, body wash, and similar bath necessities in small collapsible tubes. As you use them, you'll be able to squash them down to save space in your luggage.

Roll Your Own Duct Tape

Duct tape is one of a traveler's best friends, notes Tricia Pearsall, a Richmond, Virginia, expert on gourmet cooking for backpackers. Whether you're on the trail or traveling by car, it's useful for hundreds of repairs and emergency services, such as mending a torn tent or suitcase, standing in for an adhesive bandage, or insulating a water bottle. But a roll of duct tape is bulky and weighs close to a pound. Try this technique for making it easier to pack. Find a pencil that's at least 4 inches long and has a good eraser. Wrap duct tape around the pencil, letting the eraser stick out enough to be usable; about 10 feet of duct tape will do. Now you have enough duct tape for just about any emergency—and a writing tool to boot—all in a little package that weighs less than an ounce.

They Had NO Shame

The Shirt off Their Backs

"I know a couple who bring a whole bunch of logo T-shirts when they travel overseas and wear them every day," says Piotr Kostrzewski, owner of a custom tour business in Arlington, Virginia. "During the trip and definitely by its end, they have gifts for their guides and whomever else they meet: their used T-shirts!"

The gift they have given themselves, of course, is lighter luggage—or more space for purchases.

Sealed with a Zip

When you're traveling, camping, or hiking—especially in the vicinity of bodies of water or during foul weather—the possessions in your suitcase or backpack are always one misstep away from calamity. You could get caught in a downpour or slip and fall into a creek, or that water bottle snuggled among your T-shirts could leak. But you can weather a wet encounter

Don't Leave Home without Them

We asked experienced travelers to list their favorite carry-alongs for saving time, money, and effort. These items are lightweight, compact, and multifunctional. Here's a sampling.

- Deck of cards (cheap entertainment)
- Earplugs (for noisy hotel rooms)
- First aid kit, including aspirin and adhesive bandages (for minor emergencies)
- Fishing line, a few feet (for repairs such as stitching torn luggage)
- Flashlight, small (to place at your bedside)
- Hair ties (when a beauty parlor is out of the question)
- Multipurpose soap, in a small bottle (for cleaning on the go)
- Nail clippers (handy for cutting and filing tasks)
- Pens and highlighter (for marking your guidebook)
- Pillow, inflatable (to nap anywhere)
- Pocketknife, Swiss Army (for cork-pulling emergencies)
- Premoistened towelettes (in the absence of a lavatory)
- Rubber bands (to keep small objects bundled)
- Safety pins (to prevent overexposure in torn garments)
- Sewing kit, small (when a safety pin won't do)
- Stick-on notes (for tagging maps and guidebooks)
- Toilet paper, partial roll, flattened (you never know about public bathrooms)
- Tweezers (to remove splinters)
- Watch with alarm and compass (wrist reminder)

with a smile if you've packed everything that you want to keep dry—clothes, toilet paper, books, food—inside resealable plastic bags. The 2-gallon size are just right for folded clothes. You'll be delighted to find that the bags help you stay organized from start to finish on your trip, too. And if you're going canoeing, double-bag everything. The bags will keep your possessions dry and your pack buoyant if the worst happens.

Triple Protection, in the Bag

Trash bags are a great trouble-saving item for travelers, notes Anne Shelton, a Seattle expert on wilderness shelters and tracking. Caught in the rain? A trash bag serves as improvised rain gear: Just cut holes for your arms and head to fit through—instant poncho! You also can use a trash bag as a rain shield for anything you want to keep dry, such as your luggage or shopping bags full of goodies. Spread a bag on a park or picnic bench to protect your clothes from picking up sap or dirt. In a pinch, a trash bag can even serve as an emergency sleeping bag.

TAKING FLIGHT

Beep-Beep, Passing Through!

Airport security grows ever more complicated in our security-conscious world. If an airport security scanner beeps when you pass through, you're bound to face an aggravating, embarrassing delay as the staff checks you out. To avoid this, place your belt, wallet, loose change, pens, and anything else that's in your pockets in your briefcase or handbag before you reach the security checkpoint, suggests Chesterfield, Virginia, business traveler Peter Benwell.

When Scanners Get under Your Skin

Some travelers who have medical implants or other devices are likely to set off metal detectors at airports. Take along documentation of your condition to accelerate the screening process.

Pack Bags within Bags

Under security procedures at most airports, both carry-on bags and checked luggage are subject to inspection. One way to be prepared for those on-the-spot inspections is to pack items in resealable plastic bags. (See "Sealed with a Zip" on page 324.) Security personnel will be able to look through your items quickly and easily, accelerating such inspections and minimizing handling of your personal possessions at the same time.

Make Your Bag a Standout

There's a baggage gremlin working in every airport. Its job is to ensure that there will be five pieces of luggage identical to yours on every flight you take. A simple shortcut will eliminate time spent searching for your bag and reduce the chances that another traveler will pick up your bag by mistake. Personalize your luggage. Tie a piece of bright yarn around the handle, put your initials on the side in colored tape, sew on a distinctive patch, or add a brightly colored luggage tag.

MAXIMIZE FUN, MINIMIZE HASSLES

Hit the Sack Early

When you visit relatives who have different sleep schedules than you, you may think that you should match their lifestyle to make the visit most worthwhile. Surprisingly, though, it may work to everyone's advantage if you don't change your habits, suggests Patty Hegdal of Midlothian, Virginia, who is a grandma four times over. For example, if you're an early-to-bed-early-to-rise sort and your adult children are more nocturnal, you'll discover some benefits from maintaining your regular bedtime. When you retire early, your children will reap an hour or two of privacy, helping to keep stress to a minimum. Having preserved your sleep schedule, you'll feel splendid when you wake up the next day. And you'll enjoy some precious one-on-one time with your grandchildren while their parents snooze the morning away.

See Mickey on Tuesday

Avoid heavy traffic and long rides to major theme parks by selecting a Tuesday or Wednesday to visit. These are the days when popular parks are the least crowded. Also, when visiting theme parks, check with the front desk of your hotel to see if free shuttle service is offered. Write down the bus number and pickup and drop-off sites so you don't forget. You'll save money and parking headaches.

In a Caravan, See the Light

Driving in a caravan is tricky. If one driver gets separated from the convoy, everyone loses time trying to regroup. So if you're headed out on a group trip in several cars, ask everyone who's driving to turn on their headlights; it will be easier to spot one

5 | Captivating Car Games

All too often, our weekend trips involve several hours of driving along monotonous superhighways. Sitting and staring becomes numbing for certain parts of the anatomy, and for the mind as well. To break the monotony, engage your brains with one of the following enjoyable games.

License plate game. The object of the game is to spot a car or truck with a license plate from the state farthest away from where you are at the moment. If you're traveling with kids, bring along a map of the country to help settle arguments (but don't tell them they're learning geography at the same time).

Car colors game. This one is great for younger children. Each contestant chooses a color. The players count how many cars they can spot in that color within a specific amount of time. When time runs out, the person with the most cars wins.

Category game. Name a letter of the alphabet. Each player must name a geographical entity that begins with that letter in each of the following categories: country, state, city, river, and lake. (If you want to branch out, use other categories, such as authors, movies, fictional characters, historical figures, and so on. In any case, agree in advance on what categories you are working with.) Whoever completes the most categories wins.

Alphabet game. Each person has 5 miles of driving distance in which to look around for the letters of the alphabet—in order. A could be found on a billboard, B on the back of a truck, C on a bridge, and so on. Once 5 miles have passed, that player's turn is up, and it's the next contestant's turn. Whoever finishes the alphabet or gets farthest wins.

Window bingo. Create simple bingo cards with 16 blocks (4 rows of 4) drawn on a piece of paper. Inside each block write the name of an item that the contestant must spot outside the car window (dog, pond, airplane, and so on). The player who first spots 4 in a row (across, down, or diagonally) shouts, "Bingo!" For older kids, use more blocks and make the items to find less common.

another on the highway. When you pass through a traffic light that then changes, pull over until the others are able to catch up. Also, if more than one driver knows the way to the destination, intersperse those knowledgeable drivers with the newcomers, so they're less likely to get stranded alone.

Boy, Oh, Game Boy

Sure, playing video games for too long will turn their minds to mush. But on a long trip, loosen up the rules to preserve your sanity. Handheld video game players will mesmerize your children or grandchildren during those seemingly interminable trips. For maximum effect, buy the kids new games—but no matter how much they beg, don't allow them to play the games until you're actually on the road. That way, their video adventure will be totally new. Insist on three ground rules.

1. Turn off the sound or use headphones.
2. When an adult says something like, "Hey, look at that sixty-foot fiberglass cowboy we're driving by!" the kids must put their game players down and spend a respectable amount of time ogling the landmark.
3. Once you're back home, the regular restrictions on video games go into force.

Park Your Lunch

On an active trip, your body needs more energy than ever. If you try to save money by skipping meals, you could end up fatigued, cranky, or sick. To eat well without breaking your budget, pass up the restaurants at lunchtime and pick up some fruit and sandwich fixings at a grocery store instead. Then check your map for a nice little park and have a picnic. You'll save up to half the cost of a restaurant meal while enjoying the local sights.

Make a List, Check It Twice

Ask any businessperson: Networking provides the hottest business contacts and the surest way to find that perfect new job. So why not network to

My Favorite Shortcut

The 15-Second Postcard

Piotr Kostrzewski, owner of a custom tour business in Arlington, Virginia, tells of a traveling acquaintance who had all his postcards practically written before he left home. The traveler bought a sheet of 3-by-3-inch self-adhesive labels and wrote appropriate messages on each one: "Having a great time. Eating well. Wish you were here." On another sheet of stickers, he printed the addresses of everyone he wanted to write to. During his trip, this superefficient tourist bought picture postcards, slapped a message in the text area of each one, affixed an address label, and added a stamp. The result: 20 cards done in 5 minutes!

arrange the ideal leisure outing, too? Colleen Fischvogt, a marketing and public relations specialist in Richmond, Virginia, suggests that you start by making a list of the 10 things you most want to do when you get to your vacation destination. Then dig up the names of friends—or friends of friends—who live in or have traveled to the place you're going to visit. Discuss with them the pros and cons of your top 10 list and ask for recommendations of must-see attractions that aren't on your list. Inquire about their favorite restaurants, too. Then revise your list. This homework ensures that you won't waste time being indecisive once you have arrived at your destination, and you'll rest assured that every activity you select is a winner. With this insider information, you'll also find sites and restaurants that standard guidebooks overlook.

Hot Spots Require Special Handling

If you want to visit a popular tourist destination during your trip, make arrangements the minute you hit town. An example, says ad agency copywriter Matt Fischvogt, is the island prison Alcatraz in San Francisco. Tickets are rarely available for same-day visits; you usually have to buy them a day in advance. So on day 1 of your trip, pick up those hot tickets right away, then spend the rest of the day enjoying other sites. Make the Rock the pinnacle of day 2.

The Art of Calling Ahead

Advertising copywriter Dinesh Kapoor of Richmond, Virginia, tells the story of how he arrived at the Metropolitan Museum of Art in New York City, eager to visit a certain exhibition. To his dismay, he discovered that even though he had arrived only 4 hours before closing time, he would have to pay the price of a full day's visit. Instead, he decided to swing by the Guggenheim Museum, which operates on a donation system.

The lesson learned: Study up on the admission rules of the attraction you want to visit. You'll save yourself time, money, and aggravation.

Launder Your Money

In an unfamiliar town, it's hard to know for sure how secure your hotel room is. Who's to say, for instance, that an intruder won't ransack your quarters while you're in the shower? To preclude the vacation-spoiling possibility of being robbed, find a sporting goods store and pick up one of those waterproof plastic bags intended for boaters. They're lightweight, durable, and transparent, and they have scores of uses. In this instance, slide your money belt and camera into the plastic bag and take the bag in the shower with you.

Rubber Bands Resist Pickpockets

Having your pocket picked will surely cast a pall over your outing. While you should be pondering great works of art or charming countryside, instead you find yourself talking to bored policemen, filling out reports, calling credit card companies, and figuring out how you're going to pay for dinner. To avoid this problem, use these preventive basics at all times. Women, keep your shoulder bag pressed under one arm, with your hand on the strap. Men, put your wallet in your front pocket, or stash your cash in a money belt. Be careful in close groups. And here's a little trick you might not have considered: Wrap your wallet in rubber bands. It's very hard for even the sneakiest of fingers to slide a band-wrapped wallet out of your pocket without your knowledge.

A back-support belt is small and lightweight. Carry it with you on outings to save yourself from bleacher-back syndrome.

Look, Ma, No Legs!

Many day-trippers and campers make the mistake of lugging along a fold-up camping chair. Such chairs may feel lightweight in the store, but at the end of a long day, they can feel like a sack of bricks. And they're totally out of the question for hikers. There's an alternative to a conventional chair that will give you blessed back support whether you're sitting in a fishing boat, watching a baseball game, or lounging around the campfire. It's a back-support belt, which has a wide, cushioned band that fits around your lower back and adjustable straps that fit around your knees, providing the support. Being mostly fabric, with no legs or seat, a back-support belt is lightweight and folds up into a grapefruit-size packet. The S'portBacker by Nada-Chair sells for around $40, and other styles are available, too. (For a long event, you may still want to bring along a flat seat cushion to prevent bottom fatigue.)

Ways to Save Time on the Golf Course

Try these shortcuts for snipping minutes off your golf game without reducing your enjoyment. On a weekend trip, every minute counts!

Hop and skip. Instead of waiting for another group to finish a hole so you can play through, skip that hole entirely and play two balls on the next hole.

Travel lighter. Take only the clubs you regularly use. When your bag's lighter, you can walk faster.

No home on the range. Bypass the driving range and warm up by hitting a few extra balls on the first couple of holes instead.

Prevent putt-putting. Set a limit of three or four putts per hole. You'll save time and avoid frustration.

Set a stroke limit. Decide in advance on the maximum number of strokes allowed per hole, particularly if you're with a group of friends who take lots of time socializing between strokes.

Take the Back Nine Twice

Golf is a popular activity for a weekend getaway, but sometimes you can waste hours waiting to tee off or being stuck behind slow golfers. You can cut an hour or more off the time it takes to play 18 holes at a busy course, says avid golfer Wade Slate of Knoxville, Tennessee. "If there are crowds at tee off, skip the front nine and play the back nine twice," Wade advises. "If the back nine is crowded, consider playing the first nine twice, or play the back nine first and then the front nine." That way, you'll have time for an enjoyable round of golf without sacrificing time for sight-seeing, shopping, or other pastimes.

PHOTOGRAPHY AND VIDEOTAPING
Leave the Liquid Crystal Home

Digital cameras with those large liquid crystal display screens may be easier to take pictures with, but they're not convenient for a trip away from home. Those display screens suck up more battery power than a conventional viewfinder, says photography student Richard Haskel of Richmond, Virginia. So stick with your standard camera when you travel and save yourself the hassle of lugging extra batteries.

Customs Duty—Double Exposure

If you're planning a trip outside the United States, check your camera to see where it was made. If it's valuable equipment that's foreign-made, register the gear with U.S. Customs before you depart—unless you relish the idea of paying a duty on it when you return. Also, if you have owned your camera for a good while, have it appraised before your trip begins. If you lose the camera, an appraisal will provide bargaining power for dealing with your insurance company.

Double-Duty Camera

Traveling photographers who want their equipment to be as compact as possible should try a two-in-one digital camera, the kind that shoots both video and still photos. "It is cheaper

Running the Photographer's Obstacle Course

Running your film through an x-ray machine for carry-on luggage is a gamble in the United States. Most are not powerful enough to damage film, but some are. You should definitely be wary of the x-ray machines at foreign airports. The alternative is to carry your film and camera through the security check and have them hand-inspected. Here are some hints from Jim Blamthin, manager of corporate media relations for Kodak, to make the inspection as hassle-free as possible.

■ Strip the packaging from all unexposed film and remove the film cartridges from the plastic canisters.

■ Put the cartridges in a resealable plastic bag that you will hand to a security person. Those small disposable cameras can go through in a plastic bag, too.

■ Don't put photographic equipment in checked baggage. The handling is too rough, and the x-rays used for checked bags are much stronger than for carry-ons. In fact, they're so strong that even those lead-lined bags sold at photo shops won't necessarily protect your film.

■ Magnetic fields can damage digital images. If you have a digital camera, steer clear of TVs and monitors, electric motors, and the conveyor belts they use at security stations.

than buying two separate cameras and gives you the option of capturing the memory in two great ways," says photography student Richard Haskel of Richmond, Virginia.

Wait to See What Develops

Proud photographer that you are, you're just dying to have your film developed. But processing in foreign countries is a hit-or-miss proposition—the quality may be terrible. Avoid disappointment and wasted money and wait until you get home to have your photos processed. Besides, undeveloped rolls of film are much lighter in your luggage than stacks of prints and negatives.

TRAVELING WITH PETS

Driver's Ed for Dogs and Cats

Nothing can spoil a weekend outing faster than an unhappy pet. If Fido or Fluffy isn't accustomed to car travel, break him in gradually for a couple of weeks before your upcoming road trip. Take him with you when you use your car for errands around town. That way, he'll get used to the car's movement and learn how to behave under these circumstances. Even so, it's wise to have a backup plan in case your pet finds the trip overwhelming. Talk to your vet about prescribing a mild sedative that you can take along.

Buy Rover a Paw Pilot?

Losing a pet is always traumatic, but it can be even harder to cope with when you're on a trip. So whenever you travel with your pet, adorn its collar with a special identification tag before you leave town. The tag should include the pet's name; your name; a name, address, and phone number at your destination; and the name and phone number of a friend who could help in an emergency.

Cats Crave Classical

Unexpected car trip? For a cat, that's an instant anxiety attack. But pet fanciers tell us that soothing music has a mellowing effect on their furry friends. So next time you hit the road, introduce Muffy to the local classical radio station or your favorite cassettes or CDs of mellow music. Def Leppard? Scratch that idea.

TENT AND RV CAMPING TIPS

Leave a Quarter at Home

When you're packing for a camping trip, it's tempting to take along every piece of gear you've collected over the past couple of decades. Sure, you want to be prepared, but you'll be miserable if you have to lug around gear you don't need. Here's how to save yourself from overpacking. Lay out all the equipment you plan to pack, then choose a quarter of the items to leave at home. An example of how to cull: A poncho or rain jacket is an essential camping item. But packing rain pants is probably overkill. "I don't worry about bottoms," says Tom McKemey, a Scoutmaster from Wyndmoor, Pennsylvania. "If it's so wet that you're going to need rain pants, you're probably not going to be out there in the first place."

Make a Meal Plan

To make your next RV camping weekend a restful, relaxing getaway, prepare your meals—and snacks—before you leave. After all, there's lots more space to prepare food in your home kitchen than there is in a typical RV. And who wants to waste vacation time cooking? So tear up lettuce for salad, cut carrot and celery sticks, or make hamburger patties at home before your trip. Planning on grilled chicken? Prepare the marinade and pour it over the chicken in a container that seals tight, then pop it in your RV fridge.

Sometimes you can even do some of the cooking in advance. Want potatoes grilled on an open fire? Cook them partially in the microwave at home, then store them in the RV fridge for the trip. After a microwave headstart, potatoes will roast in a jiffy on a campfire.

Pack only what you know you'll consume while you're traveling. For example, if you'll eat only four hot dogs, don't take a whole package of wieners and buns. Transfer the precise amount you need to airtight containers or resealable plastic bags. When the weekend's over, there won't be any leftovers to unpack.

Outfit to Go

To reduce the chore of packing a camper for a weekend trip and then unpacking it when you return, longtime RV enthusiast Peter Evans suggests outfitting your camper as you would a second home. Shop flea markets and garage sales for all the dishes, pots, pans, and linens you'll need. At the beginning of the camping season, stock your RV with extra kitchen and bathroom supplies that can be left on board, such as salt, pepper, Worcestershire sauce, soap, and toothpaste. Keep enough clothes on board for a weekend—or longer—trip, and don't forget raincoats, boots, extra shoes, and other supplies for weather that isn't ideal. What's Peter's idea of packing for a trip? All he needs is a toothbrush, a few personal items, and food for the weekend, and he's good to go.

Cooking with a Can-Do Attitude

The only dishes and utensils you really need on a camping trip are one cup and spoon, says Scoutmaster Tom McKemey. Virtually any food you will prepare can be eaten out of the cup. Experienced backpacker Tricia Pearsall also points out that many objects can double for a plate in a pinch, including a pot lid, a large leaf, or even a Frisbee. Another strategy: When you open canned food to pour into a cooking pot for stew or chili, don't throw out the can. Experienced campers ladle the cooked food back into the can and eat out of it. Remember, the fewer dishes you use, the fewer dishes you'll have to wash and haul around.

Tenting Ground Rules

Camping out is fun and invigorating, but your enjoyment will be quenched fast if you awaken at midnight to discover that you're stuck in a sopping wet sleeping bag. Most campers know that laying out a ground cloth (plastic sheeting) between the bare ground and the bottom of the tent will prevent moisture from seeping through the tent floor. What many tent campers don't know is that the ground cloth should not extend beyond the edge of the tent floor. Otherwise, the edge of the ground cloth will actually catch rain running off the side of the tent and pool it under you. So always tuck the plastic an inch or so under the perimeter of the tent. Better yet, before you go camping, cut the plastic to the exact size you need—slightly smaller than the bottom of the tent—so there's no guesswork when you set up camp.

The Incredible No-Dishes Chicken Feast

This is the camp meal where you nobly volunteer to clean every pot and plate for the whole crowd—because there won't *be* any dishes! It's also a fun way to cook, so kids will love to pitch in and help. Here's how to prepare this feast.

1. Get a campfire going, using enough wood to produce a large bed of coals.

2. For each camper, lay out a sheet of heavy-duty aluminum foil about 18 inches square, shiny side up. Place a raw chicken leg and thigh in the center of each sheet.

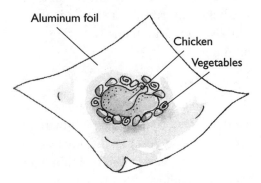

Aluminum foil

Chicken

Vegetables

3. Cut onions, potatoes, and carrots into chunks and add some to each sheet.

4. Add a tablespoon of butter, plus salt and pepper, to each sheet.

5. Grab two opposite sides of the foil and bring them together over the food. Fold the edges together at least three times.

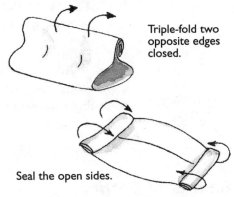

Triple-fold two opposite edges closed.

Seal the open sides.

6. Fold the two remaining open sides three times each to seal. Reseal the entire package in a second sheet of foil to protect against leaks.

7. When your campfire has produced a nice bed of red coals, place the foil packets directly on the coals. Let the packets cook for 50 minutes, turning once midway through.

8. Remove the packets using tongs or a couple of sticks. Have each camper carefully unwrap his meal (did you guess that the packets are hot?) and eat right off the foil.

How to Bag Your Dinner in the Wild

Meals prepared and eaten without dirtying a single dish—the camper's dream come true! The time-honored hot dog on a stick is a good example, notes Anne Shelton, a Seattle expert on wilderness shelters and tracking. You also can wrap potatoes and corn on the cob in foil and cook them on the edge of a fire. This technique even works for lobster and crayfish, if you can buy them fresh at your location. But for the ultimate no-fuss meal, just shell out for one of those prepackaged meals that require no refrigeration and can be heated and served in their own bags.

HINTS FOR HIKERS

A Safe Clip for Hiking

A vigorous hike is tough on your toes, particularly when you're huffing downhill and your feet slam forward in your boots with every step. If you're not careful, this constant pounding can eventually dislodge an entire toenail (often the one on your big toe). You will end up limping for the rest of the hike, with each step feeling like an electric shock to the feet. Fortunately, this agony is entirely preventable if you take one simple step in advance: Closely clip your toenails before you hit the trail.

Sweat the Details

Hikers and walkers, heed these two shortcuts for avoiding the nightmare of blisters. Sweaty feet can quickly lead to blisters, so treat your feet to a thin liner sock (a synthetic blend) under your regular sock to wick away moisture. If you're hoofing it on a warm day, keeping your feet dry can be a huge challenge. The solution: Coat your feet in antiperspirant before you go.

Glorious Gizmos

Be a Card Carrier

You probably already know about these premium camping gizmos: a Swiss Army knife and a compact Maglite flashlight. The knife has literally dozens of possible uses, and the flashlight is great for groping in your backpack in poor light. But here's another lifesaver you may not have considered: a prepaid phone card. Phone cards are small, lightweight, and worth their weight in platinum when you can't find the change to make an emergency call from a pay phone.

A Hiker's Best Friend

A hiking stick is one of the most valuable pieces of equipment for a hiker, particularly when crossing rough terrain. It acts like a third leg, helping you keep your balance. If you have loads of money to throw away, you can buy special spring-loaded walking sticks from a sporting goods company. But chances are, you can find the makings of a great hiking stick lying around in the woods. Just be sure to choose a piece of dry wood (not rotten) that is strong enough to support your weight, says Pennsylvania Scoutmaster Tom McKemey. Held vertically against the ground, the stick should reach up to your jaw. Use your pocketknife to whittle off any rough bark or sharp points (which could cause blisters) from the handhold portion of the stick.

STORING VACATION GEAR

Boxing Gear Saves Packing Time

Taking a smart approach to storing your vacation gear can cut packing time by more than 25 percent. Divide up essential gear by activity: tent, stove, and other camping gear; ski boots, goggles, and mittens; bike helmets, shorts, and repair kit. Store each type of gear in its own large, see-through plastic box (with an easy-to-remove lid) so you can view the contents at a glance. Stacked in the basement or garage, these boxes won't take up a lot of space but will keep your gear clean and organized. When it's time for a trip, just grab the boxes you need and stow them in the car. When you return home, clean and dry your gear, then put each item back in the right box so it will be ready the next time you go.

Give Your Skis a Guest Room

How you store your skis and ski boots will have a direct effect on how much time you spend in the future repairing them—or buying new ones. Each time you use your skis, wipe them down with a dry cloth and, if they're particularly dirty, clean them thoroughly. Find a spot where you can store them either lying flat or propped up on their ends. Your attic is too hot—

Ripped Tents and Backpacks

Problem:

Your tent or backpack gets ripped in the middle of your trip.

Do This Now:

Close up the hole with duct tape. It's strong enough to hold the fabric together, and it will repel water, says Anne Shelton, a Seattle wilderness expert. An alternative quick fix: Sew it up with dental floss (a superstrong material) and a canvas or tapestry needle. This needlework approach won't provide waterproofing, of course, but it will close the hole and prevent it from growing.

Do This for Good:

Back home, when you're ready to store your tent, ask the manufacturer or a sporting goods store for a repair kit. You can usually buy one that matches your torn equipment. This is the preferred approach to healing wounded gear, Anne says. Tents and backpacks are expensive, and you want them to last as long as possible. Make the repair before you toss your pack back into the crawl space. Otherwise, you're likely to forget about it and you'll have damaged equipment waiting for you the next time you go camping.

• •

your boot liners will dry-rot. And your garage is probably too damp, presenting the danger of rust. The perfect resting place? Try sliding them under the bed in your guest room.

Set Your Sleeping Bag Free

Sleeping bags are so compact in their compression sacks that it's temping to store them that way. But that could be inviting trouble. Over time, the compression can harm the bag's insulation, leaving cold spots. It's better to hang your bag loosely in a warm, dry spot.

Hassle-Free Holidays All Year Round

Traditional holiday greetings begin with either *Happy* or *Merry*, but by the time the actual event arrives, many of us are too exhausted to enjoy the celebration. Bah, humbug, we say. To lighten your load *and* your mood at the holidays, check out these shortcuts for simple party planning, staying ahead of the game, decorating (and undecorating), and shopping for gifts without losing your patience (or your pay).

HOLIDAY DECORATING

Deck the Halls in Minutes

Easy, low-cost decorating ideas are a specialty of Phyllis Cambria, co-owner of PartyPlansPlus.com. For a coffee table centerpiece you can create in less than 5 minutes, Phyllis suggests that you group unused ornaments or ornaments with the same theme (red orbs, snowmen, bells, and the like) in a crystal bowl or vase. Wrap artwork and large interior doors in wrapping paper to resemble giant presents.

Evergreen Entries

Instead of struggling to put up outdoor lights for the holidays, drape exterior doors and windows with pine or spruce branches. Branches are often available for free at a Christmas tree lot; ask the manager when you buy your tree. To secure the branches, hammer in some 2-inch nails at the top corners of door and window frames, or use small screw-in hooks. (You can leave the hooks in place year-round.) As a finishing touch, fasten a huge red bow at the top center, using a long twist tie to attach it to a branch.

Decorate Some Holiday Huggables

Do you collect stuffed animals? If so, tie brightly colored ribbons around their necks to add to the festive atmosphere.

Light Up Your Home

For a beautiful effect that will brighten up your home in mid-winter, frame large mirrors with white minilights. The double reflection is a knockout, says Phyllis Cambria, co-owner of PartyPlansPlus.com.

Whip Up an Indoor Snowstorm

Cutting out homemade snowflakes is a great activity to keep kids busy while you cook a holiday meal or deal with other holiday chores. Phyllis Cambria suggests a great way to display the results. Tie one end of a piece of white thread to each snowflake and make a very small loop in the other end of the thread. Insert the point of a pushpin through the loop and then into your ceiling. You now have a blizzard of memories. Creating a winter storm is particularly fun for Phyllis, a native New Yorker now living in Florida.

Contain Your Enthusiasm

If you're one of those jolly souls who likes to deck the halls—as well as the

The Second Time Around

Dual-Duty Poinsettias

Come February, instead of tossing out those healthy Christmas poinsettias, take advantage of their red color for a Valentine's Day display. Take the green or gold foil off the pots, replace it with pink or silver foil, and place a bowl of pink, red, and silver foil-wrapped chocolates in front of your plants.

living room, dining room, kitchen, bedrooms, and bath—your creed needs to be "Dismantle with care this year; decorate with ease next year." To make the undecorating process go smoothly, begin by investing in several oversize plastic containers. There are two logical ways to go. The first is to place each room's decor in a separate tub, properly labeling each container. This makes reassembling the merriment mighty fast next year. All you do is grab a tub and go. (Since you haven't seen the display in a whole year, being repetitive is a nonissue.) The second approach is to store items by category: candles, figurines, garland, linens and towels, and so forth. This approach favors spontaneity but allows you to achieve a balanced look effortlessly—if you designate, for example, four candles, three figurines, and one wreath per room.

Reel In Some Savings

Those reels that we wind strings of holiday lights around come in pretty handy, and Lauren Link of Milwaukee has devised a clever way to make your own, usually for free. You need a piece of foam board or heavy Styrofoam insulation. Before you rush out to buy this, check your basement. You're likely to find such boards lying around from long-ago school projects or home rehab ventures. Cut a piece 24 inches long by 8 inches wide, which will hold one set of lights tangle-free. Take a few extra minutes to carve indentations in the board to hold the cord in place more securely. This easy home project sure beats spending $5 for a commercial reel.

A foam board cut to size holds holiday lights in storage with no tangles. Small notches in the board hold the cord even more securely.

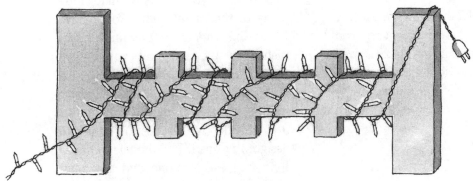

Offer Holiday Pack-Up Prizes

There's nothing more daunting than facing that big post-holiday pack-up day all alone. As a solo act, taking down the tree, boxing up lights and ornaments, wrapping delicate figurines, and folding festive linens can take hours. If persuading your family to help with the cleanup is about as likely as Santa shaving his whiskers, institute a new tradition and offer wonderful prizes as motivation. Lure each helper with an extra present that didn't make it into the December 25 pile. Or since the holiday season always includes great movie releases, treat the crew to a movie and popcorn after the last ornament disappears.

PARTY FUN

Throw Caution into the Garbage

At about the same time that holiday tunes start playing on the radio, local dollar stores begin stocking festive decorations, including colorful seasonal plastic serving platters. Buy lots of them. When you throw a party, speed up the postparty cleanup by throwing away any plastic trays with crusted-on food rather than laboring to scrub them clean. These cheap yet attractive trays are also excellent for toting donations to someone else's party. There's no worry about reclaiming your dish at the end of the evening. Just leave the leftovers and go.

The Second Time Around

Can It

After you finish eating the plain, caramel, and cheese popcorn from the oversize can that inevitably arrives every year, wash the can thoroughly. Use it to store ornaments, holiday towels, seasonal music, and other holiday items for next year. (Don't forget to label it!)

Delegate Some Dishes

If your party "to do" list is running long, reduce your tasks by delegating some of the menu items. You'll have fewer ingredients to buy and fewer dishes to prepare, and you'll save some money, too. To accomplish this feat efficiently, prepare your party menu before mailing the invitations and decide which menu items to assign. Put this list by the telephone so that as guests respond and ask what they can bring, you can give them a choice from the list. Here are three different strategies for delegating a menu.

1. Dole out all the desserts to your guests, resulting in a confectionery rainbow.
2. Assign side dishes, by category: legumes, green salads, sweet potatoes, white potatoes, pasta side dishes, breads. This approach avoids duplication but leaves room for individual creativity.
3. If it's a gathering of close friends or family, build a menu plan specifically around known specialties. After all, who wouldn't be tickled to hear that the whole family craves her special coleslaw.

Cook and Freeze for No-Fuss Parties

The moment you decide to have a holiday party, but before you even set the date, turn to the Internet for party recipes that freeze well. Type "make ahead," "appetizers" (or whatever course you desire), or similar keywords into your favorite Internet search engine for inspiration. Or invest in a cookbook based on make-ahead recipes. With these recipes in hand, choose a day during the week before your party to cook, wrap, and freeze. Then relax. The time it takes to find yummy, fast, freezable recipes will be repaid in triplicate on party day, when you can enjoy the fun rather than sweating in the kitchen.

Wrap Up Your Wineglasses

No time or budget to buy holiday wineglasses? Take glasses you already own and wrap the stems with metallic ribbon, ending with a small bow. If you use different colors of ribbon, everyone will be able to identify which glass is theirs.

My Favorite Shortcut

Inspire a Walking Party

Here's an entertaining idea suggested by Phyllis Cambria, co-owner of PartyPlansPlus.com, that even time- and money-strapped families will enjoy. Phone a few special people and invite them to join you for a leisurely stroll in a nearby park or forest preserve. That's all the planning you need to do, since Mother Nature will take care of the rest. While enjoying a walk, have everyone collect pinecones. Afterward, invite folks in for cookies and hot chocolate. Set out a decorative basket for the pinecone collection. (If it's summertime, substitute picking wildflowers for collecting pinecones, and lemonade for hot chocolate.)

Easy, Exotic Eggnog

You can serve holiday guests exotic eggnog without even breaking a sweat. Simply combine commercial eggnog with one of the following tasty twists. In each case, begin with a quart of eggnog. The amount of the added ingredients may be adjusted up or down according to taste.

- ½ cup chocolate syrup
- ¼ cup rum, brandy, or bourbon
- ¾ cup Kahlúa
- ½ can thawed frozen orange juice concentrate and ½ can cold water, plus a last-minute dollop of sherbet to taste (Substitute ginger ale, lemon-lime soda, or seltzer for water, if desired.)
- ½ cup pure maple syrup

Super-Simple Snack Mix

Here's a really tasty recipe for a party snack that you can whip up in 20 minutes or less, says Jane Ann Ellis of Columbus, Ohio. Package it for gifts or serve it at a party. Start with a large bag of oyster crackers. Add ¾ cup vegetable oil, one package (0.7 ounce) dry ranch dressing, and one teaspoon dill weed. Place all the ingredients in a large bowl and stir. Jane Ann, who's a grandmother of four, notes that if kids are helping you make this snack, just put all the ingredients in a large resealable plastic bag and have them shake it until everything is all mixed up. They'll have a blast, and you'll have a few uninterrupted minutes to clean up. Package the mix in plastic bags closed with a bow, or put it in a bowl for a special party, where it will be the best nibble around.

HAPPY HALLOWEEN

Dirt for Dessert

There's nothing better on Halloween than a creepy, crawly dessert, and here's one that's a cinch to create. Crush chocolate wafers into crumbs. In a clear plastic cup, place a scoop of chocolate ice cream and a healthy layer of crumbs, then top it off with gummy worms. Yuck!

A Fast, Fruitful Costume

In under an hour, you can transform your child into a beautiful bunch of grapes. Begin with purple leggings and a purple leotard or sweat suit. (An advantage of this costume is that the clothing can be worn long after Halloween sans decorations.) Blow up enough purple balloons to cover the clothing. Lay the clothing on a flat surface and secure the balloons to it by quickly basting through the tied-off balloon ends. Enlist your young one's help—neatness doesn't count. If desired, use purple face paint and a brown cap with green leaves stitched on to complete the costume.

No-Fuss Firefighter

A firefighter is always a popular theme for a Halloween costume. Dress your child in a yellow or red raincoat and yellow,

He's an Apple! She's a Bug!

The quickest, cheapest, and easiest homemade costume requires only poster board, grosgrain ribbon, and your imagination. Gather these materials: 2 pieces poster board; scissors; ruler; 2 yards ½-inch grosgrain ribbon; pencil; markers, crayons and/or poster paint. Then follow these directions.

1. From the 2 poster boards, cut 2 circles sized to cover your child from shoulder to mid-thigh.

2. Cut 2 pieces of ribbon for shoulder straps and 2 pieces of ribbon for underarm straps, each roughly 18 inches long.

3. Have your child hold 1 poster board in front of her body. With a pencil, mark 2 spots on the poster board, each 2 inches away from her neck.

4. Lay the boards flat and use a hole puncher to punch holes through both boards at the pencil marks.

5. Feed one piece of ribbon through the right-hand set of holes, knotting both ends to secure. Repeat on the left side.

6. Place the sandwich board on your child and use the pencil to mark 2 more sets of holes about 10 inches below the armpits. Remove the sandwich from your child, punch holes as before, and thread the remaining ribbon through each set of holes.

7. Place the sandwich board on a flat surface. Use markers, crayons, or poster paint to decorate one side. When that side is dry, flip the sandwich over and decorate the other side.

How to decorate? Use copper-colored paint to make a penny. Or paint the poster boards like an apple (complete with a worm) and dress your child in a red sweat suit and a brown cap; secure green leaves (from a dollar store) to the cap. Another idea is a ladybug: Paint the poster board red with black dots, dress your child in a red or black sweat suit and black cap, and secure 2 black pipe cleaners to the cap for antennae.

red, or black rubber boots. Visit the Halloween aisle at your favorite home store and buy a toy firefighter's hat. Let the child carry a stuffed Dalmatian if you have one in the toy chest.

Recycled Fairy Princess

Here's how to create a fantastic princess costume for next to nothing. Visit your local thrift shop and buy a frilly night-gown. Cut it to length to suit your child—there's no need to hem. Next, search through the leftover supplies from your child's last birthday party and grab a cone-shaped party hat. Wrap the hat in colored paper, then decorate it with glued-on sequins or odd buttons from your sewing kit. Cut off the tip of the hat and poke the end of a colorful oblong scarf or a crepe paper streamer through the hole. Knot the end inside the hat to secure it.

STAYING AHEAD OF THE GAME

Set a Phone-Free Hour

When the holiday season kicks into high gear and everyone begins calling with season's greetings, sometimes even the most meticulous organizer can fall behind. Here's a plan of action suggested by Illinois psychologist Dr. Jay Einhorn. Designate a daily private hour to accomplish holiday chores. If the phone rings during these 60 minutes, use the answering machine or caller ID to screen calls. Unless you suspect that the call is urgent, do not answer it. After you're caught up, set aside another block of time to brew a calming pot of chamomile tea and return the phone messages.

Index Your Card Correspondence

Does tackling your holiday greeting cards begin with a 3-hour hunt for addresses—rifling through junk drawers, random slips of paper, and various phone books? If so, set up a system for retaining addresses, and you'll end the address hunt forever. You need an index card holder, transparent tape, 3-by-5-inch index cards, and tabbed alphabetical dividers. When you receive a holiday card, cut out the envelope's return address, tape it to an index card, and file it alphabetically in the holder.

Next year you'll know exactly where to look for the addresses. Add new addresses as needed each year.

If you're computer savvy, an alternative to the index card system is to create a Christmas card address file. Each day that you receive cards, type the addresses into the file. With this approach, you'll be able to print addresses on mailing labels for next year's cards.

Shop for Shipping

When you have to ship a large gift to a faraway friend or relative, it pays to shop around, advises Colorado freelance writer Dougald MacDonald. The price can vary dramatically depending on your shipment's weight, dimensions, and time requirements, and sometimes the best deal is where you least expect it. "I had to ship a ten-foot-long sign from Maine to the Rocky Mountains, and I was told at a packaging shop that it would cost a minimum of $250," Dougald says. "I started to make my own calls and ended up shipping via Federal Express. The package left Maine on Saturday and arrived in the Rockies on Monday, and the cost was just $40."

They Had NO Shame

A Schedule-Saving Storage Idea

Shopping postholiday sales to stock up for next year is a smart money-saving shortcut. Be just as smart about where you store holiday items that you'll need long before the actual celebration day, such as greeting cards. The right place to stash these items is in the same box with the *preceding* holiday's decorations. For instance, Hanukkah candles should be stored with Halloween decorations, Christmas cards with Thanksgiving decorations, Valentine's Day cards with Christmas decorations, and so on.

Everyone's Got Mail

For the ultimate in holiday correspondence convenience, consider sending one e-mail greeting to all your Internet-connected friends. You won't even have to address each e-mail message separately, since e-mail services allow you to set up group address folders. Chicago writer Donna Shryer tells of a friend (who prefers to remain anonymous) who completed her holiday greetings last year in 15 minutes—first drafting a brief message, then e-mailing it to 25 friends in her group folder. As an added bonus, she saved close to $10 in postage.

HOLIDAY DINNERS

Down With the Door, Up With the Table

Expecting a large crowd of people for dinner and wondering how to squeeze them in around the table? Instead of scouring thrift stores for card tables, whip out your screwdriver. Use it to pop the hinge pins out of an interior door (one that you aren't planning on closing). Prop the door on two sawhorses, drape it with a tablecloth, and who will be the wiser? Be strategic: Use a door from a doorway that you'd like to keep clear so all those extra people can move easily from room to room.

Mix-and-Match Place Settings

You have dinnerware for 8, but 12 people are coming for a holiday meal. Extend your table service without a fuss by taking a trip to your local dollar store or home store. Look for an inexpensive dinnerware pattern that blends with what you already have and buy only the pieces you need. For instance, Chicagoan Donna Shryer has white dinnerware rimmed in forest green. She found plates in solid forest green at a nearby dollar store. Donna bought enough plates to be able to set her table for 12, alternating the plate patterns. (By the way, it's very chic to serve dinner on coordinated but not identical dishes.)

Flags and Flowers for the Fourth of July

Here's an easy-to-assemble centerpiece for your Fourth of July picnic table. Gather a dozen carnations in a vase. (At this time of year, you can usually find fresh red and white carnations, as well as dyed blue ones.) Insert a little greenery and several small American flags attached to thin dowel rods.

Shortcut to Sweet Potato Casserole

Sweet potato casserole is a holiday favorite. Save time by skipping the casserole prep and just bake the sweet potatoes in your oven or microwave. Then offer the gooey traditional casserole toppings on the side at the table. In small bowls, set out minimarshmallows, walnut chips, brown sugar, and plenty of butter. If applied to a hot potato, these toppings will melt and meld nicely.

4 Simple Centerpieces for Four Seasons

One large globe-shaped glass bowl, one potted ivy plant, and one plastic plant saucer are the bases for four different seasonal centerpieces. You can assemble each of these in less than 10 minutes. For each one, begin by placing the plastic saucer in the glass bowl. (You can find a large variety of glass bowls at any home store.) Set the ivy plant on the saucer.

Winter. Fill the bowl with small (2-inch-diameter) Christmas ornaments until the pot is completely hidden. Let the ivy cascade over the bowl's edges and onto your table.

Surround the outer bowl base with pine branches, then highlight the branches with randomly placed pinecones and more ornaments.

Spring. Replace the ornaments with pastel-colored Easter grass or plastic Easter eggs. Also ring the bowl with grass and eggs.

Summer. Use brightly colored citrus fruits, such as limes, lemons, and tangerines, to hide the pot.

Fall. Fill the bowl with colored leaves gathered from your yard. Ring the outer bowl base with small gourds or minipumpkins.

Roast a Breast, Not a Bird

If you love to set a beautifully browned turkey on the dinner table for carving in company, this shortcut isn't for you. But if you prefer carving in the privacy of your kitchen, here's a great time- and money-saver. Roast a turkey breast instead of a whole turkey. This cuts cooking time almost in half, and since the breast is easy to carve, you'll be done snip-snap. An added benefit is that, in today's health-conscious world, more people ask for lean white breast meat than fattier dark meat.

Stuff Your Crock-Pot

Cut back on roasting as well as serving time by cooking the stuffing in a slow cooker such as a Crock-Pot instead of stuffed inside the turkey. The turkey will cook faster, and you won't use up precious minutes transferring stuffing to a serving bowl. Also, many food safety experts recommend cooking stuffing separately because it's difficult to be certain that stuffing inside a turkey is fully cooked. In place of the stuffing,

Freeze-Ahead Pumpkin Pie

Often there's just no time to fit pie baking into the holiday rush. To solve this dilemma, make your pie ahead of time and freeze it. Here's how.

1. In a bowl, mix together 1 cup canned pumpkin, ¼ cup packed brown sugar, ¼ teaspoon salt, and 1 teaspoon pumpkin pie spice.
2. Fold in a 4-ounce container of thawed frozen whipped topping.
3. Fold in 2 cups softened vanilla ice cream and ¼ cup chocolate chips or ¼ cup chopped walnuts to make a marbled mixture.
4. Spoon the mixture into a store-bought cookie crumb piecrust and set the plate in the freezer for 3 hours.
5. Remove the plate from the freezer, cover it with plastic wrap and foil, and return it to the freezer.

On the holiday, just remove the pie from the freezer 15 minutes before serving time.

• •

insert a halved onion and some celery stalks inside the turkey cavity to lend flavor to the juices.

Dial Up a Holiday Dinner

A surprising number of specialty gourmet shops or restaurants with carryout service offer fully roasted turkeys during the holiday season. All you need to do is reheat as instructed, transfer the bird to a lovely serving platter, and garnish with fresh herbs. No one will know but you!

Kid-Pleasing Packets Keep the Peace

The kids are buzzed on sugar, bored with board games, and screaming for dinner NOW! To save yourself a major headache, plan in advance to distract those young ones while you finish assembling the sweet potato pie. A few days before the gang arrives for a holiday dinner, log on to your favorite search engine and type in "best kids sites Thanksgiving," "top kids sites Hanukkah," or "Easter coloring pages"—you get the idea. In minutes, you will find all manner of sites that have holiday-related coloring pages, mazes, jokes, games, puzzles, stories, and trivia questions, plus links to other great sites. No downloading or Internet expertise necessary. Simply click and browse until you find what you want, then print what's on your screen. Print enough pages to make an activity booklet for each child. Next, head off to the dollar store to buy a small pack of crayons or markers for each child. Instant diversion!

Enlist a Carver on the Spot

Carving the turkey is the last thing you have time for when you're coordinating a big holiday meal. To ensure that you'll have a beautifully carved bird, prepare in advance to enlist a helper. A day or two before the meal, log on to www. butterball.com and print out carving instructions, or visit the library and photocopy instructions from a cookbook. On the day of the big meal, after the turkey is properly cooked, hand the directions and the carving set to one of your gracious guests. You've just saved yourself 20 minutes, precisely when you need it most. And unless you are a practiced carver, your guest will do as good a job as you would.

GIFT SHOPPING AND GIFT GIVING

All for One and One for All

The fastest, most cost-efficient way to shop for gifts is to stock up on gender-neutral gifts en masse when they go on sale. Good examples of this type of gift are fine wines, dark-colored cashmere scarves, and fine writing utensils. With a supply of neutral but nice gifts like these, you'll have a wonderful present close at hand no matter what the occasion or who the recipient.

Ask for a Personal Sales Call

If you prefer shopping the sales for holiday gifts—and who doesn't?—here's how to take advantage of lower prices but not lose out on selection. Decide which stores most often meet your gift-giving needs and introduce yourself to the manager of each store. Ask each manager to phone you a day or two before a sale begins. That way, you can visit on day 1 of the sale, when the selection is best.

Need Gifts? Book 'Em

You may not be able to cut down on the number of names on your gift list, but you can reduce the number of shopping trips. Image consultant Susan Fignar of Itaska, Illinois, likes to select a holiday theme for as many gifts as possible—well before the season begins. The trick is to choose a gift category that allows individualized selection for both men and women, as well as easy availability at one location. For example, Susan might choose books, which means she can do all her gift shopping at one store or online at Amazon.com (www.amazon.com) or Barnes & Noble (www.bn.com). To make shopping even quicker, Susan suggests fine-tuning your theme. For example, with books, focus on inspirational books, cookbooks, or biographies. Now you're down to one stop, one store, and one aisle—but you'll still have plenty of options.

Gift Fabrics for Any Season

Commit the following list of fabrics to memory, or jot them down on a small card that will fit in your wallet.

- Wool crepe
- Rayon and rayon-blend knits
- Microfibers (especially washable suede)
- Silk (sueded, charmeuse, or silk knit)

According to Susan Fignar, these fabrics are "seasonless"—they're comfortable to wear up to 9 months out of the year. Clothes made from these fabrics are excellent gifts, and you can often find them on sale during the off season. For example, during a July sale, if you find a wool crepe blazer in Aunt Mabel's size, buy it. It will be a great Christmas gift.

Think Inside the Box

Let's face it, gift shopping is much easier if the recipient gives you a list of desired gifts. But asking for and receiving that list takes some of the romance and mystery out of the act of gift giving. To preserve the element of surprise while still enjoying the benefits of a gift list, try this simple system. Gather up some empty boxes—one for each family member. Shoe, facial tissue, or cereal boxes work well. Ask each family member to write a wish list on separate snippets of paper—one gift idea per snippet. Then have each person write his name on a box and slip the snippets inside. Now it's a game to secretly withdraw a gift slip from your sister's or spouse's box when no one is looking. There's no need to coordinate who's buying what with other family members, and plenty of anticipation

2 Timesaving Gift Traditions

Even in small families, as the kids grow into young adults, it's startling how expensive their wish lists become. Instead of exchanging gifts with your entire family, try these traditions to save time and money on gift shopping.

The Grab-Bag Tradition. Have everyone continue to buy gifts for those under 18 (or 16 or whatever age you decide), but create a grab bag gift tradition for the adults. Write each name on a slip of paper and put all the slips in a hat. Each person over age 18 pulls one name, and this is the only family member she buys a present for.

The Kids-Only Tradition. When all is said and done, isn't it the kids' gifts you most enjoy buying? Among your extended family, agree to a rule that only those under 12 will receive a gift from the aunts, uncles, and cousins. This not only reduces your shopping list but also substantially increases your budget per child.

• •

remains, as each of you wonders which gifts you might receive and from whom. Here's an extra bonus: There's no chance of duplication, since once a wish is withdrawn from a box, it's off the list.

The Great Gift Stockpile

Stockpiling gifts throughout the year is a great way to be prepared for all holidays and occasions—but only if you can find your stockpile when the time comes. Here's a three-step system for organized year-round shopping.

1. Designate one, and only one, location for stockpiled gifts. A basement corner is fine, as long as it's dry. Temperature is irrelevant.
2. Buy large plastic containers to hold your stashed gifts. New plastic outdoor garbage cans are great for zealous collectors; medium-size plastic tubs are fine for the less industrious. Label the containers with the appropriate names or general categories, such as Teachers' Gifts, Hostess Gifts, Men's Gifts, and Women's Gifts.
3. Gather a stack of 3-by-5-inch index cards, tabbed blank dividers, and a card holder. Label the dividers the same as

the plastic containers. Every time you drop a gift in a container, complete a corresponding index card, staple the receipt to the card, and file. When you need a gift, whether planned or unexpected, consult your filed cards, then seek out the gift.

Instant Gift Baskets

Gift giving is almost effortless if you plan ahead to give gift baskets and do your gift shopping in small bites here and there. At the beginning of the year, choose a few themes for gift baskets, such as travel, cooking, or computers. Then whenever you're out shopping for yourself or your family at the mall or in a department store, also swing by the departments related to your gift themes. Watch for items that are on sale and pick up a few. After 2 or 3 months of this type of stockpiling, you should have enough items ready to throw together a gift basket in 5 minutes or less.

Recycled Gifts

"A friend of mine, who will remain nameless, confessed her own gift-giving system to me," says Barbara Ellis, a writer from Berks County, Pennsylvania, who was sworn to secrecy. "She has a drawer reserved for gifts she receives, mostly the type exchanged as hostess gifts, in gift exchanges, or as party favors. When she or her husband receives something they'll never use or don't need, it goes in the drawer with a note with the giver's name. Mind you, most of these are nice gifts. But she also has joke gifts in the drawer, which are always great candidates for recycling, since opening them up is

the best part of them anyway. When she or her husband needs a gift to give, she just rummages through the drawer, picks out something suitable, and rewraps it."

Keeping notes about whom each gift came from is essential for this system: You don't want to give a gift back to the person you got it from by mistake! Also avoid recycling a gift to people who might know one another—within your bridge group or among your coworkers, for example. Instead, give it to someone unrelated, such as a neighbor or friend, so that nobody's feelings are hurt.

Easy-Shop Gifts Your Wife Will Love

At a total loss when it comes to buying presents for your wife? Here are five ideas guaranteed to please.

Go fishing. A large fishing tackle box—the kind with movable dividers—is perfect for storing buttons, beads, and other craft items, or carrying them along on a trip. (Tell her what it's for so she doesn't think you're taking her fishing!)

Plant some long-lasting flowers. Instead of a bouquet of roses, consider buying a potted orchid, a bonsai, or a terrarium as a gift, especially if your wife has a green thumb.

Hand her a hammer. A tool kit for hanging pictures and making other simple repairs may be just the ticket—especially if it fits in a kitchen drawer or under the sink. Buy a nice toolbox, then stock it with a few screwdrivers, a hammer, picture-hanging supplies, nails, and perhaps a pair of needle-nose pliers.

Get her out of the kitchen. Take responsibility for dinner one night—or several. You don't even have to cook. Just stop at the local gourmet take-out shop or a grocery store with prepared meals and pick up the meal. Make sure you get reheating instructions. And while you're at it, rent a movie you'll both enjoy and make an evening of it.

Give her a promise. Promissory notes are an old and honored tradition in many families. If you haven't tried one, it's about time. The first secret to success is figuring out what to wrap up to symbolize the gift—a hammer and some nails to represent your promise to build a garden tool storage area, or a silly picture frame in place of a fine art print, for example. What's the second secret? Make sure you follow through and deliver the present.

Presents of Mind

So many children's gifts these days involve a series, such as dolls with all sorts of clothes, train sets with endless accessories, charm bracelets, and books. Debbie Sibbitt of Bloomington, Indiana, is helping her nieces with a particular collection, so each Christmas she writes down which component she bought and files it away. The following year, she pulls out the file to double-check what she got last year. With this simple shortcut, no embarrassing duplicates find their way under the tree, and no time is wasted on returns.

Ticket, Ticket, Who's Got the Ticket?

Even if they can't write, kids can help create last-minute gifts they'll be proud to give. Just have them make tickets that can be exchanged for work projects. Tickets for chores such as setting the table, taking out the garbage, or helping with dinner are traditional. But kids also can make them for helping to shovel the driveway, walk the dog, or rake leaves for a parent, grandparent, or family friend. All will be welcome time- and labor-savers for the recipient. Cut construction paper into the appropriate size and write one chore on each ticket, then let the child decorate it. Staple the tickets into a booklet and wrap them up to make sure they're extra special.

Teens Treasure Shopping Trips

For the fussy teenager on your shopping list, don't even try to pick out a gift. Nothing will make her happier than a gift of an afternoon or evening trip to the store of her choice to pick out her own gift. (It's okay to set a dollar limit.)

Almost Last-Minute Christmas Gifts

Although a quick drive is required to procure the following gift items, you can rest assured that you'll always find them in stock, even during peak gift-giving season.

Movie madness basket. This is a gift for an avid movie renter. Buy a basket at any home store and fill it with microwave popcorn, soda, candy boxes, and a gift certificate to the place where the person rents movies.

Dinner out. Buy a gift certificate at a nice restaurant. Then ask if you can have a photocopy of the menu and use it to wrap the certificate.

Out-of-the-ordinary leather gloves. Many women have a pair of brown or black leather gloves, but what about a pair of bright pink, chartreuse, or purple gloves? It's a pure indulgence item and something most women won't buy for themselves. It's also something that is easy and quick to find at holiday time, since it's the practical black gloves that sell out first.

Hostess platter. Buy a nice chip-and-dip platter. Spice it up by adding bags of gourmet chips and a couple of bottles of salsa from a specialty food store.

Roll Out a Bottle

This shortcut is for the occasion when you literally have *no* time to stop for a gift. Pull a bottle of wine from your own collection and give it as a gift. It helps to keep a decorative wine bag on hand as wrapping, but if that's not available, stick on a bow. Although wine is an old standby, it's always appreciated and never seems to hang around for long.

Give the Gift of Time

Rather than squeezing in yet another shopping trip during December, spend a quiet half hour at home creating hand-made gift certificates, offering your time and talents to loved ones. For example, if you have a friend who's an accountant, present a certificate for a home-cooked meal at the height of tax season. Or if you enjoy afternoons with your grandkids, offer their frazzled mom a regularly scheduled afternoon off. If you have elderly friends or relatives, invite them over for lunch or dinner—or just for tea—and spend an hour or two chatting. Or take the fixings over to their house. Offer to run errands or drive them to the shopping center or doctor. Give a spring house-cleaning, or a quick pass with the vacuum cleaner, as a gift. Or plan on helping out with chores such as doing minor home repairs, replacing hard-to-reach lightbulbs, or moving and cleaning behind furniture. This strategy reduces your holiday stress by spreading your time investment over the course of the year. And most friends and family members will treasure the generous gift of your time much more than any off-the-shelf item you could find.

GIFT-WRAPPING SHORTCUTS
Gum Be Gone!

If you've ever struggled to remove those sticky price tags from a vase, candy dish, or other glass gift, you know how frustrating it can be. You can get rid of the paper, but the ugly, gummy residue seems to cling no matter what. To get rid of that gummy mess, squirt it with a bit of WD-40 or Goo Gone, and it will rub right off.

Copper plant labels make great gift labels, too (1). Wrap the tag wires around a pencil to create fancy spirals (2).

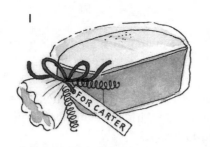
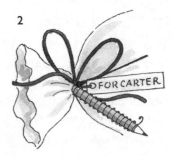

Great Gift Labels

For an inexpensive yet attractive alternative to gift cards, keep some copper plant labels on hand. These attractive, rectangular labels (available at garden centers) have a hole in one end and come with wires that allow you to attach them to any kind of package. Use a pen that has run out of ink to write your message on the soft metal.

11th-Hour Wrapping Relief

There's nothing better than looking at a deep pile of merrily wrapped gifts, sighing deeply, and saying, "I'm done!" Until the next day, when you find three more naked gifts under the bed. To finish off last-minute gifts fast, visit your local dollar or discount store and seek out festive bags and preprinted holiday boxes (they'll probably be on sale). With the gift box, all you have to do is place the gift inside, put on the lid, and encircle the box with ribbon. With a gift bag, drop in the gift, then top it off with an explosion of colored tissue paper. To do this, place the tissue paper on a flat surface, grab the center of a sheet, lift up, and place the paper point down in the bag. Do this with several sheets until the gift is completely hidden.

Smooth Solutions for Lumpy Gifts

Gifts that have odd shapes can take a long time to wrap and still end up looking lumpy. Fortunately, there are some ways to speed-wrap lumpy gifts. Put soft or small unevenly shaped gifts in an empty oatmeal canister, then wrap. Slide neckties, jewelry, or scarves into the cardboard tube from a roll of paper towels. Roll a piece of wrapping paper around the tube and tuck the edges of the paper into the tube ends. Stuff tissue paper into both ends, leaving some jutting out for a colorful accent. Roll up a magazine for which you've taken out a gift subscription and slide it inside a festive bag intended for a wine bottle. Buy a used hatbox at a thrift store or a new one at a home store and slap a bow on top. The wrapping becomes part of the gift, since the recipient can use the container to store things at home.

Stamp Out Wrapping Paper

Homemade wrapping paper adds a delightful touch to holiday gifts, and Charlene Shryer of Glenview, Illinois, has figured out a way to create an ample supply with (almost) no work on her part. Charlene invites her six grandchildren over and lets *them* make her holiday wrapping paper. She begins by rolling out inexpensive white butcher paper. Then she passes around holiday-themed rubber stamps with washable, nontoxic ink pads. The kids have a blast, and Nana gets a supply of unique, made-with-love wrapping paper.

3 Stylish Wrapping Shortcuts

The only thing standing between you and those pricey, expert gift wrappers is an ability to see wrapping paper in the most unusual places. Maria Zyble, a Milwaukee interior designer and annual family winner of the most creative wrapper award, suggests these uncommon but inexpensive ideas.

Furoshiki style. Borrow the Japanese furoshiki custom, which involves placing a gift in the center of a square piece of fabric, gathering the fabric on top of the box, and knotting opposite corners. Genuine furoshiki cloth can be expensive and difficult to find, but in its place, you can use felt (great for anyone who does crafts), a large cotton scarf, or a small tablecloth.

Kitchen style. If you're giving a kitchen tool, buy an inexpensive kitchen towel that matches the recipient's color scheme and use the towel to wrap the gift. Use adhesive tape to secure the towel as you go, then wrap ribbon around it to stabilize the wrapping.

Natural style. Go for a woodsy look by wrapping gifts in plain brown butcher paper. Fashion bows out of hardware store twine, then decorate the packages with dried flowers or pressed autumn leaves mixed with twigs gathered in your own backyard.

Too Pretty to Wrap

When you're giving an item that is a beautiful container in and of itself, why go to great lengths to wrap it? For gifts such as a woven basket, painted flowerpot, or vibrant ceramic coffee mug, use cellophane to wrap them fast and easy. You can buy clear or tinted cellophane by the roll in most stores that sell holiday wrapping paper. Just cut a piece twice as big as the container and lay it on a flat surface. Put the pretty container in the middle of the cellophane, then pull the cellophane up and around the container. Grab the "neck" of the cellophane, wrap a ribbon around it several times, and secure it with a bow.

Save time by wrapping attractive gifts in clear cellophane. Just tie the cellophane closed at the top with a bow.

A Shameless Resolution

Phew! You've reached the end of *Shameless Shortcuts*. To finish our collection of timesaving hints and tips, here's a suggestion for your next New Year's resolution. Instead of setting an extravagant or difficult goal and facing a high probability of failure, be shameless and go for something completely achievable. Turn to page 1 of this book and resolve to pick up a few more super shortcuts!

Meet Our Experts

A

Patty Allard, who operates the Furry Friends Pet Salon in Pascoag, Rhode Island, is the president of New England Pet Grooming Professionals. **John Alldredge** is the senior technical service manager at the Seal Beach, California, headquarters of Custom Building Products. **Susan Allen** is a wife and mother from Evanston, Illinois. **Todd Allerton** is a Navy Reservist in Jacksonville, Florida, who enjoys making easy snacks for himself and his daughters. **Rob Ambrosino** is a piano tuner and technician in Katy, Texas. Lifelong Minnesota resident **Dale Anderson, M.D.,** is a physician at an urgent care clinic in Minneapolis. **Wendy Andrews** is a teacher and mother of three children in Chicago. **Volena Askew** is the adult home economics supervisor in Knox County, Tennessee. **Diane Ayala** is the owner of Ayala Maquillage in Chicago.

B

Christine Bailey is a Master Gardener and organic market gardener in Germansville, Pennsylvania. **Maria Bailey** of Pompano Beach, Florida, is the owner and CEO of BlueSuitMom.com, an online resource offering work and family balance information. **Lori Baird** is the managing editor of Healthy Living Books in Queens and the editor of *Cut the Clutter and Stow the Stuff* and *Powersculpt*. **Marge Baldi** of Oakdale, New York, who works as a medical office assistant, is also a wife, mother, and grandmother. **Patty Bareford** owns Wide Open Space in Concord, Massachusetts, and is on the board of directors for New England Professional Organizers. Textile expert **Dr. Herb Barndt,** who has special expertise in stain removal, works at Philadelphia University in Philadelphia. **John Beckna** is the director of Ukrop's Pharmacy in Richmond, Virginia. **Lisa Bellistracci** is a neatnik who lives in Astoria, New York. **Jo Benwell** is a former food and nutrition lecturer at Farnham College in Surrey, England. Business executive **Peter Benwell** of Chesterfield, Virginia, travels frequently to Asia, Europe, Africa, and South America. Teacher **Chris Blackmon** enjoys using his outdoor grill at his home in Louisville, Colorado. **Jim Blamthin** is the manager of corporate media relations for Kodak in Rochester, New York. **Sue Bodmer** of Chicago is a freelance writer, wife, and mother. **Paige Boucher** is a public relations consultant and mother from Steamboat Springs, Colorado. **Judy Brown** is an organizing consultant in Yale, British Columbia. **Kat Butler** is a recently retired magazine editor from Kearny, New Jersey. **Lynn Byczynski,** author of *The Flower Farmer,* is a market gardener in Lawrence, Kansas.

C

Phyllis Cambria is co-owner of Party PlansPlus.com in Coconut Creek, Florida. **Gary Campbell** is a landscaper in Coopersburg, Pennsylvania. **Scott Campbell** is the owner of 1st Choice Plumbing in Everett, Washington. **Susan Castle** is the owner of the Magnolia Lamp Shoppe in Chattanooga, Tennessee. Writer **Tom Cavalieri** of Long Island City, New York, enjoys the challenge of keeping a small apartment organized. Registered nurse **Karen Cichocki** and her husband, **Rick,** who is a welder, live in Dyer, Indiana, with their three dogs and two cats. **Anna Cieslik** and her mother work together to make it through their busy mornings at home in Chicago. **Andrea Crawford** is a former professional shopper in New York City. College baseball coach **Ryan Crawford** of Oneonta, New York, is currently working on a master's degree. **Keith Crotz** is a former biology professor who enjoys gardening at his home in Chillicothe, Illinois. **Lori Crouch,** assistant director for the National Education Writers of America, commutes by bus in Washington, D.C. Cornell Cooperative Extension educator **Sally Cunningham,** author of *Great Garden Companions,* lives in East Aurora, New York.

D

Ralph Davis, a Web site editor for the Home and Garden Television Network, lives in Halls, Tennessee. **Lou Dawson** of Carbondale, Colorado, writes guidebooks for backcountry skiers. **Mira G. Dessy** is a homemaker and mother and also a business manager for PhoCusWright, an online research firm, in Sherman, Connecticut. Market gardeners **George and Melanie DeVault** grow organic vegetables and flowers at Pheasant Hill Farm in Vera Cruz, Pennsylvania. **Marie Devlin** is a feisty widow and retiree from Stamford, Connecticut. *Bird Talk* magazine editor **Laura Doering** shares her Long Beach, California, home with two birds and commutes daily in heavy traffic. **Tom Donnelly** is the business manager of a funeral home in Flushing, New York. **Betsy Donoghue** is a family educator and mental health coordinator at Parent-Child Development Corporation in Richmond, Virginia. Former market gardener **Cass Peterson Doolittle** is a garden writer from Flanders, New Jersey. Homemaker and mother **Diana dos Santos** lives in New York City. **Ed DuBois** is the owner of Hire a Hubby in Hartford, Vermont.

E

Fashion reporter **Sharon Edelson,** also a wife and mother of two children, lives in Woodcliff Lake, New Jersey. **Jay Einhorn, Ph.D,** is a psychologist in Evanston, Illinois. Garden writer **Barbara Ellis,** author of *Deckscaping,* tends her gardens and enjoys making crafts and gifts using materials from her small farm in Berks County, Pennsylvania. **Jane Ann Ellis** is a homemaker and grandmother from Columbus, Ohio. Naturalist **Janet Ellis** of Helena, Montana, does craft projects on her own and with her son, **Daniel Hanson. Ralph Erenzo** owns a country store and inn in Gardiner, New York. Specialty flower grower **Linda Essert-Kuchar** is the owner of My Garden Blooms in Emmaus, Pennsylvania. **Peter Evans** works as a social worker, counselor, and consultant, but in his time off, he enjoys traveling in his RV, tinkering with cars, and dabbling in a variety of projects around his small farm in Berks County, Pennsylvania.

F

Susan Fignar of Itasca, Illinois, is the president of Pur*sue, a firm that specializes in corporate image and relationship management. **Colleen Fischvogt** is a marketing and public relations specialist in Richmond, Virginia. **Matt Fischvogt** is a copywriter at Arnika, an advertising agency in Richmond, Virginia. **Eileen Fitzmaurice** enjoys browsing yard sales for items to decorate her home in Woodbridge, New Jersey. **Andrew Flach** is the author of *Combat Fat!* and a licensed weight management consultant in New York City. **Jane Fleming** of West Burlington, New York, loves to shop via mail order. **James Flynn** of Crown Point, Indiana, is an instrumentation specialist for a public utility company and has a perfect driving record. **Suzanne Flynn** is a former antiques dealer from Elizabethtown, Kentucky. **Kevin Frederick** is a computer programmer in Boulder, Colorado. **Frank and Flo Frum** are a retired couple who reside in Oceanside, California.

G

Julie Garrison is a copywriter from Boulder, Colorado. **Sue Gartner** is a wife and mother and the activities director at a senior center in Hopewell Junction, New York. Landscape designer and Master Gardener **Peg Giermek** is the owner of Nature Calls Landscaping in East Aurora, New York. United Parcel Service driver **Gigi Gonzales** shares her Claremont, California, home with three dogs. **Tommy Goodman** is a lube technician in a quick-stop shop in Knoxville, Tennessee. Master woodworker **Keith Gotschall** turns wooden bowls on a lathe in Salida, Colorado. Graphic designer and writer **Alexandra Greenwood** is from Mahopac, New York. **Bob Grimac** of Knoxville, Tennessee, is an elementary school fine arts instructor and the head of Tennessee Green.

H

Susan Hager is an interior designer in New York City. **Lucy Hall** is an innovative teenage cook who lives in Knoxville, Tennessee. **Tom Harris** is an advisor to the East Aurora Tree Board in East Aurora, New York. **Richard Haskel** is a photography and film student at Virginia Commonwealth University in Richmond, Virginia. **Connie Hatch** is a freelance writer in New York City. Catering manager **Kenny Heath**

of Seattle enjoys cooking simple meals when he's at home with his wife and family. **Pamela Heckman** is an enthusiastic container gardener from Emmaus, Pennsylvania. **Patty Hegdal** of Midlothian, Virginia, enjoys traveling to visit her four grandchildren. **Ann Davis Helke** is a sales associate at Mr. Pool in Boulder, Colorado. Dance teacher, homemaker, and mother **Eileen Herman-Haase** of Medford, Massachusetts, is co-owner of Dance Caliente. **Eric Hörst**, the author of *Training for Climbing*, is a professional trainer in Lancaster, Pennsylvania. Master Gardener **Babbidean Huber** of Amherst, New York, teaches landscape design classes.

J

Jill James is a middle school teacher and lifelong dog owner in Allen, Texas. Beauty expert **Mary Beth Janssen,** author of *Organic Beauty,* is the president of the Janssen Source in Palatine, Illinois. **Janon Johnson** is a home gardener extraordinaire from Emmaus, Pennsylvania. **Jo Johnson** is a database manager in Boulder, Colorado. **Joely Johnson,** a university media relations director and part-time yoga instructor, lives in upstate New York. **Lyle Jones** is the owner of American Porcelain and Fiberglass in Richmond, Virginia.

K

Melissa Kauffman, group editor of *Bird Talk* and *Birds USA* magazines in Mission Viejo, California, has two cockatiels. **Dinesh Kapoor** is a copywriter at Arnika, an advertising agency in Richmond, Virginia. **Kate Kearney** is a Web editor for Fine Living.com, based in Los Angeles, and also a mother from Encino, California. Retired professor of communications **Bob Kennedy** and his wife, **Joanne,** of Toano, Virginia, describe themselves as avid junk shop fans. Freelance food writer **Rose Kennedy** of Knoxville, Tennessee, enjoys leaving most of the cooking chores to her daughter, Lucy Hall. **Dr. Sarah Kirby** is an associate professor and housing specialist in the Department of Family and Consumer Sciences, North Carolina Cooperative Extension Service at North Carolina State University in Raleigh. **Kathy Kirrish** is a wife and mother from Kenilworth, Illinois. **Aimee Kocis** is a market gardener in Phoenixville, Pennsylvania. **Tim Koehler** is the president of Koehler Kitchen & Bath in Greensboro, North Carolina. **Piotr Kostrzewski** is the owner of Cross-Cultural Adventures in Arlington, Virginia. As a career woman and mother of three children, **Carol Kriebel** of Deerfield, Illinois, is a veteran of frantic mornings.

L

Mike Landkroon is a professional photographer from Stoney Creek, Ontario. **Joseph Dever Larmor** is the president and managing director of the Ulster Linen Company in New York City. **Cindy Lebow** is the president of Miracle Maids cleaning service in Brooklyn and a busy mother of six children. Family therapist **Barbara Lee** of Lake San Marcos, California, is a devoted cat owner. Corporate trainer **Jonna Lemes** recently completed a major remodeling of her house in Red Cliff, Colorado, including a new home office. **Lauren Link** of Milwaukee is a career woman and mother. **Doug Liston** is a home handyman in Worthington, Ohio. Teenager **Jenny Liston** of Columbus, Ohio, enjoys making cross-stitch projects for friends and relatives. **Susan Liston** is a mother and career woman from Columbus, Ohio. Expert tile installer **Anthony LoGiurato** is the owner of Anthony the Tileman, a tile installation business in Upper Darby, Pennsylvania. **Terry Long** is a professional dog trainer and behavior consultant in Long Beach, California. **Greg Longe** is the president and CEO of Molly Maid in Ann Arbor, Michigan.

M

Chaz Macdonald of Center Valley, Pennsylvania, travels extensively in his work as a computer specialist. Freelance writer and editor **Dougald MacDonald,** formerly a Bostonian, enjoys outdoor exercise around his neighborhood in Louisville, Colorado. **Judy MacDonald** is a grandmother and active volunteer in Yarmouth, Maine. Efficiency expert and business consultant **Lori MacDonald** manages a home office and home school for two children in Cumberland Foreside, Maine. **Justin Majors** is the owner of Majors Residential Design and Construction in Oakland, California. Expert butcher **Ed Manacek** is the owner of Elegance in Meats in Northbrook, Illinois. Apparel design consultant **JoAnn Marra** is also a home owner, wife, and doting aunt in West Bay Shore, New York. **Lillian Martin** is a licensed practical nurse who serves as school nurse at All Saints' Episcopal School in Vicksburg, Mississippi. **Ruben Masas** is the manager of Maid of Honor cleaning service in Fort Lauderdale. **Charlie Mazza** is the home-grounds/community horticulture extension leader for Cornell University in Ithaca, New York. **Charlie and Dana McGimsey** are newlyweds in Elizabethtown, Kentucky. Scoutmaster **Tom McKemey** is a retired deputy chief U.S. probation officer from Wyndmoor, Pennsylvania. **Chris McNamara** is a publisher in Mill Valley, California. **Ceil Meredith** is a jewelry designer in New York City. Professional cleaner **Patty Metheny** is the owner of Sparklin Clean in Knoxville, Tennessee. Pet expert **Arden Moore** of Oceanside, California, is a writer and speaker and the author of *The Kitten Owner's Manual.* Women's health expert **Donnica Moore, M.D.,** practices medicine in Neshanic Station, New Jersey. **Kevin Moore** is a construction worker with the U.S. Navy who lives in Laurel, Maryland, with his cat, Lager. **Pat Moore** is a professional organizer from McKenney, Virginia. **Roberta Mulliner** is a retired office manager from Cutchogue, New York, who manages her weekly errand schedule with precision. **Skip Murray** is co-owner of Murray Brothers Nursery in Orchard Park, New York.

N

Pat Neff is the owner of Swingset Corral in Oxnard, California. **Dr. Jeanette Newton Keith** is the medical director of the New Beginnings Medical Weight Management Program at the University of Chicago. **Ray Nowak** is a Master Gardener from Lackawanna, New York.

O

Carol Oddi of New Fairfield, Connecticut, commutes 132 miles daily to her job as a regulatory specialist for a veterinary product company in New Jersey. **Robyn O'Donnell** is a certified master dog groomer and the owner of the Pink Poodle Parlor in Westerly, Rhode Island. **Ethel Ondra** is an amateur woodworker from Pennsburg, Pennsylvania.

P

Consultant **Kathy Paauw** runs her own organizing and productivity firm, Paauwerfully Organized, in Seattle. **Jim Pavel** is the president of Keep Western New York Beautiful and the director of support services for the city of Buffalo. Freelance writer **Audrey Pavia** and her husband, **Randy,** enjoy training their dog on their backyard agility equipment at their Santa Ana, California, home. **Tricia Pearsall** is a backpacking gourmet-cooking expert from Richmond, Virginia. **Evelyn Petersen** of Traverse City, Michigan, is an early childhood consultant and the national spokesperson representing Hasbro and the National Parenting Center. **Kathryn Phelps** is a writer and editor in Katonah, New York. **Cindy Prince** is

a busy working mother who lives in Knoxville, Tennessee.

R

Corey Rich is a professional photographer from Sacramento, California. **Jill Richardson, DVM,** is a veterinarian for a major pet product company in Secaucus, New Jersey. Nutrition counselor **Monique Ryan** is the owner of Personal Nutrition Designs in Evanston, Illinois.

S

Natalie Salatto is a sales supervisor at Emerson Supply in Guilford, Connecticut. **Michael Scherer** is an outdoor equipment designer in Louisville, Colorado. **Chuck Schoen** is the owner of 24-7 Plumbing in Tucson. **Barry Schrager** is a professional artist and art installer in New York City. **Katherine Scott** is a mother of twins from Westerville, Ohio. **Tracy Sebastian** of Beverly Hills, California, has two "tweenage" children and a full-time job. **Steve Shadel** is a manager at McGuckin Hardware, which has served residents of Boulder, Colorado, for 50 years. **Mike Shadrack** ("The Hosta Man") is a garden lecturer and photographer who divides his time between London, England, and East Aurora, New York. **Anne Shelton** of Seattle is an expert on wilderness shelters and tracking. Glenview, Illinois, wife, mother, and grandmother **Charlene Shryer** still fields daily requests for advice from her four grown daughters. Chicagoan **Donna Shryer** is a wife, mother, professional writer, and wearer of many hats. **Stu Shryer** is a retired advertising executive from Glenview, Illinois. **Debbie Sibbitt** of Bloomington, Indiana, enjoys hosting holiday parties for all seasons. **Leslie Sinclair, DVM,** is a veterinarian in Montgomery Village, Maryland. Homemaker **Beth Slate** and her husband, **Jamie,** who is a professor at Catawba College, live in Salisbury, North Carolina. **Jim**

Slate is an avid outdoorsman and cook from Winnsboro, South Carolina. **Wade Slate** is a lawncare professional in Knoxville, Tennessee. Newspaper sportswriter **Marcia C. Smith** spends lots of time in traffic headed to sporting events both in her home area of Santa Monica, California, and in cities around the country. **Rochelle Smith** of Grand Island, New York, is a landscape designer, diagnostician, and instructor at Niagara Community College. **Rob Stanford** is a professional chef in Tampa. **Susan Steele** is an interior designer in Longmont, Colorado. Boston resident **Cathy Steever** is a staffing supervisor for Potpourri Group, a major mail-order retail company, and the mother of four children. **Myrsini Stephanides** of Astoria, New York, enjoys redecorating her home on a budget. **Jane Swanson-Nystrom** of Chicago is a career woman, wife, and mother.

T–Z

Diane Thomas is a child care provider and mother of three from Alburtis, Pennsylvania. Businessman **Arnould t'Kint** is an expert rock climber from Bloomfield Hills, Michigan. **Paul Veri** is a home handyman in Columbus, Ohio. **Laura Warshawsky** is a wife and mother from Brooklyn who works as a supervisory analyst for a securities firm. **Mikal Watson** is the director of sales at Miracle Maids in Brooklyn. Landscape designer **Sharon Webber** of Buffalo specializes in perennial garden design. **Barbara Webster** is the president of Nice N Clean Maid Service in Miami. **Benedicte Whitworth** is a well-organized housewife from Raleigh, North Carolina. **Amy Witsil** is a marketing consultant and mother of three children from Chapel Hill, North Carolina. **Paula Yurkewecz** is a psychotherapist in Oakland, California. **Flo Zack** is a longtime Master Gardener from Elma, New York. **Barbara Zagnoni** is the education director for Rowenta, a firm that manufactures high-end irons in Medford, Massachusetts. **Marylou Zarbock** is the editor of *Ferrets* magazine in Mission Viejo, California. Interior designer **Maria Zyble** of Milwaukee is a creative bargain shopper.

RECOMMENDED READING

Baird, Lori, ed. *Cut the Clutter and Stow the Stuff.* Emmaus, Pennsylvania: Rodale, 2002.

Better Homes and Gardens Books. *Decorating Ideas under $100.* Des Moines, Iowa: Meredith, 2003.

Bredenberg, Jeff, ed. *Clean It Fast, Clean It Right.* Emmaus, Pennsylvania: Rodale, 1998.

Bucks, Christine, and Fern Marshall Bradley, eds. *The Resourceful Gardener's Guide.* Emmaus, Pennsylvania: Rodale, 2001.

Crocker, Betty. *Betty Crocker's 1-2-3 Dinner.* Emmaus, Pennsylvania: Rodale, 2001.

Proulx, Earl. *Yankee Magazine's Make It Last.* Emmaus, Pennsylvania: Rodale, 1996.

_____. *Yankee Magazine's Vinegar, Duct Tape, Milk Jugs & More.* Emmaus, Pennsylvania: Rodale, 1999.

Sussman, Julie, and Stephanie Glakas-Tenet. *Dare to Repair.* New York: HarperCollins, 2002.

Yankee Magazine. *Now That's Ingenious!* Emmaus, Pennsylvania: Rodale, 2001

Index

Underscored page references indicate boxed text. **Boldface** references indicate illustrations.

Chimney starter, for lighting charcoal, 256, **256**
Chinese food, healthy choices of, 109–10
Chips
  bagging single servings of, 93
  tortilla, heating, 152–53
Chocolate
  -dipped pretzels, home-made, 286
  sauce, homemade, 285–86
  topping desserts with, 151
Chore tickets, as holiday gift, 358
Christmas lights. *See* Lights, holiday
Christmas trees, outdoor uses for, 279
Citra-Scrub, for grease stains, 227–28
Clamshells, for repelling garden pests, 320
Clay, modeling, for hand exercises, 38
Cleaning. *See also* Clutter control; Dusting; Vacuuming
  bathrooms, 34–35, 213–17, 223
  exercise from, 46–47
  involving children in, 26–27
  kitchens, 34–35, 131–36
  laundry, 35–36
  shortcuts, 23–27, 163–66
  solutions
    commercial, 24
    for glass, care with, 25
    homemade, 21–23
    soak-in time for, 25
  tools, holder for, 164
  windows, 159–60
Clean Shower, for prevent-ing hard-water de-posits, 214

Clementine baskets, for kitchen storage, 33
Clorox Clean-Up, 24
Closeout stores, 97
Closet(s)
  bedroom
    bifold doors for, 175–76
    storing craft supplies in, 297–98
  coat
    extra storage near, 18
    organizing, 18
  shelves, for clothing storage, 4–5
  space savers for, 176, 177, **177**
Closet auger, for unclogging toilet, 224–25
Clothesline, as jump rope, 38
Clothing
  accessories, storing, 4, 180–82, 181, 191
  all-season, as gift, 354
  cleanup, in children's room, 183
  exercise, 40
  laundering (*see* Laundry)
  outfit assembly, 4
  removing pet hair from, 63
  repairing, 5, 178, 179
  seasonal inventory and swapping of, 5, 178
  securing buttons on, 178–79
  selecting, 179–80, 180
  storing, 4–5, 178, 179, 180
  unwrinkling, 117, 179
Clutter control
  in bathroom, 217–18
  in bedroom, 182–84
  general household, 30–33
  in kitchen, 125–29
  in living areas, 166–69

Coat closet
  extra storage near, 18
  organizing, 18
Coat rack, for storing chil-dren's clothes, 183
Cobwebs, removing, 29
Coffee can
  as pencil and marker holder, 191
  as trash bag dispenser, 127, **127**
Coffee containers, 17–18
Coffee stirrers, as bird toy, 68
Cold air leaks, locating, 252
Comforter
  bedspread used with, 185–86
  denim cover for, 191
  warming, 185
Communication
  centers, 19, 81, 200
  issues, 112–14
Commuting shortcuts, 71–76
Compost bin, concealing, 268
Computer
  backing up data on, 209
  individualizing access to, 195
  keyboard, cleaning, 205
  keyboard commands for, 208
  mouse, cleaning, 206, **206**
  organizing photos in, 197
  printer, 211–12
  repairing, 207–8, 207
  search engines, how to use, 210–11
  wires and cables, tidying, 205–6
Condiment containers, 17
Container gardening, 305–6, 306, 308, 316–19
Containers
  baby wipe, 223

Golf, saving time in, 332, *332*

Golf bag, for carrying garden tools, 315–16

Goo Gone, for removing price tags, 359

Grape costume, for Halloween, 346–47

Grass. *See also* Lawns
low-maintenance, 273
paths, how to make, 269–70

Grater, cheese, cleaning, 133

Greased Lightning cleaner, *24*

Grease stains, 227–28

Greenhouse, how to make, *309*

Greeting cards
holiday
address file for, 348–49
e-mail in place of, *349*
storing, 349
preselected supply of, 197–98
for recording recipes, *126*

Grill
cleaning, 257
lighting, 255–56
location for, *257*

Grinder, baby food, as alternative to food processor, *148*

Grocery bags, transporting home, 76–77

Grocery basket, for weight training, 42

Grocery list, computerized, 88

Grocery shopping
avoiding marketing ploys when, *92*
best time for, 76, *91*
with children, 93–94
saving money on, 88–90, *89*, *90*, 91–93

saving time on, 90–91, *90*

Grooming
for cats, 59–60, 61–62
for dogs, 59–61, *59*
tools, storing, 59, *59*

Grout(ing)
cleaning, 217
techniques, 221–22

Guidebook, for home decor, 96–97, **97**

Gum
removing, from hair, 11
for repairing rain gutter, 277

Gutters
cleaning, 276–77
repairing, 277

Gym, factors in choosing, 120

H

Hair
accessories, storing, *191*
blow-drying, 8–9
conditioning, multitasking during, 3–4
pet, removing, 29, 62–63
removing chewing gum from, 11
spray, for applying handlebar grips, 50
styling, *9*
tangles
preventing, 112
removing, 11

Halloween
costumes, 346–48
dessert, 346

Hamburger patties, storing, in freezer, 131

Hand(s)
exercises, 38, *38*, 43, *44*
measuring with, 99, **99**
moisturizing, 76, 186

Handlebar grips, bicycle, loose, 50

Hanging plant baskets, care of, 317–19, *318*

Hard-water deposits, in shower, 214, 225

Hardwood floors, care of, 161, 162–63

Headboard
draping above, 188
redecorating, 187

Heating filters, reducing dust by checking, 28

Hedge shears, uses for, 314–15

Herbal teas, for bedtime, 120–21

Herbal vinegars, making, *289*

Herbs
growing, 302, 308, 310
tips for using, *139*

Hiking, 338–39

Holiday(s)
decorations, 341–44
dismantling, 342–43, 344
storing, *344*
dinners, 350–53
gift shopping and giving, 353–59
gift-wrapping, 359–62
Halloween, 346–48
organizing for, 348–49
parties, 344–46

Home accessories
redecorating with, 171–73
shopping for, 96–97

Home inventory, videotape for, 202–3

Home office
individualizing, 195
organizing, 193–200
saving on supplies for, *198*

Homework
study area for, 191
timing of, 111

Hose
attachment, for dog bathing, 57–58
for broken pipe repair, 245–46

Hose *continued*
  for cushioning sharp
    corners, 243
  as tool guard, 235-36
  for unclogging tub
    drain, 225
  for work sink, 243
Hosiery, preventing snags
  in, 179
Hot dogs, for dog treats,
  55-56
Hotels, protecting valu-
  ables in, 330-31
Hot tub, reducing energy
  usage by, 262-63
Household chores, calorie
  burning from, 47
Humidity, affecting piano,
  158
Husk sack, as foot warmer,
  185

I

Ice
  on walks and patios,
    melting, 278
  on windshield,
    removing, 71-72
Ice cream
  cone, preventing drips
    from, 154
  scoop, for filling muffin
    pan, 150
Ice cube(s)
  as dog treat, 65-66
  storing, in paper bags,
    130
  tray
    as reassembly aid,
      246-47
    for storing craft sup-
      plies, 296
Ice dams, removing and
  preventing, 280
ID tags, for pets, 334
Incontinence, Kegel
  exercises for,
  48-49
Index funds, 205
Ingredient substitutions,
  106, 150

Ink stains, 226
Insect pest control, in garden, 320-321
Instruction manuals, filing,
  198-99, 244
Insurance
  discounts, 203
  home, inventory for,
    202-3
Internet
  browser, purging cache
    for, 207
  forms, automatic
    completion of, 211
  holiday kid sites on,
    352-53
  instruction manuals on,
    199
  recipes from, 118, 345
  use, forwarding calls
    during, 114
Interval training workouts,
  52
Ironing, of linen, 229
Ironing board covers, 231
Iron-on patches, for sew-
  ing repairs, 178

J

Japanese beetles, killing,
  320
Jars, for workshop storage,
  242
Jewelry
  storing, 180-82, 181
    during dishwashing,
    131
Juice boxes, alternative to,
  17
Jumping rope, 38
Junk drawer organizers,
  128-29
Junk mail, trashing, 31

K

Kegel exercises, 48-49
Ketchup, in salad dressing,
  147
Keyboard
  commands, shortcut, 208
  computer, cleaning, 205

Keys, car
  alternative to, 77
  for defrosting lock,
    72-73
Kibble
  in self-feeders, 54
  storage container for, 54
Kitchen
  cleaner, homemade, 22
  cleaning, 34-35, 35
  cleanups in, 131-36
  gadgets, 148
  gifts from, 283-86, 289
  increasing counter
    space in, 33
  organizing, 125-29
  removing duplicate
    items from, 33
  retooling refrigerator in,
    129-31
Knits, delicate, hanging,
  179

L

Labels
  canning jar, making,
    286
  gift, 360, **360**
Ladder, as seed-planting
  grid, 302
Ladybug costume, for Hal-
  loween, 347
Lamp shades, redecorating
  with, 173
Landscape(ing)
  adding plants to, 269
  choosing focal point in,
    264
  concealing compost bin
    in, 268
  designing, 263-64
  door in, 271
  fallen log in, 268-69
  grass paths in, 269-70
  nature adding to, 264-65
  overgrown shrubs in,
    266-67
  perennial hedges in,
    267-68
  planting under trees,
    270-71

Tuna, with Mediterranean-style pasta, 138–39
Tuna "toothbrush," for cats, 53
Turkey
    baster, for watering seedlings, 301–2
    holiday, 351–52, 353
TV shows, videotaping, 122
TV watching
    in car, 79
    chores during, 118
    cleaning during, 163–64, 164
    exercising during, 47–49

U
Unclaimed Baggage Center, shopping at, 95
Under-bed storage, 182
Underwear, bagging, for laundering, 35–36

V
Vacations. *See* Travel
Vacuum(ing)
    dog coat, 62
    exercise from, 46
    reducing dust from, 28
    shop, as wastebasket, 239
Valance, how to make, 189, **189**
Valentine's Day decoration, 342
Valuables, protecting, on vacation, 330–31
Vanity
    bench, for bedroom, 188
    organizing, 182, 218
Vegetable oil
    for car washing, 253
    for lighting charcoal, 255
Vegetables
    as bird treats, 56
    frozen, advantages of, 145
    grilled, 137
    growing, 305–8
    quick-cooking, 145

Venetian blinds. *See* Blinds
Video(s)
    choosing, for car viewing, 79
    game players, for car trips, 329
    returns, remembering due date for, 117
Videotaping, with digital camera, 333–34
Vinegars, herbal, making, 289
Visiting relatives, sleep schedule for, 327

W
Waffles, as bread substitute, 16
Wagon, for shopping at garage sales, 98
Wainscoting, picket fencing for, 191–92
Waiting room kit, how to pack, 116
Waiting time in car, using, 78–79
Wakeup, easing children into, 10
Walking
    as exercise, 42–43, 50
    party, 345
    stick, for hikers, 339
Wallet, protecting, during travel, 331
Wallpapering, 250
Wall space, for storage, 31–32
Warranties, filing, 198–99, 244
Washcloths, kitchen, sanitizing, 35
Wastebasket
    liners for, 217
    shop vacuum canister as, 239
Water
    bottles
        frozen, for cooling lunch box, 16
        as juice containers, 17
    bowls, for ferrets, 56

exercise, 49–50
    supply, temporary, with burst pipe, 245
    valve, shutoff instructions for, 245
    for weight training, 37–38
Wax stains, 226–27
WD-40, for removing price tags, 359
Wealth, shortcuts to, 204
Weatherproofing projects, 252
Weather stripping, installing, 252
Weather Tech floor mats, for car, 247
Web sites, remembering passwords for, 209
Weeds
    as bouquet fillers, 313
    controlling
        with bed preparation, 265
        in cracks, 259–60
        in flower garden, 311
        in vegetable garden, 305–8
Weight training
    equipment for, 37–38
    slowing lifts in, 42
Wicker chair, as garden decoration, 312, **312**
Wildflower mixes, "instant meadow," 274
Wild rice mixes, substitute for, 136–37
Windex, 24
Window(s)
    blinds, cleaning, 25–26, 160, 160, **160**, 161
    cleaner, homemade, 22
    cleaning, 159–60
    frame, painting, 249
    shades
        cleaning, 161
        for concealing sewing supplies, 292
    when to clean, 25

Windshield
    cleaning, 253
    removing ice and snow
        from, 71–72
Wine, as holiday gift, 359
Wine bottle boxes, for
        shoe storage, 180
Wineglasses, decorating,
    345
Wine stains, red, 227
Winter chores, 277–80
Wire caps, as bottle cap re-
        placements, 242

Wire ties, uses for, 235
Wooden furniture
    dented, repairing, 156
    scratched, repairing,
        155–56
Workbench, organizing,
    241–44
Wrapping paper
    alternatives to, 360–61,
        361
    hand-decorated, 293, 361
    for holiday decorating,
        341

Wrapping supplies, for
        gifts, 285
Wrinkles, clothing, remov-
        ing, 117

Y
Yogurt cups, as lunch con-
        tainers, 17

Z
Zinnias, growing, 312
Zipper care, 231